P9-BBM-710

"Malchiodi understands digital media as creative and accessible tools for building therapeutic relationships. Exploring these diverse media, in the context of these healing relationships, supports clients in creating rich imagery. And examining the individual expressive qualities of particular media, as Malchiodi and her contributors do so well, enables art therapists and art therapy students to realize the potential of these materials."

—*Jane Ferris Richardson, EdD, ATR-BC, RPT-S, Associate Professor of Art Therapy, Lesley University*

"Malchiodi has done it again! This text is an accessible and comprehensive guide that invites a range of perspectives to explore meaning making from multiple technological data sources and helps to further define the evolution of art therapy in contemporary healthcare practice. Peppered with case examples and thoughtful recommendations, the authors never lose focus on the value of interpersonal relatedness and emphasize the priorities that a transforming society must have on attending to the bio-psycho-social and spiritual components of holistic and patient-centered care."

—*Juliet King, MA, ATR-BC, LPC, LMHC, Associate Professor, The George Washington University Art Therapy Graduate Program and Adjunct Associate Professor, Indiana University School of Medicine, Department of Neurology*

"Initially with Cathy Malchiodi's new publication in hand, I found myself asking, how much do I want to become familiar with digital technology in my art therapy world? Through the many examples of new media and digital applications presented in this book, the obviousness of using these modalities in our practice becomes clear. Kopytin's chapter on photo-art therapy, for example, opens up an extended accessible range of collage activities. A new milieu can be formed using the digital in our community-based and clinical practices."

—*Patricia Fenner, PhD, Senior Lecturer and Co-ordinator Master of Art Therapy, School of Psychology and Public Health, La Trobe University*

"Art therapists, practicing today, we face an ever-growing challenge as new technologies become more available and are integrated within our clinical work. Malchiodi's extensively researched handbook identifies these many challenges, including the integration of social media, conforming to professional ethical standards, and complying with mental health and health regulations, and provides an exceptionally clear guide to help us to rise to these challenges while protecting the integrity of our uniquely creative clinical focus. This is a must read for any clinician working with technology within their clinical practice."

—*Dr. Robert Irwin Wolf, ATR-BC, LCAT, LP, Professor, Graduate Art Therapy Faculty at The College of New Rochelle, and President of The Institute for Expressive Analysis*

"An absolute 'must-read' for all who seek to understand the rapidly expanding role of digital media in art therapy, including its benefits, challenges, and limitations. I highly recommend this invaluable guide!"

—*Charles Schaefer, PhD, RPT-S, Co-Founder and Director Emeritus, The Association for Play Therapy, Clovis, CA*

The Handbook of Art Therapy
and Digital Technology

The Handbook of Art Therapy and Digital Technology

Edited by Cathy Malchiodi, PhD

Foreword by Dr Val Huet

Jessica Kingsley *Publishers*
London and Philadelphia

First published in 2018
by Jessica Kingsley Publishers
73 Collier Street
London N1 9BE, UK
and
400 Market Street, Suite 400
Philadelphia, PA 19106, USA

www.jkp.com

Library of Congress Cataloging in Publication Data
Names: Malchiodi, Cathy A. editor.
Title: The handbook of art therapy and digital technology / edited by Cathy
 Malchiodi.
Description: London ; Philadelphia : Jessica Kingsley Publishers, 2018. |
 Includes bibliographical references and index.
Identifiers: LCCN 2018006131 | ISBN 9781785927928 (alk. paper)
Subjects: | MESH: Art Therapy | Computer Systems | Information Technology
Classification: LCC RC489.A72 | NLM WM 450.5.A8 | DDC 616.89/1656-
-dc23 LC record available at https://lccn.loc.gov/2018006131

British Library Cataloguing in Publication Data
A CIP catalogue record for this book is available from the British Library

ISBN 978 1 78592 792 8
eISBN 978 1 78450 774 9

Printed and bound in the United States

To all art therapists who dare
to push outside the envelope.

CONTENTS

CLINICAL AND EDUCATIONAL APPLICATIONS

FIGURES

TABLES

FOREWORD

Digital technology offers many creative opportunities for art therapists: user-friendly software programs enable easy image manipulation, filmmaking, animation, and more, which has expanded the repertoire of clinical interventions. Although this has been in many ways a positive development, digital technology has also been a source of anxiety, especially for art therapists who, like me, are "digital immigrants," born before the 1980s. Concerns such as protection of confidentiality, and etiquette and boundaries on social media platforms, have been consistently raised within our profession. Another debate has focused on the lack of the "relational, tactile and sensory experiences" (p.23) that abound when using traditional art materials.

This book is therefore an excellent and extremely timely publication where current issues of practice, research, and ethics are clearly laid out and explored. Cathy Malchiodi belongs to a small group of pioneers in this field and expertly uses her depth of understanding to address its potentials and pitfalls. The contributors to this book bring their unique experiences of different aspects of digital technology, which make for a rich, informative, and thought-provoking publication. The inclusion in each chapter of illustrative case vignettes and a table of recommendations is particularly helpful for all practitioners—digital immigrants and natives alike. In addition, innovations in practice are included, and I hope that these will be replicated and further developed worldwide to benefit our clients.

I learned a lot from this book and although primarily referencing US law and structures, I found much of its content applicable and relevant internationally. I recommend this book as an "essential reading" publication for art therapists worldwide.

Dr Val Huet, BAAT Chief Executive Officer

ACKNOWLEDGMENTS

Creating an edited book is much more than simply curating a series of chapters; it involves developing a comprehensive table of contents, finding the very best topic experts, collaborating with authors to write and revise chapters, and working with excellent support staff to craft a work worthy of publication. I am particularly proud of *The Handbook of Art Therapy and Digital Technology* because it is much more than a curated series of essays; for this reason, there are many individuals to thank for helping manifest the vision for this book.

First, I express my gratitude to the staff at Jessica Kingsley Publishers and in particular, Jane Evans, Commissioning Editor, and Hannah Snetsinger, Production Editor, for overseeing the editorial process and various aspects that go into making an edited book into a cohesive work. My thanks also go to Jessica Kingsley, who recently retired from decades in the publishing business. Jessica saw the value in publishing *Art Therapy and Computer Technology* back in 2000, far before anyone could foresee the expansion of art therapy to the digital domain. I, for one, am grateful to Jessica Kingsley for bringing so many wonderful and important books on art therapy, creative arts therapies, and expressive arts therapy to print. She has made a seminal and lasting impact on these professions through her vision, passion, and commitment.

Above all, I am indebted to the chapter authors for their contributions and for generously sharing expertise on digital media and its wide-ranging applications to the field of art therapy. If you have glanced at the contributor list, you will quickly see that these authors bring an international and culturally diverse presence to the contents of this book. In particular, I am impressed by how each author has focused on the central importance of how clients can benefit from the integration of digital technology within art-based intervention. While many authors have explored how digital technology and social networking benefit the practitioner, it is refreshing and inspiring to read about actual art psychotherapeutic applications through practical examples, experiences, and strategies that readers can immediately apply to their own work with clients.

As the editor, I am grateful to have learned so much from these outstanding authors and look forward to applying their wisdom in my own work.

Finally, I thank my husband David for buying me my first computer back in the late 1980s and starting me on a path of inquiry and discovery of all things digital. He has patiently endured the voices of artificial intelligence devices in my office and many delayed dinners when I am staring at a screen to write or edit film or immersing myself in alternative worlds via virtual reality. Thank you for making this latest book possible.

Additional resources that accompany this book can be found at www.digitalarttherapyinfo.org.

1
Foundations

INTRODUCTION TO ART THERAPY AND DIGITAL TECHNOLOGY

Cathy Malchiodi

In *Art Therapy and Computer Technology* (Malchiodi, 2000), I wrote:

> The field of art therapy, like other areas of health care, is increasingly influenced by the tremendous growth in the use of computers by professionals and the general public, the presence of the Internet, the proliferation of electronic communication, and the expansion of computer-mediated therapy. For art therapy, the strides made in computer technology and digital imagery may be even more important as they have opened up opportunities to incorporate digital media such as photography and videotape as well as computer painting and photo programs in therapy, electronic arts that can offer clients new ways to express themselves creatively. The Internet has had a significant impact on the field, creating a virtual global community of art therapists through electronic mail, online discussion groups, and real-time cyber-chats. It has made possible an international network of interchange between people with shared interests in the arts in mental health,

> medicine, and healing who might otherwise have not been in communication with each other. (p.13)

While digital technology has moved far beyond these platforms, much of this observation I made at the end of the 20th century continues to be surprisingly true. Digital communication is now ubiquitous, overtaking the workplace and daily life; social media platforms have manifested a virtual global community, making it possible for individuals to connect in ways that were not available only a decade ago. The field of art therapy is increasingly influenced by digital technology and social networking in wide-ranging ways including not only new media for creative expression, but also a variety of challenging professional and ethical issues that continue to be defined (Malchiodi and Cutcher, 2012, 2013, 2014, 2015) (see Chapter 2 for an expanded discussion).

Since the publication of the original 2000 volume, we have been living in a time of unprecedented technological advancement. Art therapy, like other allied health and mental health fields, has had to grapple with the rapid influx of electronic technologies for communication and self-expression; art therapists have met these changes often with some trepidation, wisely citing the need to increase understanding and research on the intersection between digital media and clinical applications (Asawa, 2009). Other practitioners remain focused on the ethical, clinical, and professional questions that have emerged with increased use of digital technology and social media (Alders *et al.*, 2011; Belkofer and McNutt, 2011; Malchiodi and Cutcher, 2012, 2013, 2014, 2015; Miller, 2017; Peterson, 2010). Most agree that technology is influencing the way art therapists practice in a variety of settings (Carlton, 2014; Choe, 2014, 2017; Malchiodi and Johnson, 2013), although not without a struggle to remain actively conversant with digital media and platforms (Austin, 2009).

This chapter provides an overview of digital art therapy, highlighting the precursors and the early and contemporary art therapy pioneers in the use of digital technology, and introduces readers to the key concepts integral to subsequent chapters in this book. Because software and digital platforms change so frequently, reference to specific devices, software, and programs is kept to a minimum. Instead, this chapter provides key topics in this emerging area and current issues and applications to the field of art therapy that are addressed in more detail throughout the book. Most importantly, this introduction highlights the two main areas of digital technology that impact the practice of art therapy—the use of digital media for self-expression and the influence of digital communication and social networking/social media on the field and therapeutic practice.

Defining Digital Art Therapy

Digital art therapy is a relative newcomer to art therapy methods and materials that can be defined as "all forms of technology-based media, including digital collage, illustrations, films, and photography that are used by therapists to assist clients in creating art as part of the process of therapy" (Malchiodi, 2011, p.33). It involves any activities that use computer keyboards and screens or other technological devices for image-making within the context of treatment. Equipment used to generate, modify, or manipulate images and electronic methods—such as electronic processing (computers or tablet devices), photocopying, filmmaking, videotaping, and photography in various iterations from single reflex devices to digital cameras and smartphones—are also part of the spectrum of digital art therapy methodologies (Austin, 2009; Ehinger, 2017; Malchiodi, 2000, 2011; Thong, 2007). These technologies include, but are not limited to, these currently popular forms: apps (Choe, 2017; Malchiodi, 2011; Malchiodi and Johnson, 2013) and various forms of image-creation and film editing software; animation (Austin, 2009); gaming, virtual reality (VR) and participatory environments; tablet technology (Darke, 2017); light painting (Vasquez and Laine, 2017); artificial intelligence; and digital storytelling, as well as other techno-media discussed throughout this book.

Electronic Arts: Precursors to Digital Art Therapy

Digital media were originally referred to as "electronic arts," a term used to describe the use of any electronic equipment to generate, modify, or manipulate images (Malchiodi, 2000) and to include anything from altering the size and color of an image through photocopying to filmmaking, videotaping, and hands-on photography with any type of camera. For example, magazine images and photographs can be modified by size and color and hue through the use of photocopy machines, an art-based technique made popular by such artists as Jenny Holzer and others in the late 1980s, contemporary artists who introduced the idea that images can be constructed, deconstructed, assembled, and manipulated through a variety of digital means, opening up a new range of self-expression through combining preexisting images.

Photography was a major precursor of early computer-mediated approaches to art therapy and not only includes work with any type of camera (from instant photography to 35 mm), but also included some emerging digital technology allowing anyone to directly load photographs from a digital camera into their computer and enhance color, manipulate images, and adjust size and composition (for more information on photography, see Chapters 6 and 16). Therapeutic uses of photography were introduced and developed by Krauss and Fryrear (1983), Weiser (1988, 1993), and Wolf (1976), among others, underscoring this medium as a potent modality for assessment, intervention, and self-expression.

Video emerged as a third electronic art preceding the use of computers in art therapy (McNiff and Cook, 1975; Weiser, 1988, 1993). In Chapter 5 of this book, McNiff recalls his experiences with videotape as a prelude to his early work with computer technology; he notes that in 2000:

> When portable video technology became available in the early 1970s, I was given many opportunities to use it within the art therapy program that I was coordinating in a state hospital…
>
> This early experimentation with new media took place at a time when some in art therapy insisted that the discipline should be restricted to drawing, painting, and modeling with clay. (p.87)

McNiff has been a long-time advocate of multimodal ways of working with people and naturally integrated video, photography, and performance into art therapy sessions (McNiff, 1999; McNiff and Cook, 1975). The possibilities for applications of photography and videotape expanded the vision of art therapy beyond the traditional methods of painting, drawing, and sculpture, and has set the stage for art therapists to continue to explore how computer and digital technologies can augment and enhance the creative process and self-expression.

The Twentieth Century: Computer-Mediated Art Therapy

In 1996, I observed that there were growing numbers of art therapists who saw possibilities for creative expression, therapeutic intervention, education, and online communication, pioneers who were exploring and developing the use of computer-related technologies in assessment, treatment, and intervention. In these earliest applications, inclusivity of client populations and sensitivity to individual needs, particularly people with disabilities, illnesses, or physical limitations that limit their involvement in traditional therapy, guided art therapists in exploring computers as a possibility for self-expression and therapeutic intervention.

In the 1980s, very few art therapists were writing about the use of computer technology within the practice of art therapy. Diane Weinberg (1985) was one of very few addressing the interface of art therapy and computers, with a focus on the potential of computers with patients with physical limitations such as quadriplegia, stroke, or brain trauma. Because of the population with which she worked, Weinberg was prompted to explore computer art therapy as a rehabilitative support to conventional art therapy. She used what would now be considered extremely primitive technology: an Atari 800 computer with a simple graphics program with which to draw and manipulate images.

Weinberg observed that computer art therapy offers an unusually novel and rapid approach to successful art experiences, and it has the unique advantage of being able to elicit patients' curiosity and motivation to build upon their residual strengths (1985). Although computers were comparatively simple at the time she did her work, her exploration underscored several points that still hold true today. First, computers, then and now, offer the ability to change a simple design into one of complexity, rapidly provide the possibility for different visual orientations, and easily alter color and lines. Computer programs offer step-by-step instructions and ease of operation; at the time of Weinberg's writing, she used the keyboard, a joystick (a handle that can be moved into various positions) to create images, and a light pen to trace objects or images placed on a photosensitive graphics tablet.

Weinberg also noted the possibilities computers had in monitoring patients' cognitive responses. For example, because computers have the capability to recognize and remember decisions made about composition, color, and design, they could conceivably be used to record for research purposes how patients use them to make decisions, problem-solve, and express themselves creatively. I believe that Weinberg was somewhat of a visionary with regard to possibilities for computer-mediated art therapy, particularly in the area of learning just how people interface creatively and therapeutically with technology and how it could be applied to art therapy research.

Art therapist Devorah Canter was also far ahead of the field in her vision and enthusiasm for computers' interface with art therapy. She brought live demonstrations of computer technology to national conferences and contributed some early articles and chapters (1987, 1989). Canter made a convincing case for why computers could be a medium of choice in work with children and adolescents in particular, populations that have come to know and feel comfortable with computers at an early age. For example, she noted that children and adolescents with learning disabilities experience success not achieved in other contexts through computer communication. She observed that computers foster increased concentration skills and improved self-esteem due to the experience of mastery, largely because younger clients come to know and feel comfortable with computers at an early age, noting that "sometimes it takes a modern tool like the computer to stimulate clients today" (Canter, 1989, p.314).

Twentieth-century art therapists also explored computer technology in order to develop new ways to offer individuals therapeutic experiences using drawing, painting, and photo software. Parker-Bell (1999), investigated how art therapists can use various graphics software packages as interactive and creative tools. Collie and Čubranić (Collie,1998; Collie and Čubranić, 1999) examined art therapy services as a form of telemedicine and conducted studies on just how art therapy can be effectively offered through existing telehealth and computer technology and to create distance art-based psychosocial services for people with cancer or other illnesses. McLeod (1999) pioneered the use of computers and software in her work in schools, demonstrating how this technology can enhance creative expression, not only for children and adolescents, but for people of all ages. During the 1990s, hospitals began using computer technology to enhance patients' abilities to express and cope with feelings about illness and hospitalization; pediatric programs like the Starlight Foundation[1] encouraged patients to use graphics software and to participate in electronic communication to establish social support from others beyond their hospital beds (Malchiodi and Johnson, 2013); this program now provides opportunities to experience VR for pediatric patients, an example of how technology has evolved to meet needs through new media platforms.

The Twenty-First Century: Digital Art Therapy

Since 2000, the availability of digital technology and media has exponentially enlarged capabilities for creative expression, communication, and networking; as these advancements rapidly continue to emerge, there is also an increased curiosity and discussion among art therapists about the impact and applications of digital technology on practice. This is largely due to several factors. In contrast to pre-2000, there is now wide availability of digital equipment and software for image creation and communication, not only through a computer screen, but also via personal cellular phones and other compact devices. One can create imagery by using an endless variety of painting and drawing apps, or simply manipulate images through various collage software packages, apps, or online programs. For example, it is remarkably easy now to transform preexisting images through user-friendly photo enhancement software and apps as well as Internet programs that allow the user to "clip" images for use and manipulation in art expression (Figure 1.1). There is also easily accessible online photo and film editing software and increasingly accessible devices such as computer webcams, pocket-sized film cameras, and smartphones that can both take photographs and create film footage. The currently ubiquitous

---

1   www.starlight.org

YouTube has generated video possibilities unimaginable only a decade ago. All of these developments have raised interest among art therapists and others who apply art-based methods in their work with individuals of all ages.

Figure 1.1
Image created through an online collage-creation program
Reproduced with permission from the collection of Cathy Malchiodi © 2010

The art world has also embraced digital technology as a significant part of image-making. Contemporary artists are incorporating VR, robotics, artificial intelligence, and various digital image manipulation methods in their work, integrating technologies that are currently having a major influence on society and culture. These rapidly emerging art forms not only force artists to broaden the question of what art materials are, but also impact how art therapists and those who apply art-based media to meet therapeutic goals enhance self-expression. In brief, art therapy's "palette" has expanded from what may be defined as more "low tech" materials to digital forms of self-expression and communication.

Also, it is now difficult for any practitioner to ignore that increasing numbers of art therapy clients are influenced by, and involved on a daily basis with, digital media and networking. In other words, it is impossible to compartmentalize just how digital media and networking contribute to psychosocial experiences and the role of technology in individuals' worldviews. This is particularly true in working with young clients who make up a group known as "digital natives" (individuals born after 1980 who grew up in the digital age in communities and cultures with access to technology), which now demands that those who provide intervention to children understand the possibilities, challenges, and limitations of digital technology (Prensky, 2001). This is the generation who are "native speakers" of the digital language of computers, video games, the Internet, and eventually social media. In contrast, art therapists (like myself) may be part of the slowly decreasing group known as "digital immigrants" who were born before 1980 and became familiar with digital communication and devices as adults. The emergence of digital natives not only impacts direct art therapy services, it also continues to affect the delivery of art therapy education to incoming students who are savvy consumers of technology and social networking platforms.

In response to these influences, digital and electronic media are more consistently cited in literature on art therapy materials and methods (Garner, 2017; Malchiodi, 2011; Moon, 2010), and a growing number of social networking pages and websites specifically dedicated to art therapy and digital technology now exist. As a result, art therapists and other professionals continue to explore and develop digital media approaches cited earlier in this chapter. Art therapy education is also increasingly integrating digital technology, particularly in the area of online learning, within its pedagogical frameworks. As predicted in *Art Therapy and Computer Technology* (Malchiodi, 2000), distance learning is "an area of art therapy education that is likely to grow over the next decade if demand for art therapy information and learning experiences continue to increase throughout the world" (p.29).

The Endless Debate: Relational, Tactile, and Sensory Qualities of Digital Media

Digital media involve some distinctly different relational, tactile, and sensory experiences in contrast to traditional art materials. In fact, some art therapists might say that having a "relationship" with a computer screen or tablet is counterproductive to therapy in general because it alters the human dynamic that is a significant part of reparation and recovery. While computer technology does provide the senses with images, colors, sometimes sounds and, to varying extents, touch, pencils, pastels, paints, clay, and other traditional media are quite different sensory experiences (Malchiodi, 2009).

Back in 2001, Seiden observed that technology requires a different sensibility than traditional materials; the use of digital media emphasizes conceptual and perceptual abilities over manual skills in most cases. McNiff (1999) used the phrase "virtual studio," noting that art therapy's territory is inclusive of not only traditional materials, but also those that come in the form of electronic, multimedia, and digitized formats.

More recently, Carlton (2017) posed some deeper questions about digital media:

> I would like to counter these conclusions with a few questions. Is not the base nature of touch an experience of sensory, interactive, or spatial feedback? Do not these digital media materials provide both haptic immediacy to more abstract biochemical and behavioral response experiences within and around their screens, software, and hardware? Are some persons transgressing nuanced boundaries to reach in, touch, and be affected by computer matrixes and pixels while others are not? (p.26)

In fact, some digital technology, such as virtual reality programming, taps much more than just visual senses and may stimulate kinesthetic, vestibular, interoceptive, and proprioceptive experiences through providing the perception of three-dimensional space. Even digital devices create feedback to touch in that users learn that various movements such as "swiping the screen," or the now famous Apple founder Steve Jobs' "pinch" motion, have specific results.

There are also emerging examples of how digital media may be a preferred mode of expression for some individuals; in other words, while tactile contact with materials may be beneficial for some individuals, the properties of digital media may be helpful for others. For example, the Google Project Spectrum software program (Lynch, 2016) has demonstrated benefits with individuals with autism spectrum disorders. In brief, many of these individuals have reported that the manual process of drawing is frustrating, while creating using the virtual drawing program is not only gratifying, but also makes more visual sense to them than a pencil and paper.

Finally, in determining the role of digital media in art therapy, practitioners must ultimately consider how to maximize the individual's ability and satisfaction with expression rather than have a singular focus on the art forms' physical properties. The new media have yet-to-be-imagined possibilities that may help some individuals find pathways to expression. Particular children, adolescents, and adults who may not be able to manipulate traditional art media or are uncomfortable with tactile or physical properties of paint or clay may discover the capacity to be expressive through a smartphone drawing app, collage software, or filmmaking programs via a tablet. Viewing digital media as simply additional approaches to help people achieve expressiveness introduces new options for therapeutic change and encourages all art therapists to acknowledge these "materials" as an important part of integrative practice in the 21st century.

Digital Communication, Social Media, and Social Networking

Electronic and Digital Communication

Before 2000, there was a proliferation of computer-mediated therapy and healthcare services including what was once called "Internet therapy and counseling" (interaction between a client and therapist in synchronous or asynchronous communication), telemedicine (a term still in use today for information exchange via digital means to improve patient care), and telehealth (access to assessment, education, and intervention) (see Chapter 9 for more information). These platforms eventually impacted all forms of mental health and healthcare services, including art therapy and related arts-based fields, and were the starting point for ongoing discussions about confidentiality, secure transmission of data, and boundary issues in client–therapist communications.

Today, counseling, psychology, and art therapy specifically address electronic and digital communications in their ethics codes and standards of professional practice. Play therapy, an experientially based approach, includes a specific section on computer/Internet technology in its "best practices" document (Association for Play Therapy, 2016) and the field of counseling has extensive guidelines for Internet counseling (National Board for Certified Counselors, 2016). Art therapy continues to discuss and develop guidelines not only for text data communications, but also for Internet-based therapy and supervision as well as how art expressions are electronically transmitted and digitally stored with the goals of client privacy and confidentiality. Because ethics and professional practice issues are closely connected to electronic and digital communications, Chapter 2 explores these forms of interaction, data transmission, and image storage in more depth.

Social Networking and Social Media

Digital communication has also brought about social networking (the method of digital communication to engage with others) and social media (the photographs and data you upload) through various platforms where people can transmit information in real time over the Internet via one-to-one interactions or within groups (see Chapter 13). The impact of digital communication gave birth to what we now know as social networking in the mid-1990s. It was at that time that a new frontier called the Net became accessible through home computer use and the availability of Internet service providers (ISPs). Suddenly, anyone with a computer and a telephone line could send and receive electronic mail (e-mail), and hear the now famous words, "You've got mail," and also, "Get on the Net."

This area of communication and interaction fascinated me as soon as I heard about it and I became one of the very first subscribers to what was then a new Internet provider called America Online (AOL). It was through AOL that I began to regularly communicate with another art therapist and fellow cyberspace traveler, Barbara Levy, who was extremely interested in computer technology, especially online communication and distance learning. Barbara started a creative arts therapies bulletin board, initially with an Internet service provider called Delphi, and then later expanded to what was then AOL's health and medicine section; this became an extremely active Internet bulletin board (i.e. place to post discussions) during the mid-1990s.

As a result of this growing interest, Barbara Levy and I presented "Online art therapy communication" at the 26th annual conference of the American Art Therapy Association in 1995 to provide information on our experiences with computers and communication (Malchiodi, 1996; Malchiodi and Levy, 1995). To our surprise the room was packed with attendees who were taking copious notes on everything we had to say about the Internet and live online art therapy chats we conducted during that time. For those digital natives reading this, remember that at that time, cellphones were commonly the size of a brick and sported a long antenna; many consumers still did not yet own a home computer. In retrospect, it was amazing that we were also able to include a live demonstration of online message boards and chat rooms for creative arts therapists on AOL during the presentation. As far as I can recall, this was the first live online demonstration of cyberspace for art therapists at a national art therapy conference. While I don't remember the exact content of what we presented during that hour, I do vividly remember the trauma I experienced trying to talk the hotel staff into giving us a phone connection so we could provide a real-time example of cyberspace to conference attendees. We managed to get online by using Barbara's laptop computer (a technological feat for that time period), and were able to show on a projected screen just how and where art therapists could use an Internet provider to have live, online discussions and post messages to others through bulletin boards and other venues.

At around the same time Barbara and I also hosted the first national online chat for art therapists through AOL. It was an interesting experience of several people trying to "talk" to each other through words alone typed on the screen. It was cumbersome at best, but it was exciting to see that it could be accomplished and that a group of people could communicate to each other in the cyberspace simultaneously. Following that event there was a very active message board established and facilitated by Barbara, one of the first international forums where art therapy was discussed, debated, and promoted to anyone in the world who had the computer and Internet access to participate. By the end of the 20th century, more art therapists began to explore and expand the possibilities of computer technology for communication, creativity, and therapeutic intervention through the development of Internet forums, distance learning opportunities, e-mail listservs, electronic bulletin boards, and live cyber chats.

These primitive cyber events that took place decades ago formed the foundations for the social networking and social media phenomena that exist today, including Facebook, Twitter, Instagram, Pinterest, and LinkedIn, blogs, podcasts, and web-based video communications. In all cases, social networking is designed to encourage interactions with content and other users as well as information sharing in the form of text, photographs/images, audio, and/or film.

For those individuals immersed in social media and social networking, engagement is now often routine in the form of posting personal updates, photos, or videos; commenting on others' posts and updates; writing blogs or recording podcasts; and in general, devoting time to reading or scrolling through newsfeeds, blogs, and photos, and watching videos (generally via YouTube, Facebook or other large social media platforms) (for more discussion on social media behavior, see Chapters 3, 4, and 13). In fact, individuals who have grown up with digital communications and social media now expect to communicate and express themselves far differently than in the past because of experiences with social networking, cellphones, and other devices; these trends may eventually hold true for digital immigrants who are increasingly embracing not only smartphone technology, but also Internet use as a source of news, information, and networking (Pew Research Center, 2017).

In addition to monitoring digital communications such as text messages and e-mail, it is probably safe to say that many individuals we see in therapy sessions now spend the majority of their waking hours looking at a smartphone, tablet, or computer screen. For example, the National Endowment for the Arts (NEA, 2013), a US government-funded agency, supports this observation with regard to the arts. The NEA reports that there is an overall rise in online sharing, access to and connection with creative expression, and art-related interactions among adult users. It attributes this to the characteristics of social networking and social media that provide accessible opportunities for engaging with art as well as sharing, viewing, and creating art expressions. In another research report, the Pew Research Center cites similar findings about the arts and digital access (2013). It is easy to understand that platforms like Facebook, Instagram, and others that allow for posting of images can manifest virtual environments where individuals can display their creative work, comment, collaborate, and support others or learn new approaches to art making. One example, the Art Therapy + Happiness Project which attracted over 500 participants worldwide, demonstrates that online communities are attractive to art therapists and other creatives interested in participating in virtual communities and in supporting others' creative expression (Malchiodi, 2015) (see Chapter 13 for more information). Others simply enjoy the possibilities for sharing art images, art-based approaches, and resources on platforms like Pinterest which is essentially an online, virtual "scrapbooking" platform to store links and images.

Art therapists suggest that there are benefits to social networking and social media engagement through platforms such as online communities by encouraging motivation, sharing, displaying, and exchanging actual art images (Chilton *et al.*, 2009). These virtual spaces have an influence on resilience and positivity through meaningful interactions and a perceived sense of belonging according to some studies. However, therapists who are savvy on the clinical impact of digital technology on children, teens, and adults in art therapy treatment now recognize the social isolation and impersonal nature of computer work as a challenge manifested by social media and digital devices (Klorer, 2009; Malchiodi, 2000). Digital communication and social media have also blurred the boundaries and the understanding of what is public and what is private (see Chapters 2 and 3). As Belfoker and McNutt (2011) observe, "The impact of the high levels of participation in social media, both today and in the future, is creating a multifaceted, multi-networked social construct where ideas of belonging and creativity may be profoundly and permanently transformed" (p.159).

Conclusion

Digital technology continues to evolve at what often seems like a speed-of-light pace; over a brief span of years, exciting and extraordinary possibilities for expression and communication through the rapidly changing terrains of digital technology have developed. Despite the contributions of 20th-century art therapy pioneers and more contemporary practitioners in art therapy in the forefront of exploring and initiating novel and exciting ways to use digital technology and online communications to enhance therapeutic and professional exchange, relatively little is known about art therapists' use of digital media in practice. When I first used the term "digital art therapy" in 2011, the idea of such an approach was still undeveloped and ever-evolving as technologies continued to emerge that influenced the delivery of art therapy and the therapeutic relationship itself.

Back in the 20th century, computers were labeled as difficult, too technological, and even seductive to some art therapists (Kramer *et al.*, 1995); fast-forward to today and it is becoming increasingly difficult to avoid knowing something about how this technology impacts not only therapeutic work and communication, but also how it influences the lives of the people with whom art therapists work. In contrast, Brian Austin (2009) calls for acknowledgment of technology and poses important questions for art therapists in the 21st century:

> Will our profession succumb to the fate of the sorcerer's apprentice—unschooled in and overwhelmed by the latest technological tools, and left to suffer from delusions of grandeur and flooding? Or will art therapists become technologically knowledgeable experts who embody the role of the sorcerer—where knowledge of media allows for the expression of rich symbolic content while also facilitating a therapeutic capacity to disperse the dark waters of our flooded clients? (p.85)

These questions and others underscore the content of this book and the wisdom presented by the chapter authors, not only highlighting the potential to expand art therapy into a new world of possibilities, but also illuminating the inevitable questions and challenges that come with the presence of digital technology in our work.

References

Alders, A., Beck, L., Allen, P.B. and Mosinski, B.B. (2011) Technology in art therapy: Ethical challenges. *Art Therapy 28*(4), 165–170.

Asawa, P. (2009) Art therapists' emotional reactions to the demands of technology. *Art Therapy 26*(2), 58–65.

Association for Play Therapy (2016) *Play Therapy Best Practices: Clinical, Professional and Ethical Issues.* Fresno, CA: APT.

Austin, B. (2009) Renewing the debate: Digital technology in art therapy and the creative process. *Art Therapy 26*(2), 83–85.

Belkofer, C.M. and McNutt, J.V. (2011) Understanding social media culture and its ethical challenges for art therapists. *Art Therapy 28*(4), 159–164.

Canter, D.S. (1987) The therapeutic effects of combining Apple Macintosh computers and creativity software in art therapy sessions. *Art Therapy 4*(1), 17–26.

Canter, D.S. (1989) Art therapy and computers. In H. Wadeson, J. Durkin, and D. Perach (eds.) *Advances in Art Therapy.* New York, NY: Wiley.

Carlton, N.R. (2014) Digital culture and art therapy. *The Arts in Psychotherapy 41*(1), 41–45.

Carlton, N.R. (2017) Grid + pattern: The sensory qualities of digital media. In R. Garner (ed.) *Digital Art Therapy.* London: Jessica Kingsley Publishers.

Chilton, G., Gerity, L., LaVorgna-Smith, M. and MacMichael, H.N. (2009) An online art exchange group: 14 secrets for a happy artist's life. *Art Therapy 26*(2), 66–72.

Choe, N. (2014) An exploration of the qualities and features of apps for art therapy. *The Arts in Psychotherapy 41*(2), 145–154.

Choe, N. (2017) Utilizing digital tools and apps in art therapy sessions. In R. Garner (ed.) *Digital Art Therapy.* London: Jessica Kingsley Publishers.

Collie, K. (1998) Art therapy on-line: A participatory action study of distance counselling issues. Unpublished master's thesis, University of British Columbia, Vancouver, Canada.

Collie, K. and Čubranić, D. (1999) An art therapy solution to a telehealth problem. *Art Therapy 16*(4), 186–193.

Darke, K. (2017) iPad apps and traumatic brain injury. In R. Garner (ed.) *Digital Art Therapy.* London: Jessica Kingsley Publishers.

Ehinger, J. (2017) Therapeutic technology re-envisioned. In R. Garner (ed.) *Digital Art Therapy.* London: Jessica Kingsley Publishers.

Garner, R. (ed.) (2017) *Digital Art Therapy.* London: Jessica Kingsley Publishers.

Klorer, P.G. (2009) The Effects of Technological Overload on Children: An Art Therapist's Perspective. *Journal of the American Art Therapy Association 26*(2), 80–82.

Kramer, E., Gerity, L., Henley, D. and Williams, K. (1995, November) Art and art therapy and the seductive environment. Panel presented at the 26th annual conference of the American Art Therapy Association, San Diego, CA.

Krauss, D. and Fryrear, J. (1983) *Phototherapy in Mental Health*. Springfield, IL: Charles C. Thomas.

Lynch, A. (2016, June 6) Designing a better world for all—the Project Spectrum Series Part One. Retrieved on April 1, 2018 at www.builtr.io/designing-a-better-world-for-all-the-project-spectrum-series-part-one

Malchiodi, C.A. (1996) Art therapists in cyberspace. *Art Therapy 13*(4), 230–231.

Malchiodi, C.A. (2000) *Art Therapy and Computer Technology*. London: Jessica Kingsley Publishers.

Malchiodi, C.A. (2009, November 2) Art therapy meets digital art and social media. Retrieved on April 1, 2018 at www.psychologytoday.com/blog/arts-and-health/200911/art-therapy-meets-digital-art-and-social-multimedia

Malchiodi, C.A. (2011) Materials, media and methods. In C. Malchiodi (ed.) *Handbook of Art Therapy*. New York, NY: Guilford Press.

Malchiodi, C.A. (2015, May 31) The Art Therapy + Happiness Project. Retrieved on April 1, 2018 at www.psychologytoday.com/blog/arts-and-health/201505/the-art-therapy-happiness-project

Malchiodi, C.A. and Cutcher, D. (2012) Issues and ethics of art therapy in a digital age. Retrieved on April 1, 2018 at www.digitalarttherapyinfo.com/resources/ethics-social-media-digital-art-therapy

Malchiodi, C.A. and Cutcher, D. (2013) Art therapy and ethics in a digital age. Retrieved on April 1, 2018 at www.digitalarttherapyinfo.com/resources/ethics-social-media-digital-art-therapy

Malchiodi, C.A. and Cutcher, D. (2014) Art therapy and ethics in a digital age. Retrieved on April 1, 2018 at www.digitalarttherapyinfo.com/resources/ethics-social-media-digital-art-therapy

Malchiodi, C.A. and Cutcher, D. (2015) The ethics and art therapy: How do art therapy ethics measure up? You decide! Retrieved on April 1, 2018 at www.digitalarttherapyinfo.com/resources/ethics-social-media-digital-art-therapy

Malchiodi, C.A. and Johnson, E.R. (2013) Digital art therapy with children in hospitals. In C. Malchiodi (ed.) *Art Therapy and Health Care*. New York, NY: Guilford Press.

Malchiodi, C. and Levy, B. (1995 November) Online art therapy communication. Oral presentation at the 26th annual conference of the American Art Therapy Association, San Diego, CA.

McLeod, C. (1999) Empowering creativity with computer-assisted art therapy: An introduction to available programs and techniques. *Art Therapy 16*(4), 201–205.

McNiff, S. (1999) The virtual art therapy studio. *Art Therapy 16*(4), 197–200.

McNiff, S. and Cook, C. (1975) Video art therapy. *Art Psychotherapy 2*, 55–63.

Miller, G. (2017) *The Art Therapist's Guide to Social Media*. New York, NY: Routledge.

Moon, C.H. (2010) A history of materials and media in art therapy. In C. Moon (ed.) *Materials and Media in Art Therapy*. New York, NY: Routledge.

National Board for Certified Counselors (2016) *Policy Regarding the Provision of Distance Professional Services*. Greensboro, NC: NBCC.

National Endowment for the Arts (NEA) (2013, September) *How a Nation Engages with Art: Highlights from the 2012 Survey of Public Participation in the Arts (NEA Research Report No. 57)*. Retrieved on April 1, 2018 at www.arts.gov/sites/default/files/highlights-from-2012-sppa-revised-oct-2015.pdf

Parker-Bell, B. (1999) Embracing a future with computers and art therapy. *Art Therapy 16*(4), 180–185.

Peterson, B.C. (2010) The media adoption stage model of technology for art therapy. *Art Therapy 27*(1), 26–31.

Pew Research Center (2013, January 4) *Arts Organizations and Digital Technologies*. Retrieved on April 1, 2018 at www.pewinternet.org/files/old-media/Files/Reports/2013/PIP_ArtsandTechnology_PDF.pdf

Pew Research Center (2017, May) Tech adoption climbs among older adults. Retrieved on April 1, 2018 at www.pewinternet.org/2017/05/17/tech-adoption-climbs-among-older-adults

Prensky, M. (October 2001) Digital natives, digital immigrants. *On the Horizon 9*(5), 1–6.

Seiden, D. (2001) *Mind over Matter: The Uses of Materials in Art, Education and Therapy*. Chicago IL: Magnolia Street Publishers.

Thong, S.A. (2007) Redefining the tools of art therapy. *Art Therapy 24*(2), 52–58.

Vasquez, C. and Laine, L. (2017) Therapeutic light painting photography. In R. Garner (ed.) *Digital Art Therapy*. London: Jessica Kingsley Publishers.

Weinberg, D. (1985) The potential of rehabilitative computer art therapy for the quadriplegic, cerebral vascular accident and brain trauma patient. *Art Therapy 2*(2), 66–72.

Weiser, J. (1988) PhotoTherapy: Using snapshots and photo-interactions in therapy with youth. In C. Schaefer (ed.) *Innovative Interventions in Child and Adolescent Therapy*. New York, NY: Wiley.

Weiser, J. (1993) *PhotoTherapy Techniques: Exploring the Secrets of Personal Snapshots and Family Albums*. Vancouver, Canada: PhotoTherapy Centre.

Wolf, R. (1976) The Polaroid technique: Spontaneous dialogues from the unconscious. *Art Psychotherapy 3*(3), 197–201.

2

ETHICS, DIGITAL TECHNOLOGY, AND SOCIAL MEDIA

Cathy Malchiodi, Donald Cutcher, and Kristin Belkofer

In response to the rapidly changing terrain of digital technology and social media and networking, credentialing bodies and professional associations have been forced to regularly respond with revisions and updates to their ethics codes. Art therapists are now recognized professionals in a growing number of countries throughout the world; they not only adhere to fairly universal ethics codes governing professional standards and conduct, they also may be governed by national, state, or provincial regulations. In all cases, the ubiquitous presence of digital media impacts the work of all helping professionals, no matter where they live and practice.

While this chapter cannot address every single possibility for ethics dilemmas involving art therapy, digital technology, and social media, we chose to emphasize several broad areas that all therapists should be aware of when it comes to digital media, including: digital and electronic communications; therapist–client boundaries in the digital age; online art therapy services; and the impact of social media on art therapists' client interactions and services. Because there are often no definite answers to ethics questions, this chapter's purpose is to highlight ethical issues that often have no simple or singular answers when it comes to the presence of digital technology and social media within the context of art therapy practice. Readers will also find additional ethics discussions that address specific topics and situations included in several other chapters in this book. Finally, the issues presented in this chapter are not new; see Appendix 1 for the general ethical principles for "potential cyber art therapists."

Code of Ethics and Digital Technology

As reported by Malchiodi (2000), one group of art therapists was truly ahead of the curve when it came to ethics and digital technology—the British Columbia Art Therapy Association (BCATA) in Canada. In 1999, BCATA published *Technology Guidelines: BCATA Recommendations for Ethical Practice* (Franz *et al.*, 1999) which "specifically addresses the unique concerns for art making and art images created, scanned, copied, transmitted, and/or stored via computers" (Malchiodi, 2000, p.128). The authors identified several key issues: maintenance of computer and digital technology skills; storage issues; web management and professionalism; chat lines; and scanned and digital images of client art expressions. The guidelines also discuss the uniqueness of digital images, underscoring the need for specific treatment and consent for display of art expressions on Internet platforms.

While there are many codes of ethics that have been developed by art therapy organizations throughout the world, the *Code of Ethics, Conduct and Disciplinary Procedures* prepared by the Art Therapy Credentials Board (ATCB, 2017) is the focus of this chapter because of its recent additions covering digital communications and social media. We also reference the American Counseling Association's *Code of Ethics* (ACA, 2014) because currently many art therapists in the US are licensed as mental health or professional counselors; the ACA has been at the forefront of providing guidelines and regular updates on counseling, digital technology, and social media to its professional members.

Digital and Electronic Transmittal of Client Communications and Data

All therapists who work at agencies, clinics, and hospitals, or as independent practitioners, have to follow not only ethical guidelines for transmittal of client data, but also laws and regulations about communication of sensitive or personal information. In the US, the

Health Insurance Portability and Accountability Act (HIPAA) (US Department of Health and Human Services, 2017) is legislation that provides regulations for data privacy and security regarding medical information; if you work in a location outside the US, there are likely regulations that govern transmittal of client information in your country. With regard to digital technology, HIPAA is important for two reasons. One, the HIPAA Privacy Rule, or Standards for Privacy of Individual Health Information, established standards to protect patient health information. Second, the HIPAA Security Rule, or Security Standards for Protection of Electronic Protected Health Information, establishes the standards for patient data security.

Because HIPAA includes any information collected from clients' evaluation and treatment, data includes not only information about individuals in therapy, such as history, diagnoses, and/or progress notes, but also photographs, film, and/or artwork created as part of sessions. The latter may be original artwork or digitally formatted images, and by HIPAA standards is defined as protected health information (PHI) because it may contain personally identifying characteristics or data.

Individual agencies or hospitals also may or may not set specific policies for how to manage and document this digital data received from clients via text or e-mail. There are situations where it may seem clear that documentation is needed (suicidal ideation or self-harm), while many other exchanges may not be so obvious. It is helpful to remind clients that texting or e-mailing always presents risks to confidentiality, even when systems are password protected or encrypted. HIPAA regulations always apply, so therapists must follow these regulations. This means potentially their agency as well as the therapists as clinicians, and client should know where their clinical data lives. Therapists must develop these protocols for themselves, including the proper disposal and destruction of this information from personal devices if used in professional contexts (Reamer, 2015). Therapists should also ensure that their disclosure statements and release of information forms contain specific information regarding electronic communications and digital data, including transmittal of images created during treatment.

Client Rights and Digital Artwork

While confidentiality is a priority in all psychotherapeutic relationships, digital technology as well as social networking have provided ethical challenges for many helping professionals. Here are two brief hypothetical case examples to consider which highlight some of the ethical questions that arise when client-created art expressions are publicly shared on the Internet, even when permission has been obtained.

Case Example 2.1

An art therapist conducting a Google search for art therapy with children from violent homes comes across a reference to a SlideShare[1] presentation by another practitioner on her LinkedIn page. The practitioner's SlideShare presentation contains drawings by children who have witnessed domestic violence or homicides, or have been subjected to physical or sexual abuse. Although the drawings do not have names or dates of birth on them, nonetheless several of them have idiosyncratic features that could potentially identify the child who created them; one drawing has very specific content depicting details of a violent murder. The art therapist viewing these images also discovered that she could download the presentations, including the children's drawings, or easily download screenshots of the artworks.

Case Example 2.2

An art therapist posts videos of sessions with a minor child who is identified as having a disability and uses the child's first name; there is no attempt to disguise the face of the child in the videos. The art therapist justifies the display of the videos on public social media for the stated purpose of education and also states that there is signed permission from the parents to post the videos, including the child's name, without disguise. The videos can be downloaded by viewers of the page.

---

1   A platform for publicly displaying PowerPoints on the social media site LinkedIn.

While these particular practitioners' intent may have been to educate the public about art therapy, the case examples bring up many questions and possible ethical "blind spots" about display of art expressions in a very public social media forum. For instance, even if caregivers provided consent to exhibit their children's art expressions, most do not fully understand what it means to display their children's images on platforms such as SlideShare. Unlike including images within an educational PowerPoint presentation shown to a group of professionals as part of a lecture or training session, images exhibited on the Internet can be digitally copied or manipulated. Children may sign a child assent form, but it is not likely that they will comprehend what sharing their "digital images" on social media platforms implies because of age and stage of development. In the case of the films posted to public social media, "No matter what consent was obtained or what the intent, inclusion of recordings of client sessions is really pushing the boundaries of ethics and individual welfare" (Malchiodi, 2009).

In brief, practitioners should always consider whether exhibit and display of any client art expressions is in the best interest of the individual in treatment or if they are being publicly shared for some other reason. In these case examples, therapists may be unconsciously using a public social media platform for self-promotion of art therapy services over client welfare (protection of confidential health information in the form of art expressions). In other words, in addition to considering how HIPAA impacts digital images, there are additional ethical reasons to avoid display of any client artwork, especially art expressions depicting highly charged events such as violence or abuse, on social media or other public web-based platforms. In the case of the child diagnosed with a disability, it may not be in the child's best interest over time to be identified through a specific diagnosis.

Finally, after considering the ramifications of publishing the artwork of young clients on public webpages, these art therapists may decide to delete this material from social media. While that seems like a solution, unfortunately it is not. Nothing is ever really "deleted" from the Internet and once on the Internet, these client-created art expressions can often still be retrieved. Data placed on SlideShare has often been downloaded or copied hundreds or thousands of times by visitors who may repurpose or use it in their presentations or post it elsewhere to social media. Even films that are posted on social media platforms such as Facebook can be downloaded with the right browser extension or software. So essentially, what is posted to the Internet lives on in cyberspace; it may be recoverable years later, possibly to the detriment of an individual in treatment who was entrusted to the psychotherapeutic care of an art therapist.

Informed Consent for Digital Artwork

When it first became possible to make digital copies of client-created images, it was hard to grasp all the ethical issues that could arise from the sudden ease of display of art expressions via the Internet. HIPAA, discussed in a previous section, requires signed consent for any photographs or film, including those taken with a camera, cell phone, or other device. Because text and images are transmitted in a different format than print material, electronic display and transmittal have opened up a "new area for permission to display and copyright ownership" (Malchiodi, 2000, p.129) as well as the ways that art therapists seek to promote the profession via digital images (Beck, 2009).

Therapists who seek to use client-created images in educational presentations and publications also must obtain specific informed consent and permission to reproduce any images not only for print, but for publication on Internet-based platforms. In the past, a line item might be added to a standard consent and release form to state that permission was granted for electronic display and other non-book formats. Today, the request to display images electronically is much more complicated because it is also easier for anyone to take a screenshot, download, or copy images from various media platforms.

Secure Transmittal and Storage of Client Information and Art Expressions

Case example 2.3 highlights a few of the many questions that arise when transmitting client data and art created as part of therapy.

Case Example 2.3

An art therapist provides a weekly group for a community agency with adult outpatients. The participants have all signed consent forms allowing the art therapist to take photographs of their art expressions; confidentiality is protected and no identifying information is visible on any of the images. In order to transfer and store these images, the art therapist e-mails each photograph to her secure desktop from the digital camera provided by the agency. What are some of the possible ethical challenges in transmittal of these client-created images?

Secure networks for transmittal of data are now part of most agency and hospital systems; however, it is not always possible to tell if you are using a secure network if you are using a third-party e-mail platform. This is particularly true for many of the most widely used e-mail providers; to be safe, these should never be used for transmittal of client data under any circumstances. For example, an art therapist communicating via personal e-mail with sensitive client data may be using a non-encrypted system. In brief, a non-encrypted system can be easily hacked, allowing personal e-mail to be accessed and possibly posted to other platforms.

In general, ethics codes also mandate that therapists employing communications and data transmittal technology in their practice are knowledgeable about and proficient in the digital devices they use. This often means staying current about encryption standards and new technologies, particularly if one is in independent practice. In the case example provided, were you able to arrive at a technological solution to the secure transfer of images? One way to ensure secure transfer of images is to use a USB connector or other direct transfer to a secure storage device such as a hard drive that is password protected and stored in a locked location. If the digital device (in this case, a camera) is used, after the transfer is complete the contents should be erased completely from the device.

The ATCB ethics code addresses electronic means of communication and storage; see Appendix 2 for this section of the code. Also, in Appendix 3 some sample statements for e-mail transmittals are also provided; you must also check with your workplace and local regulations to establish what is necessary by law to include in any statements you wish to use. In general, a clause that explains the risks to confidentiality, how to handle unauthorized receipt, and any specific policies or rules for responding to or terminating e-mail correspondence are standard and should be included (Zur, 2017).

Art Therapy Online

While most art therapy still takes place in face-to-face settings, the growth of telehealth and telemedicine (see Chapter 9) and other forms of digital communication are making possible more options for online or distance therapy and supervision. Online or distance art therapy can be defined as sessions that take place by video, phone, chats, instant messaging, virtual platforms, or other forms of electronic communication during a scheduled time. Some individuals choose online therapy because of convenience, lack of access due to location or transportation, disability, social phobia, or simply because of personal preferences. Global access to practitioners, supervision, and education as well as the need for more therapists and supervisors with specific credentials may be supporting a trend toward online activities.

In addition to knowledge of digital technology, online therapists should understand that relational qualities of distance therapy can be different than face-to-face sessions. For example, some individuals display a "disinhibition effect" (Suler, 2004) that may cause them to lose their inhibitions and share too much information far too quickly and discontinue therapy prematurely. Others may not engage in what is called "Internet etiquette" or "netiquette," a combination of the words "network" and "etiquette," failing to engage in appropriate and courteous interactions and responses to others. There is also the question of who is in the "virtual room"; in other words, are there unauthorized individuals who are able to see or hear what is designed to be a confidential session? Authorities on telehealth recommend that a camera scan the room prior to beginning a session to verify who is present and that the environment is secure (American Telemedicine Association, 2013).

Also, integration of art therapy into online sessions can be challenging. Currently, it is difficult to say just how many art therapists, for example, are actually conducting sessions online.

Because of the relational and unique environmental characteristics of art therapy, a distance format may be more conducive to verbal counseling than the multisensory qualities of art-based approaches. The few art therapists who currently do offer online sessions generally seem to prefer to use the time in a virtual session to discuss images created between sessions or provide various verbal approaches such as self-regulation protocols or psychotherapy techniques.

There is a lingering question about what qualifications are actually needed to provide online therapy or counseling because it may take place across jurisdictions that regulate mental health practices; for example, in the US each state regulates standards of practice for counselors and, in several states, art therapists. If a therapist is licensed in New York and a potential client lives in Iowa, can that therapist undertake online therapy with that individual? The answer to that question is still not clear. Also, art therapy is not a regulated profession throughout the US and the majority of states currently do not license art therapists. Therefore, providing services across jurisdictional boundaries may violate the jurisdictional licensure/credentialing requirements, creating an ethical violation and subsequent investigation. Until this question is finally resolved, therapists providing online sessions should clearly state, if licensed, in what jurisdiction(s) they are licensed to practice and under what state laws they practice; and if not licensed, under what credentialing body they practice.

Finally, technology-based supervision (also called "distance supervision") is regulated by both credentials bodies (for example, ATCB for art therapists in the US), national health systems, and state licensure boards for art therapists or counselors. This includes any supervisory relationship that takes place using telecommunications, e-mail, or video or audio conferencing taking place over the Internet using a variety of software applications. Like online therapy, any professional providing technology-based supervision must follow not only health privacy laws, but also any specific regulations for provision of supervision in their state or region. Providing distance supervision requires that supervisors understand the benefits and limitations of the technologies they are using; this also includes informing supervisees of any limitations of technology being employed. Additionally, there are the ethical questions about online clinical supervision, confidentiality, and secure digital transmittal of images and information. Recent discussions among professionals highlight the lack of regulatory/licensure agency acceptance of online supervision; for example, a distance supervision may not have access to the supervisee's client records or respond expediently to the supervisee's client emergencies.

Digital Accessibility and Boundary Issues

Virtual or online art therapy brings up the important questions of "digital accessibility" (how accessible am I to my clients via digital devices?) and boundary issues (how do I set boundaries for digital communication with my clients?). Some clinicians may communicate with clients via their own personal cell phones or opt for a separate "work" phone or a text messaging system. Regardless of the device through with therapists receive the communication, they are still programmed, societally and biologically, to respond to the stimuli of a text message for several reasons. It may be out of fear and anxiety that something is happening to their clients; it may be dopamine-fueled positive reinforcement because of a future booked appointment, a kind word about the session they just left, a note about successfully using a coping skill, or a child making it through the school day with praise and positive feedback. This hypervigilance is especially salient for clinicians who work within systems where they are "on-call" or are expected to be available for clients in crisis situations.

In all cases, therapists must be aware of how their thoughts, emotional states, and behaviors contribute to unhealthy technological patterns that put both clients and themselves at risk of compromised treatment, enmeshment, countertransference, and therapist burnout. When clients' emotional waves enter consciousness through words or images on our devices, the risk of being swept into their impact is high. The following is a journal reflection written by Kristin Belkofer exploring the feeling and perception of "always being connected" and "plugged in" to clients:

Case Example 2.4

9:07pm. It's late, dark, and cold as I leave the home of my final client for the evening after a difficult in-home therapy session. It's also snowing, and the roads are a mess. Since I'm pregnant, I've felt especially guilty about my attachment to my cell phone, especially while driving. My cell phone does double duty for personal and work use, as I work in people's homes and I am almost always traveling. Even though the phone is on silent, about nine new texts light up the screen, blaring louder than they would be if the phone actually made a sound. Texts 1 and 3 are from my client whose home I just left. She's explaining, in half sentences, that our conversation left her feeling anxious and alone because we are preparing for termination when I go on maternity leave. A missed call pops up. Mom of a teen client who cut so deeply last week that her leg needed to be stapled together. I swallow. She only calls when there's an emergency, and her child needs to be admitted to the hospital.

The other cluster of texts and a few e-mail notifications belong to co-therapists who work with me on cases. Assessments and prior authorizations for insurance are due. Schedules are changing. Call me back. Let me know. Cold robot tones, no time for punctuation, let alone conventions like please and thank you. Shoot...the phone number my client needs is in my iPad. Maybe I can just grab it from my bag quickly at the stoplight. I blink hard as I remember the car accident I survived last year, a missed stop sign while working, while trying to listen to Siri's directions as I navigated an unfamiliar neighborhood.

Somehow, I finish my drive home. I don't really remember the actual "drive" and that concerns me. What I do know is that behind my car drags a tangled tumbleweed of emotions: annoyance, anger, resentment, dread...and most profoundly guilt. Guilt because I know better. I know that my own anxious attachment to my devices leads to this, but it keeps happening because I haven't really committed to changing yet. I still want to see my texts—whether they be from clients or emoji-laden quips from friends—throughout my day.

9:34 pm. I'm home with my loving family and apparently 20 people need me, which oddly makes me feel alone. "Need" feels like too kind a word. My son is annoyed that I am still on my phone. I feel like my energy is being syphoned from my fingertips through imaginary cables into my phone, my iPad, my computer. My house is warm and dry, but I feel anything but safe. I am exposed and drained.

Therapists know emotions do not care about linear or logical timeframes; they have a unique professional role, as they are trusted with deeply sensitive and vulnerable expression on an everyday, often unpredictable, basis. However, even though therapists understand that emotional work does not always happen on a 9-to-5 schedule, this does not mean that they are charged with responding to emotionally charged communications (with the exception of a true emergency) in an immediate fashion. The world of e-mail and text messaging can be disorienting to the sense of time and space. All individuals now live in an age where they have constant access to counseling, either through texts to their face-to-face clinician or through online/distance counseling services which are being offered and developed at an increasing rate (Reamer, 2015). This creates a collective culture of access and availability, which—while highly effective in managing crises and working with people who would not have traditional access due to distance or mobility or location—can also rob therapists of necessary non-clinical time to reflect, regroup, and create safe space for themselves.

In addition, many feel that constant access and availability can dilute the power and meaning of a therapeutic alliance and that they open doors to unnecessary risk related to ethics, consent, privacy, and boundaries (Reamer, 2015; Sude, 2013). It's likely that therapists can all identify multiple times when clinical judgment was not at its best when they were tired or overworked. Will adding the variable of not physically seeing the client or being in a structured, expected space help this judgment? Sude (2013) elaborates on the nature of "synchronous" (thinking of the client and responding to them immediately when receiving a text from them) and "asynchronous" (lag time between responses, as in replying to a cluster of texts hours after they are received). What if a therapist sends rapid-fire "synchronous" communications, but the next time cannot respond until later? It's important to think about how this can be interpreted and if it's worth the risk clinically.

However, many clients simply feel more comfortable responding and communicating in writing, especially when building the early relationship with a therapist; this can have therapeutic benefits in itself (Sude, 2013). Keeping developmental and relational theories in mind (see Chapter 3 for more information), therapists can identify what need the clinical discourse is serving throughout the therapeutic process and identify how it can be used in a clinically appropriate and healthy way. Consider the following questions within your own practice: Can this interaction be addressed in the context of boundary setting? Will it lead to a discussion of the client's confidence in their own decisions? Does the individual simply need to feel less alone in the moment, and if so is there a transitional object that can gently replace the therapist's imagined digital presence (a journal, an app, a private Tumblr account)? These are only a few of the questions that arise in this age of digital devices and electronic communication.

Social Media and Social Networking

As discussed in Chapter 1, social media and social networking are topics now found in current mental health ethics codes. While there are numerous issues that affect 21st-century practitioners, the following general areas of social media and networking impact all therapists, including art therapists.

Therapist–Client Boundaries

Social media and networking make it more difficult to differentiate multiple roles that may lead to inadvertent exploitation or subjectivity; avoidance of multiple roles is an important part of most ethics codes. As discussed in the previous section, professional boundaries have become harder to maintain with the advent of digital technology. With social networking, "friending" clients on Facebook or adding them to contacts on other popular platforms immediately confuses boundaries. For example, in some cases this gives clients access to other individuals within the therapist's social network such as family and friends, bringing about unpredictable consequences for both therapists and clients. For more detailed information on "to accept or not to accept" a friend request via social media or networking, the Zur Institute (2017) offers a provocative and comprehensive overview for psychotherapists.

Contact Information

Because so many individuals now use e-mail to make initial contact with therapists, keeping a separate e-mail address for any social media or social networking sites is important. If you are in independent practice, use an e-mail provider that uses secure transmittal of data to protect confidentiality. If you have a website, ensure that your contact form is secure and that you use encryption standards within your website that meet the legal standards of a regulatory body like HIPAA, for example. Therapists who provide services through a clinic, agency, or hospital may have the advantage of using systems where no e-mail addresses are used and communications take place through an in-house server or patient-charting platform.

Search Engines

Chances are good that your clients will "Google" you to find out more about you; many individuals will choose a therapist, by looking them up on the Internet or even through social media. One of the most difficult questions confronting therapists is whether or not to use Google or other search engines to learn more about their clients. In the past, many therapists believed that using online platforms to search for information about clients, either before beginning treatment or during therapy, was unethical. But most professionals now agree that because the use of search engines is ubiquitous, it is a complex issue that is best addressed through informed consent at the start of therapy. Depending on your style of interaction with clients, you may be a practitioner who wants to have the option to search for further information on an individual if you have a concern about self-harm or harm to others. On the other hand, you may feel that any use of Internet searches is a violation of trust; in this case, you should state from the outset that you will not use search engines or social media to investigate individuals in treatment. In either case, it is important that clients clearly understand your policies and practices with regard to social media and search engines like Google.

The Zur Institute (2017) provides the following generic statement for inclusion with informed consent or general policies presented to clients at an initial treatment session:

> SOCIAL NETWORKING AND INTERNET SEARCHES: At times I may conduct a web search on clients before the beginning of therapy or during therapy. If you have concerns or questions regarding this practice, please discuss it with me. I do not accept friend requests from current or former clients on my psychotherapy related profiles on social networking sites due to the fact that these sites can

compromise clients' confidentiality and privacy. For the same reason, I request that clients do not communicate with me via any interactive or social networking websites.

Endorsements

Therapists in independent practice are often tempted to ask their clients for endorsements or testimonials about their services, especially upon termination; these endorsements are displayed on promotional sites including webpages and social media platforms. This is an unethical action for most helping professionals because it alters the relationship between client and therapist.

Confidentiality

Above all, confidentiality is a core value found in all mental health ethics codes. Earlier in this chapter, two case examples posed questions to consider when it comes to posting client-created artwork on the Internet, particularly on sites such as LinkedIn or Facebook. Art therapists are obviously one group of professionals who are confronted with this challenge because client-created artwork is at the core of their approach. Because so many art therapists now have social media accounts on multiple platforms, they are often tempted to post the art expressions of children, adolescents, and adults to "spread the word" about the reparative potential of art therapy. Because what is posted to the Internet and social media sites can be seen by your colleagues and in many cases possibly your clients, it is clear that in most cases, it is not advisable to share any information, including artworks created by individuals in your care. This applies not only to therapists, but also to clients who may post art expressions from therapy sessions via social networking sites. While clients own their art expressions, it is important to advise them about the inherent risks and unpredictable outcomes that may arise through posting what may be sensitive information and private communications to the Internet, particularly on social media platforms.

Social Media Policy

Having a clear social media policy is essential, but rarely discussed by most mental health professionals, including art therapists. Kolmes (2010) is one of few practitioners who have developed a social media policy that is provided to new clients in order to clarify interactions that may occur via the Internet. In fact, art therapists, who are often licensed as mental health counselors in the US, are required by the American Counseling Association (ACA, 2014) to have a social media policy if they have any type of online presence. For more detailed information, readers can visit the Zur Institute website[2] for an excellent discussion of social media's impact on the client–therapist relationship; also see Appendix 4 for a set of guidelines for developing a social media document for distribution to clients.

In summary, the Internet and social media platforms have increased online information about therapists, some of which they can control (i.e. what is on their professional website or social media pages and profiles) and some that they cannot control (information posted by others) (Zur Institute, 2017). For example, the currently ubiquitous Facebook discloses to all users that no security measures are perfect or impenetrable and that they cannot control the actions of other users who gain access to your information. For more information on the ethics of art therapy and social media as well as appropriate professional conduct via digital platforms and social networking, please see Malchiodi and Cutcher (2012, 2013, 2014, 2015) that are available through public access and download, and an excellent summary by Belkofer and McNutt (2011).

Conclusion

The ethical and legal issues presented in this chapter are only a few of the continuously emerging questions for art therapists in this digital age. It is essential that art therapists and those who introduce art-based approaches into psychotherapy recognize the impact of digital communication and social media and the inherent professional responsibilities and implications that come with technology. While the ethical and legal issues are complex and dynamic, by expanding

---

2   www.zurinstitute.com/socialnetworking.html

their range of expertise and knowledge about digital communication and social media, therapists can successfully adapt to the challenges of new media and technology and the demands that they present to therapeutic practice.

Recommendations

- Stay informed about revisions to art therapy ethics codes with regard to digital technology and social media, and also become aware of any state or regional regulations that govern digital communications and social networking platforms.

- Always give the highest priority to client confidentiality in all use of digital devices and communications, storage of data and images, and digital display of client-created art expressions. Remember that any images posted to Internet platforms are not secure and clients, especially children, often do not comprehend what it means to have their personal art expressions posted on the Internet.

- Maintain healthy boundaries with clients when using digital communication and social media; in order to support these boundaries, have a digital communications and social media policy that clearly explains your position to your clients.

- Digital technology, social media, and social networking are constantly evolving; when in doubt, contact your credentialing board, state license board, supervisors, and/ or colleagues if confronted by an ethical dilemma about digital communication or media.

References

American Counseling Association (ACA) (2014) *2014 ACA Code of Ethics*. Alexandria, VA: ACA.

American Telemedicine Association (2013) *Practice Guidelines for Video-Based Online Mental Health Services*. Rockville, MD: Substance Abuse and Mental Health Services Administration.

Art Therapy Credentials Board (ATCB) (2017) *Code of Ethics, Conduct and Disciplinary Procedures*. Greensboro, NC: ATCB.

Beck, L. (2009) Ethics and the Internet. September 20 [Blog post]. Retrieved on April 1, 2018 at www.lizbeck.net/2009/09/20/ethics-and-the-internet

Belkofer, C.M. and McNutt, J.V. (2011) Understanding social media culture and its ethical challenges for art therapists. *Art Therapy 28*(4), 159–164.

Franz, M., McCartie, S., Gold, C. and Skyward, S. (1999) *Technology Guidelines: BCATA Recommendations for Ethical Practice*. Vancouver, Canada: British Columbia Art Therapy Association.

Kolmes, K. (2010) Social media policy. Retrieved on April 1, 2018 at http://drkkolmes.com/2010/02/01/updated-private-practice-social-media-policy

Malchiodi, C.A. (2000) *Art Therapy and Computer Technology*. London: Jessica Kingsley Publishers.

Malchiodi, C.A. (2009, June 22) A Facebook fan page for your private practice? Retrieved on April 1, 2018 at www.psychologytoday.com/blog/arts-and-health/200907/facebook-fan-page-your-private-practice

Malchiodi, C.A. and Cutcher, D. (2012) Issues and ethics of art therapy in a digital age. Retrieved on April 1, 2018 at www.slideshare.net/healingarts/digital-art-therapy-and-social-media-ethics-cathy-malchiodi-phd-lpat-lpcc-reat-atrbc-and-donald-cutcher-atrbc

Malchiodi, C.A. and Cutcher, D. (2013) Art therapy and ethics in a digital age. Retrieved on April 1, 2018 at www.slideshare.net/healingarts/digital-art-therapy-and-social-media-ethics-cathy-malchiodi-phd-lpat-lpcc-reat-atrbc-and-donald-cutcher-atrbc

Malchiodi, C.A. and Cutcher, D. (2014) Art therapy and ethics in a digital age. Retrieved on April 1, 2018 at www.slideshare.net/healingarts/digital-art-therapy-and-social-media-ethics-2014-cathy-malchiodi-phd-lpat-lpcc-reat-atrbc-and-donald-cutcher-atrbc

Malchiodi, C.A. and Cutcher, D. (2015) Ethics and art therapy: How do art therapy ethics measure up? Retrieved on April 1, 2018 at www.slideshare.net/healingarts/ethics-and-digital-art-therapy-presentation-with-cathy-malchiodi-phd-and-don-cutcher-atrbc

Reamer, F.G. (2015) Clinical social work in a digital environment: Ethical and risk-management challenges. *Journal of Clinical Social Work 43*,120–132.

Sude, M. (2013) Text messaging and private practice: Ethical challenges and guidelines for developing personal best practices. *Journal of Mental Health Counseling 35*(3), 211–227.

Suler, J. (2004) The online disinhibition effect. *Cyberpsychology and Behavior 7*(3), 321–326.

US Department of Health and Human Services (2017) *Health Information Privacy*. Retrieved on April 1, 2018 at www.hhs.gov/hipaa/for-professionals/index.html

Zur, O. (2017) To accept or not to accept? How to respond when clients send "Friend Request" to their psychotherapists or counselors on social networking sites. Retrieved from www.zurinstitute.com/socialnetworking.html

3

INTERPERSONAL DOWNLOADING

The Relational and Creative Impacts of Technology and New Media in Therapy

Kristin Belkofer and Chris Belkofer

The development of digital technology is shaping the way art therapists engage with clients, connect with colleagues, and self-reflect on their roles as practitioners. The rapid technological advancements in computing technology have resulted in numerous electronic devices and social networks that have drastically impacted how information is created and shared between human beings. These "information and communication technologies and their associated social contexts" are broadly defined as new media (Lievrouw and Livingstone, 2006, p.23). In this chapter, the authors follow previous assertions within art therapy that encourage therapists to conceptualize new media as participation in a dynamic system of communication and interrelatedness in which meaning and identity are continuously created (Belkofer and McNutt, 2011; Orr, 2010; Potash, 2009).

Central to this view is the influence of new media theory, which extends beyond the development of new technologies to emphasize the intersecting social and relational impacts of digital culture (Cheong, Martin, and Macfadyen, 2012). In other words, rather than focusing on the newness of new media devices and electronic communication systems, therapists may find more footing by focusing on the relational and interpersonal impacts of new media behaviors. We believe therapists can benefit from opening their perspectives on the presence and the use of new media within therapeutic work by focusing on the potential for inter- and intra-personal growth. When considered thoughtfully, and within context, new media can be seen as an opportunity rather than a barrier or distraction. This emphasis on relational behaviors is consistent with new media scholars Lievrouw and Livingstone's (2006) call to "move away from the predominant view of 'mass media' as relatively fixed, stable and depersonalized institutional entities that have effects on people, to a view that considers what people do with media and each other" (p.8).

The first author will begin by articulating how theories of attachment, human development, social baseline, and constructivism can inform practitioners' clinical understanding of their clients' propensity for technological connection. As digital technology has entered the relational domain, the expertise on the part of therapists can offer a unique potential to clients that helps them navigate these domains on micro and macro levels. The digital realm is now an interpersonal domain: managing boundaries, practicing ethics, and promoting self-care are continual practices of the therapist's life. To succeed as their therapists, it is important to understand the dynamics underlying clients' desires for closeness, shared meaning, and access, which can manifest as collisions between our "real life, face-to-face interactions" and our presence in digital culture such as texts, e-mails, and social media.

Next, the second author will briefly describe two key concepts asserted by media scholar Henry Jenkins (2006), which are convergence culture and participatory culture. Jenkins' views influenced the second author to consider how integrating new media theories could be consistent with calls within the art therapy profession to consider more contemporary definitions of art media (Moon, 2010). As noted by Orr (2010), art therapists are beginning to see digital technology as falling "within the continuum of all media options in art therapy" (p.90). In this view, new media is imbued with creative potentials that aid creative expression akin to paper and pencils and other traditional art supplies (Seiden, 2001).

Finally, the second author will illustrate these ideas with a case example that describes how a client's attachment and engagement with his iPad helped to build a face-to-face therapeutic relationship. As opposed to seeing new media as a distraction, the art therapist reframed the iPad as an invitation to enter the client's world through his unique lens. By expanding the definition of what constitutes "real media" a client was unimpeded in asserting his creative intentions and working towards his treatment goals.

Relational Expertise in the Digital Realm

Attachment Theory

Although texting, smartphones, and apps can be a mainstay for clients of all ages, in today's American sociocultural context, this activity is especially meaningful and robust in interpersonal communication with adolescent clients. The adolescent texting pattern offers a vivid illustration of how attachment theory may be applied. For example, being aware of attachment needs in adolescents can help therapists see how the client uses texting (for better or worse) as a vehicle to strengthen and define attachment to others. Observing how these behaviors play out between the client and the helping professional can be especially helpful as it illustrates real-time behaviors related to how the client may build and negotiate trust. This behavior is certainly not exclusive to adolescents, as adult attachment styles emerge in texting as well. Pomerantz (2013) recognized the challenges to romantic relationships that texting presents as individuals have become conditioned to expect an immediate answer to any communication—no matter our proximity. An absence of this response is thus interpreted in a variety of ways depending upon the sender's attachment style.

The rapid-fire nature of texting can foster a false sense of urgency. However, it also provides a lens to assess clients' abilities to manage impulsivity, delay instant interpersonal gratification, and practice self-control (Pomerantz, 2013). Bringing awareness to this behavior ("How many times do I text? Do I express anger when I don't hear back? Do I set rules or limits?") can provide a concrete opportunity to identify maladaptive communication patterns and practice new skills. When texting includes a therapeutic relationship, there may be inevitable messiness based on the attachment issues conjured by the client–therapist dyad that are actually rooted in early childhood relationships. If a romantic relationship can feel less secure due to unanswered texts, it's not far-fetched to imagine that a similar experience can translate to the therapeutic relationship—even if the texts are not necessarily of a clinical or emotional nature.

New media interactions, although potentially messy and carrying some risk, do have the power to reveal dynamics in treatment that may not otherwise be directly addressed. For example, on a day off, I attended an art exhibit and took a picture of an animatronic sculpture that reminded me of a client who, in a previous session, had expressed how much she loved a particular animal and disclosed the meaning it represented to her. I showed her the photo the following week in treatment. Her mother responded (referring to me and my co-therapist), "See! You think they don't care about you. Clearly they do." If that simple interaction had not taken place, it is possible that the client might never have directly expressed that concern. However, I did intentionally wait to show her the image in session, rather than text it to her in "real time." Doing so protected my own off-time and personal space with my family while also enabling me to therapeutically highlight a way that she has impacted my life within appropriate boundaries.

Developmental Theory

One of the core foundational understandings of adolescent development is the need for connection and social support. Dolgin (2010) described the adolescent task of forming identity (and often multiple versions and forms of identity) which tends to emphasize interpersonal engagement in multiple social contexts such as peer groups, family, neighborhood, and co-workers. Social support is received and interpreted through these relationships, which can now be documented and saved in texts and Facebook threads. New media create the illusion that the support is ever-present. We can see and return to words of support long after they're posted, and at times even see pictures of ourselves together with friends and family that may be attached to these words. It is understandable that clients may try to "find" their therapists—an important part of their support team—on social media and may communicate with them in similar ways as they would with social media "friends," such as using social media-inspired semantics, emojis, hashtags, and so on.

The cell phone, and its function in the act of texting or communicating via social media, can be seen as a transitional object that provides comfort and security in new and unfamiliar social situations as clients build independent skills and worldviews (Dubus, 2015). In addition, texting can potentially create a person-centered narrative stream that reinforces growth and insight as well as ensuring communication while also providing an emotional distance that would not be associated with leaving a message or direct verbal expression. Perhaps it is easier for clients to ask for help and express vulnerability through a small black box of a phone. Sude (2013) also noted the role of the cell phone as a transitional object, emphasizing that texts serve as a way for the client to remain symbolically as well as literally linked with the therapist. A text conversation does not need to be active or even reciprocal, since the clients can refer back to texts from a therapist simply to feel supported, be reminded of coping skills, and continue their transition into a higher state of self-efficacy. Texts can potentially create a person-centered narrative stream that reinforces growth and insight.

Social Baseline Theory

Social baseline theory (SBT), which integrates attachment theory and physiological understanding of emotional regulation, asserts that the human brain has a "baseline tendency" to adapt to other humans and maintain connection and proximity to social resources (Beckes and Coan, 2011). According to social baseline theory, the human brain has evolved to seek connections to others in an effort to conserve cognitive resources and socially regulate emotions. Through a complex, unconscious process, the brain's neural networks communicate to its regulatory components that it can remain calm because perceived social support is present. If an individual's perception of being alone is diminished, the internalized pressure to be solely responsible for the cognitive, emotional, and behavioral tasks of survival may also be diminished. In this way, an individual's social baseline protects the self and maintains emotional regulation through perceived ever-present social support. Therefore, the brain does need to access or use all of its neural resources to manage the current difficult or stressful situation, nor does the personal resource have to be physically present.

Text messaging, for example, creates a *perception* that other people are always "close at hand" and seemingly available, which might explain the calming effect that an individual may receive from immediately texting a thought to a friend, spouse, or in this case, a therapist. Dolev-Cohen and Barak (2013) noted that, when distressed, adolescents may achieve significant emotional relief and reduced loneliness by instant messaging their peers in "real time." Applying SBT, when an individual sends a text or an instant message in a moment of distress, someone else is "there" to help manage the emotional workload even if they are only *there* in digital form.

It is possible that whether or not a person responds doesn't even matter, as long as their digital representational presence (e.g. a name, a selfie, or line of texts on a screen) appears to have received the digital attempt to connect. Social baseline theory also asserts that social relationships of all kinds—from the presence of a stranger, to the temporary yet intense work of a therapist, to long-term committed relationships—enable humans to preserve precious biological and neurological resources (Beckes and Coan, 2011). Preservation is especially salient in times of intense threat or trauma, and is illustrated when a client reaches for their phone to dial their therapist in a moment of crisis.

Constructivism

Digital culture can play a significant role in constructing meaning and sense of self in a changing world. Dubus (2015) noted that the act of texting can foster what is known as the dialogical self. The "dialogical self" refers to the abstract ability of the mind to have an internal dialogue with different, yet relational, parts of itself. These parts are seen to represent different thoughts and beliefs inherent in disparate parts of society, and offer multiple viewpoints and conflicts (Hermans, 2002). Especially significant in adolescent identity construction, the dialogical self may be involved when texters can literally refer back to the voices they express in text conversations and build insight from responses, feelings, and learned experiences.

Therapists must actively remember that adolescents are "digital natives" who have been born into an environment already shaped by a digital culture of smartphones and social media (Dubus, 2015). Conversely, there is a generational gap with digital immigrants (often their parents, possibly teachers, and other authority figures) who were raised before the proliferation of these technologies. Generational differences in new media usage and understanding have interesting implications for how digital natives and older immigrants have interpreted and constructed meaning relative to their place in society. For example, digital natives have been exposed to other cultures, beliefs, and values to an unprecedented degree due to the sprawling global connectedness of digital media (Cheong *et al.*, 2012).

The dialogical self "includes collective voices" that not only encompass the values and norms of an imagined individual thought process, but also those of an institution (Hermans, 2002). For example, a person might evaluate an individual act of behavior by asking, "What might the church think about this situation?" It is conceivable that digital culture has created more avenues for people to develop their internal voices and then to practice them in digital spaces such as social media that challenge or affirm them.

As this chapter has highlighted thus far, the therapist–client relationship can be complex, messy, and rich, similar to the ever-changing nature of text, web, and app-based communications. These digital developments can be exciting and perceived as connective and clinically effective in the moment. Their risks and implications are not always obvious. Clearly, therapists want to communicate as effectively and efficiently as possible with clients. However, those therapists who find themselves closer to the digital native end of history may have a naïve, or perhaps more lenient view of privacy, boundaries, and confidentiality that are inherent in these communications (Sude, 2013). It's imperative that no matter the professional environment, therapists create personal guidelines for ethics and practices that are rooted in their understanding of interpersonal and power dynamics in the therapeutic relationship, as well as compassion for self and clients.

Summary

Although we do not yet know fully the impact of these emerging systems and their dynamic communities, therapists may feel more grounded by revisiting their expertise and training regarding human development, social systems, and identity formation. Therapists need not solve these problems or even be digital experts to be able to draw upon their training as relational experts. However, they may benefit from exploring their own media participation guidelines as part of their self-care and their maintenance of professional work boundaries. The psychosocial theories explored here are by no means exclusive. By balancing existing psychology theory with the continual work of personal reflection and effective supervision, therapists may be well suited to manage the challenges of new media.

New Media as Creative Tools
New Media and Social Systems

New media theory incorporates the relational impacts of cultural and social systems with the evolving knowledge of electronic devices (Gane and Beer, 2008; Jenkins, 2006; Manovich, 2001; Pingree and Gitelman, 2003; Thorburn and Jenkins, 2004). Cheong *et al.* (2012) described new media as expanding "far beyond the simple proliferation of the 'new' technologies, gadgetry, or artifacts that are frequently associated with digital media" and toward an interpersonal-oriented "globally distributed web of sociotechnical relationships" (p.1). In this view, "new media" refers to an emerging and complex digital culture in which content and distribution develop organically from within a society of users. Although this culture may involve personal electronic devices, their generated and shared content, and various social or personal distribution platforms, new media also encompasses a multitude of ways to be "heard" or "seen" that translate internal experiences into digital symbols of meaning and relationships on our personal screens.

Participatory Behaviors and Convergence Culture

While "All media were once 'new media'" (Pingree and Gitelman, 2003, p.xi), we can conceptualize the new media landscape we exist in today as uniquely interactive and highly interpersonal in a way that is fundamentally different than mass media systems that existed before the invention of the computer. One key difference according to Jenkins (2006) is that new media content is experienced across multiple platforms on multiple devices, which now rarely perform one task. For example, we use our cellular phones for gaming, checking e-mail, taking pictures, and listening to music, which expands far beyond the preliminary task of talking to one another. Jenkins described the interconnectedness and ubiquity of new media as a culture of convergence. In convergence culture, information is all around us, impacting "both a change in the way media is produced and a change in the way media is consumed" (p.16).

An additional difference between old media and new media as described by Jenkins (2006) is a shift away from "older notions of passive media spectatorship" towards a "participatory culture" of media engagement (p.3). In participatory culture, media content is created and shared in dynamic and creative ways that have led to self-organizing communities who produce and curate their own media content, often outside the rules and boundaries of the commercial media systems. One example of participatory culture is fan art. Fan art is essentially creative responses to popular media. For example, there are countless examples of videos posted in response to the Star Wars franchise uploaded on YouTube. One can find user-made fully costumed short films, viewer critiques on how films in the franchise should have ended, hypothetical plot twists that explain missing links in the series, and countless variations on the movies.

In addition to creating content inspired or in response to media such as films and music, the sharing of information as well as the seeking out of interpersonal connections (such as following a blogger or even liking a post) characteristic of participatory culture are additional ways that new media extends towards social systems and complex social behaviors. As these social realities inherently involve humans, they are full of thoughts, feelings, emotions, and ideas. New media is more than mechanistic.

It is essential for therapists to appreciate that new media behaviors reference more than just consuming entertainment and are not always an escape. A great deal of emotionally salient experiences surround our digital devices. As many of us may have personally witnessed, relationships and connections can be instantly created or severed with the like of a button, the following of a page, and the posting of a comment. Sharing, viewing, and commenting on media are forms of engagement that reference our affinities and potentially reflect our identities and often our core beliefs. Through digital communication we communicate, "I believe in this!" or "This makes me angry!" without having to speak or even type a word.

Art therapists have noted the creative potential of advancements in technology as effective means of communication and creative expression (Alders, Allen, and Mosinski, 2011; Austin, 2010; Belkofer and McNutt, 2011; Orr, 2010). The following case example will illustrate how the second author expanded his definition of what constitutes appropriate media in art therapy, to deepen his therapeutic relationship with his client and promote his creative expression. Applying Belkofer and McNutt's (2011) ethical explorations of the participatory nature of new media (Jenkins, 2006) offered a treatment lens for the case example. Conceptualizing the client's involvement in new media as a participatory behavior helped inform the therapist how to leverage digital media in individual art therapy with a child to serve therapeutic goals to meet the client in the here and now.

Case Example 3.1

Kyle was an 8-year-old boy referred to art therapy because of difficulties transitioning to bedtime, low self-esteem, and excessive anxiety. Often struggling to express himself verbally, he was an excessive worrier. He would often induce the ire of his peers in his hypervigilant policing of rules and protocols for playground games such as safety during kickball and the proper order of who was next in line to play tetherball. In addition to social problems at school, Kyle's worrying impacted other areas of his life. He was hesitant to try new things and to meet new people; he was clingy with his mother in public. Bedtime required a great deal of attention and it was hard for him to settle his mind at night. For example, he would wake up concerned that his parents could be abducted by aliens.

Kyle's art therapy sessions were pleasant. He was creative and compliant, albeit hesitant, shy, and a little ambivalent. He struggled to assert himself, often looking at the floor and refraining from eye contact.

One day his mother brought an iPad to the session. "I told him that you may not allow it, but Kyle wanted to show you his favorite movie on his iPad. It's all he talked about on the way here. I'm so sorry to disrupt your session."

"Can I show you?" Kyle asked me hopefully.

It was common for my clients and their families to use their electronic devices while waiting for my sessions. However, I had never allowed them to bring devices *into* a session. I had learned in my previous work with children and adolescents with behavioral disorders that it was important to set clear limits and say "no" to testing behaviors. However, Kyle had never behaved in a defiant or oppositional manner in our previous sessions. A goal that we had developed with his family was to work on consistently expressing and asserting himself. He had never asked me for anything in such a direct manner.

"Okay," I said, "but we will need to make art too. We can't watch the whole movie the entire session and you can only show me your favorite scene."

As we walked towards my office, I began to feel guilty and anxious. I recall thinking, "Surely the art therapy gods would frown upon my watching a movie in a session. And what about the insurance panels and state licensing boards?" Being able to witness and engage in the creative expression of others is a privilege and a joy, but getting paid to watch scenes from a movie was a whole new level. How would I bill for this?

The movie, called *Real Steel,* is set in the future. Robot boxing is now the world's most popular sport. Kyle showed me two scenes from the movie. In the first, a discarded robot is found in the trash by a young boy recently united with his once estranged father. The boy and his father employ the robot to help the father pay off debts accumulated from previous lost boxing matches. As the boy and the robot struggle to reconnect, the stage is set for the robot to face off with the world champion, "Zeus." This epic battle was the second scene Kyle showed me.

Immediately, as I began watching the scenes from the movie, I shifted from perceiving his iPad as a distraction from the "real work" of art therapy towards an increased appreciation for the device as a media tool. The creative and metaphoric content that the movie provided became a catalyst in our sessions, helping to unearth the underlying content of Kyle's world that he struggled to express. Discarded robots, come-from-behind conflicts, fathers and sons struggling to connect, oh my! Kyle's creative expression blossomed as we started making masks of other robot superheroes such as Iron Man. In the safe and imaginal world of our sessions Kyle could for a few moments transform from a little boy into a powerful superhero or a protective robot.

The persona of the robot pulled Kyle out of his shell. Over several weeks of drawing robots and making robot masks, he became more expressive, confident, and assertive. Eventually, he expressed his intention to create a full-sized robot. Using the large warehouse of the private practice space to our advantage, we began to explore the grounds for found objects. We worked side-by-side gathering would-be robot materials from the dumpsters in the complex and collaborating on how to assemble the parts. Cardboard egg cartons became robot arms. Shoeboxes were made into robots' feet. Kyle beamed with pride as each creation progressed. He could hardly wait for the paint to dry and he could hardly contain his enthusiasm as he eagerly begged to take his semi-finished robot home with him. However, he also practiced patience, and frustration tolerance. He learned he had to wait. Sometimes the pieces didn't fit the way he wanted. Sometimes the glue didn't take and his robot needed to be mended.

"It's okay buddy. We can fix that," I would say.

From this example, we can see that Kyle's interest in the movie was leveraged as a creative force in art therapy. I no longer viewed media interests as a distraction from the "real work" of art therapy because I had expanded my definition of what was appropriate media. I began to conceptualize that Kyle and I were engaging in a form of new media participation consistent with the theories asserted by Jenkins (2006). Kyle's reconstruction of content from his favorite movie into his own personal art making can be thought of as a kind of fan art. The digital technology of the iPad was a creative catalyst for our sessions, inspiring his expression.

But his creative responses to the movie were also resources that allowed him to tell his own story. As noted by Jenkins (2006):

> Convergence does not occur through media appliances, however sophisticated they may become. Convergence occurs within the brains of individual consumers through their social interactions. Each of us constructs our own personal mythology from bits and fragments of information...transformed into resources through which we make sense of our everyday lives. (p.4)

Kyle's interest in the movie *Real Steel* emerged in the therapy office as he used the film to help construct his own story and *make sense* of his life. As the therapist, I was able to help him make meaningful connections between his personal world, the film, and the robots we made, but Kyle was able to drive the content of our art therapy sessions. Kyle led the construction of his robots. Through the creation of his art he was able to practice asserting his voice and experience feelings of empowerment and mastery. Exemplifying Jenkins' (2006) descriptions of participatory culture, he was able to move beyond being a mere spectator in his own therapy towards a more assertive and engaged level of participation. Kyle always "behaved" appropriately but now he was leading and fully engaged. In our therapy sessions, he was the boss. I played the role of the artist assistant, providing support and technical advice. Through our creative process he learned how to plan as well as to witness the impact of his intentions on the world.

Conclusion

In this chapter, we have attempted to illustrate how therapists can integrate emerging new media theories, foundational psychological perspectives, and relational expertise to make sense of the role of new media in therapy.

If therapists approach digital technology as a form of media change that is related to meaning making and identity formation, they can realize the potential for the relational work of digital technology. Therapists must not lose sight of the work of asking "why" within the dizzying changes of new media. In this view, new media can be understood through the "old work" of self-reflection, active listening, empathic understanding, and maintaining personal boundaries. Whether one is negotiating the therapeutic pros and cons of a pair of scissors or a smartphone, the work of the therapist essentially remains the same. As always, art therapists will benefit from asking how the client's choice of media serves the therapeutic relationship (Moon, 2010).

Working to understand the *meaning* of digital media has the potential to ground clinicians in the work of seeking a deeper understanding that is well suited to their training and skill sets. Digital technology has transitioned into a dynamic system of communications and interconnections that are emergent and ever-changing. Therapists and scholars may have yet to fully make sense of these systems, but in many ways the underlying drives of the behaviors associated with them remain familiar and universally human. For example, while the cultural practice of texting may have replaced the phone call for many people, the adolescent demand to stay connected for hours on end with their friends has not changed. As Jenkins (2006) noted, "Old media are not being displaced. Rather, their functions and status are shifted by the introduction of new technologies" (p.14). Media and media delivery systems (i.e. technology) are not the same things. It is important for therapists to appreciate that it is not just entertainment that is being shared in new media systems. "Our lives, relationships, memories, fantasies, desires also flow across media channels" (Jenkins, p.17). New media is changing how we shape our work as therapists as well as how we connect with and understand our clients.

Recommendations

To help therapists navigate the complex demands of new media change we recommend the following considerations:

- Keep in mind that new media goes beyond technological devices and also refers to social systems in which identity and meaning are made. The behavior of the client within these systems reflects their beliefs, worldviews, challenges, strengths, and skills.

- Therapeutically, the role of new media can be conceptualized as an extension of social resources and a forum to practice skills applicable to in-person relationships.

- The myriad emotional responses that can be evoked through various electronic communication systems are no less salient because they are communicated on a screen.

- For many people, new media devices are tools that help them regulate their emotions and manage their interpersonal connections. Especially when working with adolescents, therapists may benefit from a greater appreciation for how removing access to new media disconnects them from important support networks, systems, and coping strategies. The presence of alternative coping skills should be explicitly in place.

- Participation in new media may offer creative potential in the form of creating, sharing, and re-contextualizing various forms of media content.

References

Alders, A., Allen, P.B. and Mosinski, B.B. (2011) Technology in art therapy: Ethical challenges. *Art Therapy: Journal of the American Art Therapy Association 28*(4), 165–170.

Austin, B. (2010) Technology, art therapy, and psychodynamic theory: Computer animation with an adolescent in foster care. In C.H. Moon (ed.) *Materials and Media in Art Therapy: Critical Understandings of Diverse Artistic Vocabularies.* New York, NY: Routledge.

Beckes, L. and Coan, J.A. (2011) Social baseline theory: The role of social proximity in emotion and economy of action. *Social and Personality Psychology Compass 5*, 976–988.

Belkofer, C.M. and McNutt, J.V. (2011) Understanding social media culture and its ethical challenges for art therapists. *Art Therapy: Journal of the American Art Therapy Association 28*(4), 159–164.

Cheong, P.H., Martin, J.N. and Macfadyen, L.P. (2012) Introduction: Mediated intercultural communication matters: Understanding new media, dialectics, and social change. In P.H. Cheong, J.N. Martin, and L.P. Macfadyen (eds.) *New Media and Intercultural Communication: Identity, Community, and Politics.* New York, NY: Peter Lang.

Dolev-Cohen, A. and Barak, A. (2013) Adolescents' use of instant messaging as a means of emotional relief. *Computers in Human Behavior 29*(1), 58–63.

Dolgin, K. (2010) *The Adolescent: Development, Relationships, and Culture* (13th edn). New York, NY: Pearson.

Dubus, N. (2015) Texting: The third client in the room. *Journal of Clinical Social Work 43*, 209–214.

Gane, N. and Beer, D. (2008) *New Media: The Key Concepts.* New York, NY: Berg.

Hermans, H. (2002) The dialogical self as a society of mind: Introduction. *Theory and Psychology 12*(2), 147–160.

Jenkins, H. (2006) *Convergence Culture: Where Old and New Media Collide.* New York, NY: New York University Press.

Lievrouw, L.A. and Livingstone, S. (2006) Introduction to the Updated Student Edition. In L.A. Lievrouw and S. Livingstone (eds.) *Handbook of New Media: Social Shaping and Social Consequences of ICTs* (Updated Student Edition). London: Sage.

Manovich, L. (2001) *The Language of New Media.* Cambridge, MA: MIT Press.

Moon, C.H. (2010) A history of art materials and media in art therapy. In C.H. Moon (ed.) *Materials and Media in Art Therapy: Critical Understandings of Diverse Artistic Vocabularies.* New York, NY: Routledge.

Orr, P. (2010) Social remixing: Art therapy media in the digital age. In C.H. Moon (ed.) *Materials and Media in Art Therapy: Critical Understandings of Diverse Artistic Vocabularies.* New York, NY: Routledge.

Pingree, G.B. and Gitelman, L. (2003) Introduction: What's new about new media? In L. Gitelman and G.B. Pingree (eds.) *New Media,* 1740–1915. Cambridge, MA: MIT Press.

Pomerantz, S.G. (2013) Attachment and delayed gratification in the technological age [Doctoral dissertation]. Retrieved on April 1, 2018 at Seton Hall University Dissertations and Theses (ETDs) (1882).

Potash, J.S. (2009) Fast food art, talk show therapy: The impact of mass media on adolescent art therapy. *Art Therapy 26*(2), 52–57.

Seiden, D. (2001) *Mind over Matter: The Use of Materials in Art, Education and Therapy.* Chicago, IL: Mongolia Street.

Sude, M. (2013) Text messaging and private practice: Ethical challenges and guidelines for developing personal best practices. *Journal of Mental Health Counseling 35*(3), 211–227.

Thorburn, D. and Jenkins, H. (2004) Introduction: Toward an aesthetics of transition. In D. Thorburn and H. Jenkins (eds.) *Rethinking Media Change: The Aesthetics of Transition.* Cambridge, MA: MIT Press.

4

YOUR CLIENT'S BRAIN ON DIGITAL TECHNOLOGY

Cathy Malchiodi

Digital technology and social networking are changing the ways most individuals communicate, receive information, and engage in daily life. When people engage with digital devices and social media on a frequent basis, there is increasing evidence that these interactions also "rewire" our brains, altering the way we think, respond, react, and interact (Carr, 2010). Researchers like Jean Twenge (2017) propose that a new set of behaviors is emerging in "iGen" (the generation of individuals born after 1995), the direct result of "super-connection" to smartphones and social networks. She concludes that technology may have produced a generation of less rebellious individuals who are experiencing a prolonged childhood, less happiness, and a subsequent increase in loneliness and depression despite the ease and availability of being digitally connected to others.

The rapidly evolving world of digital technology and social media is not all bad of course; these advances have made possible important platforms such as telemedicine, increasingly creative, intuitive, and user-friendly software, and social connections for those who are isolated or challenged by disabilities. There is also emerging evidence that digital games and other interactive software help to enhance cognitive and physical skills, particularly in middle-aged and older adults. In our homes, we can now talk to artificial intelligence through Siri (Apple technology) or Alexa (Amazon technology) to find out the weather or the ingredients for a dinner recipe and can get a "flash briefing" on national and world news. But as digital devices and social media platforms increasingly proliferate at home and in work life, researchers continue to discover just how these technologies are impacting mental and physical health and development, and even lifespan. Because therapists are committed to the welfare of all individuals they see in treatment, it is essential for therapists to understand how digital platforms are impacting the emotional health, interpersonal relationships, and worldviews of their clients. This includes adding to one's knowledge of just how technology and social media affect development, health status, and social engagement.

Currently there is a daunting amount of information on how digital technology (the use of computers, tablets, smartphones, and other devices for communication, work, or recreation) and social networking (engagement with various social media platforms through digital devices) impact brain and body. This chapter therefore provides only a brief overview of what we know about the impact of digital technology on the brain as well as social media on human behavior, underscoring several key areas including technology-induced stress, child development, interpersonal relationships, and addiction.

Technostress

It is no surprise that the rapid growth of digital technology correlates with the level of stress-related symptoms reported by many individuals. *Technostress* is a word coined to describe the phenomenon of struggling to cope with digital and, particularly, information technologies (Riedl *et al.*, 2012); it's a common experience for any individual who uses digital devices for work, communication, or social networking on a regular basis. Technostress involves the same stress responses (activation of the sympathetic nervous system) that result from other distressful events. The occurrence of this type of stress is clearly related to how useful and reliable the technology being used actually is (Ayyagari, Grover, and Purvis, 2011). In brief, the more useful and reliable it is, the less stress people experience from it; in neuroscience terms, this means experiences with digital devices that are unpredictable or uncertain increase the brain's emotional response via the limbic system and physiological consequences to the body. Additionally, the rapid pace of change in technology alters individual experiences of technostress because any adaptation to new situations automatically increases stress responses. Fortunately, many technologies have actually become more intuitive, providing ease of use in many cases after basic functions are learned; to some extent Steve Jobs and the development of Apple devices have enhanced the proliferation of user-friendly technologies, thus reducing at least some tech-related distress.

Additionally, the physical effects of digital technology are impacting individuals in other widespread and complex ways. As neuroscientist Adam Gazzaley (2016) notes, we are now exposing our brains and bodies to an environment that requires us to do things we were not necessarily evolved to do. Many people now struggle with a deluge of data from digital sources; even after stepping away from cellphones and screens, some continue to crave the stimulation found through electronic communications (see the discussion on digital addiction below). While digital natives (i.e. individuals who grew up with digital devices) may be more adaptable to multitasking through technology, excessive multitaskers also have more trouble eliminating irrelevant information and thus experience more stress. As a result, sleep disruption and insomnia are more common in those who use digital devices during the day and especially shortly before going to bed (Twenge, Krizan, and Hisler, 2017). In fact, it has become routine for me to ask clients about their use of cellphones or computer screens when they cite insomnia or agitated sleep patterns.

All the incoming information via e-mail, texts, and social networks is changing behavior, decreasing the ability to focus and be fully in the moment with others and the environment. If being in the moment and face-to-face social connection are key to quality of life and overall health over the lifespan, technostress may already be part of the array of conditions therapists will address with many clients for the foreseeable future.

Digital Technology and Child Development

Many therapists work with children and families, making the impact of digital technology on young clients a common concern. Art therapists often consider the role digital devices play in the lives of children and adolescents in a number of specific ways, including their impact on creative expression as well as the possible applications of apps and software within the continuum of art making. All therapists, however, are concerned about the possible effects of digital devices on children's physical and psychosocial development and there are now some consistent guidelines for therapists to consider both in their work with children and adolescents and in making recommendations to parents and caregivers. The American Academy of Pediatrics (AAP) (2016) is one good source for information on the impact of digital technology on children, emphasizing the following best practices.

Children under 18 Months

Based on research that screen exposure (smartphones, tablets, computers, and television) is particularly harmful to an infant's brain, the AAP Council on Communications and Media (2016) recommends that very young children should not be exposed to screen technology of any type. In part, this recommendation is based on research that indicates that children who play independently from screen exposure are less likely to be overstimulated and also learn to entertain themselves through a variety of senses rather than just visual ones.

Children from 18 Months to 5 Years

A limit of one hour of screen exposure per day is recommended, and parents and caregivers are encouraged to co-view all media with children and provide high-quality educational digital media experiences. During this stage of child development, it is now widely accepted that digital technology not only impacts physical development of the brain, but also psychosocial development. For example, children who spend less time viewing screens are generally more socially engaged and able to self-direct free play and idle time.

Children from 6 to 12 Years

The AAP (2016) recommends that parents and caregivers do not need to supervise all digital technology with school-age children. However, children's media intake should be monitored, including the types of media viewed; for example, exposure to digital media via the Internet, social media, and even television presents content that can result in overwhelming fears and worries and impact learning due to overstimulation. While it is suggested that parents and caregivers limit screen access time to one hour per day, this can be a difficult and unrealistic expectation with digital natives. What may be more practical is to try to ensure that digital media exposure does not impact sleep and does not reduce normal physical activity and appropriate social interaction with family and friends.

Adolescents

Adolescence presents a significant challenge because youth tend to engage with digital technology and media differently and more frequently than younger children. For example, in recent years teenagers regularly use digital technology to communicate with their peers and family through texts and online chats; classroom teachers may require use of digital technology to complete homework or research, write papers, or watch educational films. Also, during this stage of development some adolescents may be attracted to technology as a career, making it difficult to restrict screen time or digital engagement. Hence restricting access or time spent with various digital platforms may be perceived as punishment rather than a legitimate health concern.

Adolescents are now using smartphones and, in particular, social networking not only to explore personal identity, but also to develop psychosocial skills and interpersonal relationships. These 21st-century modes of communication and interaction mediate adolescent psychosocial development in several ways. For example, Suler (2004) cites the term "online disinhibition effect" to describe how adolescents use digital communication to experiment with actual identity formation and engage in relationships on a psychologically safe level. Because of the range of digital communication, disinhibition effect also allows for invisibility; texting has allowed teenagers to interact without facial expression, body language, or tone of voice. This type of communication may also be asynchronous in that it occurs when electronic interactions with others do not take place in real time (e.g. as in a phone call). Disinhibition effect can decrease self-consciousness when communicating with parents, teachers, or other authority figures through digital means; for example, teenagers may test adults in ways they would not in a face-to-face conversation or say things that they would have otherwise felt uncomfortable in saying.

Suler also notes that there are other components to disinhibition effect, including *dissociative anonymity* (changing identity on the Internet in order to communicate anonymously) and *dissociative imagination* (perceiving behavior as just a game or role playing on the Internet). In other words, teenagers can create an online persona that is very different from their real day-to-day lives. However, adolescents are not the only age group that engages in these behaviors; many adults also "curate" the events of their lives, posting on social media only specific parts of their lives that imply success and positivity, thus creating false impressions and inaccurate perceptions.

Finally, recent studies on the now ubiquitous presence of smartphones in many cultures and their impact on adolescents have produced dramatic findings. When smartphone ownership crossed the 50 percent threshold in 2012 (Pew Research Center, 2017), the incidence of adolescent depression and suicide began to rise. Time spent online also affected mood; adolescents who spent five or more hours a day online were 71 percent more likely than those teens who spent less than an hour a day to have at least one risk factor for suicide (depressed mood, suicide plan, thoughts about suicide, or attempts at suicide) (Twenge, 2017). In brief, less than two hours of smartphone use is currently the recommended limit to support adolescent mental health and reduce the incidence of technology-induced depression.

Therapy in the Age of Digital Technology and Social Networks: A Case Example

In my experience as an art therapist and mental health counselor for several decades, digital communication and social networking are increasingly important experiences that clients bring into the treatment setting. Some individuals are simply struggling with technostress and the deluge of electronic communications and information that is part of their day-to-day work or profession.

For others, digital technology and/or social media have overtaken their lives in ways that have altered interpersonal relationships, emotional and physical health, and quality of life.

Case Example 4.1

Jolene [a pseudonym], age 39 years, was referred by her doctor to art therapy because of depression associated with a chronic illness. Her doctor also diagnosed Jolene with an eating disorder because of weight loss unattributed to her illness and her repulsion to most fruits and vegetables; she often wore oversized clothing to disguise her actual weight and reported that she felt uncomfortable in many social situations that involved food. During our initial session, Jolene and I discussed her struggles with her illness, depression, and perceptions about food and body image. However, I also quickly learned how much of her life revolved around the use of digital devices to access social networks. In fact, most of her time was spent on a smartphone or laptop computer and almost all of her interpersonal relationships were virtual ones. She defined her friends as individuals she met and communicated with online and referred to them as her "digital tribe." In contrast, she had only two face-to-face friendships; unlike other individuals her age, she rarely met with these individuals or participated in any recreational activities with them. Jolene shared a home with a man who she indicated was her "partner," but they rarely left the house for recreational activities because he also preferred to engage in video gaming. She explained that he was a good partner because he tolerated her "laptop in bed" and let her "check Facebook or Instagram in the middle of the night."

By the end of our first session, it was apparent that Jolene was possibly addicted to viewing and posting to social networks. When I asked her what her plans were after our meeting, she said she had to check a couple of Facebook groups she maintained and add some new posts to other networking pages she owned, including discussion groups on other social networking platforms. In fact, Jolene said that not being able to look at her smartphone while in my office was making her extremely anxious. She also explained her self-imposed rules to never let a day go by without "pinning" (Pinterest) or "tweeting" (Twitter) news; her "followers" expected her to post, according to Jolene. While Jolene emphasized that social media was "just a hobby" for her, it was clear that it occupied the majority of her life and formed her worldview, including virtual impressions of others she never actually met. Jolene clearly felt that her digital tribe sustained her in far more satisfying ways than face-to-face friendships. She also added that if a virtual relationship was unsatisfactory, she had the option to "unfriend" or even "delete" and "block" people in her social media groups whose opinions were contrary to hers or who offended her in some way.

I learned in subsequent sessions that on a couple of occasions Jolene's work supervisor reprimanded her for using the office desktop computer to access Facebook and other social media sites. Because she was no longer allowed to check social media while at work, she decided to quit her job even though it provided substantial health insurance that covered expenses associated with medication for her illness. Similar to her control over food intake, social media provided a gratifying sense of control over her life and relationships. Jolene divulged that while she believed she would live a normal lifespan, she knew that her chronic illness was progressive and that at some point she might become disabled and even homebound if she became unable to drive. Social networking was one way to stay connected to others in a predictable way in contrast to the unpredictable nature of her chronic illness. Blogging about the details of her life, posting photos of herself, and unfriending, deleting, and blocking on social networks were all actions she could control to experience a virtual sense of power.

While Jolene's engagement with digital devices and social networks is more extreme than that of many clients, her case demonstrates the numerous ways digital technology and social networking influences psychosocial behavior in the 21st century. For this reason, it is important for therapists to have at least a working knowledge of the impact of digital technology on individuals in two key areas: 1) the impact of social networking and social media on psychosocial health and 2) addiction to social networking and digital devices.

Social Networking and Social Media

It is widely agreed that social networking and media are altering the way humans communicate and form relationships. With the current focus on interpersonal neurobiology (IPNB) (also known as relational neuroscience) within psychotherapy, social networking and social media are now key factors in understanding at least part of how individuals interact with others. Some social media pioneers have gone as far as to say that these platforms may even be destroying the social fabric of society, advising people to take a regular break from all social networks (BBC News, 2017a). Others observe that social media provides self-validation and even a "hit" of dopamine (a neurotransmitter that is related to reward-seeking behavior) as a result of someone liking or commenting on a social media photo or post (BBC News, 2017b). In any case, the impact of social networks is undeniable; currently there are over 1.2 billion users of Facebook on a daily basis, spending an average of 90 minutes on social networks (Chandra, 2018). This statistic alone underscores the need for all therapists to understand how and why clients engage in these platforms and what the impact of this engagement has on overall health and wellbeing.

While not all social networking is deleterious, the potential benefits of it are complicated and often dependent on a number of factors and contexts. For example, some studies indicate that sharing honest feelings about oneself online via Facebook can potentially enhance a sense of wellbeing and perception of social support in the short term (Kim and Lee, 2011); in fact, many reclusive individuals with emotional or physical challenges may benefit from social media engagement as an experience of greater social integration (Veretilo and Billick, 2012). In contrast, there is strong evidence that social media platforms like Facebook can exacerbate negative emotions and increase hostility, rivalry, envy, and self-doubt; as previously mentioned, many users curate what they post, emphasizing only positive experiences and achievements. This inevitably can lead to negative self-comparisons and a sense that one's life is less satisfying and successful. In a large longitudinal study of 5208 participants over the span of two years, researchers Shakya and Christakis (2017) observe that overall, the use of Facebook was negatively associated with a sense of wellbeing (emotional and physical health) when compared with "offline" interactions. In all cases, the way individuals used Facebook, whether passive scrolling through posts, clicking "like," or actively posting, did not matter. The researchers conclude that "Exposure to the carefully curated images from others' lives leads to negative self-comparison, and the sheer quantity of social media interaction may detract from more meaningful real-life experiences" (p.210) and that these online social interactions are not a substitute for in-person relationships.

Research also indicates that taking a break from social networks can be good advice for some individuals, particularly for those who are experiencing depression or anxiety and other disorders that impact mood. A recent study (Tromholt, 2016) provides strong causal evidence that Facebook use, for example, negatively affects wellbeing; in brief, those who took a break from this social networking platform increased their life satisfaction and emotional positivity when compared to a control group (those who kept using Facebook). Results also underscore that the impact was significantly greater for excessive Facebook users and those individuals who tended to envy others on social media.

Chandra (2018) provides an important recommendation that therapists can introduce to clients, noting:

> We can also become more mindful and curious about social media's effects on our minds and hearts, weighing the good and bad. We should ask ourselves how social media make us feel and behave, and decide whether we need to limit our exposure to social media altogether...or simply modify our social media environment...
>
> Instead of lurking or passively scrolling through a never-ending bevy of posts, we can stop and ask ourselves important questions like, *What are my intentions?* and *What is this online realm doing to me and my relationships?*

The latter are two excellent questions to take up with our clients, especially when social media use has impacted not only mood, but the social fabric of their relationships with family, friends, and community.

Finally, social networking and social media have brought about one very serious and troubling development: cyberbullying. Cyberbullying is generally defined as bullying through the use of technology including social media, cellphones, e-mail, or anything digital or electronic (Kowalski, Limber, and Agatston, 2016); the messages communicated are intended to harass another individual with intent to cause negative consequences for another person.

While cyberbullying has been identified as a psychosocial issue for children and adolescents, adults can also experience it in various forms of online harassment, emotional abuse, and stalking. Online bullying tends to result in much more anxiety than face-to-face settings, which tend to be perceived as more contained and where the victim can clearly identify the bully. In other words, anonymity and convenience increase the incidence of cyberbullying as well as the sense of vulnerability for the victims who wonder who has witnessed their harassment and if it will happen again.

Cyberbullying is the subject of numerous studies, most of which underscore its profound impacts on psychological and emotional health and wellbeing (Kowalski *et al.*, 2016). Loss of self-efficacy, depression, and suicide are possible outcomes for many children and adolescents, especially if the problem goes unidentified and unaddressed by caregivers and helping professionals (Hinduja and Patchin, 2010). Some individuals suffer with physical ailments such as headaches, gastrointestinal pain, and/or hyperactivation in the form rapid heart rate, startle responses and elevated blood pressure; these responses are similar to trauma reactions and, in some cases, are a form of posttraumatic stress. Because of the serious mental and physical health implications associated with cyberbullying, it is essential that therapists who work with children and adolescents who display distress or depression understand the signs of online bullying in their clients.

Is It "FoMO" or an Addiction?

While in some ways we are more connected to each other than ever, we are also increasingly disengaged from direct human contact even when we are in direct proximity to each other. Think about how many times you have gone out to dinner with a partner, family, or friends only to find that everyone at your table is checking their smartphones rather than engaging in face-to-face conversation before the entrée arrives. I even have a new creative hobby now that involves taking photographs with my iPhone of people staring at their cellphones at airports (Figure 4.1). These are moments of FoMO, an acronym for "fear of missing out"; in the lives of those privileged to own a cellphone, it has become an unconscious habit to "check your phone" at increasingly frequent intervals. In fact, for many, being unable to look at one's digital device to read text messages, look at social media, or peruse the Internet feels like deprivation. This behavior reflects the basic biological need of our brains to seek those things that support a sense of safety because once that experience is felt in the body, the brain releases a bit of dopamine. When the good feeling passes, the brain goes on seeking more experiences that release the dopamine again; in other words, for many people returning to look at a smartphone for a text or a quick check of social media, the action reinforces a sense of both safety and positive reward.

Figure 4.1
Consulting the Oracle
Courtesy of Cathy Malchiodi

For some of our clients, constant engagement with digital devices to access social media or gaming may be something beyond FoMO and possibly a form of addiction. In fact, magnetic resonance imaging (MRI) research indicates that the brains of Internet users who cannot control their engagement with digital devices are similar to the brains of individuals who are addicted to drugs or alcohol. Other studies demonstrate that simply unplugging from digital technology resulted in some users experiencing physical and emotional withdrawal symptoms (Kuss, 2016).

Social media addiction is now more widely accepted as a form of addictive behavior because it is a proven mood-altering experience for many individuals. This type of addiction includes preoccupation with social media (such as Jolene's nighttime episodes). Some individuals have actual "withdrawal reactions" such as anxiety and depression when they are unable to use social networks; they may even use social media as a way to relieve negative mood, just like a person with a drug addiction may use a substance (alcohol or drug) to alleviate distress.

Conclusion

This chapter underscores the importance of staying current on the multiple ways digital technology and social networking impact the health and wellbeing of individuals of all ages. It is no longer possible for therapists to ignore that most clients come to therapy with psychosocial experiences at least partially influenced by engagement with digital devices and social media; in particular it is essential that all therapists recognize how media and devices influence mood, stress, physical responses, and interpersonal relationships. Just as meditation and physical exercise can literally change our brains, the virtual world of online interactions and electronic communications alter cognition and emotions in ways that we are just beginning to understand. We are also in the earliest stages of developing psychotherapeutic strategies to help individuals negotiate the inevitable technostress of a digital world. While it may be impossible and impractical to get our clients to disconnect from digital technology and social media, we as therapists now have a responsibility to explore and identify when and how these platforms support health and wellbeing as well as when and how they do not.

Recommendations

In order to expand clinical thinking and develop effective interventions for clients in the digital age, therapists should:

- stay informed about the impact of digital technology and social networking on emotional, psychosocial, and physical health

- consider that some forms of anxiety, stress responses, and depression may be the result of technostress due to digital devices and information overload

- when working with children and adolescents, consider how digital technology and social networking affects emotional and psychosocial development

- be aware of the role cyberbullying may play in depression, anxiety, and physical symptoms in children and adolescents

- take into account the role social networking and social media play in interpersonal relationships

- learn more about patterns of addiction to digital devices and social networking.

References

American Academy of Pediatrics (AAP) (2016, October 21) American Academy of Pediatrics announces new recommendations for children's media use. Retrieved on April 1, 2018 at www.aap.org/en-us/about-the-aap/aap-press-room/pages/american-academy-of-pediatrics-announces-new-recommendations-for-childrens-media-use.aspx

American Academy of Pediatrics Council on Communications and Media (2016) Media and young minds. *Pediatrics 138*(5), e20162591.

Ayyagari, R., Grover, V. and Purvis, R. (2011) Technostress: Technological antecedents and implications. *MIS Quarterly 35*(4), 831–858.

BBC News (2017a, December 12) "You are being programmed," former Facebook executive warns. Retrieved on April 1, 2018 at www.bbc.com/news/blogs-trending-42322746

BBC News (2017b, November 9) Facebook founding president Sean Parker sounds alarm. Retrieved on April 1, 2018 at www.bbc.com/news/av/technology-41937476/facebook-founding-president-sean-parker-sounds-alarm

Carr, N. (2010) *The Shallows: What the Internet Is Doing to Our Brain.* New York, NY: Norton and Norton.

Chandra, R. (2018, January 19) How to use social media wisely and mindfully. *Greater Good Magazine.* Retrieved on April 1, 2018 at https://greatergood.berkeley.edu/article/item/how_to_use_social_media_wisely_and_mindfully?

Gazzaley, A. (2016) *The Distracted Mind: Ancient Brains in a High-Tech World.* Cambridge, MA: MIT Press.

Hinduja, S. and Patchin, J. (2010) Bullying, cyberbullying and suicide. *Archives of Suicide Research 14*(3), 206–221.

Kim, J. and Lee, J. (2011) The Facebook paths to happiness: Effects of the number of Facebook friends and self-presentation on subjective well-being. *Cyberpsychology, Behaviour and Social Networking 14*(6), 359–364.

Kowalski, R., Limber, S. and Agatston, P. (2016) *Cyberbullying: Bullying in the Digital Age.* Hoboken, NJ: Wiley and Blackwell.

Kuss, D. (2016) Internet addiction and problematic Internet use. *World Journal of Psychiatry 6*(1), 143–176.

Pew Research Center (2017, January 12) Record shares of Americans now own smartphones, have home broadband. Retrieved on April 1, 2018 at www.pewresearch.org/fact-tank/2017/01/12/evolution-of-technology

Riedl, R., Kindermann, H., Auinger, A. and Javor, A. (2012) Technostress from a neurobiological perspective. *Business and Information Systems Engineering 4*(2), 61–69.

Shakya, H. and Christakis, N. (2017) Association of Facebook use with compromised well-being: A longitudinal study. *American Journal of Epidemiology 185*(3), 203–211.

Suler, J. (2004) The online disinhibition effect. *CyberPsychology and Behavior 7*(3), 321–326.

Tromholt, M. (2016) The Facebook experiment: Quitting Facebook leads to higher levels of well-being. *Cyberpsychology, Behaviour and Social Networking 19*(11), 661–666.

Twenge, J. (2017) *iGen: Why Today's Super-Connected Kids Are Growing Up Less Rebellious, More Tolerant, Less Happy—and Completely Unprepared for Adulthood—and What That Means for the Rest of Us.* New York, NY: Simon and Schuster.

Twenge, J., Krizan, Z. and Hisler, G. (2017) Decreases in self-reported sleep duration among US adolescents 2009–2015 and links to new media screen time. *Sleep Medicine 39*, 47–53.

Veretilo, P. and Billick, S. (2012) Psychiatric illness and Facebook: A case report. *Psychiatric Quarterly 83*(30), 385–389.

2
The Digital Toolbox— Methods and Media

5

NEW MEDIA AND THEIR EFFECTS IN ART THERAPY

Shaun McNiff

Digital Media Transcend Silos of Specialization

As someone committed to the integration of all of the arts in therapy, I have always been very comfortable and at home with the idea of art therapy. Susan K. Langer said there is only one word that gathers together painting, creative writing, music, drama, dance, and other art forms, and that word is "Art" (1957, p.14). Just as I have defined "art-based research" as inclusive of all of the arts, I feel the same way toward art therapy. Although it is institutionally a visual art therapy discipline, I am all for keeping the "art" moniker and the expansiveness it holds. And within the visual arts, I perceive photographs and video, the two primary modes of current digital art, as vital elements of "art therapy" rather than creating new and fragmenting specializations such as "digital art therapy." This inclusive idea of art therapy assumes limitless media possibilities in keeping with the spectrum of life experiences and the practice of artists worldwide. The defining feature of all, ranging from painting and drawing, the construction of objects and spaces in nature, to making video with a small and powerful new device, is the making of "art," albeit an open-ended term that lacks fixed boundaries.

I view this flexibility as an asset and the current wealth of digital possibilities will enable our discipline to fully realize its art-based medicines and powers.

I emphasize this integral notion of art and artists at the start of the discussion of digital media because these new forms of expression, especially video, are inherently multisensory; they transcend separations amongst the arts; and they naturally integrate modes of visual, kinetic, auditory, dramatic, and poetic expression. Within the visual arts, the use of digital art goes beyond traditional two- and three-dimensional materials by including live action. It is perhaps no wonder that the more conservative and restrictive thinking about the nature of art therapy has always resisted new media.

Rather than threatening the continuities of classic art materials and modes of expression, digital media enhance practice by offering distinctly different resources while also partnering with traditional art forms and helping us to appreciate them more through digital documentation and reflection. But perhaps most importantly, the introduction of digital media, so different from the more familiar substances of artistic expression, can further understanding of the need to carefully examine what every medium of expression offers to the art therapy experience. It has always been a source of consternation for me that art therapy has, with certain important exceptions, given little attention to the empirical qualities of the artistic medicines that it offers. I think this is because the discipline has not been grounded in the physical substance of the art-making experience but rather, as I will describe, operates within a paradigm that often treats all media of expression as generating data for psychological analysis and at best modes of communication furthering psychological reflection. Neither give primary attention to how the material qualities of particular media further healing. This chapter encourages looking at what the different materials do in relation to artistic and therapeutic objectives.

Two important questions are highlighted in this discussion. First, why do we use a specific art form? And, perhaps most importantly in relation to this conversation, what are the unique therapeutic qualities of digital media and how do they differ from and compare to other forms of artistic expression?

Consequently, digital media are part of a broad and holistic appreciation of the ways in which the empirical materials of artistic expression offer therapeutic possibilities and effects that correspond to their essential qualities (Hyland Moon, 2010; McNiff, 2004). The focus here on "new media" can, I hope, be considered in a way that concerns the ongoing appearance of fresh and novel materials of expression. My goal is to encourage a more comprehensive exploration of media qualities and impact with a realization that, especially in the digital realm, change and innovation happen on a daily basis. For example, many of the digital media uses that I discussed in the first edition of this book in 2001 are now dated. In this new volume, I give many examples of current digital media use in art therapy, but in a way that lends itself to change while ultimately dealing with the essential questions of media impact in a way that anticipates and supports future technologies and continuously examines their particular qualities and effects.

Early Use of Video in Art Therapy and Lasting Effects

When portable video technology became available in the early 1970s, I was given many opportunities to use it within the art therapy program that I was coordinating in a state hospital (McNiff, 1974). I am thus in a relatively unique position in having used portable and handheld video on a consistent and in-depth basis since it first became available and while it shifted from analogue to digital platforms. Early experimentation and use of video was rare since the equipment was costly, complex, and largely inaccessible, all of which has changed radically as a result of the current ubiquity of digital devices.

This early experimentation with new media took place at a time when some in art therapy insisted that the discipline should be restricted to drawing, painting, and modeling with clay. With the support of Christopher Cook who was then the Director of the Addison Gallery of American Art at Phillips Academy in Andover, Massachusetts, our state hospital studio had access to video portapaks (battery-powered self-contained analog recording systems carried with a shoulder strap), monitors, and skilled camera operators who both recorded art-making sessions with various media and also helped staff and group members learn how to use the equipment. After two years of practice within the hospital the program expanded into the art museum itself where it ran for four years in cooperation with various mental health facilities in the community. In describing why he brought a therapeutic program into the art museum, Cook said:

> I'm for the idea of art being useful. And by useful, I don't mean reducing quality. I mean that art shouldn't be just for fun and titillation, but that art has some kind of fundamental integrating capacity to make people function better... I certainly have an interest in a museum being a beautiful place. But the primary significance of a museum should be to help art get into the mainstream of life. (Newsom and Silver, 1978, p.175)

The program was inspired by Cook's vision to explore the application of new media as well as the use of the museum as a therapeutic milieu. Intrigued with how the range of practice could correspond to what was taking place in the larger context of the visual arts, we naturally integrated video into art therapy sessions (McNiff and Cook, 1975). The presence of a video camera naturally evoked the other arts, and especially performance, as responses to the medium. The media possibilities and qualities in this respect had a significant influence on my first exploration of arts integration. Everything began as a reaction to media properties. Video introduced significant and compelling ways of documenting the actions of people in our art therapy studio and evoked the presentation of life experience as art. The *medium* fostered an *integral* approach to art therapy.

Video also had the ability to inherently include the total environment of the museum—the galleries, artworks, people, and outside spaces. In this respect, it was the perfect medium to achieve Cook's goal of using the museum as a therapeutic environment that helped art connect with the mainstream of life. As I reflect back on these years of work within the museum with video, I realize that these effects happened outside the scope of our plans and immediate thoughts. The outcome was an extension of the artistic medium. Video became a kind of eco-art that included all of the things occuring within a particular place. Every small and subtle element made its contribution to the whole. The artistic use of the medium became the conduit for the art–life synthesis and therapeutic "integrating capacity" that Cook hoped to realize within the museum environment.

In assessing the work done within the museum, these effects could not have taken place without the affirming and aesthetically stimulating effects of video-playback. These environmental and spatial effects were unique in my personal video experience because within this particular program the museum space was such a significant and intentional participant in the art therapy process. We envisioned what we did as a form of artistic milieu therapy which I think has rich potential for future environmentally informed art therapy where digital media can play a similar integrating function.

Our early use of video in the 1970s concentrated on two primary features that have stayed consistent over the years and through periods of rapid change and advancement of digital technologies—the use of video to document the process of artistic expression within both individual and group situations and the making of the video as an artwork. The two principles also apply to the more recent use of digital photography.

When working with the original video recording equipment, a small number of people showed interest in mastering the technical process of shooting footage. The equipment was complicated and, although portable, it was weighty and demanded a number of technically challenging and simultaneous operations—focusing while moving the camera and following action, attending to sound quality which sometimes required microphones, carrying the equipment and tape recording portapak while using both hands and the whole body, and so forth. It took some considerable effort and skill to master these functions, but today virtually all of these challenges have been eliminated while the quality of the recording devices has exponentially advanced. With the exception of one adult group where a participant was committed to mastering videography, the recording in sessions was done by myself and the team of graduate students and museum staff working with us.

This early video experimentation in art therapy concentrated more on using the medium as a way of documenting overall group and community activity and giving individual people the opportunity to see themselves in the process of making art. The essential therapeutic effects that we experienced at that time have continued unabated through the decades and they have remained constant through the various media enhancements that have occurred. For example, in our first use of video in the early 1970s we naturally focused on the movements of a person's hands making art, both to ensure confidentiality for edited versions of video that might be shown outside the group context but also to get in close and show qualities of artistic action and touch that are not usually seen without the assistance of the camera.

The aesthetic effect of this close-up recording, often made into striking still images shown as photographs, continues to this day with considerable therapeutic power. It is impactful in every therapeutic context and it is especially valuable in situations where confidentiality is a serious concern. For example, Serena Duckrow Fonda's 2017 doctoral dissertation exploring the use of clay and filmmaking within a maximum security forensic psychiatric facility offers a compelling contemporary illustration of this process. Her work also shows the considerable therapeutic impact that results from making and showing an edited and consolidated film presentation of the video materials vs. just the raw footage. My involvement in this research has considerably influenced my appreciation of how artistically edited video significantly impacts the art therapy experience, all of which will be discussed in the chapter of this book dealing with the use of digital media in art-based research (see Chapter 20).

Paradigm Influences

Because the art therapy discipline has been largely oriented to explaining and responding to artworks within the context of narrative-based psychological theories, the field has been less concerned with the physical and emotional effects of different media. Most art therapy training programs and many art therapists still focus on the use of inexpensive and simple media such as the ubiquitous box of oil pastels and paper. I do not wish to minimize therapeutic experiences that might occur with limited resources and "poor" studios which keep us close to the basics of art making. In many cases, the box of used and broken oil pastels applied to the blank side of a used piece of paper may be the only option for expression. The quality of the art therapy experience may be enhanced by high-quality art materials, but it will never be determined exclusively by them. Meagre and humble media can generate high-quality artistic expression, but ideally every instance of art therapy practice innately strives to do the best it can in offering quality materials. What I am suggesting here is that it is common for art therapy experiences to take place without careful consideration of the impact of the media used and, often within a context where only basic art materials are used to generate images for the purpose of psychological discourse.

Art therapy has almost exclusively identified with psychological paradigms based upon narrative world views, that is, linear chains of causation and development explicated through storylines, case histories, past traumas, and the overriding values of what I call "explanationism"—if you paint that, it means this. Although I certainly appreciate the place of narrative, history, linear analysis, and chains of causation in understanding human experience, I have found that my practice of art therapy cannot be encapsulated in these concepts. I constantly observe how the most successful outcomes involve people in a process of "creating outside the lines" of psychological narrative. I am also committed to art therapy's integration of artistic and psychological processes, but in a way that reflects upon the subtler depth psychology of non-linear artistic forces and which gives significant attention to the psychological implications of media use rather than always translating artistic experiences into verbal accounts and explanations.

The creative imagination and the process of making art generate transformative and healing energies that are distinctly non-linear and always difficult, sometimes impossible, to "explain." These effects and changes are felt and experienced through our bodies as well as minds. They are also empirically present in the artistic expressions. They are *art medicines* that are typically closer to the energetic movements of nature and the body than they are to psychological concepts. Therefore, I am always exploring what media do, how they affect us differently, what qualities they convey, how they influence the circulation of energy in spaces and in people (McNiff, 2016), and how new media and new interactions amongst existing media improve practice.

Art Therapy Applications of Digital Art Media

As an advocate for digital art since it first became accessible I have to emphasize that it will never replace what I do in my studio groups where we paint and make objects with conventional art media. This is not an either-or discussion, but rather encouragement for consideration of all art therapy media resources. Traditional media have deep-rooted qualities that will always be at the core of the art therapy experience—smells, sounds, feel, wetness, weight, total bodily movement, the physical presence of objects, and the full sensory energies and sensations of a studio environment. But there are also medicines in the pixels.

Digital art has its own ways of activating and transmitting creative energies and life-changing forces. Its vibrant color, light, movement, sound, and ability to show life processes introduce palpable and potent energetic forces into the art therapy context. Digital and conventional art media share an image-base with the former expanding and enriching possibilities for therapeutic effects.

The most basic advances of digital media in relation to artistic expression arguably involve making artistic expression more accessible to all people. The current ubiquity of powerful digital devices capable of producing high-quality imagery with elemental operating skills has made it possible for people everywhere to generate expressive images. This contrasts to the worldwide attitudinal and operational obstacles to painting, drawing, sculpture, and other traditional media even in the most supportive conditions. There has been a radical shift toward an egalitarian inclusion of people in the making of digital expressions, some of which have generated media that have had significant influences on the lives of others and society.

Video Applications

In my work, the most fundamental and positive change in practice concerns the ability of digital media to express and document process. As I mention above, this aspect of digital media was primary in our first use of video over 45 years ago, but the advances in technology and tools have considerably affected the potential applications. Video affirms my longstanding emphasis on the inseparable nature of art objects and art-making processes. The object of expression is a core participant in the process during and after the completion of the physical work. The art therapy conversation separating process and product, although well intended, is out of sync with reality since "nature does not bifurcate" these elements (McNiff, 2015, pp.184–185). We can embrace and become more aware of process and lower product-oriented inhibitions and expectations by simply re-visioning the nature of the art object as an intimate other and partner (McNiff, 1992). Video affirms this complementary relationship and it adds further dimensions of processes and objects through its ability to create still images that endlessly multiply perceptions and perspectives. This wealth of imagery is a tremendous resource for art therapy in that each image expresses itself through its forms, structures, colors, and movements (Arnheim, 1954) and thus generates sources that have the potential to impact the therapeutic process in many ways.

The potential is vast and I mention only a few examples here of possibilities. I have always been fascinated with the impact of documenting various phases of the art-making process and appreciating the way in which images present themselves before we consider them "finished." Digital technology has revolutionized this process and we have only begun to explore the potential impact. Where in the past we may have had to rely on cameras to show different frames of emergence, the ability to make photographs of images from video changes everything. These images can be shown and explored individually and they can be made into a separate video of ongoing shots. The ability to witness and feel the process of art making in this encapsulated way can have a strong impact on the viewer. In addition to the fundamental energetic and visual force conveyed by the presentation, the sense of change and emergence shown through process and the different periods of formation has major metaphoric significance for therapeutic discussion and inquiry. Where possible, participants in art therapy can make these edited pieces themselves and the accessibility of the new technology makes this possible in ways that were inconceivable not long ago. In circumstances where the participants are unable to create edited videos, this can be done by therapists.

The appearance of new video devices, like a camera attached to the forehead, enables people making art to record their own process and hand movements, and this frees the therapist to witness the work without being concerned with using a camera or relying on a stationary camera location that often records less dynamic footage. However, I have consistently learned through my experience with people who can work alone without me having to constantly attend to the overall context that the use of a camera can actually enable me to get closer to the art process and the present moments of creation. The video camera becomes a focusing tool that helps me see things that I would not have otherwise experienced. The resulting video of the process becomes a form of artistic witnessing and response, all of which contribute to the whole of the therapeutic experience.

Digital Painting Software and Computer-Generated Digital Art

In the first edition of this book I described my experimentation beginning in the late 1990s with digital painting in Photoshop® and how features like the history function make it possible to capture and save progressive iterations when "painting with pixels," and how the Internet can show and communicate art objects and processes from a distance. These tools have remained largely unchanged over the years and have gotten even stronger. I believe that Photoshop® has survived and prospered as a painting medium because it closely corresponds to and in some ways enhances the process of painting with actual paint. I described how Bob Evans, an artist expert in digital media, said to me at that time (1999) that when viewing quality digital art, it is not possible to tell whether the image was made on the computer or scanned from a painting on paper or canvas. He described programs where "the computer makes the art" through programmed effects and not the person, and how the resulting work "looks like computer art" where "people express the program and not themselves." He described how "Some people can't make the leap to take over from the machine. They let the machine dominate. They can't trust the process and let the computer operate as a paint brush."

As an artist and art therapist who has been making and viewing digital paintings for over two decades, I am continuously stimulated by their perceptual qualities. My experience in making digital paintings is that the process encourages me to complement what I do on the computer by working in my studio with physical materials and vice versa. The different media feed one another. For example, I prefer painting with a mouse to a stylus, fingers, or other digital tools. The sliding process allows me to access new and spontaneous gestures—like the way Henri Matisse circumvented habitual movements by using painting and drawing tools with significantly elongated handles. We move amongst media to experience changing physical qualities and challenges that elicit new expressions from us. The quality of colors and the mouse movements contribute to the unique energetic powers of digital images. Painting with a mouse eliminates elements of pressure, both forceful and soft, that accompany the physical act of painting and drawing. These kinesthetic qualities, together with smell, touch, and texture, are clearly missing in the digital domain, but they are replaced by a remarkable ability to utilize a wide array of expressions, ranging from bold to delicate, by simply adjusting the tool. Any person is capable of making images with the broad brush strokes of an abstract expressionist or an impressionist's small strokes and patches of paint. I have been satisfied with the expressive quality of pictures that I make with the mouse because this tool prevents me from getting too tight and fussy with my movements. The mouse offers just enough control and dexterity while resisting a tendency toward excessive delineation that hampers the expressive movement of a picture.

In my work one of the most significant features of digital media is the ability to isolate and magnify details of photographs of paintings and drawings. The cropping tool can make many new paintings within a painting, often highlighting and accentuating perceptions of gestures and compositions "discovered" within the newly created frames (see Figures 5.1, 5.2, and 5.3). I have been impressed with how this viewing of details furthers an appreciation of the things that "happen" outside the controls of our more deliberate actions and thoughts. They generate a sense of freshness, wonder, and possibilities that we did not realize within our more accustomed approaches to making art. We can appreciate and engage these details as worlds unto themselves immediately and in ways that were not previously possible. These qualities and tools cry out for experimental research in art therapy (Carlton, 2014).

Figure 5.1
Harbour Bench

Figure 5.2
Sailors

Figure 5.3
Fly

Another great advantage of digital art-making is the ability to further access for physically challenged participants. A single finger can create bold and expansive gestures. The tactile features of drawing and painting with fingers become available in ways not available through traditional media. And in a most extreme instance of physical immobility, the EyeWriter® technology used by the graffiti artist Tony Quan, aka Temptl, has enabled him to paint with eye movements when his body became paralyzed.[1]

Those interested in more detailed information about using digital technology and universal design with people with special

---

1   www.npr.org/templates/story/story.php?storyId=124980282

needs might visit the CAST (Center for Applied Special Technology) website.[2] CAST has pioneered the use of technology and universal design to "expand opportunities for all people, including those with disabilities" by offering alternatives for expression and different ways of engaging materials.

Conclusion

In sum, the image-making properties of digital art can enhance many of the things we currently do within art therapy while introducing new elements to practice. However, there are things that digital media cannot do in art therapy. Exclusive reliance on any one medium or idea will always limit the full spectrum of possibilities. In addition to lacking the sensations of the studio and the ability to physically manipulate different media, computer art will never replace the three-dimensional presence of the actual thing being made. Ultimately, I am not making a case for or against digital art in relation to traditional media. Each material brings its distinct attributes to the art therapy process and, as I have emphasized, our discipline will benefit by giving closer attention to its effects and healing qualities. The world does advance through new technologies and art therapy needs to move with it. Art therapy, perhaps more than any other therapeutic modality, is perfectly suited to these new technologies. We simply need the imagination and creative resources to seize the opportunity.

---

2   www.cast.org

Recommendations

- Select any painting and take a digital photograph of it. Experiment with the crop function of whatever editing system you are using. Select many different details and discover the worlds within one painting.

- Use a digital device to film yourself creating art. Rather than focusing on the final product, consider what you learn from actually witnessing your own process of creation.

- If you have a smartphone or tablet, download some of the free drawing and painting apps (see Chapter 11 for some suggestions). Conduct your own art-based research (see Chapter 20), comparing "new media" to traditional forms of art making.

References

Arnheim, R. (1954) *Art and Visual Perception*. Berkeley, CA: University of California Press.

Carlton, N.R. (2014) Digital media use in art therapy. Doctoral dissertation. Retrieved on April 1, 2018 at ProQuest Dissertations and Theses database (UMI No. 368214).

Duckrow Fonda, S. (2017) Filmmaking as artistic inquiry: An examination of ceramic art therapy in a maximum security forensic psychiatric facility. Doctoral dissertation. Retrieved on April 1, 2018 at ProQuest Dissertations and Theses database (UMI No. 10263229).

Hyland Moon, C. (ed.) (2010) *Materials and Media in Art Therapy*. New York, NY: Routledge.

Langer, S.K. (1957) *Problems of Art*. New York, NY: Charles Scribner and Sons.

McNiff, S. (1974) *Art Therapy at Danvers*. Andover, MA: Addison Gallery of American Art.

McNiff, S. (1992) *Art as Medicine: Creating a Therapy of the Imagination*. Boston, MA: Shambhala.

McNiff, S. (2004) *Art Heals: How Creativity Cures the Soul*. Boston, MA: Shambhala.

McNiff, S. (2015) *Imagination in Action: Secrets for Unleashing Artistic Expression*. Boston, MA: Shambhala.

McNiff, S. (2016) Ch'i and artistic expression: An East Asian worldview that fits the creative process everywhere. *Creative Arts Education and Therapy: Frontiers in China—An International Academic Journal for Research and Practice 2*(2), 12–22.

McNiff, S. and Cook, C. (1975) Video art therapy. *Art Psychotherapy 2*, 55–63.

Newsom, B. and Silver, A. (eds.) (1978) The Addison Gallery of American Art: Video for special audiences. In *The Art Museum as Educator: A Collection of Studies as Guides to Practice and Policy*. Berkeley, CA: University of California Press.

6
PHOTO-ART THERAPY

Alexander Kopytin

The vibrant fields of phototherapy and therapeutic photography embrace various forms of therapeutic and health-promoting applications of photography. It is difficult to overestimate the role of photography in people's communication and creative self-expression and its influence on humanity in general, as well as clients' relationships and interaction with the world around them, and with therapists in particular. As Loewenthal (2013) puts it:

> Importantly, we are now in the digital era where the growth of digital photography, including mini movies and mobile phone cameras, together with the rapid use of photography on social networking sites such as Facebook, Flickr, YouTube and Twitter, ensure that phototherapy and its related practices now present a potentially major opportunity, not just for the older person, who still may have a family album, but as a vital way of engaging with the preferred technology of younger generations. (p.5)

The potential of implementing photography either in the form of personal snapshots and collections of photos, or pictures taken throughout or between sessions, for facilitating therapy is multifaceted. Numerous curative approaches, including various branches of expressive and creative therapies, can learn from phototherapy and from bringing photographic material and techniques into therapeutic and expressive context.

There are many forms of therapeutic applications of photography related to different schools of thought in psychotherapy. Creative arts therapists, especially art therapists, also implement photography in their work with clients, not only as photographic material for discussion, but also as a stimulus for clients' creative activity and powerful expressive medium that can be used in art therapy together with drawing, painting, clay-work, and other art forms. However, publications presenting art therapists' ways of working with photography and photographic images are still scarce. They indicate an apparent discrepancy between art therapists' rich experience of using photography as an expressive medium in their own creative endeavors and the limited scope of its applications in clinical practice (Kopytin, 2013). Not only ethical considerations, but prevailing approaches to therapy training that concentrate on "traditional" artistic media and "handmade" images rather than those produced with the use of technical equipment, together with the insufficiency of relevant information and instructions in the ways of applying photography with clients/patients in current art therapy education and literature, may explain why its rich potential is not materialized to a proper degree. That is why photo-art therapy, as a powerful integration of the potentials of handmade and digital expression, and with its special theoretical and empirical platform and appropriate ways of work, needs to be developed and brought into art therapists' daily practice.

The goal of this chapter is to stimulate thinking about photo-art therapy as a powerful integration of the potential efficacy of both handmade and digital expression. Starting with traditional approaches to phototherapy, which are primarily perceptive/ reflective and narrative techniques, photo-art therapy introduces an even wider spectrum of artistic and expressive choices. Reference to photo-art therapy as a form of digital media will also be given. These approaches will be discussed, illustrated, and explored in this chapter.

Phototherapy and Photo-Art Therapy Techniques

"PhotoTherapy techniques are *therapy practices* that use people's personal snapshots, family albums, and pictures taken by others (and the feelings, thoughts, memories, and associations these photos evoke) as catalysts to deepen insight and enhance communication during their therapy or counselling sessions (conducted by trained mental health professionals), in ways not possible using words alone."[1] Photo-art therapy techniques are art therapy practices based on a specialized adaptation of phototherapy techniques that should only be used by those with postgraduate training in art therapy, who have covered the use of photos in their training.

PhotoTherapy is defined as "a set of techniques for already competent therapists to add to their professional repertoire of counseling skills when involved in the work of helping others" (Weiser, 1999, p.xv). According to Weiser (1999), PhotoTherapy techniques can be adapted to different types of therapeutic models and client difficulties, populations, or settings depending on therapists' considerations and their belonging to a particular therapeutic approach. Weiser described five main groups of PhotoTherapy techniques that can be applied within a multiplicity of methods:

* photo-projective techniques
* self-portraits
* photos of the client by others
* photos taken or collected by the client
* albums and photo-biographical snapshots.

The photo-projective techniques make use of the spontaneous associative process of connecting a visual stimulus with conscious and unconscious meaning. Actually, any photograph can be used for this purpose since people see and understand any visual stimulus according to their beliefs and "filters of perception." Sometimes, special sets of photographs can be used to provide a standardized process for their selecting, interpreting, and comparability of response.

Self-portrait techniques are focused on exploring the client's perception of her/himself: "Here the self is addressed as perceived directly by itself, hopefully to obtain a better sense of objective self-awareness" (Weiser, 1999, pp.xix–xx).

The third group of PhotoTherapy techniques comprises photos of the client taken by others. This group of techniques helps to explore and understand how other people, such as the client's relatives,

---

1   https://phototherapy-centre.com

friends, and so on, perceive individuals and deal with "power issues around a photograph being made of a person in situations where the process was not fully under his or her, independent control" (Weiser, 1999, p.xx). Photos taken or collected by the client reflect the client's perception of the world around them, including people, nature, and social and cultural phenomena, and help to reveal her/ his relationships within the wider network of connections.

Though the fourth group of PhotoTherapy techniques usually implies picture-taking and, thus, provides a certain connection between verbal therapy and art therapy, some differences between their ways of working with photographic approaches are often emphasized. While it is more typical for verbal therapists and counselors to rely on verbal modes of communication with clients and use photos mostly as a material for discussion, art therapists give more space for artistic–expressive activities of clients with the use of photography.

The fifth group of PhotoTherapy techniques comprises albums and photo-biographical snapshots which facilitate uncovering various meanings implied in a client's biography and her/his family unit as "a self, a distinct identity apart from just the sum of those individuals who form it by virtue of birth, affiliation, choice, or whichever type of 'family' is being identified with" (Weiser, 1999, p.xxi).

Discussing the significance of working with preexisting materials in art therapy, Shaun McNiff (2004) emphasizes the role of engaging personally significant objects found in the home or natural environment in the creative process that can activate feelings and memories in a way that is less likely to occur when working with a more impersonal medium. He claims that "for most people, photographs are the preeminent carriers of these personal spirits and emotions" (p.140). He often encourages people in his studios to make objects with materials from nature and noticed how a sacred or shamanic dimension is spontaneously evoked when people reflect upon and respond creatively to objects made with materials from nature. Similarly, people can take pictures of natural objects and use them as preexisting images that evoke powerful feelings and facilitate further creative work. As McNiff (2004) puts it:

> Photographers also have the ability to make art by finding images in the world and framing them within their particular creative visions and styles...

> Instant photographs have a unique ability to create immediate images of nature, the self, and others that open us to deep reflections about our lives. (p.140)

In addition to the main five groups of PhotoTherapy techniques useful for most psychotherapy situations that art therapists can implement in their work, there are numerous related applications, among them video and multimedia art, that can aid the therapy process. Combinations of photographic and other artistic media and expressive forms can be useful to those trained in art therapy. A variety of visual–narrative techniques based on a combination of photographs and story-making—such as "digital stories," photographic diaries (photo-journaling), photo-taking assignments that include creative writing and illustrating personal stories of the client, or some cultural and archetypal themes, or poetry, or myths— are also possible. As Wheeler (2013) notes: ,

> the deceptively simple definition of contemporary phototherapy practice helps clarify the breadth and depth of practice beyond either the acts of making and viewing photographs with clients, or the passing of battered enprints (those little plastic-surfaced 6 x 4s) between client and therapist. Now the therapists are more likely to be offered a mobile phone camera gallery than prints, horizons have extended. (p.40)

Using Photography and Photographic Images in Art Therapy

Various photo-art therapy techniques may be used, depending on clients' needs and according to a treatment plan with its appropriate goals, once or many times during a course of therapy. Sometimes, photography helps to establish more direct contact with reality and emotional distance from powerful imagery; it can also stimulate imagination. In certain cases, clients may want to use photography in order to capture significant moments in therapy and their artworks, or to objectify changes that take place in them or around them.

Digital technology opens a new perspective on photo-art therapy developments. Nowadays clients often bring their skills in the use of digital technology to therapy and initiate new forms of "digital self-expression" related to mobile phone cameras. Sometimes they appear to be very creative and even more skillful in exploring new ways of digital self-expression than their therapists. "The frequent practice of the mobile phone photographers engenders in them a familiarity with the tool of their artistic expression, the cellphone camera" (Wheeler, 2013, p.45).

Case Example 6.1

A client created a series of digital artworks using his mobile phone camera. He photographed some details of his abstract expressive paintings and later elaborated on the pictures he had taken. He added images to them by drawing on the sensory screen of his smartphone with a stylus (Figure 6.1). I was surprised to see how quickly he developed his way of digital self-expression and how he revealed a high level of artistic sensitivity through these media. Most of his digital artworks were very playful and humorous (though self-disparaging humor prevailed) (Figure 6.2). He usually added brief stories to pictures. The new creative channel he discovered helped him to alleviate the pain and depressive mood evoked by breaking his love affair.

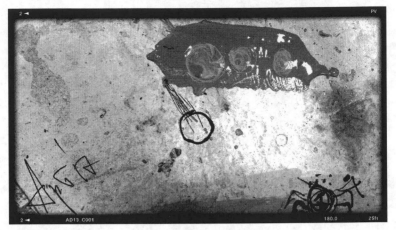

Figure 6.1
The Crab and the Blue Whale

This is an artwork created by a client drawing on a digital photograph. He accompanied the artwork with the following story: "Someday the crab and the blue whale met and fell in love, but they could not live together. Now they just see each other from [a] distance."

Figure 6.2
The Fly of the Beetle

This artwork was created by a client drawing on a digital photograph. He accompanied the artwork with the following story: "The father beetle was going home and his belly was blue and bloating with fresh air. The full moon was like a beacon leading him in the sea of night. Bumblebees and helicopters silently gave way to him. 'Why is the city so calm tonight?' he asked himself. 'Perhaps all its inhabitants went outside—to Fire Island and elsewhere...'"

Mobile devices such as smartphones require a special way of thinking about the images. Nowadays phototherapy and photo-art therapy fields are widened "by considering the interconnected actions of the phone camera, other mobile image making and viewing devices, social networking websites, online galleries and outsider art" (Wheeler, 2013, p.40). Images created on a cell phone have aesthetics that may not be appreciated by many art therapists. Such images:

> now conflate the domestic context, from which much of our photographic experience emerges, with outsider and public art contexts. The sharing of domestic images can now be more widely disseminated than those in galleries and art books from the art establishment. This outsider art practice seems to reclaim from the art establishment the capacity of anyone with a minimum of equipment to make and view art in its own context. (Wheeler, 2013, pp.42–43)

Aesthetics in this sense is grounded in the material properties of the photo or image on the smartphone screen in phototherapy (photo-art therapy), "rather than referring to some disembodied realm of judgment about beauty or truth" (MacLagan, 2002, p.7).

Though clients and groups can spontaneously come to use photography and photographic images, in some cases a therapist may stimulate them to use them by introducing certain assignments. Photo-art therapy techniques can be classified depending on particular photographic materials used (Table 6.1).

Table 6.1 Photographic materials with related artistic/creative activities that can be used in photo-art therapy

Special sets of photographic pictures used as visual stimuli provided by a therapist	Magazine pictures and those taken by clients from other sources	Personal photographs of a client/family albums	Pictures taken by clients throughout or between sessions
Active imagination leading to own handmade creations of a client	Photo-collage/ soul collage	Arranging several pictures in a composition, e.g. adding handmade details	Art journaling and other visual–narrative techniques
	Making posters		
Arranging several pictures in a composition, adding objects and handmade details (installations), etc.	Creating and inhabiting "environments" where a handmade image is included in the photograph used as a background, or vice versa	Art-journaling	Creating thematic albums, slideshows or photographic series
		Photo-collage	Photo-collage
Various visual–narrative activities	Drawing elaborations on a picture	Handmade or technical (Photoshop®) elaboration on a picture	Handmade or technical (Photoshop®) elaboration on a picture
		Visual–narrative techniques ("digital stories")	

For readers who are new to phototherapy and photo-art therapy, what follows are some case examples illustrating different ways to implement photography in their practice.

Case Example 6.2

Finding Meaning and Cohesion in Life Stories through Individual Art Making with Preexisting Personal Photographs

During a session, members of an art therapy training group were asked to make a two- or three-dimensional composition reflecting their life story and various past and present roles. Compositions were to be made using personal photographs that they were asked to bring from their homes and any art materials. They were invited to bring any personal photographs that could represent their childhood and family of origin as well as their later stages of life including their current relationships, job, and leisure activities. Group members had different cultural and professional backgrounds, but came to learn art therapy. Though most of them were Latvians, there were a few members with a Russian background and one who came from the Czech Republic to Latvia. The latter was in the process of adapting to a new cultural context.

While creating a composition, the woman from the Czech Republic cut three big circles representing past, present, and future from thick paper and then placed her personal photos together with pictures that she had taken from magazines. Her commentary is presented below.

> I made the three circles. They represent my childhood, the present period in my life, and my future. I would like to start with my childhood first... This part of my work was done with joy and ease. I'm in the roles of daughter, sister, and granddaughter here... Then I started to make my future. Doing that I recalled that in one of my therapy sessions two months ago I made my life-size self-portrait and drew a rainbow. I've drawn a rainbow today as well. Why? I think I've done so because it consists of many different colors. Maybe my "inner child" is represented as yellow; me in the role of a mother in the future is represented as pink. The color red signifies me as a wife and the color white possibly signifies something in me, what I don't understand at the moment. The last circle represents me now.
>
> My life is difficult now because I live in a new country. I play many roles at present and they are different from the roles I

played before. They are quite new for me... The center of the circle is occupied with the roles and experiences I consider to be most important. I connected all three circles together, but initially I decided not to glue them to each other. I "played" with them and moved them in different ways. This helped me to find a balance. I'm more centered now. I've put an image of the Virgin Mary in the center, because I'm going to be a mother. I also put a playing card, a joker, nearby. It signifies luck and happiness. Cards can create various combinations. This is like destiny and I trust it.

Another member of the group working on the same theme made three cones from paper and placed her personal pictures on them. As in the previous case, the cones represented her past, present, and future. Presenting her composition to the group, she said that her family experienced deportation and was sent to Siberia when Stalin occupied Latvia. She was born in Magadan, in the far east of Russia, and lived there for some years. Though she later came back to Latvia many years ago, when she selected her personal pictures at home she recalled her past and experienced strong feelings. She commented on her artworks, which included many photographs arranged around the three cones, in the following way:

I made the three cones. The first cone is my past—my family, my childhood. The second cone is my present and the third one is my future, which begins right now... I placed pictures representing the life of my family in Siberia on the first cone. These pictures evoke strong feelings in me... My parents were in hell. We lived in Magadan, but I didn't suffer. Our home was very small. I saw the sea and its presence was very positive. I remember how I tried to imagine what Latvia looked like when I was a child.

Now I show these pictures to other people for the first time in my life. In school I would have been ashamed to show them to anyone. When we came back to Latvia I was uncomfortable because children in my school were very suspicious of me...

Here is my present. I like to be alive, to feel, to meet different people, to create, to be a woman. There are my children here as well... I don't like to be in the "frames." I'm lucky to be an artist because it gives me an opportunity to move out of the "frames." I put the two photos which represent me together with my brother on this cone as well. He now lives in America. He too doesn't like to be in the "frames." Our relationship is very important to me.

I placed the cone which signifies the future on the paper with different colors and glued blue paper on top of it because I perceive my future in this color. This signifies something that is very difficult to put into words but can be perceived intuitively. I want to see the world and travel in the future and keep my connection with arts—my art and that of others.

At the end of the session, group members emphasized that in making installations using personal photographs and those taken from magazines and adding handmade images, they were able to find meaningful connections between various periods of their life, and frame and reframe their personal experiences.

A complex of therapeutic functions relating to selecting and arranging the photographs as well as adding handmade images and telling their life story helped the participants to express their feelings and come to a more coherent perception of themselves. Those functions included focusing/actualizing, containing, meaning-making, catharsis, framing/reframing, objectifying, and some others (Kopytin, 2004). The focusing/actualizing function of photography (Kopytin, 2004) was also involved in the session, when participants selected and focused on their personal photographs, evoking memories and feelings, both positive and negative. Though memories were sometimes traumatic, and powerful feelings could be overwhelming, the psychological safety and containment of feelings established in the group, together with the containing function of the photographs as symbolic containers, helped to achieve a cathartic effect and enabled participants to work successfully through past situations.

By arranging their photographs in three-dimensional compositions people were able to find, organize, and express meanings implied in the photos. Sometimes new meanings were made by finding a new place for some photographs in their relation to each other. This illustrates the framing/reframing functions found in photo-art therapy. The participants found and organized multiple meanings suggested by the photos by telling stories of their life based on their artworks which included numerous photographs, an illustration of the meaning-making function. The objectifying function helped people to find a more distanced and complex view of reality, see some typical and repeated reactions in themselves and the situations in which they were involved, as well as to see changes in their life and relationships.

This case example is also an illustration of a creative photographic approach, which, according to Simmons (2013):

provides a means to translate and evaluate personal experiences through the creation of original photographic artwork. It is a process that can help place the maker in a new relationship to their experiences, through the development of emotional distance, a term used here to describe the means whereby an experience can be understood, and its implications appreciated, from a more balanced and informed perspective. (p.54)

Case Example 6.3

Working through Personal Issues with the Use of Art-Based Techniques (Photo-Collage and Drawing Elaboration on a Picture)

The training group in this example consisted of five women and one man of different ages. It was explained that sessions would include various creative activities with an emphasis on photographs in combination with other artistic media and art forms. Sessions lasted one and a half hours. The leader proposed that the first session would include introducing members to the group through their photographs. They were asked to bring some photographs to the session, using them to "tell" others about themselves, their interests, activities, and so on. It was said that the members would decide which photographs to show, taking into account the group atmosphere. It was decided to establish two subgroups, each consisting of three group members, in order to have enough time for each participant to introduce her/himself. They were asked to show photographs to their partners and say something about themselves. It was suggested that in the introductory part of the session certain characteristic features and issues typical for each group member should be identified and one or two most significant photographs be selected as a result of discussion.

When the introductory part of the session was finished, the participants were encouraged to continue their work with one or two photographs which they found most significant. The leader explained that they could now use some art-based activities such as making a photo-collage or an artistic frame around the image, drawing around photographs or on a photograph, or arranging a protective container for a photograph in order to work through their emotions, memories, and ideas evoked by the pictures.

The leader emphasized that participants could use any materials of their choice (white and colored paper, texture, foil, various paints, buttons, personal belongings, etc.).

Two women made their artworks in the form of a container, a paper box, decorating it both inside and outside, and putting their photographs relating to their relationships with their partner/husband inside. They commented that their creations represented their need to protect their relationships and improve their emotional bonds with their loved ones. The third group member made her artistic frame in the form of a sea landscape. There was a seashore and volcano in the distance in the drawing. She explained that her frame signified feelings of freedom and energy. There was also a bird flying above the waves on the right side of the frame. Like some other members of the group, she noted that her photograph helped her to actualize valuable memories of her vacations with complex sensations and feelings evoked by her interaction with the environment.

The frame around the photograph made by a fourth group member was also in the form of a drawing. It was a drawing of an apple tree orchard in the period of harvesting, with apples in baskets. She said that the frame created a peaceful effect she associated with sensuality and joy of life. Another group member selected four photographs taken during the previous two years and created a photo-collage. She cut her figure out of the photographs and added them to a picture created from images of the environment taken from magazines. Her explanation of the artwork was as follows:

> My photo-collage concerns me and my present situation. I left my family more than three years ago, when I moved to another city and became a student. I'm in search of myself, and nature helps me to become more integrated and real. Therefore, I created a photo-collage which represents me in nature. I wanted to make my figure an integral part of the environment.
>
> I recently came back from my placement at a summer camp for children and I'm still full of impressions of how I worked with the children and was very enthusiastic and self-reliant. I put my figure at the top of my photo-collage. I'm jumping on that photograph, but when I cut my figure out of the original environment and put it in the sky, it seemed that I was flying like a bird. I put another photograph representing me at the age of 2 or 3 years sitting together with my favorite toys at the bottom of my photo-collage. I also cut my figure out of the background, which was my room, and moved it to the natural environment. I'm sitting on the top of the hill now. There are two other photographs that I used to make my photo-collage. One of them was taken when I was walking in the countryside and another one was taken when I was on a boat trip. I would like to give my photo-collage the title "My personal journey."

The only male participant in the group made his drawing around a photograph taken during a trip in the countryside together with a group of people and commented on his artwork in the following way:

> I have no family of my own and like to spend my leisure time in the countryside together with my friends. I've chosen one of the photographs taken during my holiday trip on the River Volga some years ago. You can see that I'm lying on the sand with three other members of the group and our legs are in the water.
>
> When I chose this photograph, I realized how stressed I am now and that I need an inner balance in the face of many societal demands. I started to elaborate on the photograph in order to make the natural environment bigger so that it protected me better and gave me a sense of harmony and safety. I surrounded our figures lying on the river bank with green mountains and meadows and continued the stream of water (Figure 6.3).

Figure 6.3
Drawing around a photograph taken during a trip in the natural environment

It appeared that the group participants selected photographs that concerned their most significant relationships to work on with the use of art-based techniques. It appeared that some participants were more concerned with relationships than other participants were, while others were more concerned with routes to professional and personal self-realization and finding inner harmony. Four participants emphasized their relationship with nature as playing a significant role in their attempts to cope with everyday stress and bring more meaning and quality to their life. One group participant said that artwork helped her to become more embedded in the situation presented on the photograph and actualize a wide spectrum of emotions and even physical sensations. This was in contrast to her habitual way of looking at digital photographs, when she didn't concentrate on them for long. Feelings of mutual trust and safety in the group increased at the session.

The case examples presented are illustrations of how selecting, arranging and elaborating on photographic images using artistic means can help the viewer to change their perspective on them and not only look at them in a habitual way, but also look into them. As Simmons (2013) puts it:

> Removed from their original context, photography has enabled these disparate elements to be harnessed and brought together regardless of scale, location or ownership. They have been juxtaposed to form new alliances: becoming metaphors that link internal emotional states and give them form in the material world. These signs and symbols are not rigidly fixed to a single personal interpretation, but are active and open to multiple readings… Not by looking *at* the photographs can others identify, connect with and be touched, but by looking *into* them. (pp.56–57)

Case Example 6.4

Taking Environmental Photographic Self-Portraits as a Homework Assignment

Besides personal photos, which clients bring in by invitation or on their own initiative, they may also be asked to take photographs either during or between sessions and later use them in different ways: to produce a thematic album, a slide-film, a book, or a poster, or include them in a collage or an installation. This can also help to find meaning in the environment, to better feel, understand, and personalize it and even lead to more active participation in the design and management of the space people inhabit.

Weiser (1999) presents *active PhotoTherapy* techniques as giving clients rich possibilities for creative self-expression. She often starts with extremely open-ended assignments, such as, "Go use up this roll of film on anything that catches your attention," and "Go take pictures at the park or at the..." (p.251). She also uses general wide-focus assignments such as "take at least one photo a day with the instant camera and then write about it or talk into the tape recorder about it, bringing me the week's work when you come next week" (p.251).

As a continuation of photo-art therapy activities initiated during the first two sessions with the training group (see Case Example 6.3) the participants were encouraged to take environmental photographic self-portraits as a homework assignment. They were asked to take photographs of their hand (or hands) doing something or being somewhere as a representation of themselves, a kind of photographic self-portrait. Participants could select any meaningful environment, natural or man-made object, and take photographs of their hands there in order to represent how they perceive themselves, what they like or dislike doing, to demonstrate their strengths or weaknesses, and so on.

A young woman had taken 55 photographs of her hands in different environments, starting from the River Volga embankment in the city center near the training center, and later taking photos on her way home, in the underground (Figure 6.4), and finally, in her flat where she photographed herself, both alone and together with her roommate. Photographs of her hands demonstrated her close bonds to nature (Figure 6.5), her artistic and music endeavors (Figures 6.6 and 6.7), her relationship with her roommate (Figure 6.8), and her wish to be an integral and unique being (Figure 6.9).

Fig. 6.4   Fig. 6.5   Fig. 6.6

Fig. 6.7   Fig. 6.8   Fig. 6.9

Figures 6.4–6.9
Examples of a young woman's photographs representing her perception of herself and the
world around her in response to an "environmental photographic self-portrait" assignment

Readers can see from this example that photo-taking assignments
in different environments as "active phototherapy" practice give
participants an opportunity to be involved directly with themselves
in reciprocal interaction with the environment and significant
people, materials, and processes. Unlike the usual photo-taking
assignments, environmentally based active phototherapy helps to
develop receptivity to environmental stimuli and the ability to focus
on the inner processes of body and psyche, and reveals meaningful
relational issues.

The case example illustrates the rich possibilities of active
phototherapy techniques to stimulate emotions and cognitions,
sensory, perceptive, and symbolic ways to interact with the
environment, and to reveal a photographer's relations with it. It
appears that phototherapeutic activities help to develop somatic
awareness and an embodied sense of self in one's relation to the
environment. By taking photographs of the environment, clients
become physically more active and their body becomes a vehicle
of attunement to the "environment" in the complex meaning of

this word. Often the projective nature of photography results in personal identification with objects.

The degree of mindfulness and mental focus one brings to these interactions is important. Participants were encouraged to immerse themselves in a kind of meditation while taking environmental photographs, with their absorption in physical and emotional processes on the one hand, and being attentive to the environmental stimuli on the other hand. According to Gibson's theory of affordances (1986), what clients notice and identify as relevant for them in the environment often depends on what they are looking for. As active motivated agents, clients do not passively receive environmental information. Instead, they extract and "create" meanings from and for the environment depending on their grasp of what they need. As Gibson (1986) observed, affordances are as much a part of the environment as they are of behavior.

Finally, photo-taking as an act of personalization implies perception of the environment not only as a physical and biological realm, but as a "potential space" in which symbol formation can take place. Such potential space becomes a container of symbolic forms from which different meanings and knowledge of the psyche are derived. The environment serves as a mirror that is able to reflect physical and mental phenomena and processes experienced by a photographer/artist (a client participating in sessions) shaping these phenomena and processes through expressive forms. The photo-taking assignment described in this section reinforces the phenomenon of personalization of environment (Gregory, Fried, and Slowik, 2013; Heimets, 1994) and relates to psychosocial aspects expressed through territoriality as well as through people's need to maintain a sense of belonging, ownership, and control over their space. In this case example, it was materialized by taking photographs of one's hands as a symbol of meaningful interaction with the environment. Personalization provided participants with a greater sense of ownership and control over the space, and helped to establish and maintain a sense of individuality and identity.

Conclusion

The goal of this chapter was to present some possibilities for including photography in art therapy practice and to stimulate consideration of photo-art therapy as a powerful integration of the potentials of handmade and digital expression. The rich potential of such integration is still underestimated. Publications presenting art therapists' ways of working with photography and photographic images are still scarce and indicate a certain discrepancy between art therapists' experience of using photography as an expressive medium in their own creative endeavors and the limited scope of its applications in clinical practice.

As a starting point, traditional approaches to the use of photography in therapy, which are primarily perceptive/reflective and narrative techniques, have been presented. Photo-art therapy introduces an even wider spectrum of artistic and expressive choices. Though clients and groups can spontaneously come to using photography and photographic images, various photo-art therapy techniques and art-based assignments can be introduced to reach different therapeutic and developmental goals.

Recommendations

Various art-based techniques with the use of different photographic materials that enable a wide spectrum of artistic/creative activities of clients have been presented and illustrated with brief case examples. The following recommendations, based on the literature and case examples presented, support the use of photo-art therapy:

- A combination of more traditional phototherapy techniques implying verbal commentaries and discussion and art-based activities can be helpful to "digest" meanings, emotions, and memories implied by photographs, and provide multifaceted therapeutic effects.

- Environmental possibilities of photo-art therapy and phototherapy should be taken into consideration (Kopytin, 2016). This is especially important when clients are encouraged to become involved in photo-taking assignments. Combined with a certain "environmental" sensitivity on the part of a therapist, such assignments can help to explore and change people's perception of the environment and enable them to feel in control and to appropriate it.

> - Specific mindfulness-based activities (meditative journeys in particular) can be integrated with "environmental" photo-taking assignments in order to develop a sense of physical presence in the environment and help clients to utilize sensory/kinesthetic, emotional/perceptual, and cognitive/symbolic aspects in their creative/expressive interaction with the world around them.

References

Gibson, J.J. (1986) *The Ecological Approach to Visual Perception.* Hillsdale, NJ: Lawrence Erlbaum Associates.

Gregory, L.A., Fried, Y. and Slowik, L.H. (2013) "My space": A moderated mediation model of the effect of architectural and experienced privacy and workspace personalization on emotional exhaustion at work. *Journal of Environmental Psychology 36*, 144–152.

Heimets, M. (1994) The phenomenon of personalization of the environment. *Journal of Russian and East European Psychology 32*(3), 24–32.

Kopytin, A. (2004) Photography and art therapy: An easy partnership. *Inscape: The Journal of the British Association of Art Therapists 9*(2), 49–58.

Kopytin, A. (2013) Photography and art therapy. In D. Loewenthal (ed.) *Phototherapy and Therapeutic Photography in a Digital Age.* London and New York, NY: Routledge.

Kopytin, A. (2016) Environmentally and eco-based phototherapy: Ecotherapeutic application of photography as an expressive medium. In A. Kopytin and M. Rugh (eds.) *"Green Studio": Nature and the Arts in Therapy.* New York, NY: Nova Science Publishers.

Loewenthal, D. (2013) Introducing phototherapy and therapeutic photography in a digital age. In D. Loewenthal (ed.) *Phototherapy and Therapeutic Photography in a Digital Age.* London and New York, NY: Routledge.

MacLagan, D. (2002) *Psychological Aesthetics: Painting, Feeling and Making Sense.* London: Jessica Kingsley Publishers.

McNiff, S. (2004) *Art Heals: How Creativity Cures the Soul.* Boston, MA: Shambhala.

Simmons, M. (2013) A creative photographic approach: Interpretation and healing through creative practice. In D. Loewenthal (ed.) *Phototherapy and Therapeutic Photography in a Digital Age.* London and New York, NY: Routledge.

Weiser, J. (1999) *PhotoTherapy Techniques: Exploring the Secrets of Personal Snapshots and Family Albums.* Vancouver, Canada: PhotoTherapy Centre.

Wheeler, M. (2013) Fotos, fones and fantasies. In D. Loewenthal (ed.) *Phototherapy and Therapeutic Photography in a Digital Age.* London and New York, NY: Routledge.

7

THERAPEUTIC FILMMAKING

J. Lauren Johnson

The questions "Who are you?" and "Where are you from?" can be difficult to answer, and yet in the work I do as a psychologist with Indigenous Canadians, they are of paramount importance. They can situate a person in specific life experiences, such as growing up on a First Nations reserve in Northern Alberta, or within certain identities, such as "Canadian," "Metis," "Cree," "colonizer," "oppressed." These questions can be especially important in the stories we tell about ourselves—how we see ourselves and want others to see us. They can be the opening questions in the story of our lives, and shape the futures we live into (Habermas and Bluck, 2000; McAdams, 2008).

These questions often form the basis of the initial work I do with Indigenous clients using therapeutic filmmaking. Therapeutic filmmaking is an expressive, artistic approach to counseling psychology that combines talk therapy on one hand and the creative process of film/video-making on the other (Johnson and Alderson, 2008). I have used therapeutic filmmaking in a variety of settings, such as community health centres on rural Northern Alberta First Nations reserves, a residential treatment center for at-risk Indigenous girls, a small private practice in an urban setting, and a tertiary cancer hospital in a large Canadian city. Through the use of these questions, among many others, I attempt to help my clients tell a story using words, images, movement, and sound, about themselves and the world they inhabit. I believe that it is in this storytelling, and in the exploration and expression of self inherent within it, where the therapeutic benefit of this work may be found.

Introduction

This chapter provides an overview of how I use therapeutic filmmaking by describing the approach and then presenting an illustrative case example. I have chosen to use a composite case example rather than a specific individual because many of the people I work with are in vulnerable situations; these clients are often minors who are involved in the child welfare system, forcibly separated from their families and under the guardianship of the state. They typically have histories of trauma, including physical and sexual abuse, and often struggle with posttraumatic stress disorder and addictions (Greidanus and Johnson, 2016).

Prior to delving into the case, it is first important to provide a brief overview of therapeutic filmmaking as I use it. Though filmmaking has been used therapeutically for decades (e.g. Arnott and Gushin, 1976; Furman, 1990), I specifically discuss my own approach to this technique in this chapter due to my level of familiarity with it; I welcome you to explore other approaches to this technique further. Following the discussion of therapeutic filmmaking, I describe a case wherein therapeutic filmmaking was used with an Indigenous teen girl. Then I provide a brief discussion on working with Indigenous clients and present recommendations for other practitioners interested in using therapeutic filmmaking with this population.

An Overview of Therapeutic Filmmaking

Therapeutic filmmaking roughly follows the same procedures as those involved in making any film or video (Johnson and Alderson, 2008). Typically, the process of filmmaking can be broken down into roughly five stages: 1) development, wherein the topic, idea, or story is explored and created; 2) preproduction, wherein filmmakers prepare for shooting; 3) production, which involves shooting footage on film or video; 4) post-production, which is the process of editing together the footage into a cohesive whole; and finally, 5) distribution/exhibition, wherein filmmakers share their completed films with an audience.

Differences exist between filmmaking as a creative endeavor and filmmaking as a therapeutic technique (Cohen and Johnson, 2015). Therapeutic filmmaking loosely follows the general stage-wise structure described previously. Therapeutic films are made in the context of therapy sessions that often take place for an hour at a time over a period of weeks or months, during which the client/filmmaker is engaging in personal changes that inevitably impact the story depicted in the film and require a circling back to earlier stages as the client—and therefore the story—changes. Given this, the filmmaking process is more recursive than is typical for commercial productions.

Furthermore, the content of therapeutic films tends to be different than in commercial films. In a pilot study on therapeutic filmmaking, the content of the films indicates that clients/filmmakers focus on self-reflection, self-analysis, self-observation, and observations of others in their films (Johnson and Alderson, 2008). These various vantage points provide important fodder for discussion, insight, and expression in therapy; this is intensely personal and self-reflective and is not typical in non-therapeutic filmmaking. Notable exceptions to this exist, particularly in the works of feminist filmmakers and auto-documentarians, whose work I have discussed in relation to therapeutic filmmaking in other writings (e.g. Johnson, 2007). Nevertheless, most film-goers are more familiar with the less personal content of mainstream narrative and documentary cinema, and for this reason the content of therapeutic films tends to differ from that of non-therapeutic ones.

The Stages of Therapeutic Filmmaking in Practice

As previously described, therapeutic filmmaking typically progresses through five stages of filmmaking, though the progression through these stages is recursive and non-linear. Bearing this understanding of the process in mind, it will still likely be beneficial to describe in more detail what strategies and approaches may be used by practitioners at each stage of this process. To that end, the following sections describe my approaches in working within each of these stages.

Development

The intention of this stage is to articulate a theme or topic and develop it into a framework around which the film will be built. This stage is intensely creative and involves a lot of creative prompting, brainstorming, and divergent thinking, which in turn can lead to important therapeutic conversations where the filmmaking project is set aside to discuss coping strategies or other relevant therapeutic content. For this reason, this stage of the process often takes the longest and can occur over many sessions.

Some clients come to therapy with a topic or idea already in mind, while others will need creative prompts. The questions that opened this chapter, "Who are you?" and "Where are you from?" can make excellent starting-off points to explore broad topics of interest and engage with the client's story of self. Other prompts may include questions related to the client's reason(s) for seeking therapy, what they hope to achieve as part of therapy or more generally in their ideal future, or what advice they would give themselves or others like them now that they have been through and survived their traumatic experience.

When asking clients these prompts, I often use a pad of sticky notes to jot down themes and phrases that the client generates as part of this discussion. For example, if a client responds to the question "Who are you?" with identity statements, I write down each identity statement or phrase—"Cree," "survivor," "animal lover"—on its own sticky note, and place each sticky note on a table or wall in no particular order. Towards the end of our discussion, I will then ask the client to review the sticky notes and try to organize them in a way that makes sense to them. In response, some people group the notes by themes or put them in some kind of chronological order. Sometimes the client creates a linear order out of the sticky notes, and other times clients structure them into groups or webs. When the client is satisfied with the structure they have developed, I take a picture of the structure so we can keep it in the client's digital file and refer back to it for continued development, while the sticky notes are collected together and placed in the client's paper file.

This loose structure will often become the framework around which the client's therapeutic story is developed. The form that this story takes can vary dramatically, from simply using the sticky note structure as-is to represent the story in its entirety, to having a full-fledged script with fleshed-out characters and formally written dialogue. Most clients fall somewhere in between, ending up with an outline of the story that reflects the sticky note structure and a description of specific scenes that they would like to include at various junctures in the story, but not necessarily having well-developed characters or dialogue.

Preproduction

The purpose of this stage is to prepare for production, or shooting the film, so all activity in this stage is directed towards converting the outline or script completed during development into something that can be shot with a camera. In the broader context of general filmmaking, this stage typically involves going through the script and first developing a storyboard, which depicts in picture form how each scene will be shot, resulting in something like a comic book of picture panels representing each scene in the script. From there, a typical film project will move into developing a shot list, wherein the filmmaker determines the order in which each of the comic book panels will be shot.

In a therapeutic film, breaking the script down into storyboards and shot lists is not often necessary. As such, this stage of the process typically involves going through the outline or script and discussing with the client how they want each scene represented. In this discussion, the client may choose to find existing or archival artifacts to represent a particular scene, or they may choose to shoot something new. Together, the client and therapist write down what images, audio, and/or text the client has identified to represent each scene. From this accounting of images, audio, and text, a "shot list" can be developed to identify what new video material needs to be generated and what artifacts need to be gathered. This shot list will then inform the next stage of the filmmaking process.

Production

The goal of production is to shoot the footage required to complete the film. In therapeutic filmmaking, the client spends time between sessions gathering existing materials to include in their film and either brings them into session to digitally capture or brings digital files of the existing materials to the session. If there are new scenes that need to be shot, the client either shoots them on their own or with friends or family members between sessions, or they may be shot with the therapist in session.

Opportunities for therapeutic conversations abound in this stage of the filmmaking process. The therapist may inquire into the stories and meaning behind various artifacts and creative choices, discuss decisions about what to include where and why, and help the client practice perspective-taking on a particular scene, shot, or issue. It is also often worthwhile to discuss the possible ramifications of recruiting others into helping with or being included in clients' therapeutic films. Clients may not independently reflect upon the impact of this on their wellbeing, functioning, and relationships and therefore ought to be prompted to do so. Depending on what clients may want to do with their films in the distribution/exhibition stage, it may also be worthwhile to discuss the utility of introducing release forms to any potential outside helpers. Therapeutic discussions around privacy may also be warranted.

Post-Production

Once the digital material has been gathered or shot, the process of editing together all these disparate elements into a cohesive whole can begin. The purpose of this stage is to reassemble the pieces of the film into the structure that was determined by the outline or script. This stage of the process can take some time, and may rival or surpass the development stage in length.

In this stage, the therapist works with the client to transfer all materials into a digital format and then upload these digital media into a non-linear digital editing program. Once uploaded, the therapist guides the client through the technical process of choosing, trimming, and placing media into an editing timeline. Clients have varying levels of familiarity with this process, from none at all to greater than the therapist, so the therapist needs to exercise caution in figuring out how to guide the client through this process without taking over or asserting creative control over the project.

In the process of reviewing the materials, putting them together, and adding audio (e.g. music, sound effects, voiceover) and graphics (e.g. titles, transitions, effects), there are many opportunities to engage in therapeutic conversations. Like in earlier stages, the therapist may encourage reflection and insight-development through guiding or probing questions, and use the content of the film and the client's creative choices as starting points to discuss coping skills, problem-solving strategies, and other therapeutic interventions.

The editing process can be rich with therapeutic content, discussion, and intervention. For these reasons, this stage can take an especially long time to complete, and sometimes therapy ends in this stage before the film is completely edited. This is something that I do not personally take issue with, as I am a strong proponent of therapeutic filmmaking as a process rather than a product, and I am content to follow a client's lead in determining whether a film needs to be completed or not. However, if it is, at the end of this stage of filmmaking the client will have a completed short film, and they typically take a copy home in either DVD or digital movie file format.

Distribution/Exhibition

Finally, if the client has completed all aspects of the filmmaking process and has a finished DVD or digital movie file in their possession, they may be interested in sharing the film with others. Some clients will want to share their films and others will not, preferring to keep the film as a transitional object to remind them of their therapeutic experience or an artifact to reflect upon alone in the future. For others, the sharing of the final film is an integral part of the filmmaking experience. It is imperative for the therapist to engage in thoughtful and reflective discussion with the client about the possible ramifications of sharing the film with others, whether it is specifically chosen friends or family or an audience of strangers at a film festival. It is also beneficial to discuss the parameters within which the client will want to share the film and engage in safety planning around this. Debriefing with a client after they have shared their film with others is recommended. When therapy continues long term, beyond the initial film project, the therapist may want to consider periodically rewatching the film with the client throughout the therapeutic process to reflect on their current perspectives on the film and other topics.

The therapeutic aspects of the filmmaking project stem from the conversations between the therapist and client, as well as our delving into the client's responses to questions of meaning, personal and interpersonal resources, self-representation, and hope. Therapeutic conversations take over entirely at times, leaving the creative video project aside as client and therapist focus on crisis management or coping skills. In practice, I have started working on many more therapeutic videos than have actually been completed to the exhibition stage, as my approach to this work focuses on process more than the final product. Furthermore, sometimes clients prefer to shift to other approaches as our therapeutic work progresses, and given that I work from a feminist, anti-oppressive stance it is important to me to follow my client's direction rather than impose my preferences on their therapeutic process. However, therapeutic filmmaking is a technique that can be used by a variety of practitioners operating from a variety of perspectives, and so for others it may be important to see each project through to completion and to ensure that clients experience the full filmmaking process from beginning to end.

Therapeutic Filmmaking in Practice

In order to better illustrate how therapeutic filmmaking may play out in practice, this section is dedicated to presenting a composite case example. In this section I describe a client, "Kelly," a composite character based on a variety of clients I have seen in my practice, and her therapy process from beginning to end.

Case Example 7.1

Kelly was a 15-year-old girl who was referred to me by her case worker from the Child and Family Services department on her home reservation. She was suspicious and quiet, and I found it challenging to connect with her at first. When we met, she was living in a group home on her reserve, and the care worker who dropped her off at my office provided little information to me about her life leading up to this moment. I was simply told that she needed support, and so I set about determining with Kelly what the goal of our work would be. I began by asking her simply, "Who are you?"

Kelly and I spent the first session talking about who she is, and who she wants me to see her as. She gave me permission to take notes as she spoke, so I began scrawling brief notes on themes, topics, and people she mentioned on individual sticky notes. In her discussion, she informed me about her group home, her reserve, and the family she no longer lives with but still sees often in her small community. She told me about what she enjoys: dance, ceremony, listening to the Elders' stories, singing traditional songs. She described the power of connecting with her inner self, her Elders, and her ancestors, and how much strength and wisdom they bring to her. I asked her to reflect further on these initial questions and to bring her reflections on these topics to our next session, which she agreed to.

When Kelly returned the next week, she came prepared: she brought with her recordings of sweat songs,[1] a handful of handwritten journals, and a bunch of links to YouTube videos she had discovered. We pored over these artifacts of her life and discussed why they were meaningful to her, and she told me how they fit into the story of her life. We also went through the sticky notes I had written on previously and added to them with new notes representing some of the artifacts she brought and new stories she shared. We reviewed the pile of notes, and she began organizing them into a structure that made sense to her. In this process, Kelly saw that a story was beginning to unfold that included her past, her present, and a hoped-for future for herself and her family. Using this as an organizing plot, she decided that for her film she would narrate a story that told about the abuse she had suffered, the difficulties she has faced in recovering from it, and the hope she has to live a better life in the future. We began writing a loose script of what the narration would say.

Over the next two sessions, we finished a rough copy of the script and discussed how she may want to visually represent some of the elements of her story. What parts will she reenact? What parts of her story will reference old photos she had recovered? We also recorded her scripted voiceover and uploaded it to the non-linear editing system on my office computer.

We took a break from the filmmaking project for a spell when Kelly relapsed during a family home visit over the holidays. We worked together to reestablish stability and develop a recovery plan to move forward from this relapse. She was able to connect this experience with the themes of resilience and resolve that she had originally identified in her story about herself. I encouraged her to

1   Sweat songs are traditional ceremonial songs that are sung during sweat lodge ceremonies, which Kelly received permission from the leader of her sweat lodge to audio-record and use in her video.

reflect on how she may want to work this relapse and her recovery from it into her story about herself, and to reflect on how she may want to represent this part of her experience using visuals, music, and any other relevant modalities.

Over the course of the next several sessions, Kelly and I engaged in therapeutic conversations about the role of her family in her story, about herself, about enlisting help from some people for her video project, and protecting it with firm boundaries from others. We put the project on hold a couple of times to address pressing issues when they came up, such as her shock and horror at learning of the tragic death of her cousin on another reserve. On those days, we would work on grounding her in the present and reconnecting with her body, mind, and spirit, and seeking guidance on how to move forward from this by connecting with her inter- and intrapersonal resources. Other sessions were spent reviewing video footage and photos she had taken of the natural spots around her group home where she sought solace in a private connection with the natural world, or the smiling face of the Elder who ran the weekly sweat lodge ceremony she attended.

Kelly and I fleshed out the spine of her video project with visuals: photos of herself and family members and friends, video footage we had taken of her dancing, graphics we had captured from the Internet. We layered in music around this—sweat songs and pop music and the sound of her own sweet and tentative voice speaking or singing lines she had written in her journal. We included the beautiful sound of her murmuring a prayer in the language of her people that had almost disappeared at one time in history and that was now alive and dancing on her tongue.

As we approached completion of this project, Kelly and I began discussing whether she wanted to share this video with anyone else, and what that might entail. She chose not to have a screening in session but instead wanted to take a DVD copy home and share it with her peers and the staff at the group home. We prepared for this, discussing what it might feel like for her to reveal this personal story to others, what it might feel like if the reactions weren't what she hoped for, how she could maintain her personal safety regardless of what came from this screening. As we approached the end of the project and we finalized the text of the titles and credits and ensured that she was satisfied with the transitions between scenes, we spoke more about the meaning of this story for her. I asked her how well it represented her now, and how this may have changed since the day she first started working on it several months ago. I invited her to watch the full video—only ten minutes in length, after all that hard work—with fresh eyes, like a stranger watching her own life, and to reflect on what she could learn about herself. She was able to make new connections between what she had been through and the things she wants for herself, for her family, and for the future. She also realized the necessary role that developing a spiritual connection for herself had proven to be in her recovery process. She noted that the video project had given her a reason to approach people in her community—Elders and artists and others—whom she may not have approached otherwise, and this in turn helped deepen her connection with her community, her history, and her spirituality.

Kelly and I continued to work together for two more months after she completed her video project. In that time, she shared her video with the group home and we debriefed this experience. It had gone so well that she wanted to share it with a wider circle of people within her reserve, so we discussed and prepared for this, developed safety around this, and then debriefed it afterwards. During this wider sharing, some Elders from the community told her how much her story of reconnection and resilience represented to them. From the screening of this video, she was invited by community Elders to present at a conference on Canada's efforts on reconciliation with its Indigenous people. Having gradually developed greater confidence in herself and her capacities, and having had such successful screenings of her very personal video, she agreed to make a speech at the conference. The prospect of public speaking terrified her, but she felt it was important and took the invitation from her respected Elders seriously, and in the end it proved to be a resounding success both for her personally and her community.

Our work terminated when we reached the end of our approved sessions and it was clear that Kelly was doing quite well. We had made very good progress towards our mutually determined therapeutic goals of being able to share her story of abuse, frame it in terms of resilience, and articulate a hoped-for future that she was very clearly beginning to live into. By the time our work together ended, we had seen each other for 21 sessions over the course of nine months, and had oscillated between addressing immediate crises and developing coping skills on the one hand and engaging in trauma processing and hope promotion through the creative process of filmmaking on the other. Kelly and I terminated therapy on positive terms, with her keeping a DVD copy of her video to hold onto and periodically return to, if desired, in the future.

Conclusion

Regardless of how one interprets and uses therapeutic filmmaking in one's own practice, it is important that anyone practicing this approach with Indigenous populations takes into account specific considerations in working with them (Johnson, 2015). One such consideration is to be mindful of the worldview inherent in one's own training and personal experience and how this may complement or clash with the worldview of Indigenous clients (Blackstock, 2008). To learn more about this, it is worthwhile to learn about the historical and political context of the population you are serving by delving into the region's history of colonialism and institutional oppression (e.g. residential schools, mandatory relocations, laws against spiritual or cultural practices, voting rights for Indigenous people). It is also worthwhile to learn about the precolonial language and territory maps of the region to understand the scope of cultural and land loss experienced by the Indigenous populations you intend to serve. Furthermore, it may be helpful to develop an understanding of the present-day social, economic, and political standing of the Indigenous population in your region to learn about what barriers and resources currently impact their everyday lives.

Finally, I recommend being mindful of the potential you hold as a therapist to represent oppressive institutions to your clients, and work against this by using reflective practice in an effort not to reproduce colonial relations (Wade, 1995) with Indigenous clients in your collaborative work together. In presenting this composite case example of using therapeutic filmmaking with an Indigenous teen girl, my hope is that readers will understand more about the process of therapeutic filmmaking in practical terms. For those interested in this approach, I recommend that you reflect on the question of how it may fit into your own responses to "Who are you?" and "Where do you come from?" as well as "Who are you as a practitioner?" and "Why do you do what you do?" I urge you to reflect on how you may integrate therapeutic filmmaking into your own practice in an authentic way—not as technique or strategy, but as a fitting process within your specific practice context.

I also hope that the considerations raised about working with Indigenous populations through therapeutic filmmaking help those who are interested in this work to expand their learning and understanding of what may be important to incorporate into their future practice. Though not all people working with this population need to come from an anti-oppressive stance, I do believe it is necessary to "do the work" of becoming informed about the current and historical factors that have impacted—and continue to impact—your potential clients. Importantly, my hope is that the story of Kelly helps to humanize and bring to life a sometimes misunderstood and underestimated group of people who have been amongst the strongest, most resilient, and inspiring people I have ever had the pleasure to work alongside. Though Kelly herself may not exist, the dozen or so Indigenous teen girls who contributed to this composite character do, and they are truly incredible people.

Recommendations

- Therapeutic filmmaking follows the same production process as is used by commercial filmmakers, with the same five stages of filmmaking: development, preproduction, production, post-production, and exhibition/distribution. However, therapeutic films are much shorter—typically only five to ten minutes rather than two hours long—are often made by a crew of two people (the client and therapist), and involve a lot of therapeutic conversations between the client and therapist along the way.

- When engaging in therapeutic filmmaking as a therapist, be sure to leave the creative work to the client. Rather than contributing to the creative work, help your client develop their own story by providing lots of prompts, opportunities for reflection, and conversations that encourage deeper understandings of the self.

- Safety is key; always ensure that your ethical duties as a therapist come first. This means that the film project may be put on hold or even left incomplete when pressing therapeutic concerns arise. This also means that it is imperative to engage in therapeutic discussions around issues that may impact privacy and confidentiality, such as recruiting others to help in the production process or sharing the completed film with others.

> • When working with Indigenous clients and therapeutic filmmaking, be sure that you are able to work appropriately with this population through personal and professional development. This may include learning more about the traditional beliefs and practices of the specific population you intend to work with, as well as learning more about the historical, social, economic, and political factors that may be impacting their daily lives.

References

Arnott, B. and Gushin, J. (1976) Filmmaking as a therapeutic tool. *American Journal of Art Therapy 76*(1), 29–33.

Blackstock, C. (2008) *Rooting Mental Health in an Aboriginal World View: Inspired by Many Hands, One Dream.* Ottawa, ON: The Provincial Centre of Excellence for Child and Youth Mental Health at CHEO.

Cohen, J. and Johnson, J.L. (eds.) (2015) Introduction. In *Video and Filmmaking as Psychotherapy: Research and Practice.* New York, NY: Routledge.

Furman, L. (1990) Video therapy: An alternative for the treatment of adolescents. *Arts in Psychotherapy 17*(2), 165–169.

Greidanus, E. and Johnson, J.L. (2016) Knowledge as medicine: The use and efficacy of an at-risk youth treatment program with an Aboriginal cultural education component. In T. Falkenberg and F. Deer (eds.) *Indigenous Perspectives on Education for Well-Being in Canada.* Winnipeg, MB: Education for Sustainable Well-Being Press.

Habermas, T. and Bluck, S. (2000) Getting a life: The development of the life story in adolescence. *Psychological Bulletin 126*, 748–769.

Johnson, J.L. (2007) Therapeutic filmmaking: An exploratory pilot study. Master's thesis, University of Calgary, Calgary, AB, Canada.

Johnson, J.L. (2015) Vision, story, medicine: Therapeutic filmmaking and First Nations communities. In J. Cohen and J.L. Johnson (eds.) *Video and Filmmaking as Psychotherapy: Research and Practice.* New York, NY: Routledge.

Johnson, J.L. and Alderson, K.G. (2008) Therapeutic filmmaking: An exploratory pilot study. *Arts in Psychotherapy 35*(1), 11–19.

McAdams, D.P. (2008) Personal narratives and the life story. In O. John, R. Robins, and L. Pervin (eds.) *Handbook of Personality: Theory and Research* (3rd edn). New York, NY: Guilford Press.

Wade, A. (1995) *A Persistent Spirit: Towards Understanding Aboriginal Health in British Columbia.* Canadian Western Geographical Series, 31. Victoria, BC: Western Geographical Press.

8

DIGITAL STORYTELLING AND NARRATIVE THERAPY

Bronwen Gray and Alan Young

This chapter outlines how digital storytelling can be used as a form of therapeutic healing in two different fashions: as a form of narrative therapy for those who tell the stories, and through the grouping together of stories that speak to similar experiences as a meta-narrative that helps to heal cultural wounds by challenging hegemonic values that exclude the lived experiences of minority populations. In our projects, we consider the creation of digital stories as artworks that are creative collaborations between participants, art therapists, and professional artists. The role of the artist in this process is to visually represent the spoken word in order to support the participants in de-mythologizing personal and social fiction, as a way of allowing new ways of being to emerge. This process allows the participants an opportunity to rehearse new ways of understanding their lived experiences, leading to healthy emotional growth.

The authors believe that this process can be particularly powerful for disenfranchised members of our community, who have through their life experiences internalized certain beliefs about themselves that blind them to many vital and life-enhancing experiences in their lives. It is hypothesized that the externalization of these narratives through the creation of the artworks acts as a powerful transitional space in which change can occur.

What Is Digital Storytelling?

Digital storytelling involves the layering of personal narrative with symbolic imagery to create short film clips that utilize emerging digital technologies as a medium (Gray and Young, 2011). The multimodal approach to art-making that starts with the spoken or written word and is then transformed into a visual medium provides us with opportunities to "thicken" stories and to review the original emphasis of the narrative. As Rogers states, when discussing the multimodal approach "a creative connection occurs as one art form kindles a response in another art form" allowing for the processing of information and for new meanings to be made (Rogers, 1993, p.165). As a tool for empowerment it is currently used in a wide range of educational and community settings (Hartley and McWilliam, 2009), as a technique for community engagement, and as a therapeutic medium (Clarke and Adam, 2011).

Emerging in the late 1980s as a method employed by community theatre workers (Lambert, 2002), the original aim of creating digital storytelling was to diminish the messages being produced by the mass media and entertainment industries that sought to silence or ignore marginalized communities (Burgess, 2006). Viewing the authors as "creative consumers," the power of digital technologies lies in their ability to cause major potential disruption to the dominance of commercial media, to reach mass and possibly unexpected audiences, and to be socially inclusive (Lessig, 2004; Warschauer, 2003). In our case, the final products were short animated films distributed over the Internet and in DVD format.

Storytelling, which is one of the oldest art forms in human history, has always been the primary method for ensuring that information, wisdom, and logic are transmitted from generation to generation (Czarnecki, 2009). It assists in the propagation of culture by communicating the values and customary practices of a community, providing a lens through which we see the world. Over the years, storytelling has always formed a partnership with the latest visual technologies available, from cave drawings, through to the development of the printing press, and finally through moving images in film, television, or via the Internet (Skains, 2010).

The rapid succession of media technology from printed text, through to audio-visual media, and now into digital media has had a profound effect across all aspects of culture (Skains, 2010).

Describing the emergence of digital media as a critical epoch, Skains notes how, in terms of entertainment, online activities are overtaking film and television in much the same way that these visual media overtook the printed novel. Klaebe and Bolland argue that new media technology has begun to change the very fabric of human society, because it has changed not only the way we "do" things, but our systems of communication, and correspondingly, our very ways of knowing (Klaebe and Bolland, 2007; McLuhan and Fiore, 1967).

Digital Storytelling as a Form of Narrative Therapy

White and Epston (1990, pp.11–12) believe that as we go through life, we tend to "internalize certain beliefs about ourselves that blind us to many other vital experiences in our lives." As Winslade and Monk assert, "We live our lives according to the stories we tell ourselves and the stories that others tell about us" (Winslade and Monk, 1999, p.3). Having discarded or "pruned" those events that do not fit with the dominant evolving stories that we and others tell about us, the stories become embedded into our psyche. Thus, over time and out of necessity, much of our stock of lived experience goes "unstoried" and is never expressed (White and Epston, 1990). In order to open up new ways of understanding ourselves and our place in the world, narrative therapy engages the client in a "thickening" of the story—to look at what was discarded from the script, what sits in the silences.

Narrative therapy is built on the belief that the client is not the problem but rather that they have a problem, which is distinct and can be deconstructed and then re-authored as separate from their character (Carlson, 1997). When utilized only as verbal therapy, the narrative process often involves the client in reconstructing their story with the assistance of the therapist, family, and friends, who write to the client, providing alternative points of view. However, in this instance the support and capability to engage in the reconstruction process involves an artist, who draws on the symbolism contained in the story, visually bringing it to life. As the stories are externalized the client becomes free to explore alternative and preferred knowledges, to re-author who they might be (White, 1995). Whilst writing or telling the story elicits only one way of understanding the dominant story, digital storytelling has the potential to offer up multiple new possibilities as participants become aware of how others interpret their stories. Translating it into a visual medium that can be witnessed by others allows for new ways of seeing it and acts to externalize in the most literal sense (Carlson, 1997). It works in a similar fashion to "play back" theatre, where an audience member shares a story and then a team of actors brings the story to life, creating space to awaken new perspectives.

Digital storytelling often encourages participants to use and learn new technologies to create their own digital stories, generally utilizing scrapbook aesthetics set to autobiographical narration (Klaebe and Bolland, 2007). The aim is to empower participants by upskilling them and by handing over as much of the art-making process to the individuals as possible (Benn, 1976; Goldsworthy, 2002), but this may not always be desired by, or feasible for, the participant group. For example, when we worked with women who had fled from situations of domestic violence or with people experiencing homelessness, they often did not have photos or memorabilia that could be used in the animations. For these clients, the majority of their energy was solely focused on working out where they might eat or sleep tonight, not in becoming film makers. When working with women who live with HIV, anonymity was the number one priority. As the stigma associated with the disease is so severe, most participants did not even want to use their own voices in the final product in case it identified them publicly. With no intention of reopening painful wounds, the process we use allows for these participants to take part in creating personal and communal change, by providing them with "ethical democratic access for participants, whilst maximizing relevance and impact for the intended audience" (Burgess, 2006, p.207).

Altered Lives: A Digital Storytelling Project

A number of years ago we worked on a digital storytelling project entitled Altered Lives with New Zealand women who live with HIV. The intention was to use their stories to counter the stigma that is attached to being HIV positive and to highlight the very specific issues living with HIV raises for women. Women account for more than half of the people living with HIV globally, with young women aged 15 to 24 years being the most vulnerable to infection (Bruning, Kor, and Sango, 2012). In New Zealand, approximately 400 women live with HIV (Young and Gray, 2014) and although it was once considered to be "a gay man's disease" (Brooks, 2004), the majority of new infections throughout the world now occur in women (Squire, 2003).

Studies have revealed that the stigma associated with being HIV positive has been linked to fear and isolation (Freiden *et al.*, 2006) and also to anxiety and depression (Hazra, Siberry, and Molensson, 2010). However, keeping silent about HIV status not only perpetuates cycles of shame, it also has the effect of limiting an individual's capacity to sustain their heart, mind, and soul, a capacity which is seen as essential to the self-care and wellness of women as they grow older with HIV (Plach, Stevens, and Keiger, 2005).

One of the digital stories, entitled "The Long Walk" (Young, 2012), was told by a woman who contracted HIV while living in Africa at the beginning of the epidemic in the 1980s and had been told she probably had only three years to live. After the three years passed, she decided to move back to New Zealand to be with family, so that her son, who was born before she became infected, would have family to raise him. Her animated narrative describes the moment she discovered she had contracted the virus:

> If you want to know how that long silent walk felt, it's like, if you've ever been alone in your house at night time and you thought someone was trying to break in, or if you're walking down an alleyway at night and you think someone's trying to follow you and your heart starts to pound and your head is throbbing and all the adrenalin is rushing, well that's how it felt. After seven flights of stairs I was exhausted—not from the walking but from the emotional turmoil that was going on—just holding that question, and I was absolutely petrified, because in 1990, in Africa, AIDS was a death sentence.
>
> We got to the top of the stairs and he took me into this room. Sitting in this room was a little Dutch nun in a white habit and, in her very broad accent, she started to tell me about AIDS.
>
> She took me over to the wall and there was a poster on the wall. It was a hand-drawn poster of an

African man with his shirt off. He was very buff and handsome-looking and there were four pictures of the same man[Figure 8.1]. In each of the pictures he was getting skinnier and skinnier and it was clear he was getting sick. The last picture was of a hole in the ground with a cross saying "RIP." She said, "This is what happens to you when you get AIDS. You get skinnier and skinnier and then you die." Then she stopped. She hadn't told me yet, so I said, "Have I got it?" and she said, "Yes. I'm sorry to tell you that you have." So then I said, "So what do I do?" and she said, "Three things: eat well, rest a lot, and don't have sex." That was her advice.

Figure 8.1
"You get skinnier and skinnier and then you die"—from The Long Walk
Artist Olivia Moor

Previous research into storytelling by people who live with HIV has demonstrated that the act of telling and having their stories witnessed has many health benefits for those who are HIV positive. These benefits are both mental and physical (Fair *et al.*, 2012; Gray and Young, 2011; Nichamin, 2012; Vivienne, 2012). However, when evaluating the success of this project we were keen to identify what effect the digital storytelling had on audience members— in particular what therapeutic benefits took place. As part of our research, we undertook a series of focus groups with young people aged 17 to 23 years who may or may not be sexually active, and with healthcare professionals who treat women living with HIV, and we undertook one-on-one interviews with women who were being tested for HIV.

All participants felt that the stories had the capacity to contribute to restoring dignity. They agreed that the DVD had provided them with new information about what it is like to live with HIV and had challenged the stigma and discrimination attached to this illness. All participants commented on how the DVD acted to humanize HIV. Seeing the reality of the women's lived experiences allowed the viewers to sympathize with them and reevaluate the stigma attached to being HIV positive. It became apparent that the use of digital storytelling as a process for re-authoring stories shifted the focus on to "life not death…and for HIV to be seen as life shaping not life threatening" (Squire, 2003, p.80).

One of the women who had shared her story said:

> I watched the show with my husband last night and when it finished he was crying and just held me. Isn't it weird how I thought he knew all that stuff and he did but he'd never seen it presented that way and it just made so much sense to him…in those visual images.

Figure 8.2
"and it just made sense—those visual images"—from The Long Walk
Artist Sue Lim

Among those health professionals who work with people who live with HIV, there were varying views about the therapeutic value of showing the DVD to people who are being tested for HIV or who live with HIV. One participant stated, "It is a really good tool for people when they receive a diagnosis of HIV," whereas another healthcare professional believed that "someone with a recent diagnosis is probably nowhere near emotionally ready to sit in that environment." Healthcare professionals are often seen to be the "experts of the collective grounded levels of hurt, sadness and pain, whilst those who live in pain are of course the primary experts in the sadness and hurt their communities experience" (Waldgrave, 2005, p.271).

However, while the professionals held differing opinions on the psychological states necessary to absorb the stories, the views of those being tested were unequivocal. One participant said:

> Watching this—hearing what they were saying—it is like maybe life isn't over. I just kept thinking I was going to die maybe. But like—I can still do what I want. I might just have to take pills. But then I've got epilepsy. So that is not such a big deal. I take pills anyway. So I could live with that pretty easy. And if I can live a normal life but just having to be careful—then it makes it more bearable.

Another person shared:

> You know watching the DVD and realizing that it's not a death sentence any more, it has made me feel much better. The nurse said that at the hospital, but I didn't believe her. I thought she was just trying to make me feel better. [Having watched the DVD] it seems more real now.

The fact that this participant had not been able to believe the health professional when she said that being HIV positive is not a death sentence suggests a need for messages to be shared in multiple ways, and that the creative depiction of the message through animated storytelling was an effective medium. This finding reinforces the notion that art is a way of knowing (Allen, 1995; Lambert, 2002; Moon, 2003) since the part of the brain that we use to construct a story to make sense of our experiences is very different from the part we use to listen to or view a story created for us. As Fineberg (2017) suggests, when watching or looking at art, the brain is able to perceive and creatively adapt to new realities, which is a fundamental survival skill.

Healing Cultural Wounds through Digital Storytelling

As a form of social action, digital storytelling can be understood as a creative way of enacting human rights principles, as it provides marginalized communities and individuals with free and equal opportunities to participate in society (Jacobs, 2011). Through this paradigm, digital storytelling becomes a vehicle for influencing the culture that currently excludes them (Lenz, 2008). The effect of being excluded from cultural production and representation has a pervasive effect on the human psyche as it sends strong messages about who belongs and what in this world matters (Little and Froggett, 2009; Zipes, 2006). Washington and Moxley (2008) assert that using creative means (which can include digital storytelling) as a tool for social action provides the audience with new and sometimes disturbing knowledge that may exceed their own experiences. It demands that the audience respond to what they see and hear, placing an onus on them to be part of the solution, rousing people to action (Woodruff, 2005).

The therapeutic efficacy of using art as a tool for social change within community settings is a well-established component of art therapy theory and practice (Gersie, 1995; Golub, 2005; Gray, 2012; Hocoy, 2005; Kaplan, 2007; Malchiodi, 2007). Rossetto (2012) identified that art therapists who work within this paradigm have a world view that values their connectedness to society; this interconnectivity implies a responsibility for challenging hegemonic assumptions about what and whom is valued (Gray, 2012). It acknowledges that the work we engage in is not value free or apolitical, and as such demands an active commitment that seeks to transform the lives of those members of our community who have been disenfranchised.

Self-esteem and confidence are the most commonly cited benefits by participants in community-based arts activity, with particular significance in the alleviation of mental health issues (Matarasso, 1997). Central to self-esteem is dignity, and Richard Horton, editor-in-chief of *The Lancet*, has noted the potential importance of this as a health and human rights issue (Horton, 2003). Horton argues that dignity is a global issue in healthcare and medical ethics, and that health economics must be sensitive to it. The value of using creativity to enhance social relationships is also reflected in growing evidence that good relationships and social status are major determinants of health (White, 2006). Johnathan Mann, an official with the World Health Organization, actively promotes the view that health and human rights are linked, and that these fields overlap in their desire to promote health and wellbeing whilst decreasing premature death. He states that "Injuries to individual and collective dignity may represent a hitherto unrecognized pathogenic force with a destructive capacity towards physical, mental and social well-being at least equal to that of viruses and bacteria" (as cited in Gostin, 2001, p.122).

Trent's Story

We first met Trent when he took part in a digital storytelling project we were working on with people who had experienced homelessness (Young, 2007). Trent identifies as a member of the Wamba Wamba Worka Worka Tribe, who are the traditional landowners near Swan Hill in Victoria, Australia. Indigenous Australians are ten times more likely to experience homelessness than non-Indigenous populations, and even though only 2 percent of the overall population identify as Indigenous in Australia (ABS, 2016), they account for 10 percent of Australia's homeless population (Browne-Yung *et al.*, 2016). Trent's father was a seasonal shearer, which meant that Trent sometimes lived with his parents and sometimes with his great-grandmother on the mission. Trent's father was an alcoholic who was abusive to both Trent and his mother. Trent drifted in and out of petty crime from high school. However, it wasn't until he started using heroin after a serious back injury at 25 that his criminality increased, which eventually led to him becoming homeless. He recalls that his father once asked him:

> "What do you want to be boy? You want to be black or you want to be white?" I said, "I want to be like you Dad, I want to be black." So he punched me in

the mouth and said, "If you want to be black that's fine and if you want to be white that's fine, but just remember you've got a bit of both in you."

Figure 8.3
"so he punched me in the mouth"—from Trent's Story
Artist Stephen Watkins

Working initially with an art therapist Trent was encouraged to tell his life story, which was recorded, transcribed, and then edited into a short script. Once Trent was happy with the way the script had been edited, he recorded the shortened story onto a tape, which was then sent to an animator who created a visual look and feel for the animation. Trent was invited to be a part of each of these stages of the project; however, Trent had no interest in learning how to use computer animation programs. Rather, he wanted to be a part of the process, sharing his story as a way of putting a spotlight on homelessness amongst Australia's Indigenous population.

Trent described how the beliefs within a non-Aboriginal culture of superiority affected him as a child:

> The kids used to call me Boonga and Abo, and I used to get into fights every day. Before school I'd fight, recess I'd fight, lunch I'd fight, after school I'd fight. So it was at least four different punch ons a day for me. That kind of taunting well it hurts and it stays with you, and after a while your confidence starts to suffer.

He also says:

> [Using heroin] was the start of my worst days. I
> started doing anything necessary to get that daily
> fix. Stealing cars, burgs[burglaries], whatever it took.
> Anyone can tell you it's a vicious circle. And that's
> how it was for the next two years—they were really
> desperate days.

Figure 8.4
Dark days—Trent's Story
Artist Stephen Watkins

Although Trent's story told us a great deal about the situation of
homelessness in Victoria, it also spoke to wider issues related to
colonization—a time in Australian history when the traditional
landowners were considered to be nothing more than savages,
unable to own land or organize a society (Mundine, 2016). As a
result, they were systematically starved, enslaved, and massacred
to ensure the legitimacy of white rule (Daley, 2017). His story
identified the wrongs that Indigenous Australians continue to
suffer as a result of systemic racial discrimination, which has caused
poverty, low self-esteem, and a loss of cultural traditions and identity
(Quinn, 2007). This has left a legacy of intergenerational trauma
(Atkinson, 2002) and health inequalities (Marmot, 2011). The
physical and financial violence coupled with discriminatory government policies which were inflicted upon Indigenous Australians

(Memmott, Birdsall-Jones, and Greenop, 2012) resulted in the "intractable disadvantage and the chasm of quality of life between Indigenous peoples and White Australians" (Parbury, 2016).

The question of how to apologize for the behavior of our ancestors, and for our own behavior as we reap the rewards our status provides with little sense of our white privilege, sits at the forefront of current Australian political debate (Rogers, 2017). Trent's story, and the stories we have undertaken of other Indigenous Australians, act to inform this debate in terms of restorative justice. They create clear visual messages of the issues that need to be faced. Seeing a therapist to unpack his lived experiences was undoubtedly of benefit to Trent. However, recreating his story in a manner that could be viewed by multiple audiences and in a variety of settings contributes to the process of healing cultural wounds. Indigenous Australians have expressed the importance of allowing for the development of a relationship, where those who have suffered trauma tell their stories and we listen in an empathic, genuine manner, treating the storyteller with unconditional positive regard (McKay, 2017). To date, the digital stories *Equal Service: Homelessness, Myths and Memories*, which includes Trent's Story, have been viewed on YouTube more than 7000 times.

Conclusion

Artists, either individually or whilst working alongside communities, often "tell and retell histories, some autobiographical, that attempt to depict historical stereotypes" or assumptions that have shaped collective memory and identity (Milbrandt, 2010). This allows artists to create work that is socially responsible as well as transformative and healing, or, as Gablik writes, "to make art as if the world mattered" (Gablik, 1991, p.96). This work has developed out of an instinctual belief that wherever there is affliction, suffering, and human need, art will always contain a remedy (McNiff, 1997).

Creating digital media projects that speak to identity provides multiple outcomes for therapeutic growth, both individually and collectively. For those who tell their stories, it provides an opportunity to re-author and validate lived experiences that may have been previously thought shameful or unimportant. For audience members, it provides them with new knowledge that can assist them in understanding their place in the world. More importantly, it provides the opportunity to absorb knowledge using the creative side of their brain, rather than relying entirely on the word of a perceived "expert." Finally, working on the communal level, these projects can reveal cultural wounds, which in turn provide society with an opportunity to face truths and rectify inequality.

Recommendations

- The integration of digital storytelling and narrative therapy is a powerful combination that provides participants with ways to share both individual and collective stories.

- Digital storytelling provides a way for audiences to witness narratives that present diverse worldviews, enabling viewers to more clearly understand culture as well as personal experiences.

- As a form of social action, digital storytelling is a dynamic way to provide marginalized individuals and communities an opportunity to express cultural wounds and take an active role in addressing social injustice.

References

Allen, P. (1995) *Art Is a Way of Knowing.* Boulder, CO: Shambhala.

Atkinson, J. (2002) *Trauma Trails, Recreating Song Lines: The Transgenerational Effects of Trauma in Indigenous Australia.* Melbourne, Australia: Spinifex Press.

Australian Bureau of Statistics (ABS) (2016) Prisoners in Australia 2016. Australian Government, Canberra. Retrieved on April 1, 2018 at www.abs. gov.au/ausstats/abs@.nsf/Lookup/by%20Subject/4517.0~2016~Main%20 Features~Prisoner%20characteristics,%20Australia~4

Benn, C. (1976) A new development model for social work. In P.J. Boas and J. Crawley (eds.) *Social Work in Australia: Responses to a Changing Context.* Sydney, Australia: Australian International Press.

Brooks, R. (2004) Therapeutic narrative: Illness writing and the quest for healing. Sydney eScholarship Repository, University of Sydney Postgraduate Theses. Retrieved on April 1, 2018 at http://ses.library.usyd.edu.au/handle/2123/663

Browne-Yung, K., Ziersch, A., Baum, F. and Gallagher, G. (2016) "When you sleep on a park bench, you sleep with your ears open and one eye open": Australian Aboriginal peoples' experiences of homelessness in an urban setting. *Australian Aboriginal Studies 2*, 3–17.

Bruning, J., Kor, E. and Sango, A. (2012) Women out loud. In *How Women Living with HIV Will Help the World End AIDS*. Joint United Nations Programme on HIV/AIDS (UNAIDS) (pp.15–22). Retrieved on April 1, 2018 at www.unaids.org/sites/default/files/media_asset/20121211_Women_Out_Loud_en_1.pdf

Burgess, J. (2006) Hearing ordinary voices: Cultural studies, vernacular creativity and digital storytelling. *Continuum: Journal of Media and Cultural Studies 20*(2): 201–214.

Carlson, T. (1997) Using art in narrative therapy: Enhancing therapeutic possibilities. *American Journal of Family Therapy 25*(3), 271–283.

Clarke, R. and Adam, A. (2011) Digital storytelling in Australia: Academic perspectives and reflections. *Arts and Humanities in Higher Education 11*(1), 157–176.

Czarnecki, K. (2009) Chapter 1: Storytelling in context. *Library Technology Reports 45*(7), 5–8.

Daley, P. (2017) Black diggers are hailed on Anzac Day. But the Indigenous "Great War" was in Australia. *Guardian*, April 23 2017. Retrieved on April 1, 2018 at www.theguardian.com/australia-news/2017/apr/23/black-diggers-are-hailed-on-anzac-day-but-the-indigenous-great-war-was-in-australia

Desai, D., Hamlin, J. and Mattson, R. (2010) *History as Art, Art as History: Contemporary Art and Social Studies Education*. New York, NY: Routledge.

Fair, C., Connor, L., Albright, J. and Wise, E. (2012) I'm positive, I have something to say: Assessing the impact of a creative writing group for adolescents living with HIV. *The Arts in Psychotherapy 39*(5), 383–390.

Fineberg, J. (2017) *Modern Art at the Border of Mind and Brain*. Lincoln, NE: University of Nebraska Press.

Freiden, S., Shekter, L., Chapman, G., Alimenti, A., Forbes, J. and Sheps, S. (2006) Growing up: Perspectives of children, families and service providers regarding the needs of older children with perinatally acquired HIV. *AIDS Care 188*, 1050–1053.

Gablik, S. (1991) *The Re-enactment of Art*. New York, NY: Thames and Hudson.

Gersie, A. (1995) Arts therapies practice in inner city slums: Beyond the installation of hope. *The Arts in Psychotherapy 22*(3), 207–215.

Goldsworthy, J. (2002) Resurrecting a model of integrating individual work with community development and social action. *Community Development Journal 37*(4), 327–337.

Golub, D. (2005) Social action art therapy. *Art Therapy 22*(1), 17–23.

Gostin, L. (2001) Public health, ethics, and human rights: A tribute to the late Jonathan Mann. *Journal of Law, Medicine and Ethics 28*,121–130.

Gray, B. (2012) The community fence project: A symbolic approach to healing a cultural wound on a housing estate in South Auckland. *Australian and New Zealand Journal of Art Therapy 7*(1), 52–64.

Gray, B. and Young, A. (2011) Digital storytelling and narrative therapy: A case study in working with disenfranchised communities in Australia and New Zealand. Paper presented at the 2011 Expanding Documentary Conference, Auckland, New Zealand. Retrieved on April 1, 2018 at https://www.researchgate.net/publication/325054895_Digital_storytelling_with_women_who_live_with_HIV_A_journey_for_psychic_acceptance_and_social_inclusion

Hartley, J. and McWilliam, K. (2009) *Story Circle: Digital Storytelling around the World*. London: John Wiley.

Hazra, R., Siberry, C. and Molensson, L. (2010) Growing up with HIV: Children, adolescents and young adults with perinatally acquired HIV infection. *Annual Review of Medicine 61*, 169–185.

Hocoy, D. (2005) Art therapy and social action: A transpersonal framework. *Art Therapy 22*(1), 7–16.

Horton, R. (2003) Taking dignity seriously. In R. Horton (ed.) *Second Opinion: Doctors, Diseases and Decisions in Modern Medicine*. London: Granta.

Jacobs, G. (2011) Take control or lean back: Barriers to practicing empowerment in health promotion. *Health Promotion Practice 12*(1), 94–101.

Kaplan, F. (ed.) (2007) *Art Therapy and Social Action: Treating the World's Wounds*. London: Jessica Kingsley Publishers.

Klaebe, H. and Bolland, C. (2007) Text meets technology. *Writing in Education 43*. Retrieved at http://eprints.qut.edu.au/10869/1/10869.pdf

Lambert, J. (2002) *Digital Storytelling: Capturing Lives, Creating Communities*. Berkeley, CA: Centre for Digital Storytelling.

Lenz, R. (2008) What we talk about when we talk about art therapy. *Art Therapy 25*(1), 13–14.

Lessig, L. (2004) *Free Culture: How Big Media Uses Technology and the Law to Lock Down Culture and Control Creativity*. New York, NY: Penguin.

Little, R. and Froggett, L. (2009) Making meaning in muddy waters: Representing complexity through community based storytelling. *Community Development Journal 45*(4), 458–473.

Malchiodi, C. (2007) *The Art Therapy Sourcebook* (2nd edn). New York, NY: McGraw-Hill.

Marmot, M. (2011) Social determinants and the health of Indigenous Australians. *Medical Journal of Australia 94*(10), 512–513.

Matarasso, F. (1997) *Use or Ornament*. Stroud: Comedia.

McKay, D. (2017) Uluru statement: A quick guide. Parliament of Australia. Retrieved on April 1, 2018 at www.aph.gov.au/About_Parliament/Parliamentary_Departments/Parliamentary_Library/pubs/rp/rp1617/Quick_Guides/UluruStatement

McLuhan, M. and Fiore, Q. (1967) *The Medium Is the Message: An Inventory of Effects*. New York, NY: Bantam Books.

McNiff, S. (1997) Art therapy: A spectrum of partnerships. *The Arts in Psychotherapy* *24*(1), 37–44.

Memmott, P., Birdsall-Jones, C. and Greenop, K. (2012) *Why Are Special Services Needed to Address Indigenous Homelessness?* Brisbane QLD, Australia: Institute for Social Science Research, University of Queensland, St Lucia.

Moon, B. (2003) *Essentials of Art Therapy Education and Practice* (2nd edn). Springfield, IL: Charles C. Thomas.

Mundine, N. (2016) Unfinished business. In M. Davis and M. Langton (eds.) *It's Our Country: Indigenous Arguments for Meaningful Constitutional Recognition and Reform*. Melbourne, Australia: Melbourne University Press.

Nichamin, M. (2012) Digital storytelling: A community tool to end HIV stigma. Retrieved on April 1, 2018 at http://blog.aids.gov/2012/05/digital-storytelling-a-community-tool-to-end-hiv-stigma.html

Parbury, N. (2016, July 16) It's our country: Indigenous arguments for recognition and reform. *The Australian*. Retrieved on April 1, 2018 at www.theaustralian.com.au/arts/review/its-our-country-indigenous-arguments-for-recognition-and-reform/news-story/553b4761c85731ec771cd8aadf848658

Plach, S., Stevens, P. and Keiger, S. (2005) Self-care of women growing older with HIV and/or AIDS. *Western Journal of Nursing Research 27*(5), 534–553.

Quinn, A. (2007) Reflections on intergenerational trauma: Healing as a critical intervention. *The First Peoples Child and Family Review 3*(4), 72–83.

Rogers, J. (2017) Shame, pain and melancholia for the Australian Constitution. In B. Sheils and J. Walsh (eds.) *Narcissism, Melancholia and the Subject of Community*. Basingstoke: Palgrave Macmillan.

Rogers, N. (1993) *The Creative Connection: Expressive Arts as Healing*. Palo Alto, CA: Science and Behavior Books.

Rossetto, E. (2012) A hermaneutic phenomenological study of community mural making and social action art therapy. *Art Therapy 29*(1), 19–26.

Skains, R. (2010) The shifting author-reading dynamic: Online novel communities as a bridge from print to digital literature. *Convergence 16*(1), 95–111.

Squire, C. (2003) Can an HIV positive woman find true love? Romance in the stories of women living with HIV. *Feminism and Psychology 13*(1), 73–100.

Vivienne, S. (2012) Finding my voice through positive digital storytelling. *HIV Australia 10*(1), 32–34.

Waldgrave, C. (2005) Just therapy with families on low incomes. *Child Welfare 84*(2), 265–276.

Warschauer, M. (2003) *Technology and Social Inclusion: Rethinking the Digital Divide*. Cambridge, MA: MIT Press.

Washington, O. and Moxley, D. (2008) Telling my story: From narrative to exhibit in illuminating the lived experience of homelessness among older African women. *Journal of Health Psychology 13*(2),154–165.

White, M. (1995) *Re-authoring Lives: Interviews and Essays*. Adelaide, South Australia: Dulwich Centre.

White, M. (2006) Establishing common ground in community-based arts in health. *Perspectives in Public Health 126*(3), 128–133.

White, M. and Epston, D. (1990) *Narrative Means in Therapeutic Ends*. New York, NY: Norton.

Winslade, J. and Monk, G. (1999) *Narrative Counseling in Schools: Powerful and Brief*. Thousand Oaks, CA: Corwin Press.

Woodruff, P. (2005) *First Democracy: The Challenge of an Ancient Idea*. New York, NY: Oxford University Press.

Young, A. (director) (2007) Trent's Story. On *Equal Service: Homelessness Myths and Memories*, DVD. Department of Justice, Victoria.

Young, A. (director) (2012) The Long Walk. On *Altered Lives*, DVD. Positive Women, Auckland.

Young, A. and Gray, B. (2014) Enlarging the therapeutic space: Using focus groups to determine the impact of digital storytelling from women who live with HIV. *Australian and New Zealand Journal of Art Therapy 9*(1), 29–41.

Zipes, J. (2006) The possibility of storytelling and theatre in impossible times. In M. Wilson (ed.) *Storytelling and Theatre: Contemporary Storytellers and Their Art*. Basingstoke: Palgrave Macmillan.

9

A TELEHEALTH PRIMER FOR ART THERAPY

Jedediah Walls

Telehealth is gaining a strong foothold and becoming an everyday term for many professionals in art therapy. The importance of telehealth is in part due to its ability to address problems related to access, cost, and limited distribution of providers (Nickelson, 1996). This chapter begins with an introduction to telehealth services and how they are most relevant to the practice of art therapy. Ultimately, telehealth represents the work of several different fields coming together: therapy, art therapy, communication, information science, clinical psychology, media psychology, and many others. These fields are collaborating to define what telehealth is and create telehealth services. It is important to recognize that telehealth is emerging from the work of all manner of professionals—in computers, art, and therapy—and so there is a major benefit in taking a collaborative and interdisciplinary approach to the practice.

The terminology around telehealth can seem to sprawl. Telehealth, telepsychology, telemedicine, e-therapy, the list of terms seems to grow every day. Because of this, the functional differences between telehealth, telepsychology, and telemedicine are explored in this chapter. A clear definition of telehealth is provided, as well as the means of differentiating it from related terms. While "telehealth" may be most relevant and applicable to art therapy, it is important to maintain an understanding of telehealth in general and discover resources that work across the range of terms. Best practices are assembled from many resources, providing a strong foundation for what should be considered when performing digital therapy. Three examples are provided of existing telehealth services that relate to art therapy to serve as a basis of further exploration and increase general understanding. Lastly, several recommendations are made for those who seek to engage in telehealth practice.

This chapter provides a brief overview of telehealth and telehealth-related concepts. The audience it is most suited for are art therapists and those working in related fields who are seeking a basic understanding of telehealth, those who have an initial desire to conduct telehealth services, and those who want to keep up to date on the development of digital therapy.

Clarification of Terms

The practice of telehealth is evolving constantly. The evolution of digital technologies across several fields, including psychology, telecommunications, counseling, social work, and others, has led to an amalgam of shifting terminology. Terms used include telehealth, telepsychology, telemedicine, e-counseling, and telemental health (Zur, 2012), and are often used interchangeably. For the purposes of this discussion the chapter focuses on three terms: telehealth, telepsychology, and telemedicine. All the terms, however, relate in some way to using electronic and telecommunication devices in the practice of therapy and medicine.

For art therapists, the term that is perhaps most useful is telehealth. This is because each term has a specific context and covers most needs for art therapists. To best understand what telehealth is, it is important to look at what telehealth is not, and how the other terms are used in their own unique setting. While some may think that each term is just a subset of interrelated concepts, it is important to understand how each concept overlaps with other terms and is yet its own specific domain.

Defining Telemedicine

The term telemedicine is the narrowest in scope of the three terms discussed in this chapter. This term most often refers to direct patient clinical services (Institute of Medicine, 2012). In other words, telemedicine is reserved for clinical services such as monitoring and diagnosis. Because of this, telemedicine is unique in that it is specialized for medical professionals and services. Telemedicine has the narrowest focus, affecting traditional forms of medicine and hospital services. Because of this, telemedicine has a more developed platform for insurance payments and legal protection. Legal protection centers around the idea of parity, which ensures that insurance companies offer comparable reimbursement for telemedicine-related and face-to-face practice (Andrus, 2017). Currently 42 US states have laws in place providing legal protection for telemedicine parity (State Policy Resource Center, 2017). The term telemedicine is distinctly interrelated with telehealth. While they increasingly refer to different domains, the two terms were once synonymous and used interchangeably (Nickelson, 1998). Because of this synonymous use, it is important for researchers to understand this account for both terms in their research.

Defining Telepsychology

According to the American Psychological Association (APA), telepsychology is defined as the "provision of psychological services using telecommunication technologies" (APA, 2013, p.791). It goes further by defining telecommunication as the communication, preparation, and transmission of information. How these are communicated include electrical, electromagnetic, electrochemical, electro-optical, or electronic means.

While telepsychology is a useful term for the practice of therapy services, it may not suit the needs of most art therapists. This is for the simple reason that art therapy is often considered a form of counseling employed by counselors, rather than strictly related to the field of psychology. However, documentation and study around the term alone bears mention, as the term has a very clear definition and domain outlined by the American Psychological Association. Anyone engaging in online services, regardless of their profession as a psychologist or a therapist, should read the APA's (2013) guidelines—the information provided is of the utmost importance for anyone engaging in both telepsychology and telehealth.

Defining telehealth

Telehealth is defined as the digital application of health-related services (Institute of Medicine, 2012). Additionally, it is defined as the use of telecommunications technologies to increase equality of access to healthcare (Collie and Čubranić, 1999). Telehealth can come in the form of consultation, education, and provider practices. Telehealth includes long-distance clinical healthcare, patient and professional health-related education, public health, and health administration (Health Resources and Services Administration, 2015). The practice of telehealth can take the form of advice, reminders, remote transmissions, monitoring, client care, intervention, education, live feed-based work, the use of "apps" or phone applications, and video-phone consultation. Telehealth can also involve provider practices, including distance learning/training, system integration, and online data management. It can also include inter-provider practices such as professional meetings or test sharing between clinics. Increasingly, telehealth practices are used to perform supervision services for students (Orr, 2010).

Modalities for telehealth include video conferencing and Internet communications (Collie and Čubranić, 1999). In addition, store-and-forward technologies allow the ability to play back recordings of sessions to clients, which has been shown to be useful in treating issues related to avoidance and dissociation (Malchiodi, 2009). The addition of live video technologies has allowed for innovations in clinical video telehealth (CVT) (Spooner and Baxley Lee, 2017). Overall, telehealth practices are shown to have a lot of variation in results and content, but some programs have been shown to be effective, especially when the results are compared to a group that receives no treatment and the programs involve contact with a therapist (Peñate, 2012).

Best Practices

Through the sheer amount of variation in telehealth practice, art therapists of many different modalities can find useful avenues to engage in telehealth practices. Despite claims that computers are ill-suited to therapy services, researchers contend that telehealth can be the best method of therapy for some clients, rather than a kind of substitution for face-to-face therapy (Collie and Čubranić, 1999).

Practitioners report several areas in which telehealth provides benefits for clients. These areas include the facilitation of a supportive environment, and a feeling of empowerment defined as a sense of control, liberation of choice, and emotional self-awareness (Jones, 2017). Reasons for these benefits include: 1) they can be accessed from home, 2) they include both audio and visual channels of communication, and 3) telehealth permits real-time synchronous communication (Collie and Čubranić, 1999).

Considerations of Telehealth

The APA guidelines for telepsychology provide an expansive set of guidelines. Though the guidelines are created for the psychological community they provide detail that is certainly relevant to the practice of art therapy in telehealth. While very close to the considerations provided by other authors discussed in this chapter, they cover a broader range of relevant considerations. While this is just a summary of the report, the guidelines are full of detail and consideration. A summary of the guidelines (American Psychological Association, 2013) is listed below:

1. *Competence.* The practitioner should be knowledgeable and trained not only in therapy techniques but in technical competence as well. This includes pursuing training in relevant software when available. The therapist should be able to provide clear instructions about risk, and understand the emergency resources available in the client's area.

2. *Standards of care in delivery.* This guideline asks the therapist to assess and monitor the client's progress, and understand the environment that the client is in. It also discusses the role of consultation in ensuring quality client care.

3. *Informed consent.* In addition to providing safeguards for establishing informed consent, the guideline recommends procedures for storage, security, and documentation for billing.

4. *Confidentiality.* Not only does the report address reasonable efforts to protect confidentiality, the guidelines discuss awareness of search websites and the risks involving social media.

5. *Security and transmission of data.* According to the document, it is important for those engaged in online practice to protect against viruses and hackers. Also, it is important to be aware of failure of security systems, damage to hard drives, and how to adequately manage outdated equipment issues.

6. *Disposal of data and IT.* This guideline describes considerations for how to manage data disposal in an ethical manner.

7. *Testing and assessment.* When providing assessment and testing of clients, it is necessary to ensure that high standards of quality are maintained when operating through electronic mediums. It is recommended to understand the impact of testing on diverse populations, as well as the implications of performing tests online that are intended for a face-to-face scenario.

8. *Interjurisdictional practice.* When performing therapy services online it is necessary to follow all relevant laws. A therapist must be knowledgeable about offering services across borders, and how different jurisdictions may impose regulations for clients who are temporarily out of state. It is also important to be aware of regulations that exist in the therapist's home jurisdiction for acting in environments that have no established laws.

Examples of Telehealth in Art Therapy
Creative Forces

Creative Forces: NEA Military Healing Arts Network is a program designed for military veterans and their family members who are diagnosed with traumatic brain injury and/or posttraumatic stress disorder (Creative Forces: NEA Military Healing Arts Network, n.d.). The program brings art therapists together with other creative therapsts, medical personnel, community leaders, and policy makers. The objective of Creative Forces is threefold. First, Creative Forces uses outpatient and telehealth services to place creative arts therapies at the center of client treatment. Second, the program provides community-based arts opportunities close to clinical site locations. Third, it invests in capacity-building efforts, including various forms of training manuals and research on the impacts and benefits related to treatment.

The program engages in multiple art therapies, along with music therapy and creative writing instruction. For rural clients, Creative Forces provides telehealth services in the form of video conferencing to connect patients. This allows the client to continue arts-based services beyond the in-patient treatment services provided by local hospitals and treatment programs, which enables the client to be more engaged and make better use of art therapy services. Services include supporting identity integration, externalization, and authentic self-integration, group cohesion, processing grief and loss, as well as other forms of trauma (Jones *et al.*, 2017). Research has shown that veterans treated with telehealth practices show decreases in self-reported pathology (Tuerk *et al.*, 2010).

Addressing Breast Cancer through Distance Art Groups

One project leveraged telehealth's ability to work across large distances to bring together experts who deal in art therapy, art, and telehealth to discover best practices for creating online art therapy-based support groups for women with breast cancer. The project offered group art therapy sessions online, based on evidence that support groups reduce distress and improve coping (Collie *et al.*, 2006). Two phases of research were performed. The first phase involved the creation of a computer system for Internet delivery to identify issues for continuing development. The second phase specified clinical content for distance art-based support for women with breast cancer. Participants included 25 people with expertise on breast cancer, art, art therapy, and telehealth practices. Qualitative analysis revealed a set of best practices for individuals who wish to facilitate or develop online art therapy support groups. These guidelines included information pertaining to 1) emotional expression, 2) emotional support, 3) emotional safety, and 4) accommodating individual differences.

Bravemind

While Albert "Skip" Rizzo is a clinical psychologist, not an art therapist, his work is an important addition to any discussion of digital therapies that involve images and the application of the arts in psychology. His virtual reality (VR) simulation Bravemind is at the forefront of how digital technology and art come together to perform effective therapy (Figure 9.1).

Figure 9.1
Skip Rizzo's Bravemind
Dr. Albert "Skip" Rizzo conducts a session in Bravemind with a participant

Bravemind is a virtual reality application that builds resilience in combat veterans with PTSD. The application is designed to provide exposure therapy for the veteran to help them better manage symptoms of PTSD. The VR experience itself is a virtual re-creation of a Middle-Eastern city in various settings that allows a veteran to reexperience combat conditions in an environment that is safe, under their influence, and performed with a trained practitioner (Javelin Technologies, 2012). In one of the settings, when the veteran puts on the virtual reality headset, they take on the role of a soldier inside a military vehicle, driving down a virtual Middle-Eastern city-themed road. The environment features a situation that appeals to the imagination: helicopters are heard in the distance and smoke from a damaged tank permeates the atmosphere. Soldiers surround the tank and are stationed along the road, providing just enough detail to indicate a potentially ominous situation. What happens next with Bravemind is up to what the practitioner and the client deem necessary for treatment. The program can be manipulated to make the drive continue uneventfully, or combat situations can arise. The patient uses this scenario as a means of exposure. The therapist is present, and can ask the patient about this experience to gain insight and aid assessment (Quart, 2016). Additionally, the therapist can use a nearby computer to add elements to the simulation. Those elements may take the form of simple sounds and images, such as adjusting the lighting, or they can be exposure events such as enemy combatants, explosions, or full combat simulations with wounded allies and high levels of tension. In other words, the simulation can be escalated to a severe level of exposure.

Bravemind allows soldiers to gradually immerse themselves into their traumatic experiences in an environment that they can control. The type of exposure therapy that Bravemind employs is called systematic exposure therapy. It is a form of counter conditioning that involves a process of desensitization over time (Sathe, 2014). The three steps of systematic exposure therapy are the identification of anxiety, learning coping techniques, and then using those techniques to overcome fears (Sathe, 2014). Treatment involves the gradual reliving of traumatic experiences to allow the patient to process related emotions and decondition themselves through a habituation/extinction process (USC Institute for Creative Technologies, 2017). Using a controlled, stepwise fashion, the clinician can monitor the intensity of the patient's stress response. In addition, the patient's stress response can be monitored via brain imaging and psychophysiological assessment techniques (USC Institute for Creative Technologies, 2017). The use of VR allows interactive, multisensory, immersive environments that can be tailored to a patient's needs, but also provides the ability to control, document, and measure the patient's responses (USC Institute for Creative Technologies, 2017).

Chris Merkle is a veteran who used Bravemind to help address PTSD (Quart, 2016). Merkle reported that the virtual environment allowed him to move further in his treatment than he felt he was making with a therapist alone.

Figure 9.2
Inside Bravemind

*From the participant's viewpoint, a soldier stands guard while
two Middle-Eastern men watch in the background.*

Figure 9.3
Bravemind: still image

*The participant sits in the back seat of a virtual military vehicle while two soldiers
sit in front. Ahead of them on the right a flaming wreckage can be seen.*

Figure 9.4
Veteran Telehealth

*A veteran participant in military gear stands at the ready
as a part of the exposure therapy treatment.*

Figure 9.5
Virtual Afghanistan

*In this scene from Bravemind's simulated Middle-Eastern city, a car is
on fire as members of the public gather around to investigate.*

© 2015 USC Institute for Creative Technologies
Rizzo, A. (2015). Bravemind Images [Photo]. USC Institute for Creative Technologies

Bravemind is a robust example of how art based in technology can be used to treat complex issues affecting human beings. The idea that Bravemind is a form of telehealth may raise some questions. One reason for this may be that while the client is using virtual reality gear, the therapist is still in the room. The client may not have visual access to the therapist, but the client and therapist can engage each other through speech. The assumption with telehealth is that it is concerned with fully remote practices where the clinician is not in physical proximity. However, even this assumption proves to be problematic and is not operationally defined. Bravemind's use of technology for assessment, and the ability of the therapist to use computer equipment to measure, document, and learn from the results (USC Institute for Creative Technologies, 2017) provide a basis for telehealth services. A major feature of Bravemind is the ability to monitor the client and the client's environment through a computer. In addition, virtual reality itself asks the user to place themselves in a simulated environment, which itself takes a client out of the traditional face-to-face setting. Other authors note that virtual reality can be a valid form of telehealth for assessment and treatment of mental health disorders (Zur, 2012). A therapist working with Bravemind still has direct audio contact with the client. So, while it may be an interesting exception to bring up Bravemind in a discussion on telehealth, Bravemind is setting some of the foundations in VR tools that will be used in telehealth-based assessment and treatment (see Chapter 12).

Research Needs of Telehealth

The need for basic, ground-level research in telehealth cannot be understated, especially when it comes to the practice of art therapy. The largest need is foundational research on the validity and reliability of telehealth-based assessment and diagnosis (Nickelson, 1996). How effective is telehealth diagnosis and assessment, and in what ways can assessment and diagnosis be improved through a telehealth process? In what ways are assessment and diagnosis limited? Can new assessment tools be created using telehealth (Nickelson, 1996)?

Despite its recent popularity, telehealth is still an emerging practice. Because of its relative newness there is a great need for research and evaluation. Questions that must be addressed deal with the creation of best practices and standards around which telehealth is developed and administered. Greater understanding is called for both in what standards are necessary, and how effectiveness can best be measured. In addition, qualitative and quantitative research is necessary to catalog and explore various telehealth applications, websites, and emerging software, as well as their usefulness. Ultimately these issues all can be understood as foundational research into the validity of telehealth practice.

Further, it is important to understand how different cultures understand and relate to telehealth and develop best practices for using telehealth in multicultural environments. Qualitative studies about the level of preparedness and acceptance that different cultures show towards telehealth could reveal important considerations in how telehealth technology is used in diverse environments. One such study was conducted to assess how ready one rural population was for telehealth services. Results of this study revealed factors that could lead to successful implementation with rural communities in the future (Jennett *et al.*, 2003).

Conclusion

This chapter explored telehealth as an emerging practice in the art therapy community. The term telehealth was defined and clarified regarding its association with telemedicine and telepsychology. While telepsychology is more specialized, much research that is available in telepsychology should be considered in telehealth practice regarding art therapy. Best practices and ethical guidelines provide a basis for art therapists to engage in telehealth. Three examples of telehealth involving arts or art therapy were provided. The examples were Creative Forces, a focus group of experts evaluating art therapy-based breast cancer support groups, and the VR tool Bravemind. Lastly, research requirements in telehealth were discussed. Overall, the need for foundational, ground-level research about the validity of telehealth is necessary to best understand and deploy telehealth practices.

Recommendations

- Read the APA guidelines on telepsychology (APA, 2013). The APA report has valuable information that can applied across disciplines. Understanding its nuances and recommendations can ensure safe and ethical telehealth practice.

- Be interdisciplinary. Telehealth is emerging across several industries and traditions, each with research and information that is beneficial to the practice. By taking an interdisciplinary approach, art therapists stand to gain access to a large library of research, training, and relevant material.

- Recognize that other fields will be working in art, image, and therapy. As important as it is for art therapists to look at other fields for telehealth, it is important for art therapists to realize that other disciplines will be looking to art therapy. The nature of computer technology and telehealth allows virtually any field of therapy or psychology to incorporate image, art, and art-based practices into their work.

- Mitigate the risks. Art therapists are often wary of incorporating technology and telehealth into art therapy services. However, these concerns should be used to further research and gather data for more effective practice.

References

American Psychological Association (2013) Guidelines for the practice of telepsychology. *American Psychologist 68*(9), 791–800.

Andrus, B. (2017) 2017 Telemedicine reimbursement—what you need to know. Retrieved on April 1, 2018 at http://blog.evisit.com/telemedicine-reimbursement-faqs-2017

Collie, K., Bottorff, J.L., Long, B.C. and Conati, C. (2006) Distance art groups for women with breast cancer: Guidelines and recommendations. *Supportive Care in Cancer 14*(8), 849–858.

Collie, K. and Čubranić, D. (1999) An art therapy solution to a telehealth problem. *Art Therapy 16*(4), 186–193.

Creative Forces: NEA Military Healing Arts Network (n.d.) Retrieved on April 1, 2018 at www.arts.gov/partnerships/creative-forces/frequently-asked-questions

Health Resources and Services Administration (2015) Telehealth programs. Retrieved on April 1, 2018 at www.hrsa.gov/rural-health/telehealth/index.html

Institute of Medicine (2012) *The Role of Telehealth in an Evolving Health Care Environment: Workshop Summary*. Washington, DC: National Academies Press.

Javelin Technologies (2012) *PTSD Exposure Therapy—Dr. Albert "Skip" Rizzo Interview*. Retrieved on April 1, 2018 at www.youtube.com/watch?v=OK893GmwuhM

Jennett, P., Jackson, A., Healy, T., Ho, K. *et al.* (2003) A study of a rural community's readiness for telehealth. *Journal of Telemedicine and Telecare 9*(5), 259–263.

Jones, G. (2017) Providing art therapy in palliative care using telehealth technology. Retrieved on April 1, 2018 at www.baat.org/About-BAAT/Blog/121/Providing-Art-Therapy-in-Palliative-Care-using-Telehealth-Technology

Jones, J.P., Walker, M.S., Drass, J.M. and Kaimal, G. (2017) Art therapy interventions for active duty military service members with post-traumatic stress disorder and traumatic brain injury. *International Journal of Art Therapy*. doi:10.1080/17454832.2017.1388263

Malchiodi, C. (2009) Art therapy meets digital art and social multimedia. Retrieved on April 1, 2018 at www.psychologytoday.com/blog/arts-and-health/200911/art-therapy-meets-digital-art-and-social-multimedia

Nickelson, D.W. (1996) Behavioral telehealth: Emerging practice, research, and policy opportunities. *Behavioral Sciences and the Law 14*(4), 443–457.

Nickelson, D.W. (1998) Telehealth and the evolving health care system: Strategic opportunities for professional psychology. *Professional Psychology: Research and Practice 29*(6), 527–535.

Orr, P.P. (2010) Distance supervision: Research, findings, and considerations for art therapy. *Arts in Psychotherapy 37*(2), 106–111.

Peñate, W. (2012) About the effectiveness of telehealth procedures in psychological treatments. *International Journal of Clinical and Health Psychology 12*(3), 475–487.

Quart, J. (2016) Treating PTSD with virtual reality therapy: A way to heal trauma. Retrieved on April 1, 2018 at http://abcnews.go.com/Technology/treating-ptsd-virtual-reality-therapy-heal-trauma/story?id=38742665

Sathe, S. (2014) Systematic desensitization. Retrieved on April 1, 2018 at www.slideshare.net/sanikasathe94/systematic-desensitization-32071409

Spooner, H. and Baxley Lee, J. (2017) Helping veterans build connections between creative arts therapy programs and their local arts communities through telehealth. Retrieved on April 1, 2018 at https://blog.americansforthearts.org/2017/05/05/helping-veterans-build-connections-between-creative-arts-therapy-programs-and-their-local-arts

State Policy Resource Center (2017) Retrieved on April 1, 2018 at www.americantelemed.org/policy-page/state-policy-resource-center

Tuerk, P.W., Yoder, M., Ruggiero, K.J., Gros, D.F. and Acierno, R. (2010) A pilot study of prolonged exposure therapy for posttraumatic stress disorder delivered via telehealth technology. *Journal of Traumatic Stress 23*(1), 116–123.

USC Institute for Creative Technologies (2017) Bravemind. Retrieved on April 1, 2018 at http://medvr.ict.usc.edu/projects/bravemind

Zur, O. (2012) Telepsychology or telementalhealth in the digital age: The future is here. *California Psychologist 45*(1), 13–15.

10

THE ANIMATION PROJECT

Joe Kavitski

*Introduction and Conclusion
by Brian Austin*

"I wanted the stealing, not the thing stolen."
St. Augustine

There may be several reasons why I started The Animation Project (TAP)[1] but certainly the reason TAP works with kids who break rules is that I am trying to repair something in me, and quite possibly reproduce the following true story:

I was 16. Having dropped out of high school, which my mother tolerated as long as I was employed, I was working in a local Mexican restaurant, Pancho Villas. Pancho Villas was owned by Martin Chapa. Martin, who hailed from Mexico, essentially built the restaurant himself. It was a restaurant, but it was also a home away from home for many Latin American immigrants. The staff were made up of Guatemalans, Costa Ricans, Colombians, Nicaraguans, Peruvians, Ecuadorians, Salvadorians, and Mexicans. Periodic raids by Immigration would flood the place, leaving only a few "gringos" like myself standing guard, ready to claim we were running the operation.

---

1   www.theanimationproject.org

For several years prior I was a bit of a troublemaker. I found school quite boring. The most exciting thing was skateboarding, which had no place in a classroom. Each school day began with my classmates and I meeting in a wooded area to smoke cigarettes and marijuana. Some would even drink alcohol, ingest mescaline or Quaaludes. This was how my school days began. After-school time was spent robbing houses. Evenings were reserved for parties and stealing cars.

In Pancho Villas, the delinquent attitude followed me. One evening, working as busboy, I discovered how easy it was to pocket cash from a customer's payment of their check. All I had to do was make sure the food order stub was destroyed along with the check. As least I thought I had it all figured out. Apparently there was a number system and the owner of the restaurant kept watch on it. So if check #24 and #26 were accounted for, what happened to #25? Though I was reasonably good at math, I was too thrilled by and caught up in the theft to notice.

When I arrived at work the following day, after the previous evening's lucrative shift, I was confronted by the owner of the restaurant. While I was setting up tables for the upcoming evening's seatings, Martin Chapa approached me. He said, "Brian, I know you stole money last night. Here is $150. If you ever need money all you have to do is ask me." He then walked away and never mentioned it again. Who was this man? What were his motives? Wasn't he angry? Why wasn't I fired? I had stolen money from him. What kind of response was this? I pocketed the money. Though I do not remember, I probably spent it on cocaine, pot, or alcohol. It took me several more years to "outgrow" my rebelliousness, and although I never forgot that act, I have only recently adopted it as TAP's genesis model. What I do remember very well are the feelings generated immediately after this interaction. I was, in Martin's eyes, if not yet my own, "okay." To him I was worth an investment. To him there was a profound recognition of the "need" underneath my theft. He did not make me feel like I had been bad. Then he offered me an alternative approach to stealing: ask for what you need.

The core philosophy of TAP comes from that hard-working man from Mexico, Martin Chapa. Martin Chapa expressed no judgment; he never made me feel bad. Three of TAP's core values come from this: 1) Transparency: he called it for what it was: I stole from him. 2) Development: he kept me employed even though I had stolen from him. Growth was an available option. 3) Support: I was eventually promoted to waiter, where I made a living wage.

Platform: 3D Computer-Generated Animation

What Is Animation?

Animation is an ever-expanding art form that includes numerous styles, mediums, and techniques. Popular examples include traditional 2D or classic animation such as hand-drawn or cel animation, 3D computer-generated animation, stop-motion, and collage or cut-out animation. Simply put, the animation process creates the illusion wherein still images appear to move or come alive. To understand the process, consider a series of static images or drawings in a flipbook. Each image in the series has a slight variation from the image before it that indicates a progression of movement. In the example of a passing car, the first drawing may show the car on the left side of the page. In the second drawing, the car appears a little further to the right than in the previous image. In the third drawing, the car is even more to the right, and so on, and so on. Thus, when the series of static car images is viewed quickly in chronological sequence, or flipped, the illusion is created in which the car appears to move from left to right.

Another way to think of the process is by looking at a strip of celluloid in a motion picture film. The celluloid contains individual frames, still images of whatever subject was shot by the camera. When run through a projector at a rate of 24 frames per second, the images appear to move seamlessly to the human eye.

What Is Computer-Generated Animation?

In essence, the fundamental methodology of computer-generated animation is the same as in creating a flipbook or running a strip of celluloid through a projector. A sequence of chronological still images is created, and when these still images are viewed in quick succession, they appear to move. The difference is that the content of each still image is generated digitally, and computer programs assist in creating the variations of movement from image to image, ultimately providing the illusion that the computer-generated still images are moving.

For our purposes, TAP utilizes polygonal or "box" modeling, a process that first begins with polygon meshes, 3D objects that comprises lines or edges, vertices, and faces—all of which can be manipulated. The animator can choose from an array of these meshes in the form of basic shapes, such as cubes, spheres, cylinders, cones, and so on. These shapes can then be altered—stretched, scaled, rotated, extruded, and so on—and built upon to create more complex digital assets. Cars, buildings, and even human figures can be created in polygonal modeling.

In the creation of a human character, the figure's body can be rigged with a virtual skeleton, much in the way a live, breathing person has a framework of bones. For example, let's say we created a figure named Martin. Martin's arms are at his side and we want him to point into the distance. The animator will create a keyframe at the starting and end point of that motion—1) the arm at Martin's side, and 2) the arm raised in pointing position. The sequence and position of keyframes tell the computer where to begin raising the arm and where to end the movement, as well as how long it will take for the movement to be completed.

At this stage there are two images, Martin with his arms at his side, and Martin with his raised arm. In traditional 2D cel animation, an artist would need to draw the arm elevating in slight increments so the sequence of raising the arm would appear seamless. Keeping in mind that humans perceive motion at a rate of 24 frames per second, even the basic movement of raising a character's arm would entail quite a few drawings! Luckily, with computer-generated animation software, all one has to do is set the keyframes and the computer automatically fills in the missing images between the first keyframe and the second. This process moves the 3D assets, or in this example, the character's arm, between keyframes. The animator can alter the frame rate, or number of frames viewed per second, so that movement jitter is reduced and instead appears as fluid motion to the viewer.

When the modeling phase of 3D assets and figures is complete, an animator may employ various techniques such as adding textures, shading, or light sources to give the objects a desired aesthetic or refine the object to appear more lifelike. The last step in the computer-generated 3D animation process is rendering, which processes data from the file being worked on and outputs the information to a completed digital image.

Overview of Medium

The goal of TAP's 3D Computer Animation Therapy Group is to create an original and personally meaningful digital video using computer-generated animation and polygonal modeling. To reach this goal, the following mediums are employed.

Computers

TAP holds groups onsite at each contracted location; both desktop and laptop computers are utilized. Computers must be capable of running 3D animation software. In settings where groups will be ongoing, desktop computers are installed, ideally in a room dedicated to animation production. In other locations, laptop computers are set up and put away before and after each session. Computers and equipment are then stored by each facility between sessions.

Animation Software

TAP currently uses 3DS MAX animation software manufactured by Autodesk.[2] Industry standard software for professional animators in film, video game, and virtual reality production, this program was chosen based on its polygonal modeling system as discussed above. Because this modeling technique is simple enough for participants to begin modifying shapes in the very first session, 3DS MAX is ideal software for use in TAP sessions; participants experience early success in the ability to create and move shapes, and, empowered by these successes, may then engage in learning more complicated animation techniques. This often begins a cycle in which participants continue to build self-esteem in conjunction with the understanding of new computer competency skills. As confidence continues to grow, more challenging techniques (such as working with edges or adding textures) are implemented. Mastery over new techniques contributes to increased ego strength, which in turn influences the desire to learn more techniques.

---

2   www.autodesk.com

Audio Recording Software

A variety of audio recording software may be implemented, including handheld and lavalier (wireless clip-on) microphones, recording sound directly into the computer. A handheld digital audio recorder, such as a Zoom H5 Handy Recorder (which creates and stores audio files that can then be imported to audio/video editing programs) may be utilized. Depending on the group, participants may also have the option to record audio via voice recording apps on their cell phones.

Projector

A computer-compatible projector is used for group tutorials and live animation demonstrations in early group sessions. As production continues, participants learn basic cinematography grammar and discuss camera placement and movement. Various options of how any given scene should appear are demonstrated to the group via projector and discussed. The projector serves as an important tool to help facilitate group cohesion; it allows participants to see how individual contributions may support the group process, furthering the development of interpersonal skills and teamwork.

Editing Software

Animations are edited using Adobe Premiere, in most cases by the TAP animator outside of the group in the TAP office.[3]

Population and Programming Model

TAP is a non-profit organization that serves at-risk youth, aged 12–24. A direct-service provider, TAP partners with a variety of organizations, including public, transfer, and charter schools, foster care and social service agencies, and entities serving court-involved youth, such as juvenile detention and alternative to incarceration programs.

In TAP's core curriculum, the 3D Computer Animation Therapy Group, participants collaborate as a team throughout a structured

---

3   www.adobe.com/products/premiere.html

cycle of animation production to create an original short animated video. Using a custom-designed production schedule, group members participate in key aspects of video production (scriptwriting, storyboarding, the creation of 3D models, character design, voice recording, and directing). TAP programming is unique in that sessions are co-led by a creative arts therapist and a professional animator who work as a team to create a non-threatening and safe environment. Focus is placed on fostering interpersonal skills through collaboration and teamwork. The TAP therapist assists participants in nurturing emotional coping skills such as impulse control and self-regulation throughout the development of creating an original narrative. Therapeutic interventions are introduced to safely process story content and the metaphors that arise throughout the progression of the collective story developed by the group. The TAP animator's job is to teach participants the computer animation software and manage the overall animation production.

Based on interest and level of comfort, participants may choose to participate in multiple areas of animation production or focus on a specific skill set. For example, if a participant presents as guarded or is hesitant to engage with the story-making process, he or she can concentrate on technical skill training. This flexibility allows participants to determine how they would like to contribute to the project and parallels a professional animation studio, where employees perform individual tasks while still collaborating with, and being a part of, a larger team.

Guided by the TAP animator, participants work hands-on with expensive industry-standard 3D modeling programs, software participants most likely would not be able to afford or be exposed to otherwise. The computer competencies learned in group are foundational skill sets that can then be applied toward a variety of career paths in animation and video production industries, as well as in advertising/architectural/fashion/graphic design vocations. All TAP 3D Computer Animation Therapy Groups culminate in a screening of the final animation created in session. This serves as a celebratory event to promote self-esteem and ego strength, and encourages each participant's evolution as an artist. It also allows for reflection of positive growth throughout the program while serving as an affirming and constructive termination event.

Initial TAP Group Sessions

One of the main responsibilities of the TAP group leaders is to balance the therapeutic and workforce development aspects of the program. To assist in providing this "flexibility in structure," a TAP Creed, a set of group guidelines, is recited at the beginning of each session (Figure 10.1). These guidelines are intended as an empowering approach to create a safe environment and may be revisited at any time during a session to help maintain group protocol. Participants are included in the discussion of the TAP Creed, and may add any guidelines they feel are needed to create a positive work environment. Collaborating in this way helps to establish a therapeutic alliance and allows participants to share in ownership over group guidelines.

The Animation Project

TAP animator's creed

1 we show respect
We are a team.
We need each other to create the best animation we can.

2 we take care of our technology
We respect all the equipment used in group.

3 we focus
We have a lot of work to do. *All* our
attention is focused on the project.
Text and chat outside the group.

4 we participate
A team's creativity can be more powerful
than an individual working alone.

5 we own the story
This is our story.
TAP staff will challenge the group to
make the best story possible.

6 we attend group
We want you in group.
Group members who are present may
change the story in your absence.

TAP groups also abide by the rules established by the facilities in which we operate.

Figure 10.1
The TAP Animator's Creed

The TAP Animator's Creed uses an empowering approach toward setting guidelines for group protocol, with intentional "we" language to foster team-building and group cohesion.

To additionally maintain structure, a customized production schedule is used that labels and dates each aspect of animation production to be covered throughout the entirety of the TAP group cycle (Figure 10.2). This schedule outlines clear expectations of when each aspect of production should be completed to ensure the animated video is finished by the screening date. It is also intended as a tool to assist students in developing executive functioning skills while providing consistency and ritual at the beginning and end of each session.

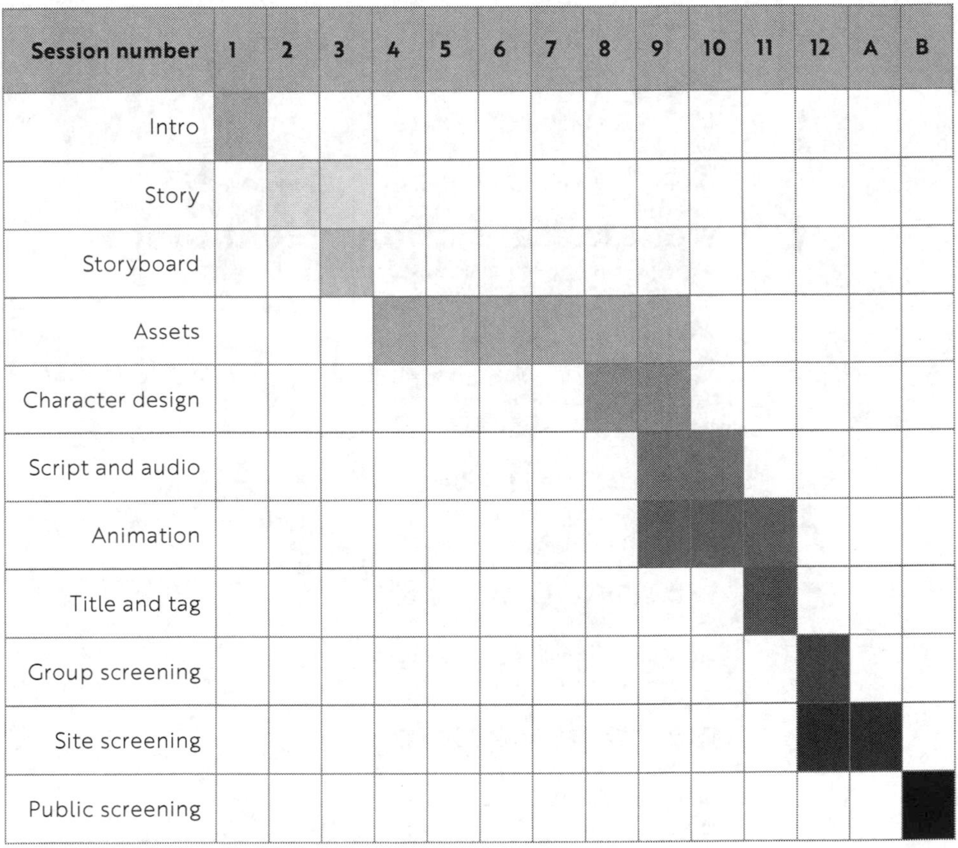

Session number	1	2	3	4	5	6	7	8	9	10	11	12	A	B
Intro	▓													
Story		▓	▓											
Storyboard			▓											
Assets				▓	▓	▓	▓							
Character design								▓						
Script and audio									▓					
Animation									▓	▓	▓			
Title and tag											▓			
Group screening												▓		
Site screening												▓	▓	
Public screening														▓

Figure 10.2
The Animation Project—production schedule

Introducing TAP to Participants: Narrative Development

TAP staff want to meet participants where they are. We accept the sagging pants, the hats worn backwards, and the profanity. Not based on any particular theoretical model, we feel that since youth in the juvenile justice system are often told what to do, where to go, and how to behave, the only way to know what they really think, want, and feel is to let them be themselves. Additionally, how can anyone develop their own way to move through the world if someone always tells them what to do, think, and feel?

The beginning of TAP narrative development differs from group to group depending on the setting and population of participants, and the personal style and approach of the TAP therapist. The narrative development process most often begins with a brainstorming session where loose ideas and themes are identified and discussed. If a group is having difficulty formulating an idea, storytelling exercises or prompts may be used. For example, the TAP therapist at an alternative-to-incarceration setting provided questions written on slips of paper that were placed in a bag and drawn at random to promote spontaneous discussion. In a probation group, images snipped from magazines were spread across a table. Participants then arranged the images to form a situation between characters, and from there developed a story.

Stories may be a non-fictional exploration, such as a transfer school's animated documentary exploring police brutality (The Animation Project, 2015a), or a narrative about environmental stressors developed by middle school students who struggled coping with the homelessness, poverty, and derelict buildings they encountered on their way to school each day (The Animation Project, 2015b). Narratives may also be fantastical in nature and feature talking inanimate objects, such as a human-hating fighter plane that earns new respect for people after a father and son fix its engine (The Animation Project, 2015c).

At times, participants may be resistant to the narrative development process and it is important for the TAP therapist to recognize and validate participant interests as a way to promote engagement. During a high school TAP session, participants initially presented as guarded and uninspired. Temporarily ceasing narrative development, the TAP therapist used the remaining time in session to talk with students about their favorite movies. As the participants excitedly discussed *Straight Outta Compton*, the TAP therapist used that information to motivate further engagement by screening a "behind the scenes" clip from *Straight Outta Compton* (Screen Slam, 2015) at the beginning of the next session. In the clip, film director

F. Gary Gray states, "When you think about N.W.A.,[4] you think about where you were when you first heard the truth…no censors, no filters, no nothing…and still today, I think that people are starving for the truth." The TAP therapist then asked the group, "What is your truth? If we were to make an animation without censors or filters, what story would you tell?" This particular group stated they wished to create a "truth story" that paralleled issues they witnessed in their own neighborhood and created the tale of a teenager who, after failing to get hired at a restaurant to help his single-parent mother pay the bills, resorts to "scamming" (a method of using blank checks at ATM machines to withdraw cash) and eventually gets arrested (The Animation Project, 2015d).

The sophistication of each story will inevitably differ from group to group. For example, in a juvenile detention setting, where there is seldom consistency of group members from week to week due to court hearings, releases, and new admittance, only one group member wished to participate in narrative development, opting to write a rap song. The project evolved into a music video, as the 3D models created by other participants served as visuals to support his song (The Animation Project, 2014a).

For some participants, developing a narrative in any shape or form may be too threatening. In such situations, participants can choose to focus on building 3D models. The final product of such a group may be a visual portfolio or highlight reel of the characters and objects they created, without audio, set to music, or with a recorded description of what was made. Such projects are still seen as a success, and participants are empowered to learn new computer skills. These TAP graduates often request another TAP cycle, then serve as mentors to new group members, taking ownership over the project and helping to lead the group to a more complex narrative.

The more TAP cycles a participant takes, the more developed his or her skill set becomes—and the final animations are reflective of this in terms of visual animation aesthetics and narrative complexity. This is evident in an alternative-to-incarceration group where participants had completed prior TAP cycles. Already familiar with 3DS Max and the process of creating a short animated video,

---

4   N.W.A. was a controversial Los Angeles-based hip-hop group formed in the mid-1980s that incorporated social commentary and personal experiences of inner-city living into their lyrics.

participants were thus able to focus more intently on deepening the story. The result was an animation they titled *True Colors* (The Animation Project, 2015e), the story of a white crayon, "Whitey," who is teased by colored crayons because his marks never show up on the standard white paper they are given. Running away, Whitey finds solace with several sticks of chalk as their physical appearance resembles his own. His marks, however, fail to show up on the chalkboard, and embarrassed, he is taunted again. Meanwhile, the colored crayons encountered a struggle of their own—black paper. After failing to make marks on the darker page, they realize Whitey's worth, apologize, and bring him back into the fold. The story of *True Colors* is saturated with themes of race, rejection, acceptance, friendship, and the struggles many of the TAP participants initially felt while trying to work as a team. It was only through multiple TAP cycles that positive group cohesion could be established to the point of exploring such themes in a safe and trusting environment. The successes of this group were many: on the therapeutic side via the social and emotional security participants demonstrated in group discussion and during scriptwriting, and on the workforce development side via the increased computer competency/animation skills needed to produce a video that exceeded their prior work, not solely in terms of conceptualization, but also in technical ability.

Working with Challenging or Provocative Narrative Content

In TAP groups, initial narrative development often begins with themes that the therapist may find challenging, including "shock value" subject matter or provocative content. While continuing to build the therapeutic alliance, the TAP therapist must not close the door on this communication, but opt to open it further. This might entail sitting with challenging content until the participants can develop a healthier outcome.

Such was the case in a transfer high school designed to support students who had fallen behind on credits or previously dropped out of school altogether. The group initially developed a chaotic narrative involving two teenagers, Shawn and Amanda, who were throwing rocks off a bridge at passing cars (The Animation Project, 2014b). When one rock smashed through a speeding car's windshield, causing it to swerve off the road and crash into a tree, the driver, Carl—a convict just released from prison—responded by pulling out a gun and shooting at the teenagers.

To include a guideline to the TAP Creed that omits excessive violence or weapons in the group narrative is an easy solution, but it is not a therapeutic intervention that would best reach the at-risk youth population we serve. Likewise, it would instill the lesson that gun violence, a reality many participants are exposed to, should not be discussed, rather than instill the benefits of open dialogue about challenging subject matter. As the therapeutic goal is to have the class come to a healthier conclusion by their own volition, the TAP therapist must guide the participants toward this outcome by gaining a clear understanding of character motives and the subsequent consequences for his or her actions.

> TAP therapist: *Carl, the driver, was just released from prison?*
>
> Participant 1: *Yeah. That's why he pulled out his gun.*
>
> TAP therapist: *Okay, then let's play this out. I'm Carl and here's my car.*
>
> [TAP therapist pulls an empty student desk to the front of the room. He sits and pretends to drive. Two students are chosen to play Shawn and Amanda. They throw rocks (crumpled notebook paper) at the car (student desk), which swerves off the road and into a tree (projector cart). The TAP therapist slumps over the desktop. Students laugh.]
>
> TAP therapist: *What's going through my mind?*
>
> Participant 1: *You're hurt. Confused. Maybe you got a concussion.*
>
> TAP therapist: *What else?*
>
> Participant 2: *You got a headache and you're all shaky. Fuzzy. You're angry.*
>
> TAP therapist: *I'm angry. Why?*
>
> Participant 2: *'Cause you just got out of jail and these kids, they smashed your car and almost killed you.*
>
> TAP therapist: *Good summary of the scene. What happens next?*

Participant 3: *You open the door and stumble out.*

Participant 1: *And then you reach beneath your seat, grab your gun and POP! POP! POP! You teach them a lesson.*

TAP therapist: *If that's the case—Shawn and Amanda—what happens to them?*

Participant 1: *They die. End of story.*

TAP therapist: *That's the end? In real life, would that really be the end?*

Participant 2: *Not if Carl murdered them. He just got out of jail, so he's got to be smart. He's not going to be waving a gun around in the middle of the street in broad daylight.*

Participant 3: *He's still angry so he might chase them, but he wouldn't start shooting.*

Participant 1: *Yeah, you got a point.*

Through dramatizing the narrative and exploring the elements of their story (theme, plot, setting, character, conflict, climax, resolution), participants are able to engage in dialogue that allows for cause/effect reality testing. Employing these techniques in this example resulted in diminished violence while still honoring each character's emotional state.

Storyboarding

Storyboards are drawn images ordered in a specific sequence that provide animators with a visual blueprint of how the final animation should look. The process of creating storyboards is helpful in both the visualization and revision of creative ideas.

For purposes of TAP groups, storyboard cards can be kept simple, with stick figures, arrows, and text to describe character action. The hand-drawn images allow participants to take a break from technology while using more traditional methods of art-making. Some participants may wish to draw more detailed storyboards and are welcome to do so, but the initial purpose is to provide participants with a visual representation of the story so it can be discussed from multiple perspectives. Later in the cycle, the storyboards will be used to help the animator set up shots with completed 3D characters and assets.

For storyboarding exercises, blank 5" x 7" index cards are used. This is preferred over 8" x 11" paper with storyboarding squares as the index cards may be laid out on a table and rearranged. As cards can be easily added or taken away, the narrative becomes visibly pliable, thus teaching participants they have control over their story, and that their story can change.

By laying out the storyboards, the TAP therapist has visual cues to delve deeper into the narrative. The image of Shawn and Amanda throwing rocks begged the question as to why they were throwing rocks in the first place. This led to the development of Shawn and Amanda's backstory, giving context to their aggressive behavior.

> TAP therapist: *Why were Shawn and Amanda throwing rocks?*
>
> Participant 1: *They were bored.*
>
> TAP therapist: *Bored?*
>
> Participant 1: *Yeah. They had nothing to do.*
>
> TAP therapist: *Couldn't they have played a game or watched TV or—*
>
> Participant 2: *Nah, they got kicked out of their house.*
>
> TAP therapist: *That seems harsh. What happened?*
>
> Participant 2: *They threw a party. Well, it wasn't even a party, just a few friends over.*
>
> TAP therapist: *And they weren't supposed to do that?*
>
> Participant 2: *Well, they didn't know. It wasn't their fault. They just had some friends over.*
>
> TAP therapist: *Man, to be kicked out of their own home? I wonder what they were feeling in that moment.*
>
> Participant 2: *It made them angry, upset.*
>
> TAP therapist: *And that's why they were throwing rocks, because they were angry?*
>
> Participant 3: *Well, you know, the streets aren't a safe place to be. You start just walking around, but sooner or later you're going to get into trouble. I don't even think they were throwing*

rocks. I think they were just on the bridge chillin' and one of them knocked a rock off by mistake.

TAP therapist: *So they didn't damage the car on purpose—it was an accident?*

Participant 3: *Yeah.*

TAP therapist: *That changes the story quite a bit, doesn't it?*

Storyboards thus provide a visual approach to creating backstory or alternate endings. They also serve as a metaphor for changing circumstances, as many participants enter group having already internalized that they cannot change their situation. Such was the case in a charter school where each participant had been expelled from their previous school and was at risk of being expelled again. When participants discussed their reluctance to participate, they explained to the TAP therapist, "We're bad and you're here to save us."

Recognizing the internalization of being "bad" was too overwhelming for some participants, so the therapist redirected this thought back to the animation, reframing the students' language into the question, "Who is a bad character that needs saving?" Working within the metaphor of this animated "bad character," the group felt safe enough to develop a story about Keyso, a teenager who had "no money and no options" but to sell drugs instead of going to school (The Animation Project, 2015f). After being arrested, Keyso was saved by an older prison inmate who pleaded with him to go back to school, start playing basketball, and get his mother out of the projects—in essence, not to make the same mistakes he had committed. When the group created storyboards and visually saw multiple decisions the character could make, the group was then able to continue articulating different outcomes for that character.

Modeling 3D Assets

"Oh, we like art therapy: it is inexpensive."
(Quote from hospital psychiatrist in response to having art therapists on the unit)

When the TAP model was being developed, the cost of adding expensive tools (computers and software) to the groups had to be justified. Pencils, markers, and paint could get at some of the issues, so why add expensive computers and software? It was theorized that technology would be attractive to both participants and funders. When pitching the program to youth we could say: come learn how to use the same software that made Grand Theft Auto (a well-known action–adventure video game). To funders who did not respond to my explanation of therapeutic needs and benefits, we could simply talk about technical skills to get their attention. On a deeper level, it was reasoned that learning how to use 3D animation software specifically, and computers in general, would add a "workforce development level" to the program that other art therapy materials could not.

During a particularly poignant TAP group, a participant disclosed that due to the high level of gang activity in his neighborhood, he was restricted to staying home after school as it was unsafe to be on the streets. "What else is there to do but play video games?" he said. "It's the only place I have some control." While the participant was correct in identifying the control he had over the video game's avatar, he was still operating in a digital world created by a team of designers. When modeling 3D assets and environments in TAP, however, participants create a new world as they see it, and they are in control of this world's shape and design. Thus, the act of 3D modeling itself is a form of communication and provides valuable information about what participants want to express in group. While the goal of building 3D environments is not necessarily autobiographical in TAP groups, this act of 3D creation often results in artwork that has personal meaning and parallels environments where the TAP session takes place.

A 15-year-old participant in a juvenile detention group created a series of buildings he titled "The Projects." In looking at the artwork, the TAP therapist noticed that the character in the image was scaled disproportionately smaller in relation to the buildings surrounding him. The TAP animator, considering the workforce development aspects of the program, demonstrated various ways to work with scaling tools, educating the participant in techniques to resize characters and assets.

After group, while TAP staff waited for the bus, it began to rain. Gazing up at the gathering rainclouds, staff noticed an imposing row of buildings that dwarfed their frames. It was no surprise when they returned to group next week and saw that the participant had opted to keep the scale of the buildings as they were originally created. In this way, the 3D world can be seen as a reflection of the real world, or as an authentic depiction of how the real word is perceived by the participant. Similarly, the creation of 3D images may also be seen as a nonverbal form of communication, as exhibited by a high school participant who modeled a park scene in group, TAP staff learning after session that a female high school student was sexually assaulted at the park across the street the night before.

It is also important to note that some participants will gravitate toward technology while others may be resistant to engaging with computers or using the animation software. Participants often exhibit varying levels of computer competency, and so the therapist must consider the technological proficiencies and interests of each participant. To navigate this, participants may be divided into "production departments" to accommodate differing interests, strengths, and comfort levels around technology and narrative development.

Creating Characters

In TAP group sessions, it is important for participants to discern the causes and effects of character behaviors in their animation. This process begins by encouraging participant ownership over the initial creating of the characters themselves—through aesthetic character design, when participants use a proprietary template developed by TAP animators to establish each character's physical attributes. Similar to creating an avatar (the "figure" or "character" the player controls in a video game), participants are presented with an arrangement of basic preconstructed characters, which participants can then customize using simple slider tools. This provides participants with a sense of control through determining the gender, clothing design, hair style, eye color, skin color, physical stature, and build of each character. Operating within the boundaries the template provides, participants are given complete control within the provided structure, ensuring the race and personality of each character are the creation of each participant, not influenced by TAP staff. This control provides valuable information about the group, as some participants invariably wish, consciously or unconsciously, to create themselves. For example, a tall male participant who was behind on credits in a transfer school was known by his peers to wear a track suit each day. When this participant created a tall character adorning the same color track suit he was wearing in class, his peers praised him for how closely he was able to create the character in his own likeness. Surprised, the participant stated he had not intentionally created the character to look like or represent himself. With a laugh, he leaned closer to the screen, verbalizing his awe.

Integrating personal attributes within characters enhances the connection participants have with their project. But also, the subsequent decisions characters make in the story may take on heightened importance as participants begin to see themselves in the narrative and can then discern how they would respond in similar situations. This supports strengthening of "cause and effect thinking" and the ability to consider consequences. In brief, the TAP therapist remains in the metaphor and safety of the story to explore a character's actions.

Sometimes a participant may also wish to work outside of the character template. In a juvenile detention facility, a female participant wished to design a more detailed character with the TAP animator. Her idea was to create a statuesque female demon, clad with horns and standing before a giant skull. Upon completion of her character, she went on to create a narrative about the demon being sent to Hell (The Animation Project, 2015g). Having lost her independence under the Devil's mandates, the demon had no choice but to overtake the Devil and develop new rules of her own as to how purgatory should be governed. The participant then modeled a megaphone and wrote a public service announcement the demon would impart to her prisoners now that she was in charge. In many ways, this story paralleled the participant's experience in the juvenile justice system, internalizing that she was an "evil kid," (a demon), sent to juvenile detention (Hell), and forced to comply with regulations against her will. The participant often felt she had no choice but to challenge frightening authority figures (the Devil), and yearned for more control over her life (overtaking the Devil and creating her own set of rules).

After completing this project, the participant's work shifted, coloring every asset she modeled pink. She created a prison cell and a courtroom, environments that paralleled her goals of having a successful court hearing and leaving the detention facility. When asked about her new color palette, she responded, "Making [3D] stuff calms me down. When I'm making stuff, I don't have to worry about my life in here. I don't think about any of it. It's the only time I can relax."

Writing the Script

Depending on the group, the script may be physically written by either the participants or the TAP therapist. Copies of the script are printed and handed out or viewed via a projector and read aloud. The narrative may still be altered at this stage; it is the group's decision whether they wish to assign roles or have one person read the script. Plot "holes," meaning gaps or inconsistencies in the story, and character decisions are reevaluated, and the TAP therapist may work with participants to act out parts. As participants play different characters or view the live action scenes, new insight can be gained into each character's emotional states. The skill of learning to name and reflect on a character's emotions in turn helps participants to better identify and express their own feelings.

In the animation *Accidental Mishaps* (The Animation Project, 2014b), Shawn and Amanda try to run away from ex-convict Carl, the driver whose windshield they broke with a falling rock. Splitting up, they each sprint down a different path of a nearby forest. Shawn trips over a fallen branch and twists his leg, his shouts of pain notifying Carl of his whereabouts. Amanda finds a cabin filled with guns, and hearing the screams of her friend, runs to his aid only to find Carl standing over his wounded body. The altercation originally culminated in a shoot-out where all characters perished, participants stating that Carl's objective was revenge—to bust up Shawn and Amanda as they had done to his car. However, when acting out the scene where Shawn is lying vulnerably on the ground, writhing in pain after injuring his leg, with Carl in a position to harm him any way he chooses, the participants instead decided he would help Shawn to his feet and assist him out of the forest.

> TAP therapist (acting as Carl): *I finally have Shawn right where I want him! Why would I help him up?*

Participant 1: *Carl wanted to hurt Shawn, right? Well, Shawn's already hurt, so he doesn't want that anymore. I guess seeing him in pain makes Carl think twice. Now he feels sorry.*

TAP therapist: *So, what is it that Carl really wants?*

Participant: *He wishes this never happened.*

Participant 2: *He wants a re-do. He wants his car back the way it was.*

Participant 3: *Nah. What he really wants is to go home. Put his past behind him.*

The rest of the group agreed, and the result was a sublimated animation where violence presented as less reactive, more regulated, and ultimately diminished by newfound empathy.

Recording Audio

When the final draft of the script is complete, roles are then assigned, often via participants volunteering to read specific parts. If multiple participants wish to read the same part, an "audition" is held to demonstrate the workforce dynamics of working actors, and participants play the role of casting directors to determine who should read each part.

When the roles are finally assigned, participants then begin recording audio. A traditional "Quiet on the set!" is used before each take to ensure clean audio is captured without background noise. Participants not recording audio themselves are given the role of directors, and can give constructive feedback after each take. Takes may also be played back for the group to hear, and participants develop interpersonal skills by working as a team to achieve the best takes possible. Participants also choose music for the animation, considering which songs fit the emotional content, theme, or pacing of a scene through either the lyrics, tempo, or general mood of a song. If lyrics contain expletives, a version of the song without lyrics can be used. Students with musical backgrounds or proficiency in audio production may play, record, or sample music to be used in the project.

Live Animation

Continuing in the role of director, participants view the assets and characters they created compiled within each scene's 3D environment. Basic cinematography grammar (types of shots and camera angles) is discussed and referenced so participants are able to communicate clearly and effectively how they envision a scene to look. Video and audio editing is conducted by the TAP animator, and typically occurs out of session.

Titles and Tags

The title is the identifying name given to the project. Participants are asked to identify what their animation is "really about," or how they would describe their animation in one sentence to a friend passing by on the street. Titles can be literal or use metaphor and humor. In *My Life in Coney Island* (The Animation Project, 2015h), a teenage narrator tells his story about day-to-day life in Coney Island where he is continually pressured to smoke weed with friends. In *Whispers of Rejection* (The Animation Project, 2015i), a bullied middle school student finds friendship with a monster he meets in the forest. *Pear Pressure* (The Animation Project, 2013) is a humorous take on peer pressure, albeit with talking fruit and vegetables.

The title is supported by a tagline, the lesson learned or moral the participants intend viewers to take away from watching their project. The tagline also provides the TAP therapist with important information as to the deeper meaning participants attribute to their work. For example, in the animation about scamming, the group titled their work, *Caught Up* (The Animation Project, 2015d), and gave it the tag, *How Far Would You Go to Protect Someone You Love?* More than just a cautionary tale about getting arrested, the participants felt their animation was really about the complicated roles many teens must take on to help their families survive.

By developing a title and tag, participants often find new meaning in their work, which then empowers them to share that wisdom with others, as well as emblazon it within themselves. Defining the moral of the animation also begins the termination process and provides closure to the production phase of the group.

Screening

The screening is held during the last session of the group cycle and serves as termination. Screenings may be held in the group room where sessions took place or may be open to the wider community, such as in a school auditorium or community center. The goal is to reward participants for all of their hard work during the group cycle and give them a celebrity experience that parallels a red-carpet Hollywood premiere. The TAP therapist facilitates and explains TAP programming to audience members, discussing the production schedule and aspects of animation production learned by the participants during group. The animation is projected onto a projector screen, and depending on the size of the exhibition space, audio speakers are provided.

After the screening, participants are called one by one and given a TAP certificate. This is also a time to publicly name a participant's strengths; the TAP therapist and animator take turns to recognize each participant's contributions to the project and celebrate the unique abilities demonstrated in group. Participants also receive a copy of the finished animation on disc, which serves as a transitional object.

**The
Animation
Project**

CERTIFICATE OF COMPLETION

_____

has successfully completed:

3D Computer Animation Group

scan here

for video

Transformation through technology
theanimationproject.org

Brian Austin, Founder

Figure 10.3
TAP Certificate of Completion
*Note the QR (quick response) barcode that contains the website URL information
of the completed animation. When scanned with a smartphone via a QR
reader app, the user is taken directly to the animated video online.*

Participants may also form a panel and speak about their project, discussing challenges encountered during the process and how they were overcome, again reiterating each participant's resiliency, compromise, and teamwork. A question and answer session is then held where participants substantiate their project and the animation process. By allowing participants to be seen, heard, and celebrated, they learn to identify with the positive decisions made in group while feeling more connected to the greater community.

Conclusion

"The child who steals an object is not
looking for the object stolen…"
D.W. Winnicott

Poised to complete a decade of service, TAP has a staff of 21, and is running animation groups in all five New York City (NYC) boroughs. In 2018, we are on target to serve 1800 participants, host 80 paid interns, and place 40 qualified participants in external internships at NYC digital design and animation studios. In closing, I offer a debt of gratitude to Martin Chapa. Mr. Chapa, your honest, non-judgmental, nurturing, and providing response to theft, delinquency, and rebellion is alive and well at The Animation Project. Muchas gracias!

Recommendations

- Set participants up for success. Participants often enter group in a vulnerable state and need to feel capable. By giving each participant the role of "professional animator," and supporting that role through use of technology, transparency, and unconditional support, participants begin to feel less vulnerable and more connected, all the while developing a sense of professional identity.

- Technology and therapeutic work go hand in hand. If participants find narrative development too overwhelming or need more distance, youth can work on modeling 3D assets or drawing storyboards, or participate in another aspect of animation production. Using animation technology provides safe distance for participants to go deeper into the therapeutic process of narrative development, while strengthening emotional regulation, impulse control, and social skills help participants prepare for workforce readiness.

- Trust the process. The therapist must be able to hold (not reject) subject matter that is challenging for the therapist and not "close the door" on disturbing or provocative content during initial narrative creation. Rather, by allowing participants to express themselves fully and safely while containing the group experience throughout narrative development and subsequent discussions, participants can begin to think critically about their decisions. The art of 3D computer animation requires focus and patience by the very nature of the medium, and this affords the TAP group time to continually examine and reshape the story to a healthier outcome.

References

Screen Slam (2015) *Straight Outta Compton: Exclusive Behind the Scenes Featurette.* Retrieved on April 1, 2018 at www.youtube.com/watch?v=HVkiwpBL6fQ

The Animation Project (2013) *Pear Pressure.* Retrieved on April 1, 2018 at www.youtube.com/watch?v=NRWpBFFY5hI

The Animation Project (2014a) *Who Will Win?* Retrieved on April 1, 2018 at www.youtube.com/watch?v=N2ASStrxXP8

The Animation Project (2014b) *Accidental Mishaps*. Retrieved on April 1, 2018 at www.youtube.com/watch?v=pjgTn-M2Apc

The Animation Project (2015a) *Where the Hammer Falls*. Retrieved on April 1, 2018 at www.youtube.com/watch?v=98bqw1Ca7tI

The Animation Project (2015b) *Going Beyond*. Retrieved on April 1, 2018 at www.youtube.com/watch?v=wr1gBPkcw9Q

The Animation Project (2015c) *Planes at War*. Retrieved on April 1, 2018 at www.youtube.com/watch?v=EscA-Km4vLMandt=123s

The Animation Project (2015d) *Caught Up*. Retrieved on April 1, 2018 at www.youtube.com/watch?v=T3nsxHkrUxk

The Animation Project (2015e) *True Colors*. Retrieved on April 1, 2018 at www.youtube.com/watch?v=B2f3xavajA4

The Animation Project (2015f) *A Baller's Life*. Retrieved on April 1, 2018 at www.youtube.com/watch?v=HMAELVM9w90

The Animation Project (2015g) *Hell PSA*. Retrieved on April 1, 2018 at www.youtube.com/watch?v=NfiTITI4tGg

The Animation Project (2015h) *My Life in Coney Island*. Retrieved on April 1, 2018 at www.youtube.com/watch?v=IBii_4iTIZ0

The Animation Project (2015i) *Whispers of Rejection*. Retrieved on April 1, 2018 at www.youtube.com/watch?v=e3SAxdz2l4k

11

THERE'S AN APP FOR THAT

Cathy Malchiodi

When I first started to explore what I called "computer art therapy" (Malchiodi, 2000), it was with the now Stone Age software called MacDraw. Honestly, it wasn't that much fun, but it was an intriguing novelty at a time when home computers were just finally in reach of consumers, agencies, and education. Creative expression was generally limited to making some rudimentary line drawings or morphing a photo of yourself or your cat into various colorful psychedelic iterations. Unless you wanted to use your computer as a form of strength training, portability from place to place was not feasible.

Fast-forward to the 21st century and I can pop a tablet (in my case, an iPad) into my bag and take it to the clinic for a client to use instead of paint and paper. While there is little research on the effectiveness of touch technology with client populations, without a doubt the current generation is comfortable with it as part of art therapy and as a language for self-expression. Apps (application programs) are a key component of tablet devices; in brief, apps are computer programs designed to provide various functions or activities. They often are preinstalled on tablets, smartphones (called a mobile app), and computers or are uploaded individually by users to a device. There are apps for word processing and spread-sheets, shopping and games, photo enhancement and art making, to name a few.

As a digital immigrant (an individual born before the digital technology age), I enjoy the wide range of arts-based apps to virtually draw, paint, assemble collages, alter photographs, and edit films (Malchiodi, 2011a) (Figures 11.1 and 11.2). As someone who studied at a school of fine arts and devoted long hours learning to use pencil, charcoal, and Conte crayon to draw from life, I am surprised at what I am experiencing via a virtual studio of touch technology. Not that long ago, image creation through digital technology was only possible through complicated and often expensive software programs, generally used by professional artists. Now anyone with access to a tablet or smartphone can create images through using a variety of apps, many of which are free to consumers.

Figure 11.1
Zoolee Cat in Repose
Created on Art Rage and modified with PhotoToaster
Courtesy of Cathy Malchiodi © 2014

Figure 11.2
Finnegan Studies the #Resist Movement
Created with iPhone and modified with PhotoToaster
Courtesy of Cathy Malchiodi © 2016

The Emerging Role of Apps in Art Therapy

The flood of apps that are available for digital art expression can be used by all ages, although sometimes it seems that the youngest of digital natives have an advantage in intuitively knowing how to use them. After all, digital tools and devices are a familiar part of their lives, but it is important not to assume that younger individuals are the only candidates for digital media and tablet technology. To date, I have used a variety of well-chosen art-making apps not only with children, adolescents, and young adults, but also adults throughout the lifespan. In some sessions, use of an app becomes the focus of the session; in other situations, an app might be used to initiate or supplement use of more traditional media such as drawing, paint, and collage.

On the other hand, many art therapists have little knowledge about the possibilities apps offer and are overwhelmed by the number of art-making apps available for digital drawing, painting, collage, and photography. In part, this has to do with a lingering resistance to technology due to the physical qualities of digital media, but also to therapeutic and ethical questions about introducing it as an approach to art therapy. For example, some observe that digital media in therapy adversely impact relational dynamics due to the overstimulating qualities of computer technology (Klorer, 2009) or decrease critical engagement in therapy (Potash, 2009). These are valid concerns, but once one becomes a digitally savvy therapist, practitioners become increasingly knowledgeable about just what apps can and cannot do, and learn how to facilitate digital art expression to enhance the therapeutic process. Engaging in one's own art-based research about how digital apps "work" and their appropriateness as a possible medium is key to realizing the possibilities for how they can enhance art therapy in specific situations.

Choe (2014) set out to study the characteristics of digital art media, including specific art apps on iPads, using a participatory design approach. Her results conclude that while there is no single app that is effective in art therapy with every individual, she did identify three distinct qualities valued by the study's participants as follows: 1) ease of use/intuitiveness, including being easy to navigate, easy to understand and user-friendly; 2) simplicity, but with robust features and options; and 3) responsiveness in terms of speed, control, and immediacy of expression. Additionally, Choe's research revealed six important features that might constitute an "ideal" art app for art therapy, including: "1) therapist's control over options; 2) creation of separate, secure portfolio folders; 3) recording of the art process; 4) integration of mixed media and multimedia; 5) assessment capability; and 6) privacy and confidentiality" (p.150). An important conclusion was derived from this data—that most of the apps reviewed in the study lack these features that may be necessary for use in clinical settings. This conclusion is not surprising because art apps have not been developed with clinical features in mind nor ethical standards (see Chapter 2); as discussed in more detail below in work with hospitalized pediatric patients, there are many potential confidentiality and storage issues that must be addressed before introducing apps via a tablet device, including the possibility of posting to social networking sites (Malchiodi and Johnson, 2013).

There is a growing consensus, albeit anecdotal for the most part, about where art apps may best serve individuals in art therapy treatment. I have used them in busy medical clinics with both adults (Malchiodi, 2011b) and children (Malchiodi and Johnson, 2013), in many cases because of infection control, as iPads are easy to clean between users; they also are preferable when an individual has allergies to multiple substances. In working with survivors of traumatic brain injury, I have also used apps as a transition to using art materials such as pencils and paintbrushes when individuals' fine motor skills are physically challenged or in recovery. Choe (2014) summarized other situations when apps may be a preferred way of introducing and supporting art making, including autism, aversion to tactile experiences, or anxiety over use of traditional art materials. In contrast, she notes that use of iPads in therapy may be contraindicated for those individuals with Internet addiction, obsessive–compulsive tendencies, or anxieties related to digital technology. As more practitioners continue to use various art apps and tablets within the context of therapy, we will continue to increase the understanding of this form of digital expression and when this type of media is best suited to supporting individual needs and goals for wellbeing.

Two Art Therapists, Two Art Therapy Apps

Choe's research underscores the types of qualities and characteristics that may contribute to art apps designed for specific use in art therapy. Two digital art therapists have already ventured into the digital terrain to create and develop art therapy apps. Matteson (2015) set out to establish a "mobile art therapy" app based on Choe's list of desirable features. The Art Therapy Draw! app includes two of those features: a portfolio option and enhanced security. Matteson developed the Art Therapy Draw! app through the framework of the first four phases of the Mobile Application Development Lifecycle Model (MADLC) (Vithani and Kumar, 2014). Participants were able to set passwords and save their images through a secure format called ArtLocker, one of the desirable features for clinical art therapy sessions. Although the sample size of expert reviewers of the app was small, the study did indicate that the Art Therapy Draw! app was easy to use and required little instruction to operate, and navigation was minimal. As with any app in development, Matteson notes that more features are needed to provide users with necessary tools and practitioners with options for use in treatment settings.

Computer Art Therapy (see Chapter 21) is an app developed by the AAA-Lab (Artificial Intelligence, Applied Statistics, Art Therapy) in Seoul, South Korea. The project is led by Professor Seong-in Kim (2017) at Korea University and a team of colleagues and students who are interested in applying technology to art therapy and measuring graphic aspects of drawings. By Western standards, analyzing artwork is not technically "art therapy," which is generally defined as a process-oriented approach. Most art therapists are interested in understanding the content of their clients' images; some practitioners help clients explore the meaning of their art expressions while others continue, like Dr. Kim's team, to search for ways to evaluate various characteristics of artwork for mental illness, cognitive and developmental disorders, and personality traits (Malchiodi, 2012).

Here is what the AAA-Lab has to say about its Computer Art Therapy app project:

> The reason why the utility of evaluation and transparency of an image falls under suspicion

is because that there is [a] lack of reliability and consistency between the evaluations from Art Therapists and a lack of validity in the result of evaluations. We developed the C_CREATES (Computer_Color Related Art Therapy Evaluation System) as one way to solve reliability and validity problems caused by the personal or subjective experiences of Art Therapists. (Kim, 2017, p.11)

Both Matteson and Kim are attempting to address the challenges of developing apps that meet the specific needs and complexities encountered in introducing digital media within art therapy sessions. However, readers can get a glimpse into app creation on one of the many user-friendly platforms now available. For example, the popular AppyPie[1] takes you through the process of app development in a series of simple steps, assisting you in creating an app without knowledge of coding. This type of app development is useful for creating mobile apps for business purposes rather than apps used to create digital art; in other words, because so many people use smartphones for information, having a mobile app for one's business is a good marketing strategy to reach a larger audience and establish "brand recognition" for your services.

Tablet Technology with Pediatric Patients

There are relatively few case examples to date that examine and explain how apps support the process of art therapy; for the purpose of this chapter, the use of tablet technology and apps in hospital settings with pediatric patients is provided as one possible clinical application. A list of several of the apps used in work with children in hospitals is included (see Box 11.1); readers are reminded that availability of apps frequently changes due to new operating systems and advances in digital media delivery and devices.

---

1   https://snappy.appypie.com/appbuilder/creator-software

Box 11.1 Recommendations for Art Apps

At the time of writing the following are examples of apps that can be applied and adapted to work with children with medical illnesses or physical challenge.

Art Rage. Painting program

Draw Something. Draw something and have your family or friends guess what it is

Finger Paint Magic. A fun virtual finger painting experience

Spin Art. User-friendly app to produce colorful spin art designs

Uzu. Award-winning app that allows users to apply different kinds of touch to the screen to create colorful designs

Virtuoso. Free piano app for music-making via virtual piano keys

Art of Glow. App that allows users to create colorful and relaxing designs

Thicket. App that is part toy, part wind chime and part spider web that provides an experience of texture, lines, and sounds

Meritum Paint. Popular app for digital finger painting

Drawing Pad. Mobile art studio designed exclusively for tablets; uses photo-realistic crayons, markers, paint brushes, colored pencils, stickers, and roller pens

Photowall. Collage app that creates images, greeting cards, wallpapers, and screensavers

Emulsion Paint. Colorful paintings through touch-screen technology

PhotoToaster. Easy way to alter and enhance photographs taken on tablets and smartphones

As previously noted, digital media offer a means of creating artwork that can be shared without putting patients at risk for spreading infection (Malchiodi and Johnson, 2013). Many art therapists who currently work with children in isolation or confined to hospital rooms use iPads or other tablet technology as one way to overcome challenges of providing art materials that may transmit infection. This is particularly helpful for patients who have very compromised immune systems such as those undergoing bone marrow transplant and so are not able to leave their room or have visitors other than immediate family.

An iPad can also become a medium to transmit images from one person to another. For example, a friend of a patient who was very concerned about her wellbeing was able to make her a "digital" art gift. Because of the risk of bringing germs into her room, he could not use traditional art materials to create her a handmade gift, but he was able to use the iPad to draw a piece of art for her. The art therapist printed it for him to see his product and then gave another copy to the patient in the bone marrow transplant unit. The patient was very excited to have a gift made by her friend and fellow patient and hung it on her wall to remind her of that support. The digital media helped these young people to connect and support each other, while keeping infection control policies intact.

Here is a different example of tablet technology with a pediatric patient (Malchiodi, 2011a). Josh, a ten-year-old boy, was admitted to a children's hospital for injuries from an all-terrain vehicle (ATV) accident. Josh underwent several painful surgical procedures and had a difficult time adjusting to his hospital stay. On three occasions, he was non-compliant with medical procedures and had to be restrained in order for nursing staff to administer medications and IVs. He did enjoy working with the art therapist and child life staff and in particular liked using an iPad to make images.

To help Josh get settled down, the art therapist introduced apps called SpinArt Studio and Spawn Glow. Both apps are easy to use and involve making colorful designs through spinning virtual paint (SpinArt) or moving colorful lines around the screen using one's fingers. Josh often became so occupied with using the iPad to make designs that the nursing staff could more easily give him injections or perform routine medical procedures without him becoming anxious or complaining about pain.

After a few days, the art therapist taught Josh about another way to make art on the iPad through an app called Doodle Buddy. The Doodle Buddy program has numerous drawing tools (colored pencil and paintbrush lines) and special effects that only require the use of a finger on the screen, like the apps previously mentioned. It is a particularly good program for children because they enjoy using these tools and effects along with the stamps that allow them to add icons for animals, environmental elements, and other objects or emoticons (such as a "smiley face"). An audio feature can be selected so that each stamp makes its own sound when the artist places a stamp on the digital artwork. Making an artwork only takes a few minutes by first selecting a background (a color or environmental scene such as a beach, mountains, or forest) and each artwork can be saved using a screenshot feature; artworks can then be printed or sent to other devices for viewing.

Josh used the Doodle Buddy over the course of several days to develop a story about one of the stamps, a sea turtle that he said had "superpowers." Superheroes are a common theme among children who are spending time in the hospital and with children in general because they are often found in cartoons, digital games, and other media. At first Josh's sea turtle was surrounded by many threatening characters, including several ominous spiders that lived on a dangerous cliff by the ocean. He mentioned that his turtle was often afraid, but learned how to make the spiders follow him into the ocean where they eventually drowned. Eventually he found a special island where he met a friendly ladybug that helped him to feel less lonely while on the island and was "very nice to talk to." They played games on the beach during sunny days together. Eventually the story ended with the sea turtle returning home to his own island of safety where he lived with other turtles at his house.

From this brief vignette, it is not difficult to conclude that Josh at least partially used the story of the sea turtle (himself), dangerous elements and entities (the discomfort of the hospitalization and psychosocial struggles), and the ladybug (the therapist), to explore and communicate his feelings during his hospital stay and eventual recovery. While the art therapist could have also introduced drawing or sculpting materials bedside, digital media are an attractive alternative for younger clients like Josh who are adept at learning how to use apps for self-expression.

Finally, tablet technology can also be used to reduce isolation by expanding a child's world when they are not able to leave their room. For example, Malchiodi and Johnson (2013) have used Skype on a laptop computer and FaceTime on an iPad to allow children to participate in events that they could not attend in person or to visit a friend in another room. This technology allowed these children to connect with others, an important element in maintaining wellness during a hospital stay.

Ethical and Legal Issues in Tablet Technology

Although ethics of digital art therapy are discussed in detail in Chapter 2, because the rapid emergence of digital technology is influencing art therapy in hospitals, a specific discussion is included here. Two areas of key importance to art therapy practice are briefly summarized: secure storage and confidentiality.

Secure Storage of Art Created with Apps and Tablet or Mobile Technology

Secure storage of images and pediatric patient data is an ongoing concern. With the advent of telehealth procedures, physicians and other professionals now routinely use handheld computers to record patient data; these devices have software that encrypts data to provide safe storage of sensitive information. Encryption does not ultimately solve all problems of secure storage, though, because devices may be synchronized with other computers that must encrypt data as well (Plovnick, 2010). For example, if a child uses tablet technology and art apps in the context of art therapy, procedures and policies for secure storage must be made in advance. They may include backup on a remote site, hard drive, or a CD or DVD, or in the form of print images. Just like the accidental breakage of a clay sculpture, if a young patient damages a laptop computer or iPad or if it malfunctions or "crashes," any artwork or confidential information created through apps may be permanently lost. A special casing for a tablet or laptop is highly recommended, to prevent not only damage but also electronic loss of artwork or data that may be impossible to recover.

Confidentiality and Tablet Technology

Confidentiality is a complex area for art therapists using any form of art expression in hospital settings, including digital technology. While there are many aspects to consider in working with pediatric patients, there are two major ones for practitioners using digital media in psychosocial care. One challenging aspect of using apps on devices like iPads with multiple children involves protecting the confidentiality of previous users. In other words, when a child uses a computer or tablet to create an art expression, any images must be stored in a way that prevents the next patient having access to them. Because online sites are recorded as "history" on most devices, this is a complex issue; it may require the therapist to constantly delete logs or anything that can be used to track the activities of the previous user.

The second major concern involves social networking sites and Internet platforms. While young clients may be encouraged to utilize social networking to enhance social support and share their stories (and art expressions) with others, participation in social media is difficult to monitor. It is challenging to advise children and adolescents about when sharing information with other young patients is helpful and when it may be counterproductive or compromising. The same holds true for display of digital photographs and films on sites such as Flickr or YouTube. Public display of these digital art forms can provide a sense of pride, mastery, and self-efficacy under certain circumstances; for a pediatric patient who is confined to bed at home or in a hospital, this type of self-expression can be critical to a sense of empowerment and connection. On the other hand, any public exhibition of art expressions by patients also brings up issues of boundaries, confidentiality, and unpredictable adverse effects. Digital art expressions, photographs, and films, in contrast to traditional art expressions, can be transmitted easily and downloaded by others who can alter their content or post them to other sites. Rice (2009) notes that cyberspace does not "forget"; once something is uploaded to a site, downloaded, or viewed, a record of the event or image is always somewhere on the Internet. In contrast, tangible art expressions (drawings, paintings, collages, or sculptures) can be securely stored or even destroyed if necessary.

Conclusion

Apps and tablet technology are changing landscapes; new technologies are constantly emerging that improve apps or change the way this technology is delivered to users. For the foreseeable future, it seems that digital media are here to stay and while apps are not the only way to create imagery, they are becoming ubiquitous for communication and expression. As art therapists and others who address the psychosocial care of individuals continue to explore digital media in their work, it is likely that new and exciting apps will emerge, including a few that are specifically designed for art therapy. Until then, practitioners must continue to explore just how the unique characteristics of digital art-making apps can enhance self-expression while also considering the limitations and risks of use. Apps will undoubtedly continue to expand individuals' artistic vocabulary—and art therapists will continue to discover the potential therapeutic and expressive uses of these fascinating digital media.

Recommendations

- Experiment with art-making apps; it is the best way to learn about their possible use in intervention and identify their limitations.

- Consider the unique confidentiality issues associated with using tablet technology with clients, and in particular children. Review Chapter 2 to identify ethical challenges and how to ensure secure transmission and storage of images created on tablets.

- Recognize that while apps can support creative expression, the use of digital devices can create technology overload in some children. Review Chapter 4 on the impact of digital technology on child and adolescent development for specific guidelines and recommendations.

References

Choe, N. (2014) An exploration of the qualities and features of art apps for art therapy. *The Arts in Psychotherapy 41*(2), 145–154.

Kim, S. (2017) *Computational Art Therapy.* Springfield, IL: Charles C. Thomas.

Klorer, P.G. (2009) The effects of technological overload on children: An art therapist's perspective. *Art Therapy 26*(2), 80–82.

Malchiodi, C.A. (2000) *Computer Art Therapy: A Virtual Studio of Possibilities.* London: Jessica Kingsley Publishers.

Malchiodi, C.A. (2011a) Art therapy materials, media, and methods. In C.A. Malchiodi (ed.) *Handbook of Art Therapy* (2nd edn). New York, NY: Guilford Press.

Malchiodi, C.A. (2011b) Art therapy with combat military. In C.A. Malchiodi (ed.) *Handbook of Art Therapy* (2nd edn). New York, NY: Guilford Press.

Malchiodi, C.A. (2012, February 26) Art therapy: There's an app for that. Retrieved on April 1, 2018 at www.psychologytoday.com/blog/the-healing-arts/201202/art-therapy-there-s-app-1

Malchiodi, C. and Johnson, E.R. (2013) Digital art therapy with children in hospitals. In C. Malchiodi (ed.) *Art Therapy and Health Care.* New York, NY: Guilford Press.

Matteson, D. (2015) Usability assessment of a mobile app for art therapy. *The Arts in Psychotherapy 43*(1), 1–6.

Plovnick, R. (2010) The progression of electronic health records and implications for psychiatry. *American Journal of Psychiatry 167*(5), 498–500.

Potash, J.S. (2009) Fast food, art, talk show therapy: The impact of mass media on adolescent art therapy. *Art Therapy 26*(2), 52–57.

Rice, J. (2009) *The Church of Facebook: How the Hyperconnected are Redefining Community.* Colorado Springs, CO: David C. Cook.

Vithani, T. and Kumar, A. (2014) Modeling the mobile application development life-cycle. In *Proceedings of the International MultiConference of Engineers and Computer Scientists* (Vol. I), IMECS, March 12–14, Hong Kong, China.

12

VIRTUAL REALITY ART THERAPY

Jeff Lohrius and Cathy Malchiodi

What **is** Virtual Reality?

In its simplest sense, virtual reality (VR) describes a three-dimensional, computer-generated, and interactive environment that can be explored by an individual. That individual essentially becomes part of the virtual world and is immersed within the VR environment with the ability to manipulate it in various ways or perform actions within it. VR uses either virtual reality headsets or multiprojected images that may be combined with environments, objects, or props. The individual using this equipment can view the artificial world and move around in it and interact in it; this is usually accomplished through a VR headset that has a small display screen directly in front of the individual's eyes or externally through specially designed rooms with large screens and projection systems. VR may include vibrations, sounds, and other sensations, also known as haptic systems.

Virtual reality was first developed at Massachusetts Institute of Technology in the mid-1960s and the core components really have not changed that much since that time. In VR, a computer generates an image, a display system produces sensory information, and a tracker device provides data on the individual user's position and orientation in space. However, in the 21st century there is much more sophistication and an increasing number of advanced features.

Virtual Reality and Mental Health

Freeman *et al.* (2017) observe:

> A technological revolution is approaching. At the forefront may be virtual reality (VR), a powerful tool for individuals to make new learning for the benefit of their psychological wellbeing... VR can produce situations that can be therapeutically helpful if used in the right way but near impossible to recreate in real life; VR allows repeated, immediately available and greater treatment input; and VR can reduce inconsistency of treatment delivery. (p.2393)

Many practitioners now believe that VR has tremendous possibilities in mental health intervention because numerous disorders involve challenges in interacting within the world; posttraumatic stress reactions, phobias, and anxiety disorders are just a few of the problems that Freeman and his team believe can be addressed through VR.

According to mental health professionals who are using VR as a treatment, the advantage is that individuals know that it is not real, but their bodies and minds respond as if it is real. In other words, people can much more easily encounter difficult situations and interactions through VR than through the real world and their ability to try out new responses and behaviors is increased. In many ways, it is similar to exposure therapy, a type of behavior therapy often used to treat anxiety and phobias (Botella *et al.*, 2015). In brief, like VR, exposure therapy involves exposing a person to something distressing, but within a safe environment in order to overcome the distress. In VR, this can involve directly encountering the feared situation via embodying a first person avatar or experiencing the fear more remotely from a third person point of view.

In particular, VR exposure therapy is also used to ameliorate posttraumatic stress disorder in individuals who are recovering from combat trauma (Valmagia *et al.*, 2016). The virtual exposure activates the memories of distressing experiences so that they can be revisited and addressed, resulting in reduced hyperactivation and other symptoms. This type of approach is believed to improve engagement with military personnel who may avoid treatment due to stigma (see Chapter 9 to read about the Bravemind program).

Pediatrics is another growing area of application for VR. For example, the Starlight Foundation (2017) uses VR to help children with cancer and other illnesses to "teleport" through immersive experiences that inspire imagination and improve quality of life while hospitalized. Starlight collaborates with media like the *Star Wars* film series, allowing children to "become" *Star Wars* characters; it incorporates Google technologies such as Google Earth and Tilt Brush for adolescent participants.

Two Art Therapists' Personal VR Journeys

Case Example 12.1

Jeff

I have always wanted to bring the new tools of digital media into the art studio (outside of the exclusive realms of game and film studios). During my graduate studies, my internship offered me an opportunity to integrate digital art tools into the existing program framework at a juvenile diversion program providing teens an alternative to going to court. I used a digital tablet, painting and photo software, and biofeedback games. Working on my thesis project, I began to see the therapeutic potential of taking an art therapy consumer from initial 2D art creation to a short final computer animation. I was inspired by the work of filmmaker Chris Landreth and his concept of psycho-realism which speaks to the expression of inner states through outer computer-animated metaphors.

The sessions progressed using the model of a computer animation pipeline. Beginning with the preliminary stages of storyboards and building clay models, the client was able to expand upon the initial imagery of an art-based evaluation and enter into a deeper relationship with the content. Next, audio was recorded of the client narrating their feelings about different elements of Self and their relationship to these parts. Unfortunately, at this point the client was dismissed from the program and needed to enter a rehab program. We were just beginning to bring the traditional images and characters into the computer to build models to be animated and would have needed a significantly greater amount of time to complete this part of the animated pipeline.

Despite not yielding a final product, the process proved to be transformative for the client. There was a creative continuum from initial concepts and symbolic equivalents to realizing those expressions in fully formed animations. You could stop anywhere along the way and realize that the process itself was effective in promoting healing, transformation, and personal growth.

After graduation, I ran a studio to help other art therapy consumers experience the healing potential of the creative continuum. Clients found digital art and computer animation compelling parts of the journey. However, I was still struggling to reach outcomes due to time constraints and technical complexity. VR was the key that would finally unlock technology's potential for expression. Not only does VR make computer painting, sculpting, and animation significantly more fast, intuitive, and accessible, it adds new dimensions of real-time interactivity and presence. I am just beginning the journey of integrating these new tools into the art therapy framework. Engaging with the technologies of my childhood, I could only dream of a day where we could step inside the imagination and be present within a work of art. Now it is a reality and VR's potential for healing, connection, and self-expression is only limited by what we can imagine.

Case Example 12.2

Cathy

My experience with VR is twofold. Since I have always been fascinated by aviation pioneer Amelia Earhart, fighter pilot Chuck Yeager, and Chesley "Sully" Sullenberger who landed a commercial plane on the Hudson River in New York, I finally took a leap of faith (and perhaps foolishness) to learn aviation. In order to become a recreational pilot, flight simulations are an important part of the training and a regular part of maintaining my aviation license through VR practice runs. In brief, a flight simulator is a VR device that artificially recreates airplane flight and various environments and flight scenarios, and it is a standard part of training. Like other types of VR, it reproduces factors such as turbulence, wind shear, cloud cover, and precipitation, giving the "pilot" the experience of vibrations and sensations of actual flight conditions. While I doubt I will ever get to experience it, my VR fantasy is to use a flight simulator to make a successful water landing just like Sully Sullenberger.

My other VR experience involves my work as an art therapist and expressive arts therapist with active military and veterans. Most of these individuals have been identified as having posttraumatic stress reactions and/or traumatic brain injury. As previously mentioned, one approach currently used within the treatment of military and veterans to resolve these conditions involves exposure therapy. As an art therapist, I have sometimes used verbal exposure therapy together with art therapy as part of interventions with returning soldiers who are challenged by posttraumatic stress reactions (Malchiodi, 2011). Many of these individuals have previously experienced VR technology that prepared them for combat through immersion in possible situations of battle and confrontation. Similarly, one of the VR programs I have used in the treatment of posttraumatic symptoms is an immersive series of virtual scenarios in an Afghan city within a desert environment, reproducing the dangers and actual events encountered by soldiers. Like the VR programs described in this chapter, it uses a headset and includes not only visuals, but also sounds, vibrations, and even smells. While I am still a novice in the use of this technology, the positive impact this type of virtual exposure has on alleviating trauma reactions is fascinating and it demonstrates the value of VR in reparation and recovery from posttraumatic stress. I look forward to more exploration on just how expressive arts can be infused into this technology.

Virtual Reality Art Therapy

VR presents an innovative new frontier of expressive, embodied, collaborative art-making tools that are highly applicable to the field of art therapy. The emerging practice of virtual reality art-making has the potential to empower, engage, and enable art therapy consumers in innovative ways. Until the very recent emergence of high-end, rotational, and position-tracking VR headsets with hand presence controllers, three-dimensional digital artistic expression required advanced software, skills, and training. In contrast to a flat, two-dimensional screen, VR art-making is immediately accessible, user-friendly, and intuitive. Like traditional art expression that occurs within three-dimensional spaces, VR is similar to creating within the "real world."

VR seamlessly allows for fluid, gestural motion of the physical body within the virtual environment through use of cameras and sensors that work in tandem with the headset and hand controls to produce a large trackable area. Additionally, hand devices offer haptic feedback such as vibration when pressing, pulling, and grasping virtual objects. The ability to utilize full-body movements to draw, paint, and sculpt within actual three-dimensional space is a natural way to convey a concept or an emotion (Felnhofer *et al.*, 2015) that was not possible with other digital tools. VR opens up the kinesthetic realm, getting clients up from their chairs, moving, and physically engaged in their art-making.

Looking into and experiencing the 3D stereoscopic, VR closely mimics real-world experience which naturally enables comprehension of scale and depth. Your body automatically relates to the virtual object through physically manipulating the object with your hands via controllers. Spatial arrangements of art scenes within the VR canvas can be used as a facet of the artwork itself (Lang, 2016). Creators can immerse themselves in their art, walk around, through, and inside their piece. "The work of art is no longer just an object to contemplate but it is one that we can explore and become part of" (Lee, 2016). Entering into their artwork, clients can explore and understand fantasies, dynamically participating in their own creative and unconscious processes (Ehinger, 2015).

VR art-making shares a number of novel aspects with other digital tools. The abilities to undo, redo, create with symmetry, and record the art process are examples of digital art components that VR art applications have integrated into their early framework. At the same time, innovative features have been introduced, such as Tilt Brush's reactive brushes which respond dynamically to sound— to give life and action to a scene, dictated by the choice of music (Lang, 2016). For example, Tilt Brush essentially allows the artist to draw and paint in 3D space by using a variety of different brushes; they range from traditional pen and brush strokes to special effects such as lightning and fire. The complexity and dynamic quality of the brush strokes can yield rich visual metaphors for art therapy clients when combined with VR.

Another element included in many VR art applications is the ability to have multiple individuals create in the same VR environment. This opens up the potential for art therapists to be part of the client's work, make third-hand interventions (Kramer, 1986), as well as conduct VR group sessions. Collaborative open studio approaches are possible that can enable individuals who live in different locations to come together within a common online VR art-making space.

Therapeutic Qualities of VR

When using VR tools for therapeutic engagement, certain characteristics stand out as unique by virtue of the inherent properties that emerge in experiencing virtual reality. The ability to identify these attributes allows the art therapist to leverage consciously create conditions and directives that play into the strengths of VR. The following section describes the therapeutic qualities of VR that can support art therapy.

Presence/Immersion in VR Space

The most compelling attribute of virtual reality is the sense of being viscerally present and immersed in a distinct virtual place. By donning the VR headset, clients enter another space without distraction; attention and concentration on the task at hand are enhanced. This environment can be personally absorbing, containing only tools, materials, and an infinite canvas that are ideal for art creation. In this sense, VR can act as spatial container, offering a safe haven and refuge for rehearsing new behaviors. From personal experience and work with clients, wearing a VR headset creates an intimate space that can facilitate therapeutic transformations infinitely more nuanced and malleable than being confined to the material space of the office or studio. For example, a scene from the client's life or possible scenarios or challenges can be created with VR art tools and then inhabited, rearranged, and transformed. Externalizing internal parts, emotions, and memories can also be explored in this way, similar to exposure therapy.

The VR space can potentially act as a holding environment that has characteristics which support positive attachment experiences.

Synesthetic feedback can transmit a sense of repair and re-patterning of early attachment wounds. For example, apps such as Tilt Brush allow for a dynamic movement of brushstrokes that can be synchronized to a nurturing sound such as a heartbeat through use of audio reactive brushes.

Shared VR Space

VR is powerful in shaping shared therapeutic connection with another individual or group. This allows the art therapist to enter creators' artwork and witness its creation; for example, this can include watching the client create the work in 360-degree volumetric space. Once the art is complete, therapist and client can experience, occupy, and explore the artwork together.

Some VR apps also allow for the possibility of multiple individuals participating in art-making within the same virtual space. This creates options for shared collaboration in the form of an art therapy group or open studio approach. Right now the options for creating a virtual avatar for self-representation are limited in VR art apps. As additional features are added, how individuals present themselves in the virtual art space will add additional layers of self-expression.

Scale

When you are present in a virtual space at true 1:1 human scale, there is a strong visceral effect with regard to size. Every object and brushstroke is self-referential and can be manipulated to be tiny or enormous. Clients may also want to scale an image of a challenging person, situation, or environment down to fit safely in the palm of their hand. Conversely, they may scale a VR representation of themselves up large to feel more agency and power. The fact that scale becomes immediately malleable can be a potent force in the therapeutic art process.

Scale is also important with regard to the size of the actual VR artwork. The client can create an entire world over multiple sessions that can span huge virtual distances. Some apps contain a teleport option to travel around work that is too big to walk around. Viewers can be invited to explore and discover rather than just look and observe.

Body Movement/Interaction

Unlike other media, VR provides the experience of becoming more fully present as an actively engaged participant. Creating art in VR is very gestural and the user immediately feels their body fully involved in the art-making process. There is a sense that you are physically part of the artwork or that it is an extension of your form. Clients can engage in embodied learning that includes cognitive activity and increased use of senses, reinforcing growth and change in a holistic way.

The ability to have your hands within virtual space opens up therapeutic possibilities. Moving, holding, and manipulating virtual objects is extremely intuitive and lifelike. Performing these actions digitally on a 2D screen contains a level of abstraction that disengages the user from the creation process. To hold a tool or object and manipulate it in space feels direct and lifelike, allowing the user to feel present and connected. When creating a human figure in VR there is the ability to just step inside the drawing, painting, or sculpture to get a feeling of embodying the form, proportions, and pose. This is a poignant and emotional process that connects the artist intimately in a representational way. The process approximates a body tracing or making a papier-mâché body mold, but then being able to virtually transform the figure.

Physics

In VR, real-life physics are completely malleable with regard to properties such as gravity, weight, and mass. Making actions in VR with hands and body—pushing, pulling, grasping, throwing—can display novel characteristics. For example, a normally heavy object may float or an individual may be capable of flying.

Playing with the laws of nature may heighten awareness about the rules that govern personal behavior. For example, exploring and experiencing pliability within the VR environment can impact users' real-world mindset and behavior; rigidity and limited thinking can be expanded and transformed through the empowering plasticity of virtual reality creation.

Perspective

Taking different perspectives and points of view is an important component of therapeutic change. Participating in a VR environment naturally enhances possibilities for experiencing different perspectives. Many VR art apps feature camera modes that users can position third-person angles (e.g. outside the viewer, higher in perceived space, and looking down at an avatar or at a "floating-above view"). Individuals can see themselves creating from this vantage point if they look at a second two-dimensional screen. Spectators within the VR space and watching on screen can witness the artist create. VR art-making becomes a kind of performance art when configured this way.

When creating a first-person avatar and navigating in VR space, many social worlds allow you to "jump out" into a third-person point of view. This allows the user to navigate between being in a direct embodied relationship and a feeling of watching from a distance (while still controlling the avatar). While VR art apps are still at a basic level and do not have multiple avatars, at some point they will have this feature.

Conducting an Initial Virtual Reality Art Therapy Session

Once you understand the expressive power and potential of VR art-making and have the equipment to make it possible, how do you facilitate a therapeutic experience for another? Here are some preliminary steps for getting clients inside and immersed in the VR world, feeling comfortable with the equipment and free to move and create.

Introduction to VR Art through Google Cardboard

The easiest way for VR art therapy consumers to understand art-making is to experience it firsthand right at the start of a consultation. As a practitioner, you could provide complimentary Google Cardboards (as business cards) or just have one on hand for this purpose. There are a number of good websites and apps to show

VR art. This provides a good foundation for introducing the higher-level art-making equipment.

Calibrating Equipment

The next step is to introduce the head-mounted display (HMD), sensors, and hand presence touch controllers. The first thing to show the client are the various straps and how to adjust the headset for a comfortable fit. Then explain what to expect from looking into the lenses and adjust them so that the client can see clearly. Lastly, explain sensor layout, the guardian system, and where to move around. Modern HMDs such as the Oculus Rift make setup very easy and fast, which is important when working within the time constraints of a consultation.

Introductory VR Art-Making Experience

With many great VR art application options, it's helpful to briefly explore what initially appeals to the client. Apps such as Tilt Brush and Quill are good choices for drawing and painting. For building and sculpting, Blocks and Medium are accessible apps to start with. There are also animation apps such as AnimVR and Tvori that allow for brushstroke, object, and camera movement. Some clients may be more hesitant to jump in and create. Self-image and identity-altering apps such as Mindshow and EmbodyMe may be a more comfortable introduction to VR and its creative possibilities.

Finishing Artwork, Witnessing, and Checking In

At this point the VR art therapy consumer has viewed examples of virtual reality artwork, has gotten comfortable with the equipment involved, and has had an initial experience creating art in VR. The next step is to check in with them with regard to how the consultation went and how you can support and empower them through further sessions. Witnessing the artwork together and sharing insights is a good way to conclude.

Ways to View Virtual Reality Artwork with Google Cardboard

Google Cardboard (Figure 12.1) is a very powerful tool for artists and art therapists for this reason: it allows the viewer to *view* art that was created in VR to really get an experience of what it looks like even if they don't yet have access to the high-end tools to *create* it. The following sections will give readers some basic ideas about how to use Cardboard, which is available for purchase online for less than $10 USD. Several apps and websites have emerged that allow users to both upload VR art made with high-end equipment and contemplate the art in VR with a Google Cardboard viewer. If you don't yet have access to a headset and hand presence controllers, this is a great entry way into the virtual world of VR art.

Figure 12.1
Google Cardboard

Sketchfab

SketchFab is a large repository of 3D art that is available both as a website and an app. To view artwork is as simple as clicking on a piece and waiting for the file to load. One thing to keep in mind is that sometimes there is a large amount of data to load the file and it could take some time depending on the Internet connection speed. Some of the elements that have to be rendered are polygons, textures, colors, lighting, and sometimes animation. Once you have Google Cardboard and a smartphone available, you can click the VR viewer icon in the lower right-hand corner. When you hover over the icon it will say "View in VR," which will enter you into VR mode. Your phone will change into a split screen and have an arrow in the top left corner, instructing you how to insert the phone into the Google Cardboard.

Google Poly

Poly is a website that was created by Google to host VR art that was made in their VR apps Tilt Brush and Blocks. Once you click on a piece, the navigation to view the artwork on your screen is exactly the same as Sketchfab. To enter VR mode, you click on the VR viewer icon. Some artists allow their creation to use a feature called "remix." When a piece is made public and remixable, any other user can save the file, open it in their version of Tilt Brush or Blocks, and then proceed to add their own creative touches to it. Once this is done, the user can upload the new version, which is a fun way to play with interpretation and perspective, acting as a type of response art. Sometimes an individual will start a piece with a single element and encourage multiple users to remix it, creating a chain of creative collaboration.

Instamuseum

Instamuseum is an interesting website created by Sketchfab that allows the user to upload their Instagram images and create a 3D virtual art gallery to house them. Once you connect your Sketchfab account you can enter your Instagram information and choose from a few options for how your layout should look. The algorithm will take a few minutes to build your gallery and then give you a web address link to view the finished product. Once you visit your new page, navigating your artwork on screen or in VR is the same as any other file in Sketchfab.

Conclusion

This is a very brief overview of VR and its many possibilities to enhance the delivery and practice of art therapy. As noted earlier in the chapter, VR presents an innovative new frontier of expressive, embodied, and collaborative art-making tools to support therapeutic engagement and self-exploration. Like traditional art expression that occurs within three-dimensional spaces, VR is similar to creating within the "real world," yet also provides the unique experience of being immersed within the artistic and therapeutic process. We are currently on the threshold of numerous and far-reaching innovations in the area of VR and it is exciting to see these possibilities becoming a part of the virtual art therapy digital toolbox.

Recommendations

- Google Cardboard is a great place to start your own personal experiences with VR. You will quickly begin to understand the immense possibilities that more sophisticated VR technology offers our work as art therapists.

- Learn more about current uses of VR in exposure therapy and mental health; this brief chapter provides a few starting points, including applications for posttraumatic stress and hospitalized children.

- Consider the embodied experiences VR has to offer and how these types of multisensory experiences can support therapeutic engagement and rehearsal of positive behaviors and responses, and provide new learning opportunities for clients.

References

Botella, C., Serrano, B., Baños, R.M. and Garcia-Palacios, A. (2015) Virtual reality exposure-based therapy for the treatment of post-traumatic stress disorder: A review of its efficacy, the adequacy of the treatment protocol, and its acceptability. *Neuropsychiatry Disorders and Treatment 11*, 2533–2545.

Ehinger, J. (2015) Filming the fantasy: Green screen technology from novelty to psychotherapy. In L.J. Cohen, J.L. Johnson, with P.P. Orr (eds.) *Video and Filmmaking as Psychotherapy: Research and Practice*. New York, NY: Routledge.

Felnhofer, A., Kothgassner, O., Mareike Schmidt, M., Heinzle, A. *et al.* (2015) Is virtual reality emotionally arousing? Investigating five emotion inducing virtual park scenarios. *International Journal of Human-Computer Studies 82*, 48–56.

Freeman, D., Reeve, S., Robinson, A., Ehlers, A. *et al.* (2017) Virtual reality in the assessment, understanding, and treatment of mental health disorders. *Psychological Medicine 47*, 2393–2400.

Kramer, E. (1986) The art therapist's third hand: Reflections on art, art therapy, and society at large. *American Journal of Art Therapy 24*, 71–86.

Lang, B. (2016, September 11) Artists are taking to "Tilt Brush" with incredible results. Retrieved on April 1, 2018 at www.roadtovr.com/artists-taking-to-tilt-brush-with-incredible-results-virtual-reality-art

Lee, C. (2016, December 3) Painting a new perspective: How virtual reality is transforming art. Retrieved on April 1, 2018 at www.techradar.com/news/painting-a-new-perspective-how-virtual-reality-is-transforming-art

Malchiodi, C.A. (2011) Art therapy with combat military. In C.A. Malchiodi (ed.) *Handbook of Art Therapy* (2nd edn). New York, NY: Guilford Press.

Starlight Foundation (2017) Starlight VR. Retrieved on April 1, 2018 at www.starlight.org/starlight-programs/starlight-vr

Valmagia, L., Letif, L., Kempton, M. and Rus-Calafel, M. (2016) Virtual reality in the psychological treatment for mental health problems: A systemic review of recent evidence. *Psychiatry Research 236*, 189–195.

13

SOCIAL NETWORKING PLATFORMS AND SOCIAL MEDIA

Cathy Malchiodi

Social networking platforms are technically not "tools" found in a proverbial digital art therapy toolbox. In fact, most art therapists and mental health professionals may not have perceived social networks and social media beyond forms of communication and information sharing. Art therapists, just like counselors and psychotherapists, usually use social networking platforms to communicate with colleagues and to promote their services as well as widen public exposure of the field of art therapy. In other words, social networking is used as a way to advertise to the marketplace, elevate status in the eyes of peers, build independent practices and consultation services, and promote the value of their field to the public. This is understandable because art therapy as a profession is often still misunderstood; social networking is also a relatively low-cost way to promote one's services and reach an extensive audience through available digital media.

Additionally, art therapists use social networking to display personal artwork for response from peers (Malchiodi, 2009) and in somewhat altruistic ways for the purpose of sending art supplies or even handcrafted items to support those in need. For example, Operation Sock Monkey (2017) assists with humanitarian efforts through volunteer-created sock monkeys (dolls crafted from socks) that are sent to children and adults around the world. But as mental healthcare professionals, art therapists' purpose in social networking and social media is beyond simply leveraging it for personal gain or carrying out charitable "arts as social action" programming. The purpose of art therapy is to provide psychotherapeutic services to others; therefore, it is essential to understand how we can use social networking with their therapeutic interests in mind.

Considering the widespread use of social networks and social media by clients and their undeniable role in 21st-century human interactions, these platforms may actually support therapeutic goals for some individuals. But can practitioners successfully integrate social networking platforms within the framework of an art psychotherapeutic relationship? The short answer is this—it's complicated. However, as telehealth, virtual reality, digital storytelling, and other digital media continue to expand, it is likely that at least some art therapy services will involve not only digital technology but also social networking platforms.

As discussed earlier in this volume, practitioners have focused on the ethical, clinical, and professional questions that have emerged with increased use of social networking and social media (Alders *et al.*, 2011; Belkofer and McNutt, 2011; Malchiodi and Cutcher, 2012, 2013, 2014, 2015; Miller, 2017); readers are referred to Chapters 2, 3, and 4 in this book for a broader discussion of those issues. This chapter instead explores the intersection between social networks to support actual art therapy services to clients and how these platforms, applications, and sites may become part of the psychotherapeutic process for individuals seen in treatment. A brief review of current social networks and recommendations for practitioners is presented as well as several examples of how social networking can be adapted for use with client populations.

An Overview of Social Networking Platforms, Applications, and Sites

As discussed in Chapter 1, social networking is the use of digital communication to engage with others while social media are actually the information (text, images, films) you upload through various social networking platforms. These two terms are often used interchangeably to describe creation and exchanges of user-generated content through digital means. Forms of social networking and social media include, but are not limited to:

* sites such as Facebook and LinkedIn
* blogging platforms such as Wordpress and Blogger
* microblogging sites such as Twitter and Tumblr
* instant messaging applications such as Facebook Messenger and Snapchat
* communication platforms such as Skype, Zoom, and FaceTime
* content-sharing sites such as YouTube, Flickr, Digg, Pinterest, and Instagram
* discussion sites such as Yahoo! Groups and Google Hangouts
* online course development and content management platforms such as Moodle, Thinkific, and Teachable
* livestreaming such as Facebook Live, Periscope, and Lifestreaming
* virtual worlds such as Second Life
* online support group platforms such as Daily Strength, Turn2me, and Anxiety and Depression Association of America (ADAA) Online Support.

These platforms, applications, and sites continue to change and also disappear completely as newer technologies emerge and preferred ways of digital communication evolve over time. Because the majority of individuals now use one or more forms of social networking or media to communicate (Pew Research Center, 2017), therapists should have a working knowledge of them in case a technology-based approach is compatible with client needs and preferred ways of communication.

A Brief Review of Ethics and Social Networking

Because social networking is a rapidly evolving domain for communication and connection, art therapists and mental health professionals are still determining just how to integrate these platforms into work with clients. As discussed in Chapter 2, art therapy and counseling ethics codes have only recently been revised to include guidelines on social networking and social media. Before determining if social networking platforms can be integrated into one's psychotherapeutic work, it is important for all practitioners to review the following key practices:

* Carefully examine the role of social networking in your personal and professional life and establish separate social media accounts for professional and personal information sharing.
* Learn about privacy settings on your social media accounts and do a periodic "check-up" to see if your privacy settings are meeting your needs and current ethics codes.
* Create your own social media policy and consent for clients (see Appendix 4).
* Keep track of changes to social networking and social media rules and regulations as determined by your credentials and licensing boards.

Finally, remember that the Health Insurance Portability and Accountability Act (HIPAA) of 1996 (US Department of Health and Human Services, 2017) (see Chapter 2) plays a central role in any communication with clients via social networks or applications of social networking and social media within the framework of therapy in the US; always consult with your country's regulations for transmission or exchange of client data. The key issue in the use of any digital communication is the possibility of invasion of privacy or breach of confidentiality; in brief, therapists ensure that social media communication does not include any content from therapy sessions or diagnostic information. HIPAA does, however, allow clients to authorize informal communication with therapists if written permission is given. While most therapists prefer to interact with their clients through more secure forms of communication, there will undoubtedly be more individuals who wish to use them as ways to relay information to helping professionals as social networking continues to proliferate. Kaplan (2011) notes that although therapists may hesitate to use social media, in some cases the "question should be asked, 'is this particular tool the best way to help this specific client with this specific need?'" (p.4). In other words, some situations may call for traditional methods of interaction while others may involve technology; in all cases, the goal is always to protect the client and to keep that individual's best interests in mind.

Social Networking and Social Support

One of the key reasons social networks may have a place in art therapy is because there is some evidence that they can enhance a sense of social support for some individuals. Social support is key to maintaining physical and mental health over the lifespan; it is well accepted that it increases the quality of life, providing protective effects with multiple positive outcomes. More recently we have learned that it is also necessary to enhance resilience when exposed to stress or traumatic events, decreasing symptoms of trauma-induced disorders (Masten, 2014). In brief, social support provides a sense of belonging, increased feelings of self-worth, and a sense of security through access to assistance, advice, or guidance. Many of these experiences can now be found through connection and communication with others via many online social networking sites (Wright, 2016).

While we still do not completely understand the impact of social networking and social media on human relationships (see Chapter 4 for a detailed discussion), it is clear that it can be a positive form of social support in specific situations. For example, some individuals struggling with anxiety or depression appreciate anonymous peer-to-peer support through connecting with other people who are having the same experience. For individuals living with illness in rural areas, online networking with a helping professional may be the only means to access treatment if disability and distance are barriers to regular office visits. This type of networking may take place via telemedicine, as described in Chapters 9 and 18, or may utilize other forms of digital communication such as specially designed private groups (see examples later in this chapter).

I often recommend reputable support group sites as a possible adjunct to treatment because I have personally experienced online social support firsthand and can vouch for at least some of the value found in some social networking groups. As a result of a family member diagnosed with a rare disease, I recently began to search the Internet, not only for information on the condition but also for any help for caregivers and family members of patients. Fortunately, there was not only a good source of reliable medical information, there happened to be a "closed group" (membership through screening by the group administrator) that I subsequently joined as a caregiver. The group's day-to-day dynamics have provided a learning experience about how much networking groups can contribute to the lives of those facing challenging situations. While a survivor of cancer can find face-to-face support in most locations, people with rare illnesses cannot and find themselves feeling that no one, including medical personnel, can really understand their struggles, symptoms, and psychosocial challenges. Similarly, my husband who is a research scientist facilitated a support group for individuals with another relatively rare condition through a secure social network that used an online "bulletin board." Patients and their families could post information, share stories, and ask questions; the online board also served as a way to track individuals who had this disease or were at genetic risk of being diagnosed with it in the future.

The more widely known social networking sites like Facebook have a wide array of support groups. If you and your clients talk about online support groups, remind them that even when joining groups on a platform like Facebook, what others can see depends on how they have their privacy settings set and whether the group is open (anyone can see the discussions) or closed (participants are admitted by request or invitation and discussions cannot be viewed by the public). Even when joining a closed group, others may be able to see that they are participants in these groups. When clients tell me they have joined a closed group, I remind them that nothing posted on the Internet is totally private and to consider what types of information they are sharing (e.g. test results and diagnosis or location and personal data).

As an art therapist, I also have a discussion with clients about sharing artwork online in support groups or various creativity groups (e.g. visual journaling groups). These groups can provide tremendous encouragement and empowerment to participants; on the other hand, any images posted to any social network platform, even when deleted, become part of the Internet or may be downloaded by others. In particular, I ask clients not to post images created during their art therapy treatment, emphasizing that these images are really part of their "medical record." I realize that this is difficult for many clients because social networking provides a place to exhibit artwork that clients may be proud of or want to share because the images tell their stories of reparation and recovery to others. But sharing any images created in the course of therapy in even a secure online forum has its risks and it is essential that therapists have this discussion with clients to explore the pros and cons of digital sharing.

Art Therapy + Happiness Project

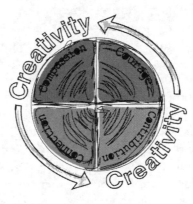

Figure 13.1
Art Therapy + Happiness Project logo
Design courtesy of Josh Kale[1]

The Art Therapy + Happiness Project (ATHP) (2012; Malchiodi, 2015) is an example of utilizing a social networking format to bring together a self-selected community of art makers; it specifically focuses on the intersection between visual self-expression and positivity. It is based on principles found in positivity psychology (Seligman, 2012), resilience research (Masten, 2014), and self-compassion (Neff, 2011). The course logo (Figure 13.1) represents the conceptual framework and four positive forces emphasized within the curriculum— connection, compassion, courage, and contribution—and the overarching experience of the creative process. Three art therapists (the author and art therapists Janet McLeod and Emily Johnson Welsh) co-facilitate the programming. To date the program has been offered three times with up to 500 individuals participating in the online platform. This description introduces ATHP to potential

---

1   www.joshkale.com

participants through social networking platforms such as Facebook, LinkedIn, and Twitter, various blogs, and electronic newsletters:

> We believe that art making can make us "happier" through four positive forces that help us to be more resilient when challenged by life events, big and small. These Four Positive Forces are: *Connection, Compassion, Contribution and Courage*. We all can use our own *Creativity* as a positive force that inspires and motivates us to deeply *Connect* with others, experience *Compassion* for others and ourselves, make *Contributions* that are meaningful and life-affirming, and have the *Courage* to tell our stories and speak our truths. In the Art Therapy + Happiness Project, we will be rolling out new activities, techniques and ideas to stimulate your creativity and positivity through the next 4 months. You will be able to download print materials, view films that inspire and teach concepts, view photos and images created by participants, and interact with like-minded creative spirits from around the world. (Trauma-Informed Practices and Expressive Arts Therapy Institute, 2012–2018)

This is just one example of the many activities introduced to the group, using the conceptual framework illustrated in the course logo (Figure 13.1) from the course site:

> Where do you find community, connection, courage and contribution? These four positive forces, as described by Cathy Malchiodi, can help us be more resilient when challenged by life events, big and small. This community focuses on these as key elements that can be framed, shaped, and informed by creativity in our lives. For this first activity, please introduce yourself to the group through these four words and create your own Wheel of Creativity. The image of the wheel, whether described as a circle, mandala, pie, plate or lens is prevalent in both our cultural and natural worlds! This shape is believed to bring balance, movement, and focus when used in art

> making. (Trauma-Informed Practices and Expressive
> Arts Therapy Institute, 2012–2018)

While the ATHP integrates best practices that underscore approaches found in art therapy, the program is not intended as psychotherapy and includes a disclaimer that explains this to all participants. Some basic guidelines for participation are also necessary at the outset of any online programming that involves participant interaction, including the right to remove anyone who violates the community rules for "netiquette" (networking etiquette) with other individuals participating in the program. Facilitators can draft these guidelines based on the needs, intent, and structure of an online group. However, there are a variety of good models already available for online participation; there is an evolving *Code of Conduct* found on Creative Commons (2018) that outlines basic guidelines for communication and behavior and can be revised to fit specific programming or online communities.

Like many similar online artmaking communities, ATHP is self-guided; that is, it is up to participants how much they wish to engage in various art processes and activities. Here is a sample description that introduced this concept to participants:

> This course is self-guided—that means you can participate as much or as little as you want to. There are a number of projects that you can visit by clicking on the links in the menu. We will be adding new projects as we go along and these will also appear in the menu. All projects will remain available for viewing and participation until the end of the year. In order to keep you informed about new projects, we will be sending you regular e-mails to prompt you to return to the Art Therapy + Happiness Project website so that you can see the new content. Each project has a description of the activities and many of the projects have downloadable documents that you can print out from your computer. Each section also has a "sharing and comments" feature so you can post images and comments on your own process and reply to others in our community.[2]

---

2   https://www.trauma-informedpractice.com/online-live-courses/art-therapy-happiness-project/

Although the majority of ATHP takes place online through participants' posting of images and comments, one of the most popular features of the program is a periodic "art swap" conducted through regular mail. Those members of the community who want to exchange art sign up to do so, committing to create and mail a small artwork to a specific group of individuals who, in turn, send art to them. The art swap items are designed to fit into a regular letter-sized envelope to reduce costs of postage for participants. Interestingly, although most of the ATHP experience took place through digital communication and social networking, the popularity of the art swaps underscores that participants still crave the person-to-person connection found through receiving an "old-fashioned" way of communicating—a letter that contains a tangible art object that one can touch, hold, and view in real time as opposed to virtual communication and relationships.

One thing I have learned from developing and launching a variety of online learning and participatory experiences is something very common to virtual platforms: only a subset of those who register for an online course or even a support group will actually participate and stay with the program. However, this does not mean that participants are not accessing the material; they just may not feel comfortable in posting comments or images to the program site. Also, because online learning like ATHP is self-guided, people do find it more difficult to stay focused and attentive; one of the challenges of online programs is long-term participation. Weekly or bi-weekly updates with information about current content and links to new activities and documents can help to keep participants involved. However, if your online programming is free (no fee charged), then there is often a very high attrition rate, possibly because a monetary investment, even a small one, encourages people to "get what they paid for."

Finally, ATHP uses a social networking platform known as Ning, which allows people to upload images and contribute to discussions. Participants are notified by e-mail from the site each time a new project or activity is introduced by the facilitators.

"Drip content" is another option and is available on some education and learning management platforms; in other words, the facilitator can preset time frames to send notifications (drip) about new activities and content automatically. This allows the facilitator to install an entire course curriculum, yet only allows participants to access it at specific times (e.g. once a week, bi-weekly, or monthly).

Resiliency and Art Therapy Group for Military Partners/Spouses

Based on what I continue to learn from ATHP, I have developed additional online programming specifically for client populations. Part of my work as an art therapist involves developing expressive arts "resiliency" programs for active military personnel and their families. One of the more successful parts of that programming is an ongoing group for wives of soldiers, many of whom have to manage homes and children on their own while a service member is on duty.

Because many of the participants had moved away from the base where we held our original resiliency group, they suggested that they could benefit from staying in touch with others with whom they had formed connections. To address this need, I received permission to set up a platform for a time-limited group to be conducted online. In creating such a group, my first consideration was technology—secure, user-friendly, and reliable. Fortunately, the military base where I see clients was able to set up a secure platform similar to the one used in ATHP, but with video features so that the six group members could see not only me but also each other.

Commitment and follow-through is strong within military personnel and their families, so group members agreed to participate in all eight online sessions. An activity and short reading about resilience was provided each week before the scheduled online video session, so our time together in online sessions was used to discuss what was learned and to share art images, rather than make art as we did during the face-to-face resiliency groups. While this was somewhat of a drawback, participants decided that they would rather use the time online to share stories and hear from each other; they valued the chance to share their creative output and were motivated by others to complete assignments to share with others via video. Like ATHP, participants also requested an art swap based on the one they had experienced in the original face-to-face group; this particular swap involved the creation of decorated playing cards based on the themes of self-compassion and courage (Figure 13.2). While video communication was appreciated by participants, most also indicated that the swap helped them to feel connected to others in the group through the tangible creations that reminded them of the emotional support they received from each other.

Figure 13.2
Decorated playing cards for online resiliency program "art swap"
Images courtesy of Cathy Malchiodi

A Moodle-Based Psychoeducational Group for Chronic Pain Patients

Moodle (*m*odular *o*bject *o*riented *d*ynamic *l*earning *e*nvironment) is a free, open-source learning management system that is available to anyone who wants to set up distance education, and is used by universities and businesses. It has customizable features that include a variety of options to load text, post documents, films, and PowerPoints, add quizzes, request short feedback responses, and upload assignments including images. Groups and "galleries" can be included so that users can interact and post comments and questions. Numerous plugins are available that can extend the features of a Moodle site; these plugins can be downloaded free of charge from the Moodle website.[3] While Moodle is a no-cost platform that can be accessed by anyone, it is important to understand that it does involve an initial steep learning curve. There are online tutorials

---

3   www.moodle.org

that are helpful because Moodle does require some advanced understanding to construct an effective course or learning experience. Once learned, however, it is quite versatile and is, for the most part, user-friendly for participants.

At the request of a pain management clinic, I designed a psychoeducational program for patients with chronic pain issues using Moodle as the platform; like the resiliency programming described in the previous section, a secure, password-protected site was used and only individuals who were cleared by the clinic were given access. These patients had a variety of conditions resulting in back, hip, or joint pain to headaches such as migraines or tension-related conditions. Because Moodle can be structured to allow users to participate as individual learners, patients who registered for the program could access it at their own pace and remain anonymous to other users. The program included six "modules" (topics) ranging from self-assessment of pain to mind–body techniques; each module provided a downloadable summary of the topics covered and additional self-care strategies.

An optional part of the program involved several hands-on art activities, including using body outlines to track pain and simple drawing exercises for stress relief. Patients who participated in the online activities had the option to post their work to the site for review by the facilitator or share comments and impressions in a group forum open to all participants. While not all participants chose to use this option, for those who did, it added a dimension to their experience and learning. Surprisingly, several of these participants decided to opt for art therapy services as a result because they were surprised at what they learned about their pain and its management through simple drawing activities and online sharing with cohorts.

Conclusion

Social networking is now a ubiquitous presence, not only in personal communications but also in professional interactions with many clients. Fortunately, there is emerging evidence that it provides benefits to the practice of art therapy, although it also brings challenges. While art therapists may simply see social networking and social media as platforms to advertise services or promote the profession, when we keep our clients' needs as our first priority, our understanding and exploration of how social networks may help clients will continue to emerge. I hope this brief overview and examples of psychoeducational and therapeutic applications inspires more therapists to explore and design new platforms and to consider the multiple ways that we can provide support to our clients through creative, engaging, user-friendly, secure, and ethical social networking experiences.

Recommendations

- Rather than viewing social networking and social media as platforms for self-promotion, marketing, or social action, consider the possibilities for how to use these means of digital communication in the service of clients.

- Explore the variety of online support groups to learn more about how these forms of digital communication can enhance social support for some client populations.

- Periodically review your credentials and/or license board current regulations for social networking and social media interactions with clients. Also, review your own social network accounts and review your privacy settings.

- Participate in an online artmaking community through social networking; firsthand experience is an excellent way to learn more about how or if a social networking platform may be beneficial to your clients and under what circumstances.

References

Alders, A., Beck, L., Allen, P.B. and Mosinski, B.B. (2011) Technology in art therapy: Ethical challenges. *Art Therapy* 28(4), 165–170.

Art Therapy + Happiness Project (ATHP) (2012) Welcome to the Art Therapy + Happiness Project. Retrieved on April 1, 2018 at www.trauma-informed practice.com

Belkofer, C.M. and McNutt, J.V. (2011) Understanding social media culture and its ethical challenges for art therapists. *Art Therapy* 28(4), 159–164.

Creative Commons (2018) *Code of Conduct*. Retrieved on April 1, 2018 at https:// wiki.creativecommons.org/wiki/Slack/Code_of_Conduct

Kaplan, D. (2011) Legal and ethical issues surrounding the use of social media. *Counseling and Human Development 43*(8), 4–13.

Malchiodi, C.A. (2009, November 2) Art therapy meets digital art and social media. Retrieved on April 1, 2018 at www.psychologytoday.com/blog/arts-and-health/200911/art-therapy-meets-digital-art-and-social-multimedia

Malchiodi, C.A. (2015, May 31) The Art Therapy + Happiness Project. Retrieved on April 1, 2018 at www.psychologytoday.com/blog/arts-and-health/201505/the-art-therapy-happiness-project

Malchiodi, C.A. and Cutcher, D. (2012) Issues and ethics of art therapy in a digital age. Retrieved on April 1, 2018 at www.slideshare.net/healingarts/digital-art-therapy2012-presentation-by-cathy-malchiodi-phd-and-don-cutcher-atrbc

Malchiodi, C.A. and Cutcher, D. (2013) Art therapy and ethics in a digital age. Retrieved on April 1, 2018 at www.slideshare.net/healingarts/digital-art-therapy-and-social-media-ethics-cathy-malchiodi-phd-lpat-lpcc-reat-atrbc-and-donald-cutcher-atrbc

Malchiodi, C.A. and Cutcher, D. (2014) Art therapy and ethics in a digital age. Retrieved on April 1, 2018 at www.slideshare.net/healingarts/digital-art-therapy-and-social-media-ethics-2014-cathy-malchiodi-phd-lpat-lpcc-reat-atrbc-and-donald-cutcher-atrbc

Malchiodi, C.A. and Cutcher, D. (2015) Ethics and art therapy: How do art therapy ethics measure up? Retrieved on April 1, 2018 at www.slideshare.net/healingarts/ethics-and-digital-art-therapy-presentation-with-cathy-malchiodi-phd-and-don-cutcher-atrbc

Masten, A. (2014) *Ordinary Magic: Resilience in Development.* New York, NY: Guilford Publications.

Miller, G. (2017) *The Art Therapist's Guide to Social Media.* New York, NY: Routledge.

Neff, K. (2011) *Self-Compassion: The Proven Power of Being Kind to Yourself.* New York, NY: HarperCollins.

Operation Sock Monkey (2017) About OSM. Retrieved on April 1, 2018 at www.operationsockmonkey.com/about

Pew Research Center (2017, May 17) Tech adoption climbs among older adults. Retrieved on April 1, 2018 at www.pewinternet.org/2017/05/17/tech-adoption-climbs-among-older-adults/#

Seligman, M. (2012) *Flourish: A Visionary New Understanding of Happiness and Well-Being.* New York, NY: Simon and Schuster.

Trauma-Informed Practices and Expressive Arts Therapy Institute (2012–2018) Art Therapy + Happiness Project. Retrieved at www.trauma-informedpractice.com/online-live-courses/art-therapy-happiness-project

US Department of Health and Human Services (2017) Health information privacy. Retrieved on April 1, 2018 at www.hhs.gov/hipaa/index.html

Wright, K. (2016) Social networks, interpersonal social support, and health outcomes: A health communication perspective. *Frontiers in Communication 1*. doi: 10.3389/fcomm.2016.00010

3

Clinical and Educational Applications

14

UTILIZING DIGITAL ART THERAPY WITH HOSPITALIZED YOUTH

Mary K. Kometiani

The role of normalized and prevalent technology has changed current society and how people live; individuals are reading, learning, socializing, creating, and communicating through modern technology in daily life. Children are going online at a young age, accessing media in an entirely different way; they are experiencing a social and technological revolution (Hicks, Grimson, and Smith, 2013). Therefore, clinicians must possess flexibility, creativity, and openness in their therapeutic practice while providing the best treatment for patients. Because contemporary society has influenced the way therapists practice, digital art therapy should be examined and evaluated for its healing potential and the numerous benefits to a wide range of clients including hospitalized youth.

Art therapists have been writing about the importance of using digital art therapy in the clinical setting for the past several years (Carlton, 2014; Choe, 2014; Malchiodi, 2009). In a busy and advanced setting like a pediatric medical hospital, utilizing digital art in art therapy services is a fundamental and often preferred method because of its convenience and options for bedside application, ease of sanitization for hygienic purposes, mobility, and affordability. Facilitating art in technology draws on an ever-increasing range of art applications (apps), appropriate for all age groups from beginners to advanced fine artists.

Digital art making offers many of the same features as conventional art media (Malchiodi and Johnson, 2013), if not more possibilities through vast color choices, multimedia options, widespread sharing, and in using an extensive number of images found on the Internet for collages. Digital art media provide an avenue for success-orientated art making, an effortless way to fix errors, and maximum artistic freedom, all in a compact format that is easily operated and offers a large memory for storage (Darewych, Carlton, and Farrugie, 2015). They have the advantage of lack of odor, mess, and texture, a benefit for tactile-sensitive patients, while promoting autonomy for individuals with developmental disabilities who may be intimidated or unable to work in traditional media. Digital media are preferred for clients who are overwhelmed by sensory stimulation or who may consume non-food objects (Alders *et al.*, 2016). Digital art therapy is recommended for individuals with intellectual disabilities and sensory issues, and those who are not able to use art supplies during treatment due to infection risks, paralysis, body positioning, or lack of stamina.

This chapter provides an overview of several digital art apps and how hospitalized youth have benefited from using technology in art therapy. Several case examples are given of applied digital art therapy. Lastly, the chapter explains some of the ethical considerations and unique challenges of using digital art therapy in the hospital setting and provides recommendations for best practices.

Digital Art Therapy with Hospitalized Youth

It is widely accepted that creative art therapy improves the quality of life in pediatric patients (Madden *et al.*, 2010). Research has demonstrated that art therapy improves patient mood and decreases pain, stress, and nausea (Chapman *et al.*, 2001; Madden *et al.*, 2010; Siegel *et al.*, 2016). Art therapy is an effective and dynamic avenue that addresses issues of anxiety and the emotional impact of medical diagnosis (Nesbitt and Tabatt-Haussmann, 2008). Medical art therapy communicates patients' needs, wishes, and experiences in a meaningful form of response to hospitalization; this aids in the patients' mastery over disturbing events and transforms their sense of wellbeing (Councill, 2012). Whether the art therapy session leads to an expressive artwork or just some mark making, art is a tangible response to illness, reflecting on life beyond hospitalization (Councill, 2012). Medical art therapy has clear and compelling benefits including symptom management, emotional catharsis, and providing meaning.

Like medical art therapy, digital art therapy provides experiences similar to traditional art therapy in hospital settings, including:

- active and engaging processes that address pain, aggression, exhaustion, stress, nausea, and depression experienced by pediatric patients
- choices (apps, paint programs, photography, film) and opportunities for expression of feelings and reflection about diagnosis and hospitalization
- stimulation during times of boredom
- normalization of medical experiences
- empowerment by giving pediatric patients control
- promoting medical treatment compliance
- hope in the future by giving children and youth relevant ways to express reactions to medical procedures, hospitalization, and illness
- improvement of quality of life and personal wellbeing.

There are generally two broad approaches to using digital art therapy in the hospital setting: stimulation and/or relaxation, and psychotherapeutic digital art making. First, digital technology can simply be stimulating and/or relaxing for pediatric patients. This includes experiences of what may be only brief engagements with colors, lines, textures, sounds; apps may serve as ways to relax during painful procedures, prevent boredom, or initiate the therapeutic relationship by appealing to the patients' interests. As a way to reduce stress and provide an opportunity for self-regulation, art therapy apps can be explored.

Case Example 14.1

Jocelyn, aged nine, was referred to art therapy during her hospitalization to manage her pain crisis from her sickle cell anemia diagnosis. She was extremely apprehensive about receiving needle sticks; the art therapist provided her with the iPad as a form of relaxation to exhibit control over her anxiety. She engaged with the Bloom app, allowing her to choose colors and sound, and focus on creating a pattern composition rather than her stress and pain. This allowed Jocelyn an opportunity to support her self-regulation skills, reduced her tension in preparation for the upcoming medical procedure, and encouraged treatment compliance.

Psychotherapeutic digital art making has the same goals as art therapy with traditional media; it engages the patient fully in therapy and the artwork represents the individual's innermost thoughts and feelings. The hand-held device makes this type of art perhaps even more personal than paper formats as every move is deliberately made determined by the individual, starting with the color and size of image. This form of digital art therapy is personally affirming and can help make meaning out of the hospitalization while coping with the many facets of illness.

When Jocelyn's disease progressed, she received a bone marrow transplant and was in isolation for weeks, with restrictions to protect her from infection. The tablet was a safe alternative that could be easily sanitized as it posed little infection risk. Jocelyn was an expressive and enthusiastic patient, interested in art therapy even when her energy was low and she was in pain. There were times when she could barely sit up in bed from her discomfort, so traditional art supplies would have been too difficult for her to use and would have required too much energy.

When provided with an iPad, Jocelyn frequently engaged with the Educational ZoLO Creative Play Sculpture app that supplied a gallery of colorful shapes and symbols to choose and manipulate. She often used the decorative figures to symbolize her family and their traditions of gathering together, and made several images of her mother with her siblings at meal times as this was a sacred time for her family to gather (Figure 14.1). Digital art became the way for her to cope with being apart from her family unit due to her illness and treatment, and to express her feelings of loss that accompanied her hospitalization. The art therapist facilitated spontaneous opportunities for her to create remembrances of feeling loved, secure, and together with her family. Jocelyn was able to express her emotional needs in the art therapy session and, through her vibrant digital art, maintain a lively connection with her family who could not be present due to caring for her siblings.

Figure 14.1
Jocelyn's collage of her family dinner

Digital Art Therapy Media with Hospitalized Youth

Drawing and Painting

Digital drawings and paintings offer techniques and settings that are similar to traditional art supplies with children and adolescents in hospitals. These drawings and paintings can be created with a finger, mouth stick, mouse, stylus, and/or digital brush. Depending on the art app used, different settings allow for variations in opacity, pigments, layering, and thickness. The pressure used in drawing and painting are replicated in the process and there are often ways to adjust the precision as well as add smudges to blur the lines within the digital drawing. In technology, the undo feature is very helpful in painting and drawing, making digital errors easy to fix.

Using one's finger in art making is similar to using traditional drawing materials (Diggs, Lubas, and De Leo, 2015) while using a stylus replicates drawing, erasing, and shading. An art pen stylus provides pressure sensitivity and tilt sensitivity to drawing movements, and a pencil stylus allows for a tactile experience similar to a pencil, providing ways to shade, change line thickness, and adjust pressure, very much like an ordinary pencil. The stylus can serve both as a tool for drawing and for erasing, making artists feel as if they are using a lead pencil (Diggs *et al.*, 2015). These tools allow precision in detail and are receptive to the patient's force and speed. Used in coordination with an art app, brushes have the following options: straight brush tip, angled brush tip, or precision tip for different mark makings and control while creating. Although such tools are not required for digital art therapy, they can enhance the experience of art making and technique skill-building.

Flexible, mobile devices have transformed the lives of those who have severe medical issues, providing new avenues for recovery and a new sense of control and empowerment. For those with motor control impairment, there are plenty of adaptive tools available for digital art making too. There are various options for mouth sticks that patients can use to direct movement and control. Adaptive stylus straps for an individual's hand enable a better grip and make drawing easier for those who have fine motor control issues. In addition, a "light pen," a mechanism that uses a light detector to select choices and make art on a tablet, is helpful for those who do not have the ability to put pressure on the screen (Malchiodi and Johnson, 2013). There are also advanced ways to use voice control and speech recognition with technology. These devices serve a population often overlooked and underserved; these clients require accommodating tools to participate in art therapy.

Case Example 14.2

Palliative care patient Destiny was a six-year-old who had been diagnosed when she was a toddler with the rare neurological disorder transverse myelitis and was left paralyzed as a result. Although she was not able to move her hands to make art, Destiny was quite an artist as she was able to manipulate a mouth stick with her tongue and mouth in various ways to achieve different techniques with painting. Destiny enjoyed using the iPad art apps for drawing and painting and would often paint colorful images of the outdoors. Her images of rainbows and cloudy skies were symbols of peace and beauty. Although she was not able to participate in typical outdoor activities, art allowed her a powerful means to express herself, feel supported, and develop a new sense of mastery. Her art making and creations brought her family together as they encouraged her, recognizing her strengths and ability, and shared in appreciating her creative vision. Art allowed her to make the unbearable bearable; her images communicated her acceptance of her illness through the cohesion and inclusion of the vibrant colors. She showed keen interaction with nature and her images reflected that she was not only a witness but also was a part of the beautiful, living world.

Collage

Collage is a non-threatening, effective, engaging, adaptable, and expressive medium; collage facilitates storytelling through both the conscious and unconscious minds in addition to expressing emotions and thoughts (Diggs *et al.*, 2015).

Case Example 14.3

Sarah, an eight-year-old girl, had been in a car accident and suffered from trauma and severe laceration. She underwent many surgeries to repair her abdomen; she had a drain site closed with tubes and bottle, and besides difficulty managing her pain, she could not sit up for many therapy sessions during her long hospitalization. Using the iPad for collage, she was able to effectively engage with art making even with her restricted movement and while lying down in her hospital bed. As she was hospitalized for many months and missed celebrating a lot of holidays, digital collage was a way of celebrating with her family and friends from afar by making their photos and holiday icons into cards as presents. Sarah's collage work facilitated candid storytelling about her loved ones, providing her with an opportunity to express feelings of empowerment and hope for discharge from the hospital and her reunion with her family.

Photography, Film, and Video

Digital photography is cost effective and allows for simple editing and instantaneous results without requiring the use of darkroom and chemicals (Peterson, 2010). Special effects such as cropping the image, changing color scheme and tones, adding text, editing faces to enhance or drastically change appearances, and other manipulations are easily applied, experimented with, and adapted. A benefit of using digital photography is that the young patient can demonstrate many different techniques on the original image but can always go back to the original with the undo function; this is not possible without the use of digital technology (Thong, 2007). Digital photography also offers many possibilities for alterations such as adding color modification filters and changing color saturation, in addition to offering the possibility of addressing several therapeutic medical art therapy goals. Using digital photography in art therapy is an expression of the perspective of the patient, a form of reflection and meaning making; the art offers a sense of control, and builds skill in a developmentally appropriate manner while learning new technology (Malchiodi and Johnson, 2013). Image metaphor and the emphasis on perspective in photography are also useful tools for the art therapist when processing the picture with clients.

Case Example 14.4

Mike, an adolescent diagnosed with end stage renal disease, received dialysis three times a week while waiting for a kidney replacement. During his dialysis treatments, he suffered from pain, cramping, decrease in blood pressure, and fatigue. The position of his arms, which were restricted by tubes that carried blood to and from the machine, affected his mobility, making it difficult for him to engage with traditional art supplies while receiving dialysis. Patients who have end stage renal disease are at higher risk for impaired health-related quality of life, psychosocial complexity, and lower educational achievement because the disease and its management have a profound effect on the physical and emotional functioning of daily life (Tjaden et al., 2016). Art therapy goals for individuals on dialysis focus on providing coping strategies, stress management, active listening and support, medical compliance, and self-expression (Schreibman, 2013).

The art therapist was always welcomed by Mike during his dialysis treatments and provided a supportive presence and active listening to Mike, who revealed that spirituality and prayer were very important to him. However, there were times when he was not feeling well enough to create art or when the machines, and the medical procedures the staff needed to do, would not permit him to physically participate. When he did participate in art therapy, he seemed to prefer simple and efficient ways to engage before his fatigue overpowered him, disengaging him from a session.

During a memorable session, Mike expressed his connection to his dialysis room. As he had spent countless hours in this dialysis room, he felt an attachment to the mural of an eagle against a background of light blue clouds. He sensed a connection to the bird and its symbolism as he felt the eagle's presence through his treatment. He expressed an interest in wanting to use the eagle as a subject in his art. Using the Doodle Booth app, Mike cropped a photograph of the mural for his desired perspective. The app also enabled him to add decorative elements to the photo; he typed part of his favorite Bible verse: "but those who hope in the Lord will renew their strength. They will soar on wings like eagles; they will run and not grow weary; they will walk and not be faint" (Isaiah 40:30, New International Version). This quote connected Mike's stages of treatment to his faith; his art symbolized the hope he maintained in regard to receiving a kidney and his continued patience and fortitude while progressing in his treatment journey.

All photos represent a type of self-portrait and are a reflection of past and future personal narratives (Weiser, 1999), and Mike's digital art portraying the photograph of the dialysis room mural clearly represented his focus on his dreams and goals for the future. Mike's artwork (see Figure 14.2) provided him the means to process his situation and his hope that he could endure his illness and live fully in the future. The metaphor of the eagle in his self-portrait symbolized his eventual freedom from his disease and its seemingly endless treatment schedule; he hoped to soar like the eagle pictured in the image.

Figure 14.2
Mike's self-portrait of hope and freedom

Film

Kid Pix Studio is a multimedia workspace available for computers and is a current and popular program for filmmaking. While engaging in this program, young artists may use many different tools to create a virtual show: draw with pencil, line device, paint bucket; add a background setting, stamps, text that speaks, characters that move and talk, and sounds that unify the animation of the entire piece created. Children can use this program to quickly create a short movie after making several choices.

Case Example 14.5

The consequences of not attending school regularly because of frequent scheduled medical appointments created the basis for psychosocial issues for Mike; as a result, he developed a strong imagination and fantasy life. Watching movies was one way he connected to others and to a life outside his home and the hospital. He enjoyed action movies about superheroes and he was particularly drawn to Kid Pix Studio. Using this program, he was able to create a setting, characters, and a battle plot of good versus evil just by making several clicks on the computer.

Mike used movie making as a way of making sense of his disease progression and the battle for health he endured. He used his imagination to represent the attack on his physical being. Aggression is a normal response to the effects of diagnosis, and art therapy is a way to make meaning out of the pain (Councill, 2012). The art therapist witnessed a high level of allegory and metaphor in Mike when he was involved with digital art, communicating his aggression and will to fight against his disease and cope with the physical symptoms. With technology, Mike was able to vent his anger response and remain hopeful by expressing his personal grief over the many losses he encountered due to his illness and make meaning from his journey to overcome the struggle.

Video

Video therapy is a way for the patient to combine storytelling, music, art, and video production to benefit a patient's situation (Kreitler, Oppenheim, and Segev-Shoham, 2012). The patient develops an idea, writes a script, designs the setting, and edits the final film. Using visual storytelling allows the patient to assume the many roles of the author, performer, executor, director, editor, and broadcaster (Kreitler *et al.*, 2012). Video art therapy can help to alleviate anxiety and provide pain management. Unconscious communication is achieved through symbolism while the art provides a fun and satisfying opportunity for mood enhancement and quality-of-life improvement. The ego is strengthened through learning new skills and using a coping strategy (Kreitler *et al.*, 2012). Using the video format in art therapy allows reconnection to emotions as well as adding depth to the metaphor of the movie; this process quickly achieves a therapeutic rapport between the client and art therapy (Alders *et al.*, 2016).

Case Example 14.6

The iMovie app (installed on most Apple operating systems) is an easy approach to movie making with patients that provides a way of processing what is distressing.

Ava, who had been hospitalized for several weeks, was going through many tests as the doctors attempted to identify her illness. She had been suffering from several unusual side effects and had experienced difficulty in keeping up with her school routine due to her symptoms. This eight-year-old patient communicated that she wanted to make a movie about bullying because she was having issues with acceptance from the other students due to the lack of regular socialization and missing so much school. The art therapist supported her through several sessions as she developed the plot, organized her characters from her stuffed animals and handmade puppets, created a background, and assisted with filming her work.

In the movie, Ava's puppets acted out scenes showing a bully harassing a student followed by an intervention from the teacher and an expression of remorse from the bullying student. During this filming, Ava admitted that she had been bullied and how this had negatively affected her self-esteem and self-image. This concise yet evocative movie gave Ava the freedom to be the author, director, and actor, and powerfully and eloquently portrayed her most distressing personal issue. Once the video was complete, the therapist and client were able to watch the video together in a private screening party, and Ava expressed enthusiasm for sharing her video with her family and friends in the future.

Making a movie on a personally relevant topic enabled Ava to give voice to her narrative and construct her own ending. This was an empowering and validating experience that improved her quality of life. Her purpose behind the movie was in sharing her story and in expressing her feelings from this personal and global disturbance; she also communicated to others the effects of bullying and her hope that this troubling practice would discontinue in her school for the wellbeing of other victims.

As these diverse examples demonstrate, digital art provides a modern form of self-expression that addresses medical art therapy goals of treatment compliance, sensory stimulation, pain and stress management, emotional articulation, procedural support, skill building, and empowerment, while providing a sense of control, and normalizing a painful and isolating experience. There is a spectrum of art apps that allows for rapport building and creative expression to communicate the internal worlds of pediatric patients and their difficult and personal medical journeys. While the practices for digital art therapy are only briefly described in this chapter, there is unlimited potential regarding the different uses and applications. Digital art therapy provides an active, engaging process in a flexible format that provides hope, healing, and improved quality of life to children who need it most.

Guidelines for Digital Art Therapy in Medical Settings

As they would do with the introduction of other new art techniques or different art supplies, medical art therapists should familiarize themselves with the materials and tools in order to foresee any issues that might arise in terms of safe and appropriate application, especially in the hospital setting where therapy can be interrupted and private session time is greatly valued. The role of the art therapist does not change, but with digital media, the art therapist must learn about the apps and operation of the various tools: undo, zoom, palette options, text insertion, and additional decorative elements. Adequate preparation by the therapist will ensure that the patient experiences the full sense of the possibilities of digital art in even a brief medical art therapy session. Technology is ever-evolving and requires dedication to stay informed because of the fast evolution of apps, innovation of technological devices, and because the engagement process takes time to learn and master (Malchiodi and Johnson, 2013). The patient will feel confident that the therapist can facilitate the full use of the device as the patient explores the capability of the application and his or her own feelings.

One major challenge in using digital art in the hospital setting is that the work can easily be obliterated and the unfortunate potential for technical difficulty is always present. This unwelcomed loss can be an additional burden on youth who are already facing many losses due to diagnosis and hospitalization. In addition to feeling uncertain about technology and burdened by fear of malfunction (Asawa, 2009), some art therapists might see digital art as isolating, separating the patient from the therapist (Diggs *et al.*, 2015). Sometimes in a medical art therapy session, when a bedbound client holds the iPad, it can be difficult for the art therapist to observe all of the details of the creative process, and a balance is needed between paying attention and hovering when using digital media. Due to its compact size and how the patient holds the tablet, digital art may detach the patient somewhat from the art therapist and the desired experience in the process.

In clinical populations where a choice can be made, the therapist must bear in mind that the lack of sensory involvement with touch and smell can be drawbacks with using technology. However, in the medical setting this can be a preferred approach as patients' senses may be more sensitive. Other criticisms may be that digital art on an iPad is too orderly and is limited in size, although the compact nature of the tablet may be preferred if the patient is immobile or confined to a hospital bed. The lack of mess and the ability to provide infection control are tangible advantages for engaging with digital art in the hospital. Although some art therapists might find the characteristics of digital art being clean, compact, odorless, and contained a challenge, these reasons strengthen the argument for digital art therapy in the medical setting.

Finally, due to the harsh sanitization supplies that are used in the hospital setting, as well as providing the utmost protection for the equipment as it is carried and handled, an all-terrain case is recommended for the iPad. Such cases are resistant to shock, shattering, dust, and water. The hinged plugs protect the ports, connectors, and buttons and the durability of the iPad. The case may also provide a stand that allows the iPad to sit on a table or a lap at an angle comfortable for art making.

Ethical Considerations Impacting Digital Art in Medical Art Therapy

The Art Therapy Credentials Board's (ATCB) (2016) ethics require that art therapists provide an environment that is safe and protective of clients' confidentiality. Medical art therapists are required to protect patient identity at all times, and they must be careful using technological devices, especially in the hospital setting when going from room to room to provide art therapy. Art therapists need to practice utmost caution regarding confidentiality of patient information when using technology in hospitals; this becomes a challenge because some medical units are similar to small communities in that patients know each other, their families, and their medical histories.

When art therapists interact with or store anything that identifies a patient, they are required to use caution and to protect this information. Art therapists should always make sure to check that all of the artwork has been removed from the tablet or device before another session. The iPad can save photos to multiple sources and files, and clinicians should routinely make sure that images have been removed from the app, photo album, and anywhere else the photo might have been uploaded. According to standards of best practice, art expressions are required to be stored in a secure and unidentifiable manner and art therapists are required to inform clients how and where the artwork is stored (AATA, 2013). Therapists are encouraged to keep secure copies of patient artwork on a hard drive or device that is secured and not available to other clients (Alders *et al.*, 2016). Art therapists must inform patients and their guardians of confidentiality and where the respective digital artwork is stored; this can be difficult in a pediatric medical setting because parents are not required to be present during therapy sessions. Additionally, hospitals may have their own regulations for digital artwork storage and art therapists are also required to follow those guidelines.

Conclusion

It is difficult to ignore the computer as an obvious art medium (Thong, 2007) anywhere technology is part of the therapeutic environment. Indeed, technology has changed today's world quickly and drastically and it is challenging to foresee what possibilities will be available in future technological advancements and how they will impact the practice of art therapy. Medical art therapists are encouraged not to overlook this necessary and pivotal change in our field; they should respond to the power of technology and embrace the changes that will inevitably come to our profession and our future clients, especially pediatric medical patients whose ability to participate is enhanced by the advances of creating digital art.

For hospitalized youth, digital devices and software offer unlimited options for making choices, and making these decisions is often the best way to experience control and mastery. Whether through engaging in design composition to channel anxiety, expressing one's faith and hope in the future or a personal struggle, symbolically portraying one's aggression resulting from the effects of a serious medical diagnosis, or illustrating one's perspective of presence in the world, the case examples in this chapter confirm the remarkable capacity of digital art therapy with pediatric medical patients. These young patients are creating and engaging with a contemporary art medium and giving voice to their fears, dreams, and hopes. Digital art offers vast potential for art therapists and their clients and it clearly broadens the tools and widens the practice of medical art therapy. Digital media has the capability to become a principal art therapy tool, restricted only by ethical obligations and imagination (Peterson, 2010). The artist has always embraced new vision, and technology is the lens of the present day.

Recommendations

- Recognize that digital art offers many advantages that can provide meaningful and expressive opportunities for hospitalized patients, including: flexibility; compact size; prompt results; ease of sanitization; limitless choices; multimedia options; lack of odor, mess, and texture.

- Increase your understanding of technological adaptive digital art tools and programs. Digital art especially benefits those who are not be able to use traditional art supplies during treatment due to infection risks, paralysis, or lack of energy as well as those who have intellectual disabilities and sensory issues.

- Like traditional art psychotherapy, digital art psychotherapy produces artwork that represents the individual's innermost thoughts and feelings. It is an effective outlet for anxiety, pain, stress, depression, and aggression in hospitalized youth.

- Be aware that digital art therapy presents ethical challenges within the hospital setting for patient privacy protection; practice caution to ensure confidentiality and use appropriate digital artwork storage.

References

Alders, A., Beck, L., Allen, P.B. and Mosinski, B. (2016) Technology in art therapy: Ethical challenges. *Art Therapy 28*(4), 165–170.

American Art Therapy Association (AATA) (2013, December) Ethical principles for art therapists. Retrieved on April 1, 2018 at www.arttherapy.org/upload/ethicalprinciples.pdf

Art Therapy Credentials Board (ATCB) (2016, September) *Code of Ethics, Conduct, and Disciplinary Procedures.* Retrieved at www.atcb.org/resource/pdf/2016-ATCB-Code-of-Ethics-Conduct-DisciplinaryProcedures.pdf

Asawa, P. (2009) Art therapists' emotional reactions to the demands of technology. *Art Therapy: Journal of the American Art Therapy Association 26*(2), 58–65.

Carlton, N.R. (2014) Digital culture and art therapy. *The Arts in Psychotherapy 41*, 41–45.

Chapman, L., Morabito, D., Ladakakos, C., Schreier, H. and Knudson, M. (2001) The effectiveness of art therapy interventions in reducing post traumatic stress disorder (PTSD) symptoms in pediatric trauma patients. *Art Therapy 18*(2), 100–104.

Choe, S. (2014) An exploration of the qualities and features of art apps for art therapy. *The Arts in Psychotherapy 41*, 145–154.

Councill, T. (2012) Medical art therapy with children. In C.A. Malchiodi (ed.) *Handbook of Art Therapy* (2nd edn). New York, NY: Guilford Press.

Darewych, O.H., Carlton, N.R. and Farrugie, K.W. (2015) Digital technology use in art therapy with adults with developmental disabilities. *Journal of Developmental Disabilities 21*(2), 95–102.

Diggs, L.A., Lubas, M. and De Leo, G. (2015) Use of technology and software applications for therapeutic collage making. *International Journal of Art Therapy 20*(1), 2–13.

Hicks, P., Grimson, J.B. and Smith, O.P. (2013) With a little help from my friends: Experiences of building a virtual community for children with cancer. *Journal of Community Informatics 9*(2). Retrieved on April 1, 2018 at http://ci-journal.net/index.php/ciej/article/view/840

Kreitler, S., Oppenheim, D. and Segev-Shoham, E. (2012) Fantasy, art therapies, and other expressive and creative psychosocial interventions. In S. Kreitler, M.W. Ben-Arush, and A. Martin (eds.) *Pediatric Psycho-Oncology: Psychosocial Aspects and Clinical Interventions* (2nd edn). Chichester: Wiley-Blackwell.

Madden, J., Mowry, P., Gao, D., Cullen, M. and Foreman, N. (2010) Creative arts therapy improves quality of life for pediatric brain tumor patients receiving out-patient chemotherapy. *Journal of Pediatric Oncology Nursing 27*(3), 133–145.

Malchiodi, C. (2009) Art therapy meets digital art and social media. Retrieved on April 1, 2018 at www.psychologytoday.com/blog/arts-and-health/200911/art-therapy-meets-digital-art-and-social-multimedia

Malchiodi, C.A. and Johnson, E.R. (2013) Digital art therapy with hospitalized children. In C.A. Malchiodi (ed.) *Art Therapy and Healthcare*. New York, NY: Guilford Press.

Nesbitt, L.L. and Tabatt-Haussmann, K. (2008) The role of creative arts therapies in the treatment of pediatric hematology and oncology patients. *Primary Psychiatry 15*(7), 56–62.

Peterson, B.C. (2010) The media adoption state model of technology for art therapy. *Art Therapy 27*(1), 26–31.

Schreibman, R.C. (2013) Art therapy and hemodialysis: Coping creatively with kidney failure. In C.A. Malchiodi (ed.) *Art Therapy and Healthcare*. New York, NY: Guilford Press.

Siegel, J., Iida, H., Rachlin, K. and Yount, G. (2016) Expressive arts therapy with hospitalized children: A pilot study of co-creating healing sock creatures. *Journal of Pediatric Nursing 31*, 92–98.

Thong, S.A. (2007) Redefining the tools of art therapy. *Art Therapy 24*(2), 52–58.

Tjaden, L.A., Grootenhuis, M.A., Noordzij, M. and Groothoff, J.W. (2016) Health-related quality of life in patients with pediatric onset of end-stage renal disease: State of the art and recommendations for clinical practice. *Pediatric Nephrology 31*, 1579–1591.

Weiser, J. (1999) *PhotoTherapy Techniques: Exploring the Secrets of Personal Snapshots and Family Albums* (2nd edn). Vancouver, Canada: PhotoTherapy Centre Press.

15

EXPRESSIVE REMIX THERAPY

Engaging Adolescents through the Use of Digital Media Art

Jeffrey Jamerson

This chapter will highlight examples of creative engagement using digital media in a model that I call expressive remix therapy (ERT). I describe and showcase how digital media art is utilized to engage adolescents both therapeutically and educationally. The digital examples can be accessed via URL links and are examples of what one can do using digital media technology/art as a tool with your clients/students.

I have worked with youth in the foster care system for more than 25 years. In the early years of my career I occupied several direct care positions and later in my career I have enjoyed a leadership role in various child welfare programs and services. Throughout my time as a member of direct care staff and supervisor I have envisioned various ways to creatively engage foster youth therapeutically and educationally. Currently I am a vice president at a nonprofit that provides an array of services for children and families in the Los Angeles, California area. Our team of workers are constantly trying to find effective ways to engage youth in services. So much of mental health and child welfare service delivery is "prescribed" to clients by mental health and child welfare professionals and paraprofessionals. At times this prescriptive approach leaves little room for voice and choice by the client or consumer. It is rooted in left-brain thinking and is predicated on a linear process of problem solving.

I believe the preferred language and self-expression of children and youth occur through play and art. However, coming from a world dominated by prescribed models of therapy (evidence-based practices or EBP), I have rarely seen models in child welfare and mental health that come out of expressive play and art. I believe expressive remix therapy is a progressive step in the direction of play- and art-based services for children and youth. It's an approach that utilizes the whole brain and puts an emphasis on art and play as well. As discussed earlier, expressive remix therapy is a mash-up of sorts—not of music, but of academic disciplines. Imagine blending narrative therapy, expressive arts therapy, and digital media art together; that is what ERT is: a blending of those three disciplines.

Expressive Remix Therapy

The key word in *expressive remix therapy* (ERT) is not *expressive* or *therapy*, although these are very powerful words in and of themselves. The key word is *remix*. I view remix as analogous to reframe, rewrite, or revise. It is the process of taking something already in existence and changing it up with a creative twist, transforming the mundane into something novel and fresh. The classic reference of remix comes from the domain of music production. Below is an example of how remix is used in the world of music with soon-to-follow examples of how we use it in expressive remix and narrative therapy.

Before a DJ can create a remix or a mash-up she needs to have an idea of what existing elements to use together. She needs to imagine how different parts of different songs will sound once blended. Then she takes her imagined idea and puts it together, testing it out to see if it is something new, something different that will spark a sense of awe in the listener.

This was illustrated by one of the more famous mash-ups of modern times through the hands of the artist–producer Danger Mouse. Brown (2016) relates how Danger Mouse took works from two seminal artists from different genres and times and mashed them together to create an eclectic innovative album. Danger Mouse took the remixed looped instrumental music from the Beatles' acclaimed *White Album* and the flavor-driven acapella lyrics from Jay-Z's *Black Album*, and mashed them together to generate what he called the *Grey Album*. Most listeners were in a state of bewilderment when they first heard Mouse's *Grey Album* because it was a simple concept yet profound in execution and production (Brown, 2016).

So it is with the approach described in this chapter. Although I am not Danger Mouse, and I am not using music to complete a mash-up, I have envisioned how using certain elements from the disciplines of art therapy, narrative therapy, and digital media art can be blended together to generate a novel modality, a mash-up, that serves and supports adolescent youth. As individual songs in a music mash-up can stand alone and generate a positive response from listeners and dancers, so each discipline discussed above is able to achieve its desired goals of engaging clients/students both therapeutically and educationally. However, with that said, there is also the expectation that the new mash-up or remix will amplify a positive response from practitioners and participants of the expressive remix model. It all starts here with the elements, so let us take a good look at them and see how they fit together in a narrative mash-up.

The Central Role of Stories in ERT

The central theme of ERT is to tell stories and then to remix those stories using digital media, creating art in the process. Words and narratives are not objective facts—they are nuanced, they take on the "color" of the beholder so to say. In other words, they are plastic, dynamic, and mutable. They can be shifted or morphed at the creative will of the person, again like a DJ creatively (re)mixes a standard song. It is my hope that the reader will take away or acquire one or more of the deliverables below:

* Learn how to create new forms of digital art.
* Develop a skill set to remix stories using digital media art.
* Acquire an enhanced ability to reflect/analyze the storytelling process.

An Example of ERT *in vivo*

You might ask, what does this look like *in vivo*? Below is a story I wrote based on a life-changing experience. The first step in the process begins with writing the story down and then figuring out different ways to creatively express (or remix) the story. This story is about a trip I took that was incredibly impactful for me. In 1985, with no job and very little money, I had a dream of visiting Africa. Within a year's time, my best friend and I embarked on a journey that would serve as a catalyst for a major transformation in my life. Here is part of that story.

> Imagine all your sensory detectors simultaneously giving you alarming information, sensations that were out of your normal day-to-day experience. This was my reality when the Dutch KLM 747 airplane that I had just spent five hours on came to an abrupt halt on the tarmac of a relatively small airport in Liberia, West Africa. I peered around as passengers arose from their seats to gather belongings from overhead compartments. I followed suit. An African man next to me smiled and said, "I see you've never been here before." With a puzzled look I responded, "How do you know?"
>
> He let out a small chuckle and said with a deep Liberian accent, "Well, first of all you're wearing a long-sleeve shirt." I pondered this for a moment as the airplane door opened, revealing a dark and moonless night. My mind raced as I walked down the airplane aisle towards the open door, as beads of sweat appeared on my brow. Questions swirled! How could it be this hot at night? Why was it so dark outside? Where was the airport? Then a few lights came into focus, "Oh, there it is," I thought as I located a small terminal across the tarmac.
>
> To blow off some much-needed anxiety I took in a deep breath and instantly noticed that a musty charred scent filled the air. At that point, I realized I was no longer in America. I was no longer in my hometown of Pasadena, California! Once inside the airport my eyes adjusted to the homogeneous sea of black faces, and to the sounds of unfamiliar dialects. This was my first night of what would become seven beautiful and life-changing months in West Africa.

Figure 15.1 shows this story expressed or remixed as a word cloud (an image composed of words used in a particular text or subject, in which the size of each word indicates its frequency or importance). I took the text from the story and pasted it into a digital program to give me the creative picture below. This digital program or application uses an algorithm that gives a weighted preference to duplicated words. The larger words in the picture appear more often in the story. Remixing narratives as word clouds can reveal an important reality about what we say, such as, what are the dominant words being used in our discourse?

Figure 15.1
African adventure word cloud

Again, ERT helps a client create a narrative that can be remixed in multiple artistic ways; it is simply retelling a story in a nuanced manner. In short, I call this *narrative plasticity*; a narrative is malleable, much like clay in the hands of a potter. This nuanced experience of narrative is a form of self-empowerment because one realizes that one is not at the beck and call of narratives, specifically of dramatic or traumatic narratives, but that narratives are at the beck and call of the person who is creatively engaging them in a remix session.

Integrating ERT with Art-Based Approaches

Expressive remix therapy as a modality is effective because it expands the toolkit of professionals. Because of expressive remix therapy, a greater number of therapeutic techniques can be used to bring about a change; if the idea is to shift or change the story, why not use digital art to help accomplish this task? Specifically, this can be done by using images, pictures, and symbols.

Is it not said, "A picture is worth a thousand words"? Remix therapy uses pictures and words; it uses techniques similar to traditional art therapy but goes a step further and digitizes or animates images to create livelier forms of art narrative with which a client or participant can connect. Remember the story of my journey to Africa? The first remix was a word cloud. The link below is the same story now remixed as a kinetic typography piece using three different iPad apps (MegaPhoto, AutoRap, and Pinnacle Pro). I created the audio version of this piece by reading the words from the "Africa" word cloud above into the iPad app AutoRap. AutoRap takes spoken words and arranges them into song.[1]

Another digital intervention that we have utilized with youth is "the animated mask." This intervention blends the use of digital media with a more traditional form of tactile art using techniques like painting and collaging. For example, a participant takes a cardboard mask and decorates it using tissue paper, paint, magazine clippings, various forms of cloth, and beads (Figure 15.2).[2]

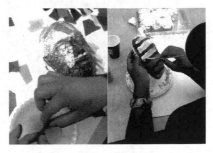

Figure 15.2
Mask-making activity

---

1   www.dropbox.com/s/r51lgkvqe8iv8yr/Africa.mp4?dl=0
2   www.youtube.com/watch?v=aSp2DJ6Hl84andfeature=youtu.be

Digital Media as an Educational Tool for Workforce Development

Youth today are natural experts when it comes to social media. In many respects they are more comfortable texting than chatting face to face. It is second nature for them to navigate Twitter, Snapchat, Instagram, Tumblr, YouTube, Flickr, and more. I began to see this shift while working with clients in school settings in 2006; as a result, I asked myself, why not use the technology that youth are connected to, to deliver service? (Jamerson, 2013).

Apparently, I was not the only one who asked this question, particularly within the realm of education. In 2014 I attended a national conference called DML (Digital Media Learning), held in Los Angeles, California. I was one of 400 attendees there to see how the use of digital media learning is being applied in various inner cities across the United States. The keynote speaker for the event was CNN political partner and columnist Van Jones. In his opening address, he highlighted how a shift in the landscape for employment and career opportunities in the technology field was ever increasing and would become more abundant in the next five years.

Van Jones said there would not be enough qualified people to fill emerging tech positions. He then juxtaposed this by stating how millions of young people of color, mostly African Americans, vie for jobs in professional sports and entertainment that only have a few hundred openings. He went on to tell a personal story of what he says when he meets urban youth who are on a quest to become rappers and hip-hop stars. Van Jones says to many youth like this, "Don't show me your rap, show me your app!" This statement signifies a hopeful shift in the consciousness of young people of color to an industry that has a greater upside than the already saturated industries of sports and entertainment.

Portions of Chicago's urban area have gone through a metamorphosis as small groups called "hives" have begun to surface. Imagine the YMCA or Boys and Girls Club shifting their youth support programming to include an outlet or space for youth to come in and learn about digital technology development. Libraries throughout the city have followed suit by offering weekly classes on coding, robotics, digital music production, and graphic design.

The youth who engage in these classes earn something called a "digital badge," which is a way of acquiring a form of acknowledgement that they possess a skill competency in a certain digital area. With these digital badges, youth can show proof of accomplishment in a digital area to tech companies such as Pandora, Facebook, and Twitter. In the recent past, companies like these would only hire college graduates and very few of these college graduates were youth from inner cities. However, this is changing and so are the interests of Chicago's inner-city youth. Where youth once engaged in after-school activities like sports, they now join digital tech hives instead. For example:

> Hive Chicago is comprised of 85 youth-development focused organizations such as museums, libraries, advocacy groups, higher education institutions, after-school programs and tech start-ups… Guided by the design values of Connected Learning, Hive Chicago programs: engage youth around their personal interests, peer culture and civic participation; focus on production-centered, hands-on making and skill building; harness digital media, technology, and the web to broaden and diversify learning opportunities; offer meaningful and supportive interactions with peers and mentors; and link equitable and accessible learning experiences with schools and communities. (Hive Chicago, 2018)

While in attendance at the digital media learning conference I noticed that much of the talk and many of the workshops were geared around empowering youth in digital learning, literacy, and competency. In the book *The Digital Youth Network: Cultivating Digital Media Citizenship in Urban Communities* (Barron *et al.*, 2014), the authors write:

> The DYN learning model can best be explained as a collection of overlapping affinity spaces within a larger community context. Through a mix of during-school, after-school, and online spaces, DYN provides youth opportunities to develop and apply digital media literacy in ways that are personally and academically meaningful to them. Guided by more experienced student peers and professional adult artists who are also mentors trained in elements of

pedagogy, students produce digital artifacts, share their products, and demonstrate digital media skills and understandings...

The ultimate goal of the DYN learning motto is to prepare students for productive careers, prosperous lives, and civic engagement in the twenty-first century. Three dispositions are cultivated that together are referred to as "digital media citizenship." The curriculum demands that students become (1) critical consumers of digital media; (2) constructive producers of digital media; and (3) social advocates for better futures. (pp.22–23)

Post-Structuralism, Story Control, and Empowerment

Post-structuralism and social justice are two underlying forces of nature that give direction and influence on both narrative therapy and ERT. Seeing the world through a post-structural lens empowers one to control their own story! However, there is a philosophical difference between a structuralist view and a post-structuralist view as each view directly influences the way one sees and acts within the world of helping services in fields such as therapy, social work, and education. The website for the Evanston Family Therapy Center shows a contrasting view of the differences. Below is a comparison adapted from the Evanston Family Therapy Center website.[3]

Structuralist view

- Classifies participants into types or groups.
- Experts have control to make the story.
- Experts interpret and give meaning to participant stories.

Post-structuralist view

- Values a person's self-identity.
- Participants have voice and choice of story construction.
- Participants have power and control of story interpretation.

---

3 www.narrativetherapychicago.com/narrative-worldview/

In short, post-structuralism is an evolutionary step beyond structuralism. This evolutionary step shifts the power of discourse from the so-called expert to the individual receiving the service. Localized and particular stories are very important and it is good to see that post-structuralist forms of inquiry pay attention to personal story.

In light of this shift the quintessential question in ERT is, "Who controls my story?" The quintessential answer, discovered by participants in ERT is, "OMG (Oh my God), I control my story!" This realization is a revelation of sorts that is discovered when a story is externalized and remixed using digital media art. As discussed earlier, although people subjectively construct stories, they are also intensely prone to embrace conventional stories that are part of the status quo of the time and culture.

The embrace of such stories (i.e. other people's stories) can sometimes be toxic and can lead to experiences of social oppression and personal depression. For example, foster youth who have navigated the child welfare system will tend to acquire what I call a *personal pseudo story* in the form of many layers of documentation that appear in their mental health charts. This personal pseudo story is constructed and dictated by the many professionals and paraprofessionals who encounter and work with the foster youth.

A typical or average child welfare or mental health chart can be anywhere from half an inch to two inches thick, including various forms of documentation of everyone else's story of who and what the foster youth is. In other words, social workers, therapists, foster parents, teachers, psychiatrists, and so on, all give their opinion—a story—about the foster youth, and this is what I call a personal pseudo story. The helping professionals create a discourse that foster youth participate in. Combs and Freedman (2012) say it this way:

> In any social group, small or large, we are all participants in each other's stories. We each shape, and are shaped by, the beliefs, intentions, and actions of others. Collectively, we participate in discourses. Rachel Hare-Mustin (1994) defines discourses as "a system of statements, practices, and institutional structures that share common values." ... For post-structuralists, no one is in a position to be an objective expert on someone else's experience. (p.1036)

The challenge here is that not all helping professionals see themselves as post-structuralists; indeed, many still see themselves as experts on other people's situations.

Many foster youth also yield to and embrace the discourses, invisible norms, and expectations of professionals in the child welfare system. Here are examples of bits and pieces of labels (or discourses) that make it into the personal pseudo story of foster youth. These bits and pieces, although constructed from professionals and paraprofessionals, are over time embraced by the foster youth in the form of "I am" statements. For example, it is not uncommon to hear foster youth verbalize the psychobabble coined by their helpers. These verbalizations may include statements such as, "I am a victim of abuse," "I am a victim of neglect," "I have a mental illness," "I am bipolar," "I need medication to be stable," "I am a special education student," "I am not wanted," and so on.

These labels may constitute a form of social oppression, albeit an inadvertent form of social oppression. Intentional or not, the labels return to the central question at hand, "Who controls my story?" After navigating narrative therapy and ERT the answer is, "No, they don't control my story. I control my story." Through a post-structuralist frame such as narrative therapy or ERT, a movement or shift is made away from inadvertent social oppression to purposeful social justice, where the justice experienced occurs because the foster youth learns to gain control of his or her own story. Combs and Freedman (2012) suggest:

> For us it illustrates how people can assert a position as privileged authors of their own lives.
>
> Narrative therapists believe that people give meaning to their lives and relationships through stories. As narrative therapists, we are interested in joining with people who consult (clients) in what White often called "rich story development." We work to facilitate the development, telling, and retelling of stories from people's lives that speak of experiences and intentions that they prefer. Through these tellings, we facilitate experience of possibilities not apparent in the problem story. We are not focused on solving problems, but rather on helping people immerse themselves in life stories that offer different

possibilities and directions than those offered by the problem stories. From within the stories, people's relationships to problems change. (p.1034)

Engaging Adolescent Foster Youth with Digital Media Art

My place of employment has a digital media lab where we offer digital media workshops for adolescent youth. Like the before-mentioned DYN and Hive model, we engage youth working through a post-structuralist lens, teaching them to create their own stories and then remix those stories using digital media. Youth have participated in workshops that range from making beats (music production with Ableton software), digital collage (with Adobe Photoshop®), animated mask, digital storytelling (using iMovie), and superhero creation. The digital media lab is shown in Figures 15.3 and 15.4; Figure 15.5 shows the logic model.

Figure 15.3	Figure 15.4
Beat making 1 in digital media lab (DML)	Beat making 2 in DML

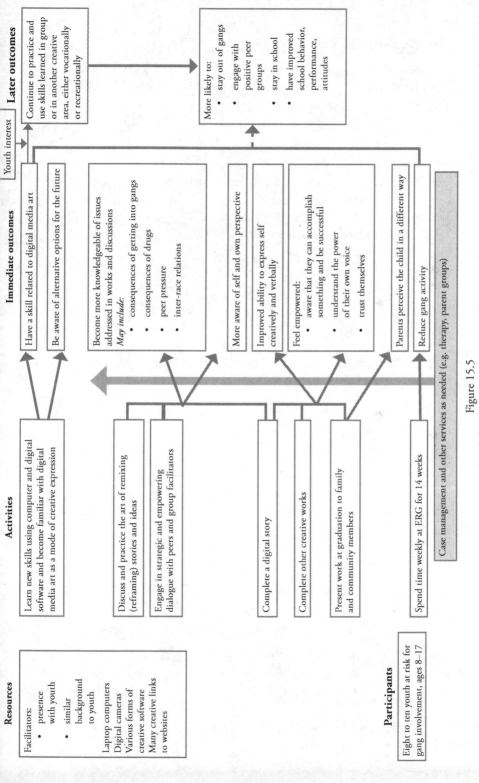

Figure 15.5

Detailed expressive remix group model

Expressive Remix Group Outline

This section provides readers with an ERT outline of weekly activities, including participant goals, objectives and some URL links to video examples of digital activities.[4]

Creative Excursion 1: Digital Storytelling

Week 1: Discuss group dynamics, make rules, explain and demonstrate digital stories.
Week 2: Begin digital storytelling projects.
Week 3: Complete digital storytelling projects.

Creative Excursion 2: Animated Mask

Week 4: Complete CE1, begin creating masks after group facilitator demonstrates process.
Week 5: Paint masks.
Week 6: Complete therapeutic worksheets, use answers as a script to animate the masks.

Creative Excursion 3: Comic Voice, Magazine Cover, Movie Poster

Week 7: Complete CE2. Facilitator demonstrates creation of a comic strip utilizing an informative theme (e.g. bullying, gang violence, teen pregnancy). Participants create their comic strip storylines with the theme as a backdrop.
Week 8: Create mock magazine cover based on their theme from the previous week or on storyline of digital story from CE1.
Week 9: Create mock advertising poster for digital story.

Creative Excursion 4: Virtual World Creation

Week 10: Complete CE3. Facilitator shows examples of virtual world creation. Participants work with software to create a positively themed virtual world.

---

4   www.youtube.com/watch?v=TD02w83CSWoandfeature=youtu.be

Week 11: Participants begin to create their own virtual worlds.
Week 12: Continue virtual world creation, complete project.

Creative Showcase Theatre

Week 13: Complete CE4. Family and friends invited to session to observe and admire the creative art participants have designed.

Participant Goals and Objectives

* Become familiar with digital media art as a mode of creative expression.
* Learn new skills using iPads, smartphones, and digital software.
* Discuss and practice the art of remixing (reframing) stories and ideas.
* Become engaged in strategic and empowering dialogue with peers and group facilitators.
* Complete a digital story from beginning to end.

Digital resources include, but are not limited to, various forms of hardware (iPads, laptop computers, smartphones, and digital cameras); creative software programs; and links to digital art websites and tutorials.

It is not uncommon for individuals who have not had a lot of experience using technology to be intimidated and this has been true with some participants in ERT. In my experience, I felt it was important to conduct orientations and tutorials for participants before they engaged in a digital creative excursion. It was also great to see how many participants took the initial idea of the remix assignment and literally remixed it into something more artistic and rewarding than my original thought. This type of remix—a remix of the remix—occurred in every group session, once again giving credence to the notion of the element of surprise involved when one creates art.

Conclusion

Digital art created in the ERT group has much in common with other forms of art created in therapy as well as art created educationally. In many respects, one of the central occurrences of making art is the element of surprise with what actually gets created. In facilitating the expressive remix group and seeing others facilitate, I have been pleasantly surprised on more than one occasion by the digital art that has been created by participants. What is even more rewarding is seeing the participants' reactions to their digital art creations. Many are speechless after making digital art and when they do finally speak, they express how much fun the process was and that it was easier than their initial expectations.

I hope you find success navigating the world of digital media art in therapy and education with your clients and/or students. I wish you the best as you move the field of helping services forward with innovation.

Recommendations

- Learn how to create new forms of digital art.

- Develop a skill set to remix stories using digital media art.

- Acquire an enhanced ability to reflect on the storytelling process; narrative therapy, post-structuralism and social action are three key concepts in this process.

References

Barron, B., Gomez, K., Pinkard, N. and Martin, C. (2014) *The Digital Youth Network: Cultivating Digital Media Citizenship in Urban Communities.* Cambridge, MA: MIT Press.

Brown, M. (2016) Danger Mouse | biography, albums, and streaming radio. Retrieved on April 1, 2018 at www.allmusic.com/artist/danger-mouse-mn0000674440/biography

Combs, G. and Freedman, J. (2012) Narrative, poststructuralism, and social justice: Current practices in narrative therapy. *The Counseling Psychologist 40*(7), 1033–1060.

Hive Chicago (2018) About Hive Chicago. Retrieved on May 15, 2018 at https://hivechicago.org/about

Jamerson, J. (2013) Expressive remix therapy: Using digital media art in therapeutic group sessions with children and adolescents. *Creative Nursing 19*(4), 182–188.

16

THE ONE PROJECT
Therapeutic Photography with Adults

Bryce Evans

When it comes to helping people to heal, there is an essential first step that often provides a larger hurdle than is necessary for the individual or their counselor/therapist: communication. Our modern society has been mostly focused on words (across many different languages around the world) to express, communicate, and connect so that we can grow and evolve as individuals and as a collective. Problems arise when we encounter the limitations of the words that we're so accustomed to using, especially when this is paired alongside deep personal pain, shame, or trauma.

This is the problem I found myself facing as a teenager dealing with deep depression and anxiety, unable to communicate what I was suffering from and therefore lacking access to the proper resources. It led me to pick up a camera and start releasing it all through my photos as a sort of last resort, opening up a whole new world of possibilities for expressing and reflecting on these ideas, thoughts, and pieces of myself that were repressed for a long time.

After years of working through my own issues in this way, I discovered a specific process that I had built and used, only partially aware of what I was doing at the time. Looking back, I was able to see a set of steps and specific techniques that I utilized with my photography and creative writing that allowed me an easier way to get started talking about depression and anxiety, while working to become more comfortable talking about it and diving deeper into introspection of my identity and its relationship with those issues.

The body of work I created during that time became known as a photo series titled "one," later evolving to become The One Project.[1] There was a lack of conversation at the time around the therapeutic power of photography and how it, along with creative writing, could help provide simple and accessible tools for anyone to use in overcoming issues that are difficult to talk about. This chapter explores how therapeutic photography supports mental health wellness through The One Project, a platform for helping individuals experience healing through personal photography.

A Global Trend in Communication and Therapeutic Expression

Just as I was able to use my photos to help put words to the depression and anxiety I was experiencing, The One Project was a major step to putting context and structure towards something already happening all around the world. With the increase of Internet access and high-quality camera phones, more and more photos were being taken and shared, massively compounding each year into unthinkable numbers.

As people began to take more photos, many stumbled upon the therapeutic benefits of the practice, just like myself—whether they were fully conscious of using it for that purpose or not. You may find yourself going out for a walk with your camera on a day where you're particularly stressed, not thinking directly about how the act of photography is helping you and still gaining those benefits. Or perhaps you start to see a trend and pattern in your recent photos (e.g. a new preference for black and white) that you realize connects with grief of losing a loved one, starting to see how taking the photos helped you through the process. Participant Melanie Hood observes:

> Photography has been one of the best things I have ever done for my mental health. It helped me get through the empty nest syndrome, the passing of my mother and also helped me process and make sense of past childhood trauma.

I found countless people coming across the project and immediately connecting the dots, *seeing how photography had a large hand in their own personal growth and healing*. Wherever they were in the world or whatever their first language was, people were able to take photos to

---

1   https://theoneproject.co

express what they were struggling with and others could connect or empathize, regardless of language or physical barriers. I believe that as we become more connected, both online and offline, the importance of this will only grow. While this type of expression opens doors for verbal communication, there's immense value that can come from simply sharing or seeing a photo that speaks to your soul.

Therapeutic Photography

Therapeutic photography involves taking, analyzing, and using photos for the purpose of personal healing, growth, or understanding, whether done consciously or unconsciously. By actively constructing, analyzing, and reflecting on photographs by pairing this with creative writing, you are able to learn more about yourself and how you see the world. Art expression helps people express experiences that are too difficult to put into words, such as a diagnosis of cancer or the intense web of feelings that can come with depression or anxiety. Photography is one of the most accessible and least threatening forms of art and creativity that anyone can use to express themselves and find healing.

A person's perspective on themselves and the world can be gradually explored and changed through the process of taking photographs, analyzing them, and discussing them with others. This becomes increasingly important as people gain the ability to explore, share, reflect on, and start to actively create the stories that they tell about themselves, the people in their life, and the world around them. By creating photos that tell stories you cannot put into words which then become works that you are proud of, you can start to develop a sense of mastery. Similarly, sharing your photographs and getting positive feedback from others can help you continue to build confidence and become more comfortable expressing your opinions, thoughts, and story with others. The wide range of benefits involved in these techniques and practices come together to provide many of the changes needed to help bring people back up from a deep depression, calm and control anxieties, and work proactively to keep these issues from lasting or coming back again.

For many people, the act of taking or editing the photos is very therapeutic, and working with your photos afterwards can also be (asking questions about them, writing stories about them, and more). Your photos from the past can also provide powerful insights and reminders as you continue throughout life, showing you how your perspective of yourself and the world has changed over time and/or how you have grown as a person.

The Original One Project

When I started to develop the first version of The One Project and discover the therapeutic power of photography for myself, it was during the process of exploring the depression and anxiety I'd been suffering from for years. Through the use of many stories (a photo paired with a title and short paragraph of poetic, creative writing), I started to delve into thoughts that had bounced around my head for far too long without external examination. I started to create concepts that fit the various themes that I felt I needed to explore, including: school/graduation/careers; wealth/money/material things/happiness; relationships/breakups; Internet/friendships/human connection; school/bullying/depression; and dreams/darkness/loneliness/suicide. During the creation of each photo, I felt I was relieving pressure and feeling a weight lifted off me, while simultaneously gaining a third-person perspective on these issues and stories that had haunted me for so long. In brief, I gained control and a better understanding of my struggles.

All of this occurred largely on my own and with little communication with others about the true reasons behind the work; I slowly added more people into the process to be models in the photos. It was still a very personal process aided by a select few who were willing to help. From these simple interactions, I began to see how people were able to connect and understand the core of what I was doing, applying it to their life and opening the doors for deep healing, conversations, and connection.

Through these slow, tiny, and gradual steps—ones that may be seen as unnecessary—I was able to push past the inertia of being silent and doing nothing about these issues for so long: a position that I believe far too many people are in, especially when suffering from depression and anxiety. Each step helped me to become more comfortable in expressing myself around these topics (whether in private or public) and built my confidence, while I continued to learn more about what I was going through, why I may be suffering in this way, and *realizing that I wasn't the only one.*

Starting in 2010 as the first photography community for depression and anxiety, The One Project is now a global movement and collection of online wellness tools to help people become the best version of their authentic self. It includes a private online platform using therapeutic photography techniques to connect people and help others suffering from depression and anxiety; it is available globally and no previous camera skills are required. The One Project also provides opportunities for learning how to use therapeutic photography through free online courses and contribute to a community-curated collection of tools for mental health wellness. It's a simple process that many others have followed which can help give clearer steps and guidelines for people to follow when working on their own issues, with a therapist or on their own.

Figure 16.1
The Lavish Façade
Courtesy of Bryce Evans

Figure 16.2
Back to One
Courtesy of Bryce Evans

Figure 16.3
Lost and Looking for Direction
Courtesy of Bryce Evans

How Photography Can Be Therapeutically Beneficial

While there are many ways that photography can be a form of self-help, here are a few of the therapeutic benefits I discovered through The One Project:

- *Connecting with nature and environments.* Photography often provides a motivation to get outside and connect with nature. As you begin taking photos, there's a pull that comes to find new and unique views—alternate perspectives—which will lead people outside of their door, their neighbourhood, and often their city. It encourages movement (exercise) and allows us to get "out of our heads."

- *Self-expression and reflection.* Photographs are forms of self-expression and reflection that can provide not only therapeutic benefits, but also powerful personal insights into who you are and your worldview. When patterns start to emerge in the way that you compose or edit your photographs, it can simply be a personal preference or may be an indicator of something more meaningful. Photos can act as reminders, showing how perspectives have changed over time.

- *Shifting perspective.* When taking photos, you are literally looking through a new (or different) lens, which can become a metaphor for the shift in perspective that it can bring for you. Photography allows you to step outside of that to see different perspectives, more beauty, and more possibilities. Something as simple as a small shift in perspective can have a profound impact on your life—especially when compounded with further changes over time.

* *Searching for beauty.* When you have a camera in your hand, you naturally begin searching for beauty in the world more often. For example, the mundane can start to take on new meaning and light for you as your eye becomes more trained to find the next photo.

* *Non-verbal communication.* Photography acts as non-verbal communication. Like art expression, photography as a form of non-verbal communication can be a much easier way to express what's too hard to put into words. Also, many people respond to others' photos, observing, "Wow, this is exactly how I feel!" or "Seeing this image made me feel less alone, I now know there are others struggling in the same way I am. Thank you." When talking about a photo, it can spark an incredibly powerful conversation that enhances your level of comfort in talking about your own personal struggles.

* *Accessing mindfulness, flow, and focus.* Photography can be a form of mindfulness (present state awareness), similar to meditation. It helps you to focus externally, rather than getting caught up in the thoughts racing through your mind. The same can happen during the editing or review process of looking through your images: you can find yourself "there" again in that space or that moment. Also, often when you're taking photos, you can find yourself in "flow," which brings many health benefits similar to meditation, like calming the mind and providing relief from stress.

* *Gaining control.* When holding a camera to take photos, you regain a sense of control. You have full control over what is in the frame (and what isn't), along with all the settings that come with your camera when in manual mode to present the view in the way that you want. In this sense, photography can be an accessible way for people to start to gain back control of their creative voice.

* *Experiencing positive feedback.* When we do share our photos, it can be a great way for us to gain positive feedback from our friends, loved ones, and other people from around

the world. Sharing your photographic work and receiving positive feedback continues to help build confidence, opens you up to sharing your creative voice, and motivates you to continue the process.

- *Helping establish social bonds.* Photography can be a very social activity, encouraging you to reach out and establish relationships with people. For example, when trying to capture someone's portrait up close, you will naturally have to go over and ask them if it is okay. In a similar way, your camera can be a great excuse to connect with people and overcome social anxiety.
- *Connecting to the unconscious.* Photography can be a connection to your unconscious mind, helping you to discover powerful personal insights.

Conclusion

As mentioned, I believe the largest barrier that holds most people back from getting the help that they need—whether it's through friends and family or professional support—is not a lack of information, it's communication. While there are issues in funding and lack of resources around mental health in many countries, causing millions of people to not get the support and care that they need, there are significantly more who do not enter those doors or start the conversation in the first place. For some, that can be a lack of understanding of what they're dealing with, as silence can only increase the difficulty of learning or uncovering the issues. Others may be fearful of stigma or unsure of how to put words to what they are struggling with without facing a backlash, judgment, or shame from others. This is the space that I believe therapeutic photography best serves.

By embracing therapeutic photography as an additional tool and method within the larger space of art therapy and wellness, we are able to alleviate the strain on our limited resources and infrastructure for health, while allowing individuals to be empowered in their own healing and growth—with or without professional support.

Recommendations

- Therapeutic photography and programs like The One Project help individuals start expressing difficult issues.

- Provide accessible tools for individuals to work through their own personal therapeutic process and recommend professional help when required.

- Integrate therapeutic photography into the clinical therapy practice as ways to encourage examination, conversation, and reflection or recommended as assignments in between sessions with clients.

17

DIBAAJIMOWIN (STORIES)

Health Promotion through Digitalized Oral Stories

Debra Johnson-Fuller and Elizabeth Warson

Digital storytelling is one of many culturally responsive technological approaches in Indian country in the US that has been effective in communicating health topics as well as promoting a sense of wellbeing, creating meaning-making experiences for viewers and participants alike (Haigh and Hardy, 2011). Digital stories are typically two to three minutes in duration and incorporate multimedia sources from video, text, animation, and voice narration, and often utilize free software programs. Digital storytelling workshops are designed to train participants in creating their own story in a collaborative and supportive environment. Within the cancer community, digital storytelling has proven to be an effective empowering and life-affirming approach (Høybye, Johansen, and Tjørnhøj-Thomsen, 2005), demonstrating results such as an increased sense of wellbeing through these shared experiences (O'Neill and Hardy, 2008).

Digital storytelling has been a catalyst for communicating perceptions of illness and wellness within the medical community (O'Neill and Hardy, 2008). Since 2009, Indigenous communities have gravitated toward this digital format because of their strong oral tradition, due in part to the foundational work of nDigiDreams.[1] There is a paucity of evidence-based research on the effects of

---

1 http://ndigidreams.com/ds.html

digital storytelling on health promotion and education. Collateral observations from the work of nDigiDreams and their partners suggest that Native people have responded favorably to these digital shared stories and shown a preference for accessing these stories over textual or didactic sources.

For American Indians and Alaska Natives disease prevention and awareness are more about healing ourselves as a community. Acceptance of chronic disease conditions and their impact on individuals, families, and communities involves a deeper understanding of the comorbidity of psychological and physiological illness among Native people (Bombay, Matheson, and Anisman, 2009). The aim of digitalized oral stories is to empower community members with the capacity to tell and retell, define and redefine their place in tribal history, their orientation regarding diseases and wellness, their approach to medicine and the medical industry, their understanding of themselves and their community, as people capable of shaping their own responses to the changing landscape of health and wellness. Within Indigenous communities, digitalized oral stories comprise an innovative and culturally responsive approach to create and harness a constellation of understandings, capacities, and awareness that regenerate as technologies mature, disease states change, and as medicine progresses. In this respect, digital storytelling has proven to be a catalyst for communicating perceptions of illness and wellness within Native communities and the medical community (O'Neill and Hardy, 2008).

Within the cancer community, digital storytelling has proven to be an effective empowering and life-affirming approach (Høybye *et al.*, 2005), demonstrating results such as an increased sense of wellbeing through these shared experiences (O'Neill and Hardy, 2008). This is significant because American Indians and Alaska Natives experience cultural and geographic barriers preventing them from accessing quality healthcare (Office of Minority Health, 2016). Nationally, programs such as Patient Voices (O'Neill and Hardy, 2008) and the American Indian and Alaska Native Health archives associated with the National Library of Medicine[2] have provided a forum for viewing health-related stories; however, the impact of these stories on health promotion and cancer education in Native communities has not been fully realized. Since 2011, The Fond du Lac Band of Lake

2   https://americanindianhealth.nlm.nih.gov

Superior Chippewa has been in the forefront of digital storytelling, largely because of their ongoing collaboration with a woman-owned and Indigenous-focused consulting and digital storytelling training company, nDigiDreams. Through a grant from the National Library of Medicine, nDigiDreams was able to partner with the Min No Aya Win Human Services Center on a one-year health-related digital storytelling grant. This funding opportunity enabled first author Debra Johnson-Fuller, cancer health educator, to successfully create and implement a health-related digital storytelling curriculum for the Fond du Lac Human Services Division.

Significance

Chronic Illness and Cancer in Minnesota Tribes

According to the Centers for Disease Control and Prevention (CDC) (2012), there are four primary health risk behaviors that cause chronic disease: 1) lack of exercise; 2) poor nutrition; 3) tobacco use; and 4) drinking alcohol. Of these, tobacco is the leading cause of cancer, which is the second leading cause of death, and a challenge for Minnesota tribes with a smoking rate over 50 percent (Fond du Lac Band, 2012). Although cancer can be a preventable disease through healthy lifestyle choices and regular screenings, the American Indian population in Northern Minnesota are twice as likely to experience high rates of cancer disease and mortality than any other racial/ethnic group.

Minnesota tribal communities comprise seven Chippewa bands from the Ojibwe reservations as well as four Dakota communities. Within the Chippewa bands, cancer control initiatives are disparate, not coordinated, and address a variety of issues.

Art Therapy with American Indians and Alaska Natives

Presently, there are only two art therapists conducting research in Indian country. One is Dr. Cueva, a registered nurse and cancer educator, who has been researching culturally relevant art-based interventions as part of her ACS(American Cancer Society)-funded Arts-based Cancer Education with Alaska Native People (2011) and

CHR Cancer Education Module (Cueva *et al.*, 2010). The other is second author of this chapter Elizabeth Warson, who also focuses on cultural relevancy in devising and implementing art-based psychosocial interventions specific to stress and pain management for cancer survivors and their family members (Warson, 2008, 2012a, 2012b). Both researchers consider a relationally based Native perspective of wellness comprising the interrelationship between mind, body, spirit, and context in their approach (Cross, 1997, 2001; Hodge, Limb, and Cross, 2009).

Innovation

Within the past decade, the practice of digital storytelling has emerged as a culturally responsive research method in health promotion (Gubrium, 2009). "Digital stories can influence indigenous healthiness and resilience by offering a means of owning and being able to tell one's story" (Gubrium, 2009, p.187). As an innovative community-based participatory research (CBPR) approach, digital storytelling is situated in context to author, and shared meanings emerge through the storying process. Digital stories are co-created in workshop settings, fostering a sense of connection through shared understanding. The digitalized oral stories workshop format transcends traditional focus group methods by incorporating a participant-led agenda (Gubrium, 2009). In terms of Native communities, story circles are an integral component to the digital storytelling process.

Since 2011, the Fond du Lac Band of the Lake Superior Chippewa have been co-constructing digital storytelling programs for their community through their ongoing collaboration with nDigiDreams. This partnership launched a funded project through the National Library of Medicine, resulting in multiple training sessions and workshops and a culminating archive of digital stories focused on Native health and wellness. The Fond du Lac Band has since implemented digital storytelling as part of their Fond du Lac Men's Group through cancer health educator and tribal member Debra Johnson-Fuller, leading to the creation of a digital storytelling curriculum.

As a complement to this innovative technological approach, the participants maintain visual journals as a means to process thoughts, feelings, and perceptions referenced during the story circles and shared voluntarily as part of the Appreciative Inquiry (AI). Warson (2012a, 2012b; Mercer, Warson, and Zao, 2010) has conducted several visual journaling studies exploring the emergent themes from entries created by American Indian cancer survivors and their family members. In addition, the inclusion of visual journaling in the digital storytelling workshops will foster, and ideally sustain, self-care practices resulting from the workshop experience. PhotoTherapy techniques are included in the storyboarding process to enhance the narrative co-authoring. The authors draw specifically on Dr. Weiser's (1999) publications on PhotoTherapy techniques, encompassing five recommended approaches: photos by the clients, photos of the client, self-portraits, family photos and albums, and photo projectives. The inclusion of art therapy interventions in the digital storytelling curriculum enhances the technological innovation and provides a means to sustain self-care practices resulting from the workshop experience.

Multimedia approaches in the field of art therapy are on the rise, consisting of telehealth applications (Collie *et al.*, 2006), computer-based digital artmaking (Orr, 2012), and iPad applications (Malchiodi, 2012). These creative tools, paired with phototherapy techniques, have improved the delivery of services, provided accommodation for individuals with disabilities, and created a new forum for the storying process, among other benefits.

Approach

Digitalized Oral Stories Workshop Format

Deborah Johnson-Fuller's digitalized oral stories workshop format was designed for the Fond du Lac Band of the Lake Superior Chippewa, incorporating a group orientation, referred to as a story circle. Individual mentors or story gatherers, trained in digital storytelling, are paired up with a participant to co-create the story.

The workshop format follows the participatory method outlined by Gubrium (2009) and is conducted over a three-day period at a retreat center. This tranquil retreat setting allows for participants to engage in an intensive workshop with support staff. Balancing self-care with didactic instruction, this environment fosters a "safe" place to share cancer stories in a supportive group setting. The retreats are typically offered on a quarterly basis with a maximum of ten participants and an equal number of "story gatherers" or mentors. Prior to the workshop, participants meet individually with their mentors to digitally record a "draft" of their cancer story and bring in photos, videos, or images to be scanned.

The group workshops are divided into six phases over the three-day workshop: phase one is an overview of the digital storytelling process and review of sample stories. The main facilitator, Debra Johnson-Fuller, visually demonstrates the seven elements of digital storytelling, comprising point of view, dramatic question, emotional content, voice, soundtrack/music, economy, and pacing (Lambert, 2006).

Phase two focuses on the co-creation of a script emerging from the shared storying process from the story circle group. The format for the story circle mirrors Yalom's (2005) existential group therapy format in terms of providing a safe and supportive environment to discuss emergent themes.

Phase three is more instructional, providing an overview of the software and hands-on demonstration. The aim of phase three is to incorporate the insights and collaborative sharing from the story circle using technological elements.

Phase four is geared toward finalizing the scripts of their stories to incorporate into a final draft; a voice recording of their story is created using free editing software, such as Sound Studio or Audacity. During this phase, the story gatherers work individually with the participants to demonstrate the voice recording software.

Phase five considers the visual layout or menu for the digital story. The story gatherers assist participants in creating a storyboard using collage elements and phototherapy techniques to align holistically with the narrated scripts.

The final phase is geared toward the final edit using Movie Maker or a comparable program. A hands-on demonstration of the software and editing features is conducted with the aim of producing a digital story for the final story circle. A digital story screening is provided for participants directly involved in the workshops with a final story circle to provide closure. Final edits to their story may be required and are conducted through as-needed follow-up appointments with Debra Johnson-Fuller at the Min No Aya Win Human Services Center.

Program Participants

The participants are American Indian and Alaska Native cancer survivors aged 21–85, male and female, who reside in rural or urban tribal communities in Minnesota. The workshops include individuals with all types cancers and no limitation in terms of years of survivorship. Participant recruitment for the workshops relies on the partnerships developed through the cancer education program through the Fond du Lac Band. Approximately ten participants attend one of three workshops, a total of 30 participants a year.

Evaluation Methods

To evaluate the efficacy of the digital storytelling, with respect to improved qualitative of life factors (QOL) and cancer knowledge, the authors will be collecting pre- and post-SF-36v2 Health Surveys, that is, a 36-item survey to measure functional health and wellbeing from the patient's perspective (Ware *et al.*, 2000). Eight health domains are considered: physical functioning, role-physical, bodily pain, general health, vitality, social functioning, role-emotional, and mental health (Ware *et al.*, 2000). This is a generic measure and has been translated in more than 50 countries as a part of the International Quality of Life Assessment (IQOLA) project. Published reliability statistics exceed the minimum standard of 0.80 and for mental health and physical scores, 0.90 (Ware *et al.*, 2000). The SF-36v2 will be administered as a baseline measure once a week for a total of three weeks prior to the workshop. In addition, the SF-36 will be administered as a pre- and post-measure on day one and day three of the workshop.

In collaboration with a three-member advisory committee, a pre- and post-cancer knowledge survey will be created based on valid existing models and then modified for cultural relevancy for Minnesota tribes.

Appreciative Inquiry

Through Appreciative Inquiry, the prevailing perceptions regarding health education and promotion and beliefs that are likely to affect the quality of life factors for American Indian cancer patients will be explored. An established qualitative baseline (pre-interview) and an evaluation of the program (post-interview) will be included to explore the prevailing perceptions regarding cancer education, health promotion and cultural beliefs that are likely to affect the quality of life for members of Minnesota tribes. This evaluative approach incorporates an assets- or strengths-based model to conducting individual interviews, referred to as Appreciative Inquiry. Appreciative Inquiry attempts to use ways of asking questions to foster positive relationships, utilizing a cycle of four processes (Cooperrider and Whitney, 2001):

- *Discovery*: the identification of processes that are effective and, in this instance, culturally relevant (appreciating).
- *Dream*: the envisioning of processes that would work well (envisioning results).
- *Design*: planning and prioritizing processes that would work well through collaboration and community involvement (co-constructing).
- *Destiny*: implementing what has been envisioned (sustaining).

This method of strengths-based evaluation reinforces Native values of generosity, courage, respect, and wisdom.

Mentor Training

Digital storytelling training for four mentors or story gatherers is typically conducted in two phases. The first phase consists of five days of training comprising the successful completion of the trainer's own digital story and an understanding of their role as mentor or story gatherers. The second phase considers the experiential learning from participant interaction and mentoring under Debra Johnson-Fuller. A follow-up training session is conducted upon completion of the first retreat to evaluate participant interaction and competencies with the digital format and occurs on site. The aim of the training is to have the story gatherers conduct digital workshops for their respective communities and to engage in program evaluation. Once trainers have completed their initial training, they will have access to a hard copy of the curriculum. Copies of the existing curriculum cannot be disseminated to the general public without this training.

Digital Storytelling Training and Resources

There is a plethora of free resources on the Internet that utilize digital storytelling "tools," from storytelling websites to apps primarily serving educational settings (Pappas, 2013). Huson *et al.* (n.d.) have a helpful iPad resource that was instrumental in establishing a digital storytelling program in a school-based setting where Warson facilitated groups as a behavioral health specialist. To elevate the effectiveness of the digital storytelling, Johnson-Fuller was consulted to facilitate a three-hour onsite workshop with Warson for her high school students at an alternative high school in Colorado. This hands-on training provided a foundation for facilitating a digital storytelling group, laid the groundwork for a participatory approach with students, and created a meaning-making experience through the use of iPads, apps, microphone, and a computer.

Facilitating a digital storytelling workshop as a participatory approach in health promotion and human services requires additional training, supervision, curriculum development, and evaluative methods. This chapter focuses primarily on "situating" a digital storytelling workshop with the guidance of Native American advisory members, community members, and mentors to provide a co-constructed, participatory, and sustainable approach to health promotion (Warson, 2008). Johnson-Fuller's successful implementation of digitalized oral stories for Native American cancer survivors is evident in the National Library of Medicine, American Indian Health (n.d.).

Since 1993, the StoryCenter, formerly the Center for Digital Storytelling,[3] has been known as the premier "space" for digital storytelling: their "methods of group process and story creation serve as reflective practice, a professional development tool, a pedagogical strategy, and as a vehicle for education, community mobilization, and advocacy" (n.d.). The StoryCenter's list of offerings ranges from their standard three-day workshop to online webinars, master classes, and facilitators' intensive.

Since 2011, The Fond du Lac Band of Lake Superior Chippewa has been in the forefront of digital storytelling, largely because of their ongoing collaboration with nDigiDreams. Through a grant from the National Library of Medicine, nDigiDreams was able to partner with The Min No Aya Win Human Services Center on a one-year health-related digital storytelling grant. This funding

---

3   www.storycenter.org

opportunity enabled Debra Johnson-Fuller to successfully create and implement a health-related digital storytelling curriculum for the Fond du Lac Human Services Division.

Recommendations

- Exploring your own story is paramount to understanding the inherent meaning-making process of digital storytelling. This process entails scripting out a two-page written narrative, collecting images, and creating a storyboard, thereby allowing you to "plot" out ideas beforehand.

- Experimenting with free apps and available electronic devices is highly recommended before investing in equipment, software, downloads, and training/tutorial programs. Digital stories can be created using accessible electronic devices such as smartphones and tablets.

- Understand the possibilities of digital storytelling as an agent of social change, personal healing and exploration, as well as group process. The process of co-constructing a digital story can be a transformational meaning-making experience in and of itself.

References

Bombay, A., Matheson, K. and Anisman, H. (2009) Intergenerational trauma: Convergence of multiple processes among First Nations peoples in Canada. *International Journal of Indigenous Health 5*(3), 6–47.

Centers for Disease Control and Prevention (CDC) (2012) Chronic disease prevention and health promotion. Retrieved on April 1, 2018 at www.cdc.gov/chronicdisease/overview/index.htm

Collie, K., Bottorff, J.L., Long, B.C. and Conati, C. (2006) Distance art groups for women with breast cancer: Guidelines and recommendations. *Journal of Supportive Care in Cancer 14*(8), 849–858.

Cooperrider, D.L. and Whitney, D. (2001) A positive revolution in change: Appreciative Inquiry. *Public Administration and Public Policy 87*, 611–630.

Cross, T. (1997) Understanding the relational worldview in Indian families (Part I). *Pathways Practice Digest 12*, 4.

Cross, T. (2001) Spirituality and mental health: A Native American perspective. *Focal Point 15*, 37–38.

Cueva, M., Kuhnley, R., Stueckermann, C., Lanier, A.P. and McMahon, P. (2010) *Understanding Cancer: Cancer Education Module.* Anchorage, AK: Indian Health Service.

Cueva, M. (2011) "Bringing What's on the Inside Out": Arts-Based Cancer Education with Alaska Native Peoples. *Pimatisiwin: A Journal of Aboriginal and Indigenous Community Health 9*(1), 1–22.

Fond du Lac Band (2012) Fond du Lac Wiidookaage Comprehensive Cancer Program. Retrieved on April 1, 2018 at ftp://ftp.cdc.gov/pub/Publications/Cancer/ccc/fond_du_lac_ccc_plan_2007_2012.pdf

Haigh, C. and Hardy, P. (2011) Tell me a story: A conceptual exploration of storytelling in healthcare education. *Nurse Education Today 31*(4), 408–411.

Hodge, D.R., Limb, G.E. and Cross, T.L. (2009) Moving from colonization toward balance and harmony: A Native American perspective on wellness. *Social Work 54*, 211–219.

Høybye, M.T., Johansen, C. and Tjørnhøj-Thomsen, T. (2005) Online interaction. Effects of storytelling in an internet breast cancer support group. *Psycho-Oncology 14*(3), 211–220.

Huson, C. *et al.* (n.d.) Digital storytelling with the iPad. Retrieved on April 1, 2018 at https://sites.google.com/site/digitalstorytellingwiththeipad/home

Gubrium, A. (2009) Digital storytelling: An emergent method for health promotion and research and practice. *Society for Public Health Education 10*(2), 186–192.

Lambert, J. (2006) *Digital Storytelling: Capturing Lives, Creating Community.* Minneapolis, MN: Life on the Water.

Malchiodi, C.A. (2012, February 26) Art therapy: There's an app for that. Retrieved on April 1, 2018 at www.psychologytoday.com/blog/the-healing-arts/201202/art-therapy-there-s-app-1

Mercer, P., Warson, E. and Zao, J. (2010) Visual Journaling: An intervention to influence stress, anxiety, and affect levels in medical students. *The Arts in Psychotherapy 37*(2), 143–148.

National Library of Medicine (n.d.) American Indian health. Retrieved on April 1, 2018 at https://americanindianhealth.nlm.nih.gov/cancer.html

nDigiDreams (n.d.) Digital storytelling. Retrieved on April 1, 2018 at http://ndigidreams.com/ds.html

Office of Minority Health (2016) Surveillance for health behaviors of American Indians and Alaska Natives: Findings from the Behavioral Risk Factor Surveillance System, 1997–2000. Retrieved at https://minorityhealth.hhs.gov/omh/content.aspx?ID=3442

O'Neill, F. and Hardy, P. (2008) Designing patient-shaped healthcare: Hearing patient voices. *White Rose Health Innovation Partnership Technology Bulletin.* Retrieved on April 1, 2018 at www.patientvoices.org.uk/pdf/articles/wrhip14.pdf

Orr, P. (2012) Technology use in art therapy practice: 2004 and 2011 comparison. *The Arts in Psychotherapy 39*, 234–238.

Pappas, C. (2013) 18 free digital storytelling tools for teachers and students. eLearning Industry. Retrieved from https://elearningindustry.com/18-free-digital-storytelling-tools-for-teachers-and-students

Ware, J.E. with Snow, K., Kosinski M. and Gandek, B. (2000) *SF-36 Health Survey: Manual and Interpretation Guide*. Boston, MA: Quality Metric.

Warson, E. (2008) Art-based narrative inquiry with Native American breast cancer survivors. Doctoral dissertation, Colorado State University. Dissertation International Abstract Section A: Humanities and Social Sciences, 70(2-A), 2009, 487.

Warson, E. (2012a) Healing across cultures: Arts in healthcare with American Indian and Alaska Native cancer survivors. In C. Malchiodi (ed.) *Art Therapy and Health Care*. New York, NY: Guilford.

Warson, E. (2012b) Healing pathways: Art therapy for American Indian cancer survivors. *Journal of Cancer Education 27*(1), S47–56.

Weiser, J. (1999) *PhotoTherapy Techniques: Exploring the Secrets of Personal Snapshots and Family Albums* (2nd edn). Vancouver, Canada: The PhotoTherapy Centre.

Yalom (2005) *Theory and Practice of Group Psychotherapy* (5th edn). New York, NY: Basic Books.

18

GROUP ART THERAPY AND TELEMEDICINE

*Gudrun Jones, Rachel Rahman,
and Martine Robson*

The psychological impact of a cancer diagnosis is well documented as patients negotiate their own health perceptions, challenges to their self-identity, managing the emotions of those around them, and the need to make numerous decisions about their treatment (e.g. Blake-Mortimer *et al.*, 1999). As a result, psychosocial support has consistently demonstrated positive effects for patient outcomes during this time (Spiegel, 2002). Specifically, group psychotherapy has been shown to be highly effective in supporting the psychological adaptation of patient groups and enhancing quality of life and cancer survival (Blake-Mortimer *et al.*, 1999; National Institute of Clinical Excellence, 2009).

However, for patients undergoing chemotherapy, attending group therapy in person can be ill-advised due to immunosuppression (Chang, Khort, and Maeker, 2014). In addition, the side effects of treatment, such as tiredness and nausea, can limit a patient's ability to socialise and engage fully in daily activities. With the added complexity of living in a rural location, with increased travel distances to reach an appropriate group psychotherapy session, the benefits and likelihood of patients attending become more questionable.

This was our situation in rural Wales, where patients receiving chemotherapy received limited or no psychosocial support. Given that for some clients, telemedicine was the preferred option rather than a mere substitute for face-to-face therapy (Collie and Čubranić, 1999), we had an interesting opportunity to develop a much-needed service. Our need to use telemedicine offered an opportunity to overcome a number of the challenges of providing face-to-face psychosocial support. Telemedicine allows a client to use a laptop or home computer to talk to and see a therapist who is in a different location. We were not completely new to the idea of using telemedicine, having previously developed a successful service to link the palliative care team to individuals in their own home as part of a previous research project run by local university (Keenan *et al.*, 2016). We were encouraged by the positive patient responses, and I as the art therapist discovered to my relief that I was able to develop a good rapport with the patients who I was connecting to; however, doing this with a group seemed far more daunting.

I, the lead author, have traditionally been involved in providing a two-core approach that includes psychodynamic art therapy as well as "first aid" cognitive behavioral therapy (CBT), working to level 2 of the National Institute of Clinical Excellence Guidelines (NICE, 2004) for using CBT techniques in cancer care. I was aware from running group art therapy sessions in person with other clinical groups that the quality of communication is critical. Art therapy aims to provide a safe, supportive, and consistent place where patients can discuss their issues and experiences of living with a cancer diagnosis. The creation of art work offers an additional vehicle for communicating and sharing meaningful experiences through symbol and metaphor. It can offer a place to express thoughts and feelings that are not voiced elsewhere, providing a welcome safe space where negative or angry feelings can be expressed without overburdening family or friends.

I have run art therapy groups in different ways over the years depending on the needs of the client group, including brief or longer-term, slow, and open groups. I have used a directive approach, providing clients with themes and visual exercises, and with groups who have worked together on joint images, as well as a more traditional non-directive, psychodynamic art therapy approach, which allows clients' own ideas and themes to emerge in the moment. However, I was aware that communicating remotely via technology can create a very different dynamic. I am sure that we have all sat in videoconference meetings where communication is stilted, with awkward stop-starts, and overlapping talk. This was not the type of space I wanted to create and I questioned how effectively people would be able to communicate and develop a space for open and frank conversation. I knew I would have to think carefully about what types of activities would be possible in a remote space as well as consider how conversation was going to flow and facilitate the relationships between patients themselves. Needless to say, I was full of trepidation. This was going to be a new experience, exploring a new territory without much of a map to negotiate the technology.

In this chapter, we present a combination of patient interview data and my own therapeutic reflections on a collaborative research project with our local university's psychology deployment to discuss how delivering group art therapy via telemedicine influenced communication between my patients and me and between group members. We also discuss how this influenced communication outside of our closed therapeutic space for patients and therapist.

The Telemedicine Infrastructure

In order to provide the necessary technology for group participation, all participants were given use of a laptop which was loaded with videoconferencing software supported by the health board. Patients had to open the software and enter a number followed by a pin number to enter the remote videoconferencing room. We met with patients face to face to introduce them to the processes and trialled connecting via the software. This took a few problematic weeks of trials and panicked conversations with technicians about overcoming firewalls before patients were connecting in with ease.

Later in the project, the opportunity to use a popular videoconferencing software program which was being considered for adoption by the local health board arose. This worked well in one-to-one trials and involved a relatively easy login for patients who just needed to accept a meeting invitation via e-mail, and click on a link which downloaded the software automatically and connected them to the virtual meeting room. In reality, downloading required patients to accept certain terms and conditions, and patients admitted that without the support of the research assistant, they would have found the process daunting and confusing. It also became apparent that while one-to-one connections worked well, the broadband width available to our rural patients was inadequate to support group connections. Patients dropped out intermittently, some were unable to maintain a video link, and one was unable to connect at all. As a result, we reverted to the original videoconference software for the remainder of the sessions.

The Virtual Art Therapy Space

During this initial phase, we recruited enough people to run two small groups offering weekly sessions for eight weeks. The names used in this chapter are all pseudonyms to protect identity. The first group included two women, Sian and Sheila, aged between 45 and 55 and living close to the local hospital. The second included a man—Ashley, aged 69—and two women—Kate, in her 60s and Gemma, in her late 30s. These participants lived in much more remote locations, between half an hour and an hour away from the hospital.

An art pack was delivered to each participant which included an A4 (210mm x 297mm) spiral-bound journal, chalks, pastels, paint, brushes, glue, and a variety of colored paper. The journal and the materials were theirs to keep for personal use and reference, and use outside the sessions.

Each of the eight sessions lasted an hour and half, and followed a regular pattern. The art therapy sessions began with a sharing round, including discussion of topics that covered the whole range of emotions and experience accompanying a cancer diagnosis, day-to-day concerns, and thoughts about the future. This was followed by a period of approximately 20 minutes when patients made or drew their images using a chosen theme. Participants then shared their work and each session ended with a five-minute relaxation exercise.

The research team interviewed participants before, midway through, and after the art therapy groups to record their expectations, concerns, and experiences. The interviews were semi-structured in nature and used an interview schedule to guide the topics for discussion, but allowed participants the freedom to deviate and elaborate on topics that were particularly relevant to them. Interviews typically lasted between 30 minutes and an hour, depending on the health of the participant, and were audio recorded to allow verbatim transcripts of the interview to be made for analysis.

Technological Challenges of Telemedicine Art Therapy Sessions

While patients were connecting from the comfort of their own homes, I was aware that I was in a meeting room without the usual paraphernalia of an art therapy room around me. Reflecting on this emphasized the defining characteristic of a telemedicine art therapy session—the focus was the screen and the voices of the participants rather than the therapists' environment. I questioned whether the same supportive interpersonal relationships could develop between members of the group and me as the therapist when we were all so remote from one another. Coming to the first session of any group holds many anxieties for participants about the others in the group, and in their pre-therapy interviews participants expressed concerns about what they would hear and say. They wondered whether the sessions would help them, whether sharing and hearing other people's stories about cancer might make them feel worse, or if their own stories would be discouraging or difficult for other patients to hear. I was very anxious about the technology failing, thus isolating people further by cutting them off abruptly. What would the quality of the communication be between the group members who would meet for the first time in a virtual therapy room? How would they relate to each other? Would there be enough time for everyone to speak? Would they be able to say what they wanted to say? Anxiety levels were very high for all of us.

The first few connections for both cohorts were technologically disastrous and my worst nightmare came alive before me. As a therapist, this was the worst possible feeling as the comfortable supportive space I was trying to create felt increasingly out of my control. I lost audio and visual connections with people and so had to keep reintroducing conversation as people rejoined, and yet I tried to persevere to offer those in the virtual space the therapy I had promised. Despite this, the candid discussions and sharing that followed the making of rich and emotive images indicated that, even via the imperfect telemedicine technology, the group had developed into a safe space for participants to share their experiences and art work. Despite being inexperienced in making art, clients showed ingenuity and confidence in interpreting themes and describing their experiences. This in turn gave me confidence to pursue this way of working, with technology as a partner in therapy.

Confidentiality

In order to preserve a sense of confidentiality and safe boundaries, I suggested to participants in their information pack that they clear a quiet place for themselves in their home for the duration of the session. In reality, this was not always possible and there were glimpses of participants' home life, often depending on where in the home access to Wi-Fi or an Internet connection was located. This meant that a family member's animals or the arrival of the postman or district nurse could become unexpected parts of sessions. Reflecting on the boundaries of the therapy space, I am reminded that these are not the typical spaces in which art therapy takes place. However, it became important that these interruptions during therapy sessions be identified and shared with the group, and any anticipated interruptions be mentioned to keep the therapy space as secure and confidential as possible.

In art therapy, the therapist is traditionally the caretaker of the visual work until such time as the therapy comes to an end. It struck me when I first began working via telemedicine how much I invested in that role and how much I missed reflecting on the art works as I put them away after sessions. In our sessions, the length of time the art work was viewed was limited; the therapist and the group were dependent on the art maker to provide a verbal description. While I missed the tactile experience of observing the work being made, I was surprised to learn from participant interviews that this was not so for participants, who valued the privacy the technology offered. Many discussed how they enjoyed the 20 minutes when the others were "there" on screen, but not intruding into their space while they created and shared their art. Not being observed by others meant that they felt more relaxed and confident about their art work and some talked about taking inspiration from their own surroundings that held personal meaning for them.

Examples of Patient Expressions Shared via Telemedicine Art Therapy Sessions

I have always found that metaphors using containers of any kind allow an interesting use of language and description of states of mind, and can encourage playful and creative thinking by the maker. Containers such as boxes, boats, treasure chests, houses, and rooms come to mind. A container for feelings and experiences has an outside and inside and can hold things within, or feelings can be depicted spilling out or escaping. I have always found this theme a rich source of ideas and for exploration. In *The Book of Symbols* (Ronnberg and Martin, 2010) a boat, for example, evokes ideas of means of travel. The authors observe that "Thus the ship has often been experienced as an aspect of the great feminine, as Mother or beloved, the strengths and vulnerabilities of whose holding body the captain or navigator" must intimately know (p.450).

When faced with a period of illness and treatment, managing and building relationships with the medical team, family, and friends, feelings of loss of control and powerlessness are common. In this first session, the metaphor of a boat enabled discussions about personal journeys, their own resources, isolation, sources of support, and difficulties. It gave permission for creative play with ideas relating to the type of vessel, navigation of weather conditions, and location. I hoped the metaphor of a boat would support patients to share something of their character, to say a little about their current feelings about themselves and their situation. Using these images would also give me an idea about how much personal or emotional information they wanted to share. Through this process, my questions about how the sessions would work were clearly answered in the quality of the sharing in the very first session.

The challenge of managing communication with family and friends was a common theme in the interviews as well as patients' art work. Sian's drawing was related to communication on several levels. She was pleased with her drawing because it was able to express the emotions and experiences associated with her diagnosis and treatment, and also reflected her negotiation of closeness and communication with others. Her boat was alone in choppy seas with some other boats in the distance representing family and friends. She had a radio so could call for help if she needed, but she said she wanted to be alone in the boat. For her, having choice and control about when she wanted or accepted help were very important. In this session, there was group discussion about the often overwhelming nature of the care friends and family wanted to give and how difficult it is to explain the need sometimes to be alone to come to terms with the illness, without offending or appearing ungrateful. Interview data also revealed a sense of control that participants enjoyed through the remote connection, finding it easier to manage communication from their own home and to decide whether and when to connect.

Where the telehealth technology had failed temporarily for Kate, e-mail enabled the written word to be shared, which demonstrated the need to have as a possibility a variety of ways of connecting digitally or electronically at or after each session.

Reflections

In my canoe, alone far away from home
Why a canoe? Maybe there's only room for me
A part of me craves isolation, yet I
tell others of my situation,
I am angry, angry this disease is sly, unforgiving, cruel
No symptoms, month after month, what a fool
Don't worry, be happy, stay sane
Stay stable, keep calm, keep able
Days of tiredness, just hours of feeling okay,
Not full of energy but enough to get up and about
To smile and see the good around me
Why alone, I think I need to be just me
It's my control key.

In this poem, Kate explores the solitariness of her condition and experience through the image of a canoe. There is a tension between her need to be alone, to maintain her fragile control and balance, and her desire to reach out to and connect with others that resonated strongly with the other patients, who asked for copies of Kate's poem. Another group member, in her mid-point interview, referred to Kate's poetry, and said that she had shown it to family members to help them understand how she was feeling, in an example of how the meaningful communication in the telehealth sessions affected and facilitated communication with others in patients' lives.

The Role of the Art Therapist in Telemedicine Groups

Despite the depth of engagement in the session, I was still left questioning whether the fragility of the technological connection was going to make people feel worse, and following the initial session of both groups, I felt that I could not put the clients through another session like it. It had been almost unbearable for me, so I could only imagine how people who were unwell after chemotherapy must have felt. Surely, they would not be able to bond as a group with us connecting in this unreliable manner. At the end, I had to ask them whether they wanted to carry on. To my amazement, they all said yes. They had clearly connected with each other and benefited from that tenuous contact. But my heart sank, as I was not sure I could cope with the continual risk of connectivity failure. I was very conscious that the situation echoed the fragility and uncertainty that their illness, treatments, and test results can cause, and I was having a direct experience of this through the difficulties with the technology. However, at their request, we persevered.

Over the weeks I began to feel more confident that the virtual group had engaged with creative processes. The sharing of thoughts and ideas around the work gave an insight into each person's thinking and approach to their illness and experience. I was pleased and excited to find that the image-making came into its own and provided a rich layer of sharing in the group. The communication between the participants was meaningful and this felt great, but I had one misgiving—was I actually needed in this forum?

The groups communicated so well, and the conversation was rich and expressive. I barely needed to say a word! I wondered whether these groups would work just as well as a peer forum without me. Many of my patients tell me about online forums for people with cancer, which can be a valuable source of support. However, by the end of the research study, patients explicitly discussed the role of the therapist in the sessions. The nature of technology limited the size of the groups to two to four patients and in the early interviews, the idea of such a small group brought out patients' anxieties about having to manage each other's emotions and stories. Despite my experience of a diminished role, later in the sessions patients talked about how the therapist was vital for relieving them of the burden they would otherwise have felt to manage communication with other group members. The therapist was able to take responsibility for other people's emotions so that they didn't have to.

Interestingly, patients made a point of discussing the power balance. I was not seen as being "in charge" or "leading" and was referred to as an "equal" in the relationship. It appeared as though the remoteness of the technology and patients being in their own surroundings removed a number of the power dynamics we often hear about in healthcare contexts. Perhaps contrary to my own beliefs that a lack of control of the therapeutic space was going to be perceived badly by patients, this in fact created a new type of relationship which the patients appeared to appreciate.

The Benefits of Group Telemedicine Communication

While the therapeutic relationship generated meaningful conversation, I remained interested in how effectively the group members were able to bond with each other when connecting remotely. Each patient had a different type of cancer and was at a different stage of the disease, and they were of different ages and backgrounds. Patients discussed this in their interviews with the researchers, explored how they would relate to other group members and what effect hearing their different experiences at different stages of their cancer would have.

Despite assumptions that computer-mediated communication is less effective or "real" than face-to-face interactions, it became apparent through patient interviews that the telehealth group created a unique space for frank and open discussion. Patients found relief from the anxiety they felt about sharing their feelings with loved ones or friends, but they did not want this group to forge life-long friendships. For those with later-stage or recurring cancer came concerns about creating anxieties for those who had a new diagnosis. Similarly, for those who were recovering came concern about being seen as "a fake" or taking the place of someone who was in more need of support. Many referred to the benefit of having a designated number of sessions resulting in an easy closure to the relationships developed. Interestingly, four of the five patients articulated how they would not have joined a face-to-face group through shyness or for fear of the added commitment that this would bring. The distance offered by the technology was seen as an opportunity to share openly and honestly, but with the freedom to disconnect if they needed to.

Initially, we wondered how this would affect the relationships that developed and the quality of communication that evolved. However, in later interviews the open communication did appear to facilitate close relationships between the group's members. Patients discussed holding group members in their thoughts throughout the week, reflecting on conversations, and wondering how others were coping. For example, Gemma was unable to connect visually and her health limited her ability to connect at all in some weeks, but this changed nothing about her membership of the group in their eyes. The concerns about differing cancer stages had become a benefit of the group, with those at later stages taking comfort from being able to guide peers through the chemotherapy process, while those earlier in their illnesses gained strength and motivation from conversations with others who were surviving and thriving having completed their chemotherapy, albeit with their own challenges.

The nature of the communication itself through technology also contributed an interesting dimension to the group. It was not possible to hold conversations in the usual manner with overlapping talk and interruptions. Our previous concern had been that this would create an artificial and awkward interaction. Some participants, particularly those who were aware of being in close geographical proximity to one another, discussed during an early interview how they would have enjoyed meeting in person, perhaps indicating that face-to-face interaction is assumed to be superior to computer-mediated communication. These participants actually briefly met one another in person when waiting for clinical appointments. As they reflected later, this hurried interaction gave them a new appreciation of the privacy and comfort of meeting remotely from their own home. The telehealth technology had created a new kind of space, at once public and private. In this space, they had felt free enough to agree to throw off the wigs that both were wearing, having discovered that they both hated the feel of wearing them! Of course, a similar relationship might have developed had they met during a conventional therapy session. But what was becoming clear was that communication via the technology was not necessarily a poor relation to its face-to-face counterpart.

Patients' reflections highlighted other previously unconsidered benefits of communication via technology to the group dynamic and therapeutic process. Interrupting and talking over each other is common in face-to-face group therapy sessions, which sometimes has to be managed by the therapist. In telehealth, talking at the same time is not possible, and even noises of agreement or sympathy that typically indicate active listening break up the sound quality. As patients became aware that overlapping talk caused delays in conversation, turn-taking and listening without interrupting became a natural part of the conversation. The technology thus created a unique space for listening and speaking. Patients commented that freedom from needing to respond allowed them to listen more deeply to what each person was saying rather than being concerned about how they could contribute to the conversation. Some participants had anticipated dominant voices or opinions in their pre-session interview, fears which proved unfounded and were minimized due to this format. For example, one participant who was small in stature related her experiences of sometimes feeling intimidated or dominated by the physical presence of others in a group setting. The telehealth screen equalizes physical presence in its head-and-shoulder perspectives of fellow group members, which for this participant reduced her sense of risk when connecting remotely.

There were also other benefits from participants' physical remoteness, something that is usually considered a barrier to communication. Two participants, for example, confided during interviews that they would not have considered attending a group therapy session in person, through shyness or a dislike of interacting with groups of people.

In summary, what initially appeared to be a technological limitation seemed to result in more focused, meaningful, and respectful communication as group members consciously limited unnecessary responses and allowed space for each other's talk to unfold.

Conclusion

In conclusion, these two groups have shown that technologically mediated communication can be meaningful, close, caring, supportive, humorous, cheeky, fun, and at the same time allow for serious discussion about fear, loss, depression, and anxiety as a result of diagnosis and treatment side effects. The process of setting up, delivering, and evaluating a novel service for patients using technology at the core of delivery was exhausting and challenging, but ultimately very rewarding. Our experiences have highlighted some overarching observations and recommendations which we share below.

Clearly, this type of service is not going to meet everyone's needs, but it appears to have reached a group who would not have engaged in group therapy had it not been offered in this manner, not just because of their immunosuppressed status, but also because of the pressure of face-to-face group dynamics and fears of being made to feel worse by hearing others' stories about illness. Participants valued the privacy and control the technology offered, and they were more confident to make art work without being observed. The virtual connection perhaps allowed inhibitions to be dropped more easily and the sharing to be more candid.

In terms of the art work, visual or written work produced at each session, there were more similarities than differences between face-to-face and virtual art therapy sessions. In doing this project, I have learned that digital technology offers different ways of providing a space to make art work or explore through a creative process. Now and in the future, telehealth offers new and different ways of providing psychological support through remote and electronic means.

Recommendations

- *Telemedicine offers accessibility to art therapy services.* Working through a rural health board where financial restrictions limit access to psychological support, telemedicine offers a better use of resources, cutting down on travel for both health professionals and patients. It is a technology more familiar in countries such as Canada and Australia where patients in rural areas cannot access the services of professionals, including art therapists. But it clearly also has applications in the provision of psychological support and therapy; we encourage art therapists and other professionals to explore the possibilities of telemedicine.

- *Technical infrastructure is not always a barrier.* While there may be a lack of technical support in a small rural hospital, this study has identified that psychosocial therapy has been possible and has been beneficial to those patients who received such support through telehealth.

- *Telehealth technology changes over time.* Telehealth and digital technology are fast moving, but being able to work alongside a local university offers opportunities to develop small explorative research studies that can add to the body of knowledge for future studies. Collie and Čubranić (1999) encourage art therapists to engage in small research projects such as this one.

References

Blake-Mortimer, J., Gore-Felton, C., Kimerling, R., Turner-Cobb, J.M. and Spiegel, D. (1999) Improving the quality and quantity of life among patients with cancer: A review of the effectiveness of group psychotherapy. *European Journal of Cancer 35*(11), 1581–1586.

Chang, S., Khort, H. and Maeker, H.T. (2014) Monitoring the immune competence of cancer patients to predict outcome. *Cancer Immunology and Immunotherapy 63*(7), 713–719.

Collie, K. and Čubranić, D. (1999) An art therapy solution to a telehealth problem. *Art Therapy 16*(4), 186–193.

Keenan, J., Rahman, R. and Hudson, J. (2016) *Experiences of palliative care patients accessing psychosocial support through telehealth.* Conference proceedings at the European Health Psychology Society and BPS Division of Health Psychology Annual Conference 2016. Aberdeen.

National Institute of Clinical Excellence (2004) *Improving Supportive and Palliative Care for Adults with Cancer.* Cancer Service Guideline CSG4. London: NICE.

National Institute of Clinical Excellence (2009) *Early and Locally Advanced Breast Cancer: Diagnosis and Treatment.* Guideline CG80. London: NICE.

Ronnberg, A. and Martin, K. (eds.) (2010) *The Book of Symbols: Reflections on Archetypal Images.* Köln: Taschen.

Spiegel, D. (2002) Effects of psychotherapy on cancer survival. *Nature Reviews Cancer 2*(5), 383–389.

19

DIGITAL DEVICES AS CREATIVE EXPRESSIVE TOOLS FOR ADULTS WITH AUTISM

Olena Darewych

Humans across the globe express their thoughts and emotions in many different ways. One may express their ideas in words while another may convey their feelings through a drawing or movement. In today's information and communication technology age, portable digital devices are one of the preferred means of daily expression for individuals in industrialized societies. In the clinical arena, the potential for integrating digital technology as an expressive medium within art therapy practice for hospitalized children (Malchiodi and Johnson, 2013), individuals with learning disabilities (Hallas and Cleaves, 2017), older adults with dementia (Mihailidis *et al.*, 2010), and young adults with autism spectrum disorder (L'Esperance, 2017) is now being recognized.

Autism Spectrum Disorder and Digital Technology

Autism spectrum disorder (ASD) is a neurodevelopmental disorder and rates of ASD are rising in the Western world. According to the Centers for Disease Control and Prevention (2016) in the United States, each year 1 in 68 children is diagnosed with ASD by the age of 8. Consequently, higher numbers of art therapists in North America are working with children, adolescents, and adults with ASD. Individuals with ASD tend to exhibit deficits in verbal and non-verbal communication, imagination, social engagement, and symbolic representation, with repetitive interests and behaviors such as rocking, hand flapping, and self-talk (American Psychiatric Association, 2013). Certain individuals with ASD also demonstrate difficulties with executive function: organizing and sequencing thoughts and actions (Hill, 2004), along with anxiety associated with their social relational challenges (Gillot and Standen, 2007). Further, some struggle with tactile and olfactory sensory issues. Those with low sensory sensitivity often yearn to interact with a variety of tactile stimulating objects and prefer listening to music while creating art, whereas those with high sensory sensitivity tend to reject textured and scented art materials and favor making art in silence (Bogdashina, 2016).

Since the integration of digital technology into art therapy sessions is a cutting-edge phenomenon, research exploring this modern therapeutic trend for individuals with ASD is just beginning to flourish. In one recent qualitative phenomenological study, Darewych, Carlton, and Farrugie (2015) explored digital technology use in art therapy as a new art medium for adults with ASD and other developmental disabilities who at the time of the study were enrolled in a traditional group art therapy program at a Canadian community-based autism centre. Study participants attended five one-hour weekly individual digital art therapy sessions grounded in a combined person-centred (Rogers, 1951) and strengths-based (Niemic, Shogren, and Wehmeyer, 2017) theoretical approach. The art therapist who facilitated the sessions continuously engaged in strengths-spotting through observing participants' creative, communicative, and digital abilities. The semi-structured sessions were geared towards each adult's level of cognitive and physical needs and divided into three segments: warm-up activity, art-based intervention, and closure activity.

Each session commenced with a paper-based check-in nine-emoji feeling faces chart (angry, happy, loving, mellow, sad, silly, sneaky, surprised, unhappy) and closed with a check-out nine-emoji feeling faces chart. During the sessions, participants created on two password-protected portable digital devices: a Lenovo Yoga 13.3-inch Windows 8 touchscreen Ultrabook™ and a Samsung 7-inch Galaxy Tab 3 Android touch tablet. The Windows 8 laptop was selected due to its large screen, easel-like table positioning, password-protected folders and instant printing feature. The Android tablet was included because not all the selected creative applications (apps) were compatible with the Windows 8 platform.

The following five art-making apps were introduced to participants: ArtRage, Fresh Paint, Crayola Art Studio, Coloring Mandalas, Sand Draw, and Zen Brush, and the following four creative game activity applications were introduced during the warm-up and closure segments to maintain and strengthen participants' cognitive patterning, problem-solving, and sequencing skills: GS Kids! Shapes and Colors, Number Link, Puzzle Touch, and Sticker Tales. Participants could create on the digital canvases with a round-tip stylus, a Nomad brush stylus, or their fingers. Participants had a choice to create digital art in silence or with background music. One key study finding supported Alders' and her colleagues (2011) notion that individuals with ASD with high sensory sensitivity interact more effectively with mess-free and texture-free digital canvases than traditional tactile art mediums.

The following section of this chapter presents a case example illustrating Max's (pseudonym) lived experience participating in the aforementioned digital art therapy study sessions. The case highlights Max's digital art-making process, the shift of traditional art-based interventions onto the digital canvas, the role of the therapist, the positive therapeutic outcomes, and the intermittent technical glitches encountered along the creative journey.

Case Example 19.1

Max, a 24-year-old adult with ASD, volunteered to partake in five weekly one-hour individual digital art therapy sessions. He was a cheerful individual with verbal and written expressive communication abilities. His speech included some repetitive language. He was comfortable with making eye contact with others, although social interaction in a group setting was a challenge for him. As an individual with moderate sensory sensitivities, he enjoyed attending the traditional group art therapy sessions where he engaged in routine art activities and created with acrylic paint and pastels. Completing multistep sequencing art projects was not easy for him. At home, he played video games on his computer.

Max's digital art therapy sessions took place at the autism center in a private room where the bright fluorescent buzzing lights were dimmed and a basket of grounding objects (e.g. fuzzy ball, Slinky, felt squares) was available should he require a sensory break from digital art making. A color inkjet printer was present in the room, allowing Max to print his digital artwork during each session should he desire. Prior to commencing the study sessions, Max attended a digital trial-run session during which the art therapist assessed his comfort level with using the two portable digital devices and art-making apps. During the trial-run session, Max gravitated towards the Fresh Paint art-making app with its drop-down toolbox which included virtual acrylic paint, chalk, crayons, pastels, pen, pencil, and watercolor paint. He did not find the Android Zen Brush drawing app appealing due to its limited inkbrush color palette.

Session One

In session one, Max was invited to sit in front of a table where the Windows 8 laptop was set up in its easel position. He began by completing the paper-based emoji chart. Max circled "happy," for he was looking forward to attending a new college course for individuals with developmental disabilities. The warm-up activity encouraged him to play with Number Link, a Sudoku-like puzzle game app with different levels of difficulty. The aim of the game is to link pairs of colored numbers without crossing the lines and leaving any empty squares on the board. Immediately, Max named all the colors on the grid and with his index finger independently completed Level 1, which he found challenging.

After completing the Number Link game, he was ready to engage in art making. The art therapist directed Max to create a scribble drawing (Cane, 1951) using the Fresh Paint app. The scribble drawing art-based intervention allowed the therapist to examine Max's imaginative capability in developing symbolic representations of people, places, and objects not present to his visual sense from his spontaneous scribble lines. With a round-tip stylus and with his eyes closed, Max painted a red scribble on the smooth-textured digital canvas. After a few seconds, he opened his eyes, viewed the scribble and stated, "Looks like flowers to me." He then developed his scribble into orange flowers and titled his image "Flowers" (see Figure 19.1). When asked what he liked about painting with Fresh Paint he stated, "It was easy. It's fun. I like using my finger and stylus." Near the end of the session, Max experimented with Sticker Tales, a Windows 8 picture-making app that allows an individual to create pictures by placing stickers (e.g. land animals, marine fish) on preset background scenes (e.g. farm, under water). He completed one farm scene and then was ready to move on.

For his close-out emoji chart, Max circled "mellow" and verbally emphasized how he enjoyed creating digital art during today's session.

Figure 19.1
Flowers

Session Two

In session two, Max circled "happy" on his check-in emoji chart for he was looking forward to Thanksgiving weekend. The warm-up activity allowed Max to experiment with Puzzle Touch, a creative Windows 8 puzzle game app that allows one to create simple (12-piece) to complex (300-piece) jigsaw puzzles with the images provided or pictures imported into the app. The built-in clock allows the user to time themselves. At once, Max stated, "I like puzzles." The art therapist opened the app and showed him the collection of puzzle images.

Max eagerly picked an animal image and with the round-tip stylus began to complete a 12-piece puzzle.

While working on the puzzle, Max asked to listen to music. Together, the art therapist and Max searched for and downloaded one of his favorite songs from a free YouTube clip. Max hummed and sang to the music while creating his puzzle. He completed the 12-piece puzzle in one minute. Max enjoyed the digital puzzle activity so much that he asked to create another puzzle with a Puzzle Touch nature image. This time, the art therapist challenged Max to complete a 24-piece puzzle which he was able to execute in two minutes. After completing the second puzzle, Max independently opened one of the fixed Puzzle Touch city images and challenged himself to complete a 24-piece puzzle. The art therapist sat back and witnessed Max smile and accomplish the 24-piece puzzle.

Max was then directed by the art therapist to review basic shapes using the GS Kids! Shapes N Colors app. He appreciated reciting all the shapes but was not drawn to the app due to its child-oriented design. At that moment, the art therapist opened the Fresh Paint app for Max and asked him to draw shapes using his working memory. Max painted orange circles, squares, and triangles (see Figure 19.2).

Figure 19.2
Shapes

Next, the art therapist directed him to draw a house or a tree or a person (H-T-P) (Buck, 1948). It is theorized that the H-T-P image may symbolically mirror the artist's identity. Using Fresh Paint, Max chose a digital black pen, and with the round-tip stylus drew a square house with a triangular roof and triangular windows while listening to the music downloaded from YouTube (Darewych et al., 2015). Afterwards, Max asked to create a free drawing. When he completed his free drawing, the art therapist taught Max how to save and print his digital house drawing and free drawing.

The closure activity for the second session was to use Number Link or Puzzle Touch. Max enthusiastically chose Puzzle Touch and worked on a fourth puzzle. His ability to complete a range of puzzles that challenge in different ways in one session increased his level of self-confidence. His check-out feeling on the emoji chart was "happy" and his end-of-session remark was, "It's fun using the computer. It's fun listening to music."

Session Three

In session three, Max circled "happy" on his check-in emoji chart and for the warm-up activity was permitted to create a free drawing using Fresh Paint. He independently opened Fresh Paint from the laptop's desktop, selected a wide paintbrush, and commenced painting the entire digital canvas red, as this was his favorite color. The process of painting the entire touchscreen surface with one color seemed to ground him. He then used the paint dry option to add a second, blue layer to his painting, which he titled "Red and Blue" (see Figure 19.3). He appreciated the app's multiple paint layer brushstrokes width options.

When he finished his free drawing, the art therapist presented the Android tablet to Max and introduced him to the meditative Coloring Mandala app with its simple circular design templates. Max excitedly selected a mandala template and with the automatic color fill-in option added blue, green, gray, orange, and red to the small circles (see Figure 19.4). While coloring and zooming in and out with his finger, he joyfully uttered, "Oh cool! So awesome! Concentrating on it." Max was proud of his mandala creation and asked to print his mandala. He clicked the print button but the wireless network between the laptop and printer ceased, leaving Max to wait until the following session to receive a tangible copy of this digital painting.

For the closing session segment, Max elected to play with Puzzle Touch. The art therapist asked if he was interested in importing and transforming his "Red and Blue" painting into a puzzle. Max immediately exclaimed, "Yes!" The art therapist demonstrated how to import the digital painting into a 12-piece puzzle, which he silently executed in one minute.

At the end of the session, Max's check-out emoji was "excited," for the music band One Direction was coming to town and he was looking forward to attending the concert.

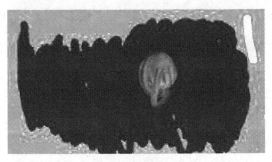

Figure 19.3
Red and blue

Figure 19.4
Mandala

Session Four

In session four, Max cheerfully entered the therapy room, sat down in his usual chair, and with a pen circled "happy" on his check-in emoji chart. Instantly, Max asked to view images of the music band One Direction. Together, Max and the art therapist opened Google and searched for the images. While viewing the images and listening to One Direction music from YouTube clips, Max shared his experience of attending last week's music concert and stated that during the concert, "I never stopped singing." Max seemingly enjoyed the opportunity to reflect upon his feelings and recent memory of the musical event with the art therapist.

Next, the art therapist offered Max the Android tablet to explore Sand Draw, a drawing app which allows one to doodle and add stickers of beach objects on a sand grain backdrop. In the clinical setting, Sand Draw simulates a sandplay therapy sandbox without the tactile sensory element. Max created a few quick sand drawings, and did not save any of his drawings, as he enjoyed clicking the delete image button which caused a virtual wave with ocean sound to wipe away his sand doodles. While he doodled, he stated, "That is so much fun! I like drawing in the sand."

For the closure activity, Max asked to continue doodling with Sand Draw. At the end of the session, the art therapist asked Max what he liked about today's session. He replied, "Drawing in the sand. I like you." Additionally, the art therapist reminded Max that next week would be the last digital art therapy session. Hence, Max circled "sad" on his emoji chart due to the fact that the digital art therapy sessions were coming to an end.

Session Five

In session five, Max quickly circled "happy" on his check-in emoji chart and for the warm-up activity promptly chose to create a free drawing on the laptop using Fresh Paint without listening to background music. He independently selected a thin paintbrush and commenced painting the entire digital canvas red. Once again, painting the entire canvas one color seemed to ground him. After independently saving his red painting, the art therapist asked Max to draw his favorite kind of day (AFKD) (Manning, 1987). Rather than drawing, Max chose to write the following words on the digital canvas to the best of his ability: "One Direction," "art class," and "I like you" (see Figure 19.5). He verbally informed the art therapist that listening to music and attending the art program at the autism centre were his favorite activities, and that he was fond of the art therapist's presence in the digital art therapy sessions.

At the end of the session, Max independently printed his AKFD and decided not to complete the check-out emoji chart. Instead, he verbally informed the art therapist that he was feeling sad that the digital art therapy sessions were coming to a close. During the closure dialogue when the art therapist questioned which medium he preferred creating with, traditional or digital, Max specified both. He also emphasized that he favored the undivided attention he was receiving from the art therapist in the individual digital art therapy sessions compared to the traditional art therapy group sessions. Though the digital art therapy sessions came to an end, Max continued attending the traditional group art therapy sessions at the autism centre.

At the end of the fifth and final session, the art therapist saved Max's digital images to a USB drive which was transferred to a locked filing cabinet located in the principal researcher's office.

Figure 19.5
My favorite kind of day

Summary

Max participated in five weekly individual digital art therapy study sessions. Throughout the entire one-hour semi-structured sessions, he displayed a sense of comfort while interacting with the two digital portable devices and shifted from one creative activity to another with ease. He preferred painting on the digital canvases with a round-tip stylus and with music playing in the background from the downloaded YouTube clips. Fresh Paint was his favorite art-making app due to its drop-down toolbox with a variety of art instruments, multiple layered painting feature, and eraser tool to correct mistakes. His least favorite art-making app was Zen Brush due to its limited color palette. He found the problem-solving Number Link game difficult. He effortlessly completed the traditional art therapy interventions on the digital canvas. The scribble drawing (Cane, 1951) encouraged his imaginative thinking abilities, the H-T-P (Buck, 1948) helped him gain a sense of self, and AFKD (Manning, 1987) sparked his mental images of significant events and people in his current life. By session three, Max took on a more active role in navigating the apps, saving artwork, and printing his digital paintings, which in turn allowed him to gain a greater sense of control over the digital devices.

The art-making apps permitted Max to maintain his visual and auditory processing skills as well as his fine motor skills of drawing and writing, but did not allow him to develop his manipulative skills such as cutting paper with scissors, threading beads, and rolling clay. The Puzzle Touch creative activity app helped him strengthen his problem-solving, pattern and color recognition, and sequencing skills (see Table 19.1). The check-in and check-out emoji feeling charts helped Max verbally and non-verbally externalize his internal feelings and thoughts around current life events and issues with the art therapist.

Table 19.1 Max's digital art therapy sessions

Session		Creative activity	Application (app) name	Skills development
1	Warm-up	Pattern game	Windows 8, Android Number Link	Pattern and color recognition, problem solving
	Art intervention	Scribble drawing (Cane, 1951)	Windows 8, Fresh Paint	Creativity, imagination, communication, fine motor
	Closure	Non-social sticker pictures	Windows 8, Sticker Tales	Color, pattern, and symbol recognition
2	Warm-up	Puzzle creation Shapes creations	Windows 8, Fresh Paint Windows 8 GS Kids! Shapes N Colors	Pattern and color recognition, problem solving Non-social symbolic
	Art intervention	House-tree-person (H-T-P) (Buck, 1948)	Windows 8, Fresh Paint	Creativity, self-concept, communication
	Closure	Puzzle creation	Windows 8, Fresh Paint	problem solving, auditory processing
3	Warm-up	Spontaneous art	Windows 8, Fresh Paint	Creativity, fine motor
	Art intervention	Mandala	Android Coloring Mandalas	Attention
	Closure	Puzzle creation	Windows 8 Puzzle Touch	Problem solving

cont.

Session		Creative activity	Application (app) name	Skills development
4	Warm-up	Music band images	YouTube	Social symbolic, auditory processing
	Art intervention	Sand play	Android Sand Draw	Creativity, imagination, communication, non-social symbolic
	Closure	Mandala	Android Coloring Mandalas	Focus-oriented
5	Warm-up	Spontaneous art to music	Windows 8, Fresh Paint	Creativity, fine motor
	Art intervention	A favorite kind of day (AFKD; Manning, 1987)	Windows 8, Fresh Paint	Imagination, communication, symbolic
	Closure	Spontaneous art and writing	Windows 8, Fresh Paint	Communication

Similar to traditional art therapy sessions, the role of the art therapist during each digital art therapy session was to provide Max with a safe and supportive therapeutic environment, establish a healthy client–therapist relationship, witness his creative process unfold, assess his cognitive and physical strengths and limitations, guide him towards creative, cognitive, and emotional growth, and assist him with new art medium challenges when they presented themselves.

Overall, the digital art therapy sessions permitted Max to undergo verbal and non-verbal self-expression, expand his digital skills, connect with the world with his auditory and visual senses, utilize his imagination, and gain a feeling of self-worth.

Conclusion

In the 21st century, digital devices are orthodox expressive tools for individuals of all ages with and without developmental disabilities and will remain so in our fast-changing technological age. Tech-savvy clients are now expecting their therapist to be technologically competent and trained in administering digitally oriented clinical interventions. Thus, the field of art therapy has to make changes accordingly. Art therapists and art therapy program faculties have an ethical obligation to remain current with new clinical theoretical frameworks, tools, and interventions (Corey *et al.*, 2015).

Austrian pediatrician Hans Asperger, known for his earlier work with children with autism, made a provocative statement in his 1953 German publication: that the clinician and educator working with individuals with ASD "has to become somehow 'autistic'" (as cited in Silberman, 2016, p.106). In other words, the art therapist must be comfortable making minimal eye contact and communicating non-verbally with their clients with ASD and providing a low sensory clinical environment for those with high sensory sensitivity. Requesting that certain individuals with ASD continuously make eye contact, connect with tactile sensory-stimulating art materials, and engage in verbal self-reflective dialogues may intensify their level of anxiety. Further, since certain individuals with ASD prefer connecting with places and objects rather than with self and people due to their social engagement issues, art therapists need to respect such clients' greater physical and psychological attraction towards a creative digital device than to a therapist. Under such clinical circumstances, the client intrinsically connects with the art therapist by means of the creative mess-free digital device.

Autism research continues to accentuate that ASD causes considerable health loss in an individual across their lifespan (Hirvikoski *et al.*, 2016). As a result, art therapists need to implement creative therapeutic programs for children, adolescents, adults, and older adults with ASD that enable them to engage in meaningful creative activities, which, in turn, can mitigate any levels of anxiety, depression, and societal isolation, and improve their psychological health and wellbeing.

In the field of art therapy, research exploring digital technology in art therapy remains sparse but new research findings are indicating that digital technology has the potential to be a valid creative therapeutic tool to improve the wellbeing of individuals with ASD and other developmental disabilities. Thus, the author calls upon art therapists, creative arts therapists, and expressive arts therapists to embrace contemporary digital touchscreen devices with creativity, curiosity, and courage.

Recommendations

- *Explore the benefits and limitations in digital technology with individuals with ASD.* Researchers should continue exploring the benefits and limitations of digital touchscreen devices as creative and skill-building tools for individuals with ASD and other developmental disabilities.

- *Recognize that the digital canvas may be a "preferred medium."* In a recent mixed-methods study by Darewych, Newton, and Farrugie (2017) investigating imagination in adults with medium- to high-functioning ASD utilizing art-based assessments, study participants had a choice to complete their drawings with traditional or digital media. Interestingly, the preferred medium by the participants was the digital canvas.

- *Collaborate with app developers to create software for use in therapy.* Since a large number of user-friendly art-making and creative activity apps have been developed for children and youth, there is a need for the art therapist–researcher to collaborate with app developers to design simple software programs for adult clinical populations.

- *Attend to strengths over deficits through both traditional media and digital media.* Future clinical directions might include clients' blending of traditional media with digital media in art therapy sessions. It is important that art therapists design and implement clinical programs that attend to the strengths of their clients with ASD and other developmental disabilities rather than their deficits.

References

Alders, A., Beck, L., Allen, P. and Mosinski, B. (2011) Technology in art therapy: Ethical challenges. *Art Therapy 28*(4), 165–170.

American Psychiatric Association (2013) *Diagnostic and Statistical Manual of Mental Disorders* (5th edn). Arlington, VA: American Psychiatric Publishing.

Bogdashina, O. (2016) *Sensory Perceptual Issues in Autism and Asperger Syndrome: Different Sensory Experiences—Different Perceptual Worlds* (2nd edn). London: Jessica Kingsley Publishers.

Buck, J.N. (1948) The H-T-P technique: A qualitative and quantitative scoring manual. *Journal of Clinical Psychology Monograph 4*, 1–120.

Cane, F. (1951) *The Artist in Each of Us*. Craftsbury Common, VT: Art Therapy.

Centers for Disease Control and Prevention (2016) New data on autism: Five important facts to know. Retrieved at www.cdc.gov/features/new-autism-data/index.html

Corey, G., Schneider Corey, M., Corey, C. and Callanan, P. (2015) *Issues and Ethics in the Helping Professions* (9th edn). Belmont, CA: Brooks/Cole.

Darewych, O.H., Carlton, N.R. and Farrugie, K.W. (2015) Digital technology use in art therapy with adults with developmental disabilities. *Journal on Developmental Disabilities 21*(2), 96–102.

Darewych, O.H., Newton, N. and Farrugie, K.W. (2017) Investigating imagination in adults with autism with art-based assessments. *Journal on Developmental Disabilities 23*(2), 25–34.

Gillot, A. and Standen, P.J. (2007) Levels of anxiety and sources of stress in adults in autism. *Journal of Intellectual Disabilities 11*(4), 359–370.

Hallas, P. and Cleaves, L. (2017) "It's not all fun": Introducing digital technology to meet the emotional and mental health needs of adults with learning disabilities. *International Journal of Art Therapy 22*(2), 73–83.

Hill, E.L. (2004) Executive dysfunction in autism. *Trends in Cognitive Sciences 8*, 26–32.

Hirvikoski, T., Mittendorfer-Rutz, E., Boman, M., Larsson, H., Lichtenstien, P. and Bolte, S. (2016) Premature mortality in autism spectrum disorder. *British Journal of Psychiatry 208*(3), 232–238.

L'Esperance, N. (2017) Art therapy and technology: Islands of brilliance. In R.L. Garner (ed.) *Digital Art Therapy: Materials, Methods, and Application*. London: Jessica Kingsley Publishers.

Malchiodi, C.A. and Johnson, E.R. (2013) Digital art therapy with hospitalized children. In C.A. Malchiodi (ed.) *Art Therapy and Health Care*. New York, NY: Guilford Press.

Manning, T.M. (1987) Aggression depicted in abused children's drawings. *The Arts in Psychotherapy 14*, 15–24.

Mihailidis, A., Blunsden, S., Boger, J., Richards, B. *et al.* (2010) Towards the development of a technology for art therapy and dementia: Definitions of needs and design constraints. *The Arts in Psychotherapy 37*(4), 293–300.

Niemic, R.M., Shogren, K.A. and Wehmeyer, M.L. (2017) Character strengths and intellectual and developmental disability: A strengths-based approach to positive psychology. *Education and Training in Autism and Developmental Disabilities 52*(1), 13–25.

Rogers, C.R. (1951) *Client-Centered Therapy: Its Current Practice, Implications and Theory*. Boston, MA: Houghton-Mifflin.

Silberman, S. (2016) *NeuroTribes: The Legacy of Autism and the Future of Neurodiversity*. New York, NY: Avery.

20

USING DIGITAL MEDIA IN ART-BASED RESEARCH

Shaun McNiff

An exploration of the contributions of digital media to art-based research first requires a description of the framework informing this approach to inquiry. What is the nature of research, the concepts informing it, and the purpose for doing it? How do we define art-based research? What is the paradigm within which we operate? What are the objectives of our research?

After establishing this context, we can look more specifically not only at what digital media, and video in particular, can offer, but how they can significantly determine the nature of the research process and outcomes. Video offers art therapy the opportunity to document live action and combine the persistent dualities of *process* and *product* into a more integral approach to research and practice. This chapter will also explore how the editing of video footage and the creation of an aesthetically engaging presentation of the experimental process and its outcomes are defining features of art-based research which supplant exclusive reliance on linear analysis with the making of something new and the showing of art as evidence.

The Nature of Research within an Art-Based Paradigm

There are clear differences within art therapy and other disciplines as to the fundamental nature of "research" and therefore this process cannot be taken for granted. I approach research as disciplined and systematic inquiry and in the case of art therapy, it is based in art. This simple and direct definition of research offers a practical alternative to the social science bifurcation of quantitative and qualitative inquiry and the myriad categories of the latter, all of which are seeking legitimization within a paradigm that does not align with artistic practice and which I believe generates considerable confusion regarding how to best advance art therapy efficacy.

I define art-based research (McNiff, 1998, 2013) as the use of art-making, in all artistic disciplines, as a primary form of inquiry by the person conducting the research, either alone or with others. The distinctive feature of art-based research is the realization that artistic expression offers modes of communication and understanding that are inaccessible to linear and logical reason and language, the same rationale for the use of art in therapy, which paradoxically is forgotten and contradicted by art therapy when it comes to research. This happens because art therapy tends to be intent on justifying itself according to the dominant scientific paradigm, which only furthers the feared marginalization because first, art and its depths cannot be explained and reduced to science, and second, because the social/human sciences have not been effective in generating law-like principles (MacIntyre, 2007). Ironically, art-based research can help social science establish a more effective approach to inquiry which accepts the unpredictability of human experience and thus focuses on perfecting practice and ways of engaging life situations rather than the impossible task of reducing them to rules and laws.

And perhaps most essentially, art is the evidence in the practice of art-based research (McNiff, 2014a). Rather than insisting that artistic outcomes be translated into scientific categories and measurements that cannot convey their nature, art therapy needs to believe that art speaks for itself and then work more systematically to perfect and maximize these art-based communications, trusting that intelligent and open decision makers, as I have experienced, will see the evidence and maybe even be transformed by it.

Making the case for generating, examining, and presenting artistic evidence involves inevitable dissonance with prevailing assumptions about doing research. In my experience there have been three consistent impediments even within situations where art-based inquiry is supported.

In just about every academic context where research involving human experience is conducted, it is assumed that the person conducting the study will first collect "data" and then "analyze" it with the goal of identifying "themes." These assumptions and stock approaches hinder artistic inquiry. In the practice of art-based research, art objects and expressive actions are compromised and lessened when reduced exclusively to the notion of "data." Within art-based research art is created and not just collected. I greatly respect the generation and use of data in relation to certain forms of inquiry, understanding, and decision-making, and I have worked closely with data (numbers, opinions, trends, and so forth) throughout my career, especially when in leadership roles. But an art object is a living and expressive entity that, like a person, holds complexities, change, and infinitely variable possibilities for relationship. Thus, I cannot simply approach it as data to be collected and analyzed according to a formula of some kind.

Second, analysis is part of the interpretative process and not the whole of it. Analytic processes function within the realm of linear and logical thought, separating factors from the more integral context, and break things down into parts. The interpretation of art is more than analysis alone. It is a more holistic process of reflection and relationship between the object and the person, a dynamic exchange that creates *new life* and understanding resulting from the reciprocal engagement. Art objects and expressive actions express themselves through their material properties and features and they are not simply inert material to be transmuted into constituent parts. Thus, in art-based research we do not assume that "data analysis" is the exclusive and fundamental mode of operation. We see ourselves as often analyzing, but arguably more essentially interpreting, engaging, reflecting, imagining, and co-creating in close relationship with the objects and processes emerging from the research activities.

Finally, themes have their place in art and life, but not every element of an artistic expression can be reduced to a theme and its narrative prejudice. Art-based research also opens to patterns, structures, essential elements, forces or energies, expressions, and various other factors inherent to art that are beyond the scope of themes alone. Thus, the way that academic research in art therapy is assumed to be based upon data and theme analysis hopefully demonstrates how exclusive reliance on a particular research paradigm is a restriction that arguably should be presented in the "limitations" section of the standard APA format. Hence, how do we generate artistic evidence and document our art-based experimentation as to how art heals and changes people and situations? And how can we most effectively communicate these outcomes to others? Based on my experience with today's art materials and communication systems, both of these questions suggest the use of digital media in art-based research. But before describing ways of using these tools within the research process, it is important to also address the ultimate purpose and goals of research and the conceptual framework within which we operate.

The Importance of Practitioner Research

Everything that I have done in art therapy has been closely tied to research that is inseparable from practice, what I call *practitioner research*. With my first art therapy experiences, I kept records of art expressions and made detailed and systematic notes documenting what we did in sessions and how people responded. From the start, I have been focused on perfecting practice and trying to do things in ways that reliably help others. Every session over the course of my career has been characterized by practical and empirical experimentation, reflection, and assessment with an overall goal of advancing my own practice with others and trying to discover and document things that can be of use to students and other art therapists. I am always exploring how art heals, both in relation to the process of creating and our engagement with art objects, alone and with others. It is a process of inquiry based in doing the work. Again, the objective of this practitioner research is perfecting how we operate and serve others.

There is a pervasive assumption today that research is separate from practice and conducted by academically trained "researchers" who bring a certain distance and purported objectivity to the enterprise. These notions also pervade the art therapy discipline and generate considerable confusion that essentially results from a fundamental paradigm conflict that is rarely named. Pioneers of psychotherapy and art therapy practice established these disciplines through their individual and collective practitioner research. They studied what they did with others, systematically examining therapeutic processes and outcomes, with the goal of making methods available to others.

It is assumed that the manner, style, experience, and skill of the therapists conducting the research will influence outcomes, yet the primary emphasis of practitioner research is focused on the mode of practice and its ability to *transcend* these individual circumstances and become an entity unto itself. For example, my experimentation with responding to paintings through movement is based in my practice but the research is intended to not only perfect what I do but then communicate the outcomes to others who can use the methods. The mode of practice is unequivocally empirical, autonomous, and transpersonal. Reality is an interplay of participants at every level of experience with nothing being capable of complete isolation from the foundational interdependence of all things. Thus those who insist that experimental research with a particular therapeutic method should be conducted by a person other than the therapist exploring the practice are, first, at odds with reality; second, assuming the presence of a more objective context that does not exist; and third, eliminating the very heart of the inquiry which is informed by the vision, skill, and commitment of the practitioner committed to perfecting a method.

The goal of my research is to establish empirical methods and approaches to practice that exist autonomously and hopefully in sync with universal and common aspects of artistic expression and human experience. Once these methods are established and communicated, I assume that they will be used in infinitely varied ways based upon the styles and interests of individual therapists, the needs of participants in the particular therapeutic situations, and the forces within a specific context or environment. Thus, the goal is to advance practice with empirical structures which may have universal value, like the movement response to a painting, but that are implemented in ways that are unique due to the inherent variability and unpredictability of human experience. Other examples of empirical methods that have emerged from art-based inquiry are the current exploration of art-making by art therapists as a mode of inquiry and understanding in supervision and reflection on practice (Fish, 2006, 2016) and the closely related process of art-making by therapists during sessions as a companion process (Lett, 2016; Moon, 1997). We perfect these methods by doing them ourselves alone and with others and the introduction of video and digital media to these areas of inquiry will exponentially increase the range of research issues and methods.

Video Captures Empirical Process and Outcomes

Video enables us to document, record, and perceive live action and artistic processes. This happens simultaneously from varied perspectives. Rather than just reflecting on artistic processes through notes and memory after the fact, the video footage complements these modes of documentation with a lasting record of the actual actions that can be continuously revisited and examined. The process of artistic expression is thus made permanent and palpable, just like the presence of the finished art object. We have access to *empirical forms of both process and product*, and in relation to the former, video technology enables us to show the various iterations of the art object through still images made with screen shots. In this respect, the art object is made manifest not just as a final form, but through its ongoing emanation.

The use of video in research in this respect helps to transcend the unnecessary bifurcation of process and product that historically permeates art therapy. It establishes a more integral stance with regard to their interdependence, furthering the realization that the object is protean and a necessary partner to process that cannot exist without it. In this respect, video documentation of art-making enables the exploration of questions and issues related to the *progressive emergence of visual images*. The recording process shows how all forms of visual art are enactments, movements, and live actions in time and space just like the performing arts.

In contrast to video applications, the tendency to present outcomes and evidence through still visual images is deeply ingrained in art therapy, dominating the literature and professional presentations at every level. I have continued it myself through my own publications (McNiff, 1992, 2004, 2009). This pattern is an extension of the way the established academic practices of an era determine thought and communication. It is, however, interesting that the emergent digital media and especially video have not yet fully exercised their influence and potential impact on practice and research. There are a number of reasons for this, and perhaps the most significant is the hegemony of the social science paradigm and its assumptions about research within the art therapy community.

Art therapy journal publications in recent years, with certain notable exceptions, have actually moved farther away from even the discipline's historic presentation of still images. There is a preponderance of graphs, tables, quantifications of survey questions pervaded with bias, assumptions, and opinion, all presented in jargon and concepts that look and sound very distant from the art-making process and its outcomes. Art therapy keeps emphasizing the importance of process, yet it is rarely shown in publications and research. In contrast, art-based research informed by an artistic paradigm takes a different direction and does its best to get as close as possible to the actual experience of artistic expression in both documenting processes and showing outcomes (McNiff, 2014b).

When we discovered through our experiments in the early 1970s (McNiff and Cook, 1975; McNiff, 1981) that video is to human action what the microscope is to biology and the telescope to astronomy, we were concentrating on how to use the medium in art therapy practice, as I have described in Chapter 5. These uses of digital art-making tools have continued unabated, but it is only recently that I myself have begun to encourage the use of video as a primary mode of inquiry in all of the art-based research that I supervise.

I think the reasons for this delay are in some ways attributable to the static conventions of formal academic research. Even within art-based inquiry there has been a tendency to show still visual images and then describe processes with words, in keeping with past practice. We do this in spite of the realization that: discursive language and narrative cannot convey the sensory and energetic dimensions of creative expression as experienced by the person making art; these felt experiences cannot be reduced to the thoughts and words of the person observing them; and perhaps most importantly, whatever is translated into words is often a construction and expression of a particular person. The verbal descriptions may miss the inherent and empirical qualities of the action. Thus, why not try to *let the action speak for itself* in a more direct and complete way, all the while realizing that even video recordings present a point of view which does not present the complete experience, but nevertheless is much closer than a verbal account. Where it may be difficult in terms of time and resources within the demanding context of art therapy professional practice to conduct this type of careful study, it belies logic why it does not become the focus of academic research.

There are perhaps three primary reasons for a recent shift toward the digital documentation of process in my supervision of doctoral research: 1) the increased credibility and interest in art-based research in keeping with the principles described above; 2) the accessibly and common use of high-quality digital recording devices (small hand-held and wearable cameras) together with greatly simplified editing technologies; and 3) the increasing interest in exploring the immediate effects of empirical artistic processes versus more speculative questions. The convergence of these and other factors has resulted in the use of video to document action and to also generate an extensive range of still images that can be captured through screen shots. In short, the properties of the artistic medium have dramatically influenced the nature of research and the questions and issues that it addresses.

Rather than attempt a comprehensive overview of video usage in art-based research, I acknowledge the vast range of possiblities. I also offer a detailed vignette of a hypothetical example of developing an art-based research question and method of inquiry using video in Ross Prior's (2018) *Using Art as Research in Learning and Teaching* (McNiff, 2018). Thus, potential questions and methods are as large as art itself. Based on my experience with video and digital media over the course of their existence, it can also be said with certainty that the particular ways of using the technology will grow and change significantly in sync with broad usage and technological advances. Therefore, I concentrate here on two fundamental aspects of video use that are likely to persist and offer opportunities for approaching research in distinctly different ways—the ability of video to document action and the role of the editing process in reflecting upon and interpreting processes and presenting the work.

Using Video to Document Process

The common practice in the use of video in art-based research that I supervise involves the person conducting the research first experimenting alone to directly experience, test, and perfect a particular research method before engaging co-researchers (participants in the experimental process; research "with" vs. "on" people (Reason, 2003)) in a subsequent phase of inquiry. Through this solo experimentation the research question/s and methods of inquiry are refined. The work alone is pivotal to artistic inquiry since a primary premise of the approach to research is that I do not want to ask someone to do something that I do not do myself and also, if I want to know a particular artistic process and how to perfect it, then it makes sense to do it. In addition to developing new methods of practice, art-based studies explore the qualities and effects of various materials used in art therapy. Video recording plays an essential role in that the person conducting the research is not completely alone—the camera operates as witness and offers independent evidence together with a record of what happened.

Both the solo sessions and those that follow with others are videotaped with multiple cameras. For example, a fixed camera on a tripod can be adjusted to document, in the case of painting, drawing, or object making, the whole two-dimensional surface or the complete object. A wearable camera on the artist's forehead can be used to follow eye movements and provide close-up footage of the hands at work. A camera may also be used by the person conducting the research while working with a co-researcher. This results in footage from vantage points not captured by the other cameras; interestingly enough, using a camera may enhance the focus of witnessing another person work rather than limiting or obstructing a more complete perspective.

The artistic use of the camera by a researcher is yet another distinguishing feature of video-assisted art-based research. Where the skillful use of the camera in art therapy practice influences the expressiveness of the resulting video, the same applies to its use in research. Quality footage and editing as discussed below have an impact on outcomes and the ability of the video presentation to affect others. The artistic presentation of art-based research is one of many factors demonstrating the illusory assumptions of objectivity in human experience. Even if a still camera records a completely mechanical and verbatim video, the camera operates from a particular position in space and the perceptual qualities of the footage, in this case a bland attempt at a literal account, impact the viewer with their structural features. So why not improve the expression of the medium? These issues and realities in turn contribute to the infinite possibilities for conducting art-based research with digital media.

Video as an Artistic Mode of Reflecting on Research Processes

As important as it is to capture video footage of live action, the process of editing video as a mode of artistic interpretation and reflection on the experimental activity truly distinguishes art-based research from conventional social science approaches. Reflecting upon video footage and the process of editing illustrate how a more complete process of interpretation and artistic presentation happens within art-based research.

When people ask, "How do we reflect on video footage documenting a particular session, series of sessions, or a particular moment in time," I say *artistically*, like a filmmaker who approaches the editing process with the objective of shaping the most impactful aesthetic outcome. The editor as artist *makes something new*—perhaps the most fundamental distinction from analyzing what exists.

A common feature of the research that I supervise is the creation of a five- to seven-minute edited video synthesizing a sequence of sessions with an individual co-researcher. This video is often shown in a final or culminating session reviewing all of the previous work. The viewing of the video gives the co-researcher the opportunity to contribute to the overall process of interpreting the work as a whole and identifying essential elements and outcomes. If the previous sessions involved the making of visual artworks, these expressions will also be physically present in the final reflective session. The edited video adds a dynamic and live element that enables the co-researcher to see and relive the previous work. As in the use of video in therapy, the showing of the edited video can serve as an affirmation of the co-researcher's contributions. It is also likely to stimulate reflection, insights, and comments. Again, as in art therapy sessions, a compact and aesthetically stimulating video is more likely to generate creative and insightful reactions than a long and literal showing. Even when a co-researcher is willing to watch hours of footage, it is debatable whether this will be as productive as watching a terse and *carefully crafted distillation*.

The artistic bias of editing is an accepted part of the process because, as stated above, any presentation, including the most mechanical and literal showing, is presented from a point of view. The objective of the video is thus the furthering of a depth of engagement between the research participants and the materials they are examining. I find that the editing process and the creation of concise documentation also helps to keep the person conducting the inquiry focused on the research questions and it prevents tangential deviations.

One of the challenges in making a terse video synthesis of a series of sessions is selecting what will be shown. Even when viewing a relatively short period of action, the possibilities for editing clips can be vast, especially when stills are shown together with pauses that hold a poignant gesture or image for sustained viewing. As I mention above, the video interpretation and editing involve analysis, but it is more than identifying existing parts. It is essentially a process of aesthetic construction and creative expression, a making of art, rather than simply collecting data, that brings something into existence, something that did not previously exist.

I encourage making pure and simple video that gives the clearest and most expressive showing of overt and subtle action, emphasizing the values of *cinéma vérité*, which is characterized as direct observation of life that allows the action to speak for itself without artificial devices or commentary. I am learning that those editing video footage need to be reminded of these objectives when they start adding music, for example, or other sounds or images that were not present during the session. Video reflection and documentation are not about entertainment or making a show. I also discourage showing any explicit written or spoken conclusions in edited videos that will be shown to co-researchers with the goal of engaging them in the process of reflecting on the experimental work. As I have emphasized, the person editing the footage will be making selections and interpretations in determining what will constitute the final video. This bias is inherent to creating and it is acknowledged in every aspect of the research, yet it is distinctly different from making categorical comments within a review process intended to invite the responses and insights of the research participants.

In helping researchers make selections from footage documenting hours of sessions and often doubled or tripled through the use of multiple cameras, I encourage them to view the work repeatedly over an extended period of time, to essentially live with the video. I urge them to identify *poignant and decisive moments* (Cartier-Bresson), sequences that may inform or reinforce their original ideas, but also ones that may contest them or add something completely new and unexpected in keeping with how the creative process always produces outcomes not known or planned at the beginning. Raw footage is viewed repeatedly in much the same way as reflecting on audio recordings and transcripts of interviews. But in contrast to text-based interview dialogue, video generates gestures, pauses, and other subtle expressions outside the scope of narrative.

The video footage of art-making sessions will usually involve dialogue and verbal reflection involving all of the people participating in the experimental process. The final reflective viewing of the video is also recorded and transcripts are made from all of the spoken discussion. I encourage people to examine the text repeatedly just as they view the raw footage. The increasingly standardized use of computer technology to code an interview for key words can be helpful in organizing the contents of a text and identifying patterns, but these methods are mechanical and limited to quantifying repeated words that may sometimes simply reflect a person's speech habits, good and bad. As I say to students, these tools cannot replace the more essential reading and reading of a text and being immersed in a relationship with it over time where the overt and subtle features act upon our sensibilities.

Art-based researchers may also use their own artistic responses to the viewing of the video in order to further the identification of essential elements and outcomes. If the research sessions involve work with paint, ink, or clay, the person conducting the research will respond and reflect upon the footage of the sessions by becoming involved in the same type of artistic expression. This corresponding artistic activity serves as a physical, bodily, tactile, and multisensory form of interpretation and understanding whereby action and feel invariably offer distinct modes of understanding. The art-making is also videotaped and viewed repeatedly as a way of furthering the identification of insights and outcomes.

After making selections of footage and constructing an edited video from the various clips, I encourage an artistic organization of the whole. In many cases it will be appropriate to show a sequence of action as it occurred within a session or in a sequence of sessions. But ultimately, I support an artistic construction that maximizes expressive impact, and this may deviate from literal and linear documentation. Various devices such as multiple frames on a screen may also be used to both condense and multiply effects, all of which are informed by the goal of enabling the medium to make its contribution to understanding within its kinetic and multisensory nature.

Bringing It All Together

Art-based research using video also tends to make a culminating video that presents the entire research process as part of a dissertation or thesis and for public showing. All of the editing processes used to make a video, synthesizing sessions with an individual co-researcher, apply to creating an edited video showing the whole research process. In a research project involving the visual arts we often use footage focusing on hands and bodies at work without identifying the person, for the purpose of confidentiality. However, even when co-researchers agree to be identified and credited for their participation, we discover how a close-up showing of the manipulation of materials actually heightens and focuses the impact and clarity of the presentation.

The final video presentation of the whole study also concentrates on a concise distillation of essential outcomes, usually involving no more than 12 minutes of video. The effort to capture fundamental principles through the editing process furthers the overall precision and communicability of the research. In the case of a doctoral dissertation, the video presentation complements the overall written text which is in keeping with conventional standards. The video and text work together. They complement one another. The written identification of outcomes in a terse format furthers a comparable distillation in the editing process and vice versa. However, we conclusively see that an artistically produced video presents compelling evidence that can stand on its own without an accompanying academic text and we work to achieve this goal throughout the editing process. The final research will hopefully be presented in various venues with different time demands and limits.

The *artistically engaging video* documenting outcomes is the lynchpin or hub of the research and it generates ensuing possibilities for many different ways of experiencing and studying the overall research that extends from it. This creative shaping of the video through the editing process and experiencing discoveries not anticipated in the research plan is another distinguishing property of art-based research. Rather than analyzing data according to a preexisting concept, the editing process builds upon the previous sessions. The edited video elucidates what went before, but as with the artistic process, it generates yet another artistic response and contribution in a sequence of creations, as Jung would say, imagining it all further.

Conclusion

Video provides opportunities for a more complete and multisensory process of expression, one that transcends words and narrative and that corresponds more closely to the multisensory gestalt of art therapy processes, again the very things that we identify to justify the use of art therapy as a complement to verbal therapeutic practice. As with art therapy practice, we naturally attempt to select poignant and decisive moments from the ongoing movement of experience, moments that encapsulate what we consider to be essential elements from the extensive flux of a particular session or dialogue.

The tangible presence of the finished art object and the exclusive emphasis on it throughout history has resulted in the obfuscation and avoidance of the dynamic, kinesthetic, tactile, and temporal features of the acts of creation. Video turns the tables on these limits and unites the visual arts with other dynamic art forms happening in a particular time and space. And most importantly the features and capabilities of artistic media such as video will in the future significantly influence the kinds of research questions and issues that will arise in the future, together with the methods used to explore them. The medium is the message and more—it shapes thought, experience, the process of inquiry, outcomes, and our shared sense of actuality and significance.

Recommendations

· Start practicing by videotaping yourself while making art with any medium and simply focus on the process of creation without a particular research question or direction.

· Capture no more than ten minutes of footage with a wearable camera and with a camera on a tripod focused on the hands at work. Use this footage as a basis for exploring the methods and principles discussed in this chapter.

· Trust the process—practice will help you understand the medium and its properties and prepare to use it in formal research activities.

References

Fish, B. (2006) Image-based narrative enquiry of response art in art therapy. Doctoral dissertation. Retrieved on April 1, 2018 at ProQuest Dissertations and Theses database (UMI No. 3228081).

Fish, B. (2016) *Art-Based Supervision: Cultivating Therapeutic Insight through Imagery*. New York, NY: Routledge.

Lett, W. (2016) *Creative Arts Companioning in Coconstruction of Meanings*. Melbourne, Australia: MIECAT Institute.

MacIntyre, A. (2007) *After Virtue: A Study in Moral Theory* (3rd edn). Notre Dame, IN: University of Notre Dame Press.

McNiff, S. (1981) Video enactment in the expressive therapies. In J. Fryrear and B. Fleshman (eds.) *Videotherapy in Mental Health*. Springfield, IL: Charles C. Thomas.

McNiff, S. (1992) *Art as Medicine: Creating a Therapy of the Imagination*. Boston, MA: Shambhala.

McNiff, S. (1998) *Art-Based Research*. London: Jessica Kingsley Publishers.

McNiff, S. (2004) *Art Heals: How Creativity Cures the Soul*. Boston, MA: Shambhala Publications.

McNiff, S. (2009) *Integrating the Arts in Therapy*. Springfield, IL: Charles C. Thomas.

McNiff, S. (2013) *Art as Research: Opportunities and Challenges*. Chicago, IL: University of Chicago Press.

McNiff, S. (2014a) Art speaking for itself: Evidence that inspires and convinces. *Journal of Applied Arts and Health* 5(2), 255–262.

McNiff, S. (2014b) Presentations that look and feel like the arts in therapy: Keeping creative tension with psychology. *Australian and New Zealand Journal of Arts Therapy 9*(1), 89–94.

McNiff, S. (2018) Doing art-based research: An advising scenario. In R. Prior (ed.) *Using Art as Research in Learning and Teaching.* Chicago, IL: University of Chicago Press.

McNiff, S. and Cook, C. (1975) Video art therapy. *Art Psychotherapy 2,* 55–63.

Moon, B. (1997) Welcome to the studio: The role of responsive art making in art therapy. Unpublished doctoral dissertation, Union Institute, Cincinnati, OH.

Prior, R. (ed.) (2018) *Using Art as Research in Learning and Teaching.* Chicago, IL: University of Chicago Press.

Reason, P. (2003) Doing co-operative inquiry. In J. Smith (ed.) *Qualitative Psychology: A Practical Guide to Methods.* London: Sage Publications.

21

COMPUTATIONAL ART THERAPY IN ART THERAPY ASSESSMENT AND RESEARCH

Seong-in Kim

Knowledge in art therapy is largely empirical, heuristic, and subjective, based on an art therapist's individual professional expertise and experience. This nature of art therapy makes decision-making complex and difficult for art therapists. In this sense, art therapy is analogous to such areas as economic demand forecasting, weather forecasting, diagnosis of diseases, or judicial sentencing (Kim *et al.*, 1992). The use of computer technologies in these areas, especially artificial intelligence, the purpose of which is to make computers that can imitate intellectual actions of human beings, even to think, learn, and improve by themselves, is already in progress and has yielded significant results.

Computer systems can provide a way to overcome the limitations of conventional art therapy assessments such as subjective evaluation, dictionary-type one-to-one interpretation, and even contradictory interpretation, by building a structured and systematic knowledge of art therapy. An interdisciplinary approach incorporating computer science with art therapy using art as a medium can significantly expand the potential and value of art therapy. Art therapy, accompanied by scientific thought and supported by state-of-the-art computer technology, can achieve its greatest effect in its purpose of improving and enhancing the physical, mental, and emotional wellbeing of individuals of all ages.

The primary goal of computational art therapy (CAT) is to provide objective and quantitative evaluation of elements and systematic interpretation of art, computerize art therapy tools, and develop new methodologies for the improvement of practice and theory, and thus establish art therapy as a science. CAT is defined as art therapy that actively utilizes various computer technologies including quantitative statistical methods. It is different from the limited use of computers as a tool for generating drawings or communication media for remote sessions. Furthermore, it applies computer technology such as artificial intelligence to evaluate and interpret drawings.

This chapter explains the key principles involved in CAT and demonstrates how it can be applied specifically to enhance several contemporary art therapy assessments. For a more comprehensive understanding of CAT and its applications, therapists are encouraged to read *Computational Art Therapy* (Kim, 2017) for more detailed information; this chapter summarizes the prologue in that publication.

The Need for Computational Art Therapy

Present Status of Computer Technologies in Art Therapy

Since the advent of mankind's first computer in 1946, computer technology has made remarkable progress and greatly influenced human society. Various fields including manufacturing, design, education, medicine, and law have progressed remarkably by adopting rapidly changing computer technologies. Compared with other fields, art therapy has been relatively slow in adopting computer technology. But several studies have gone beyond the above practice, using computer systems for evaluating drawings (Kim, Bae, and Lee, 2007; Kim, 2010; Kim *et al.*, 2012; Mattson, 2012) and interpreting drawings (Kim *et al.*, 2006, 2009). This line of research is still scarce, however.

Problems and Difficulties in Art Therapy

One of the reasons for this limited state of research and the slow adoption of computer technology is the lack of art therapists' knowledge about state-of-the-art computer technology. Some practicing art therapists were initially skeptical about the effectiveness of technological tools, just like in other fields that depend on human expertise and skill. Asawa (2009) reported that most art therapists' responses to computer technologies were anxiety and fear. Another reason is that the field of art therapy could be classified as a domain in which well-defined algorithms or an objective means for finding a solution hardly exist. Gussak and Nyce (1999) pointed out that art therapy is eclectic in practice and theory and not reducible to a single set of algorithms.

Solving problems with computers requires scientific methods based on quantification. Since it is seemingly difficult, if not impossible, to quantify the process of art therapy, the field has not paid enough attention to using computers to their fullest extent. It has also been widely believed in the field that the ability to reason qualitatively, which is essential in art therapy, cannot be specified as a computer program. Many art therapists still claim that their evaluation of elements of drawings and interpretation regarding drawers' psychological states are complex and not amenable to quantification.

Computer Technologies as a Solution

Lord Kelvin, in the 19th century, emphasized the importance of quantification, stating that "measuring whatever it is and expressing it in numbers may be the beginning of knowledge advanced to the stage of science" (Thomson, 1889). Simple computer algorithms such as color analysis and edge extraction can provide basic building blocks for objectification and quantification of art evaluation.

A number of art therapists have already acknowledged that a scientific approach is essential to resolving implicit ambiguity and uncertainty in art therapy and stressed that the academic sustainability of art therapy depends on science (Kaplan, 2000). Kaplan (1998) stated that subjective impressions need to be carefully evaluated in light of existing empirical evidence. She argued that, although science may continue to be unable to provide all the answers to problems related to human minds, rapid progress is being made, and hence the subjective nature of human emotions can be better interpreted in the light of science based on empirical evidence. Gantt (2004) argued that we can develop scientifically sound and clinically effective art-based assessments. Various techniques in artificial intelligence, expert systems, computer algorithms, and statistical models are emerging as useful methods to overcome the limitations of art therapy.

Furthermore, recent progress in artificial intelligence research allows computers to solve problems where objectification and quantification are difficult or even impossible. Artificial intelligence enables computers to reason with expert knowledge like humans. In the past, we used computers only for problems that were obviously quantifiable, where we could write a sequence of instructions (i.e. an algorithm) to solve them. However, we can now make computers use human experts' knowledge and experience to solve problems with uncertain or imperfect specifications. Kim (2008) claimed that art therapists should embrace techniques in artificial intelligence to assist their practice and theory.

Computer Technologies Relevant to Art Therapy
Built-In Functions of a Computer

First-generation computers were able to process 10^2 instructions per second. Current PCs can process 10^{12} instructions per second. The ability to process a huge number of instructions per second makes software faster, saving art therapists' time and effort in many aspects. First-generation computers were able to store several thousand characters, compared with more than 10^{12} characters (10^8 pages of news articles) nowadays. The ability to store a huge amount of information allows art therapists to store not only clients' drawings but video recordings of the art drawing process and evaluation results, and to retrieve them at any time. Today, the size of the population with access to the Internet is estimated to be bigger than one billion. Progress in communication technology facilitates opinion and information sharing with clients as well as remote drawing of art and its evaluation and interpretation, making remote art therapy a realistic option.

Computers represent a drawing by splitting it into pixels (e.g. using 1280 pixels horizontally and 960 pixels vertically, a total of 1,228,800 pixels). The color of a pixel can be any of 256 x 256 x 256 = 16,777,216 colors. There are a number of software tools for drawing on the display (e.g. Corel Painter, Tux Paint, InkScape, and CADian to name only a few). Photoshop® is one of the most well-known software tools for drawing. Such advances in computer graphics provide a novel way to generate drawings and a finer scale of information in drawings, computerize art evaluation and interpretation, facilitate new art therapy assessments, and improve the reliability and validity of art therapy assessments.

Techniques of Digital Image Processing

Digital image processing in pattern recognition is a subfield of cognitive science, which is about recognizing characters, speech, or shapes using computational machines. Blurring and clustering, which are techniques of digital image processing, can be used to quantify the areas of each color and the length of edges in a drawing. Blurring and clustering are methods for removing noise and finer details not intended by the drawer of the digital image. Edges are locations (pixels) where the color change occurs. Figure 21.1 shows how the computer recognizes colors and extracts edges between colors through blurring and clustering. For a detailed explanation, see Kim (2017).

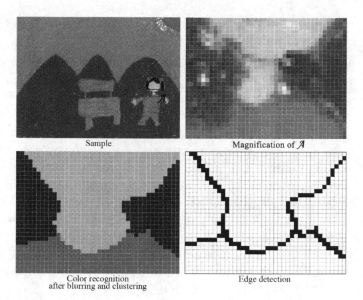

Sample   Magnification of $\mathcal{A}$

Color recognition
after blurring and clustering   Edge detection

Figure 21.1

Color recognition and edge detection by a computer after blurring and clustering

Computer Algorithms

A computer algorithm is a sequence of instructions or computational methods to solve a given problem. For example, a computer algorithm for removing background color to determine a *main color* of a drawing can be devised. Here the *main color* may be defined as the most important one that expresses the drawing's theme. The algorithm might be as follows:

- *Step 1*. Limit the candidates for *main color* to three which have large values of A (number of pixels x number of clusters). Here, a cluster refers to a contiguous area of the same color, not separated by different colors.

- *Step 2*. Remove colors with clusters that have a relatively long edge on the paper boundary.

- *Step 3*. Select the color with maximum A.

Expert Systems

Artificial intelligence is about making machines such as computers or robots able to complete complex tasks such as adapting to new situations, learning from past experiences, and recognizing things that are unique to human intelligence. Expert systems are one of the most successful subfields of artificial intelligence, where the focus is on capturing human expert knowledge to enable computers to reason and make decisions. Some expert systems are capable of learning as well, automatically accumulating and improving knowledge.

In expert systems, human expert knowledge is stored in the knowledge base, which is continuously updated. For example, they can store, accumulate, and update newly discovered knowledge on the relationship between the elements of a drawing and the psychological state of the drawer in many of the commonly used art therapy assessments, such as the Diagnostic Drawing Series (DDS) (Cohen, 1986/1994) or the Formal Elements Art Therapy Scale (FEATS) (Gantt and Tabone, 1998), and the rating system Person Picking an Apple from a Tree (PPAT) (Gantt, 1990). The MATLab (MATrix Laboratory) can be used for the development of expert systems. Figure 21.2 shows the architecture of an expert system.

Figure 21.2
The architecture of an expert system

Statistical Methods

Various statistical methods are applied to art evaluation and art interpretation. The analysis of variance is used to examine the relationship between an element and an interpretation; other methods can be used to determine the consistency of evaluations of drawings by human raters and those done by expert sustems, and grades and measures evaluations in ranks. Regression analysis is applied to develop systems for evaluation of an element from other elements, and systems for predicting a psychological state from the evaluation results of drawings. The coefficient of determination is a measure for the appropriateness of a particular regression model. Figure 21.3 shows two regression models where the element *prominence of color* is estimated from either only the element *number of used colors* or both the elements *number of used colors* and *area colored* in number of pixels. Readers not familiar with basic statistical methods are encouraged to refer to textbooks such as Walpole and Myers (2006). Statistical software packages such as Statistical Package for the Social Science (SPSS) or Statistical Analysis System (SAS) can be used to replace time-consuming calculations.

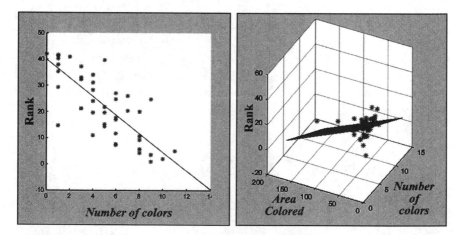

Figure 21.3
Illustration of regressions

Bayesian Network

The Bayesian network is a technique for artificial intelligence. It graphically represents the probabilistic cause-and-effect relationship using a set of random variables as nodes and their conditional probabilities as edges in a directed acyclic graph. The Bayesian network allows us to encode knowledge that is not deterministic. For example, a traditional deterministic interpretation of art is that "children suffering from attention deficit hyperactivity disorder (ADHD) tend to draw a full picture using more than 90 percent of the paper." Using the Bayesian network, we can make a more quantitative expression such as "children with ADHD will draw a full picture with a probability of 0.75, whereas normal children draw such a picture with a probability of 0.1."

In summary, we can make the computer perform an art evaluation by combining the built-in functions of a computer, techniques of digital image processing, computer algorithms, expert systems, statistical methods, and Bayesian networks to analyze, measure, or rate elements of drawings. Furthermore, we can computerize existing art therapy assessments (tools) of evaluation or develop new elements (art evaluation). Again, these computer technologies can be used to interpret drawings. Here, art interpretation refers to inferring the drawer's psychological state based on the art evaluation results of formal and generic elements of drawings. Through active application of various computer technologies, we can make the art therapist's knowledge more structured and systematic, rather than diversified and subjective, and sometimes even inconsistent and self-contradictory.

Computerized Art Evaluation

A Computer System for Art Evaluation, C_CREATES

A computer system for art evaluation, the Computer_Color-Related Elements Art Therapy Evaluation System (C_CREATES) (Kim *et al.*, 2007; Kim, 2010) applies various computer technologies to art evaluation and compares it with some representative art therapy assessments such as the DDS, the PPAT, the Descriptive Assessment of Psychiatric Artwork (DAPA) (Hacking, 1999), and the Face Stimulus Assessments (FSA) (Betts, 2003).

Noting that many elements of evaluation are concerned directly or indirectly with the color in a drawing and also that evaluation of some elements can be computerized, Kim *et al.* (2007) and Kim (2010) developed C_CREATES for art evaluation. C_CREATES proposes new elements that are color related and can be computerized. All of its 19 elements, listed below, are evaluated automatically and quantitatively by computer technologies. "Color-related elements" are not limited to elements directly related to colors, such as *number of used colors*, but include elements indirectly related to colors, elements which are formed during the process of color analysis such as *length of edges*,[1] *number of clusters*,[2] and *area of colored convex hull*.[3] The elements in art therapy assessments are listed in *italics* throughout the chapter. See Kim (2017) for more detailed explanations and examples of terminologies used in digital image processing and statistical analysis, such as edge, cluster, convex hull, and regression functions.

These elements are classified into two categories depending on the presence or absence of absolute objectivity. The first category includes elements which can be evaluated objectively such that the results of evaluation can not be disputed; these are basic elements. The second category includes elements whose evaluation results are consistent but can be somewhat subjective depending on the way evaluation methods are constructed; these are applied elements. These elements can be evaluated based on the evaluation results of the basic elements using regression analysis, computer algorithms, and expert systems.

For example, *variety of colors* is evaluated in rank by the following computer algorithm:

* *Step 1.* The one having a higher *number of used colors* is ranked higher for *variety of color* than one with fewer colors.
* *Step 2.* When two drawings are found to have the same *number of used colors*, the one with the greater *length of edges* is ranked higher.

---

1   The edge consists of pixels which differ in color from their neighboring pixels.
2   A cluster refers to a contiguous area colored with the same color, not separated by different colors.
3   The convex hull refers to the area which includes all pixels on the line within two points of the area.

Likewise, the *main color* and the *placement* are evaluated by appropriately devised computer algorithms.

Prominence of color is, for example, statistically rated by the following regression function:

Prominence of color (grade) = 1.201 + 0.247 (*number of used color*) + 0.002 (*number of clusters*) + 0.376 x 10^{-6} (*area of colored convex hull*)

Likewise, the *details*, the *space usage*, and the *concentration* are rated by regression functions appropriately developed.

A software package of the C_CREATES is available (Kim, 2017), which art therapy practitioners can easily use via their computer to access technologies to help them obtain a more reliable analysis. Practitioners can thus save time and effort in their practice, easily enhancing the quality of their practice. Figure 21.4A illustrates its evaluation process of the 19 elements in graphs and Figure 21.4B shows its evaluation results in statistics.

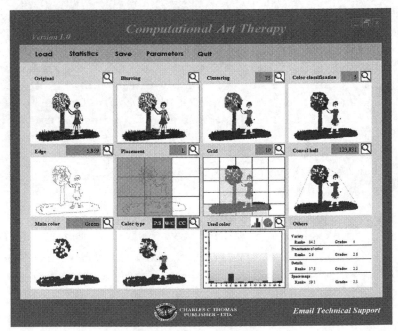

A. Evaluation process

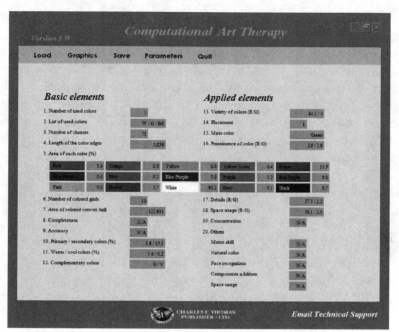

B. Evaluation results

Figures 21.4A and 21.4B
Evaluation results of elements by C_CREATES

Comparison of the C_CREATES with Other Art Therapy Assessments

The DDS is designed to gather clinical information about a client in a single session (Brooke, 2004). It evaluates 23 elements. The PPAT is intended to provide a method for understanding and examining the non-symbolic aspects of art and to demonstrate how the structural characteristics of a drawing furnish information about a drawer's clinical state and his or her psychiatric diagnosis (Brooke, 2004). It has 14 elements. The DAPA includes five elements. As additional elements, the first picture drawn by clients in the FSA considers five elements.

Thus, the total number of elements considered in the four traditional art therapy assessments, the DDS, the PPAT, the DAPA, and the FSA is 47. Some of them, such as *integration, line quality*, and *space usage*, are listed in both the DDS and the PPAT. However, some are the same elements under different names, such as *idiosyncratic color* in the DDS and *color fit* in the PPAT. Thus, there are actually 30 elements. Meanwhile the C_CREATES evaluates 19 elements. For example, *number of used colors*, classified into a quantitative element in the traditional assessments and classified into a basic element in the C_CREATES, is counted by the pixels of each color. The information is more detailed because it identifies both the existence of each color and the *area of each color*. As another example, *space usage* is evaluated not only in the quantitative number of the colored area but also in grade, rank, or percentile.

The comparison of elements in conventional assessments and the C_CREATES is summarized in the list below, which indicates in parentheses if the elements also exist in the the DDS, the FEATS, the DAPA, or FSA, or if they are newly proposed in the C_CREATES. The elements considered in conventional assessments but not in the C_CREATES include 1) *line quality*, 2) *abstract symbols*, 3) *person*, and 4) *implied energy*. The elements considered in C_CREATES but not in conventional assessments include 1) *area of each color*, 2) *main/subsidiary colors*, 3) *number of clusters*, 4) *accuracy*, and 5) *concentration*.

Basic elements

- *Number of used colors* (DAPA, DDS, FEATS)
- *List of colors* (DAPA, DDS, FEATS)
- *Number of clusters* (new)
- *Length of edges* (new)
- *Area of each color* (new)
- *Number of colored grids* (new)
- *Area of colored convex hull* (new)
- *Completeness* (new)
- *Accuracy* (new)
- *Primary/secondary colors* (new)
- *Warm/cool colors* (new)
- *Complementary colors* (new)

Applied elements

- *Variety of colors* (new)
- *Main/subsidiary/background colors* (new)

* *Placement* (DDS)
* *Prominence of colors* (FEATS)
* *Details* (FEATS)
* *Space usage* (DAPA, DDS, FEATS)
* *Degree of concentration* (new)

Reliability of Evaluation

All evaluations of elements in the DDS and the FEATS are more or less subjective and their results may differ depending on the raters. Even when concrete descriptors for evaluating all levels of each of the elements were provided, the evaluation process is time consuming and there still remains a probability of some inaccuracy. Thus, we always face the problem of low inter-rater reliability or inconsistency between raters. High reliability requires special training, especially for the evaluation of qualitative elements. For example, the diagnostic interpretation of the DDS is difficult without the recommended training (Brooke, 2004).

Inter-rater reliability in the DDS was found unsatisfactory by Fowler and Ardon (2002) as they felt that ratings were too heavily dependent on experience. Although they agreed that the handbook and training were clear and precise, their work suggested that clarification and precision were insufficient in practice. Brooke (2004) reported on the reliability of the PPAT that aside from *perseveration*, with moderate correlation of 0.57, 0.74, and 0.52, the correlation for other scales was 0.74 and higher.

In most cases, the computer systems including the C_CREATES automatically provide information that is ultimately accurate and detailed, which is something human raters cannot do. For the 12 basic elements, the C_CREATES provides perfectly accurate measurements. Also, the C_CREATES can provide not only the measurement but also the grade, rank, or percentile. Moreover, there are elements that can be provided only by the C_CREATES, not by human raters. For a simple example, raters cannot measure the *area of each color*.

Now, for the seven applied elements we examine reliabilities between human raters and the C_CREATES as well as the reliabilities among human raters. Kim and Hameed (2009) reported high reliability of *variety of colors* between two human raters and moderate reliability between the raters and the computer system for the sample size of 52: The Rank (Spearman) Correlation Coefficient (RCC) (Walpole and Myers, 2006) between the raters was $R_s = 0.825$. The RCC between the computer system and Rater-1 ($R_s = 0.759$) was found to be higher than between the computer system and Rater-2 ($R_s = 0.662$). All the reliability measures in evaluation of other applied elements show the usability of the C_CREATES (Kim, 2017).

Merits of the CAT for Art Evaluation

In conclusion, the relative merits of the CAT system for art evaluation compared to conventional art therapy assessments are as follows: 1) objective—it provides objective information acceptable by art therapists; 2) consistent—it always provides the same results for the same drawing; 3) quantitative— it provides a result in quantitative terms and also in grade or percentile when desired; 4) detail—it provides more detailed information than conventional assessments do; 5) automatic—it provides information automatically so as to save the time and effort of art therapists; 6) instantaneous—it provides information in a short time so as to save art therapists time.

Computerized Art Interpretation

The purpose of the DDS and the PPAT is to gather clinical information on a person's clinical state and psychiatric diagnosis. They do not interpret drawings, but only investigate the correlations between elements in a drawing and psychiatric symptoms. For example, in the DDS, light *pressure*, included *animals* in the free drawing, and disintegrated *trees* differentiated, at a significance level below 0.05, the dysthymia patients group; in the PPAT, *prominence of color*, *details of objects and environment*, and *line quality* differentiated children with ADHD from children with no learning or behavioral problems (Munley, 2002).

There have been several attempts to computerize art interpretation (Kim, 2017). We introduce below two studies on determining psychological status or disorders based on the results of C_CREATES evaluation of elements using computer technologies. One uses an expert system and the other uses a regression model.

An Expert System for the Interpretation of DAP (Draw a Person test)

We introduce a prototype model of the expert system to demonstrate the possibility of applying an artificial intelligence system to art therapy diagnosis. The model has decision-making processes composed of standard diagnosis, psychological diagnosis, and feedback (Kim *et al.*, 2006).

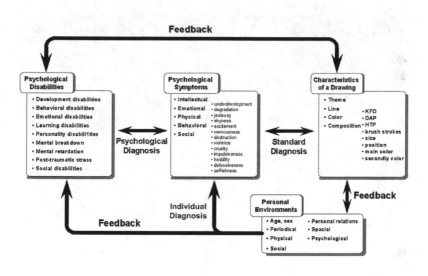

Figure 21.5
The Feedback Process

In Table 21.1 a small part of knowledge used for this prototype expert system is represented in written form. In the process of developing an expert system, abstract knowledge is turned into specific and concrete knowledge in a written form to constitute a knowledge base. This representation process of the system has the advantage of providing a basis for transforming a subjective diagnosis into an objective one. Furthermore, new methods may be developed in the representation process to offer important grounds for theoretical developments in art psychotherapy, facilitating more scientific diagnoses.

The model shows how similarities and contradictions in a mass of knowledge in art therapy are thoroughly reviewed, evaluated, classified, and organized to improve the quality of the knowledge base. Apart from being capable of synthesizing expert opinions from numerous sources, the proposed system can also effectively reconcile conflicting pieces of information and organize them in a systematic manner.

Table 21.1 A part of the knowledge in the expert system

Code	If–then rule
[S.1-1-1]	IF large or full size, THEN hyperactivity, activation, impulsivity, defensiveness, expansion of self-ego, expansive delusion
[S.1-2-1]	IF *placement* skewed to the left, THEN impulsivity, desire to change, extrovert
[S.1-4-2]	IF large head, THEN compensation for anxiety
[S.1-4-5]	IF hair emphasis, THEN dogmatic, defensiveness, hysteric
[S.1-4-8]	IF eyes emphasis, THEN unrest, tension, suspicion, defensive, paranoia
[S.1-4-12]	IF no mouth, THEN frustration, inability, contraction, lack/difficulties of personal relationship, conflict
[F.3-1-1]	IF communication problems with parents, THEN cause of psychological disorder
[I.1-1-7]	IF large head and age under 6, THEN [S.1-4-2] not applicable
[P.2-1-2]	IF impulsivity, careless, diffuseness, THEN attention deficit
[P.2-2-2]	IF bad relationship with people, THEN attention deficit hyperactivity disorder (ADHD)
[P.2-2-3]	IF attention deficit, hyperactivity, THEN ADHD

Figure 21.5 is a sample drawing by a child who has been diagnosed with a psychological disorder (Shin *et al.*, 2002). The child is six years old and has communication problems with his parents. Information is fed into a computer through the user interface. In the figure, a cellophane sheet overlaps with the left side of the drawing paper.

The drawing takes up the entire space. We can gather the following elements from this drawing:

* full picture
* skewed to the left side
* big head
* emphasis on hair
* emphasis on eyes
* big ears
* omission of mouth.

Specific personal environments are as follows:

* age six
* communication problems with his parents.

After three types of diagnosis—standard, psychological, and individual—the tentative conclusion is that this child may have ADHD. A tentative conclusion that can be drawn from the psychological diagnosis of symptoms invoking knowledge [P.2-1-2], [P.2-2-2], and [P.2-2-3] (see Table 21.1) is that this child may have ADHD. In the feedback process, the background knowledge [F.3-1-1] that the child had communication problems with his parents further supports the likely diagnosis of ADHD. No further feedback exists in this simple case. Hence the entire process of establishing the diagnosis of ADHD can be clearly and systematically documented by the system.

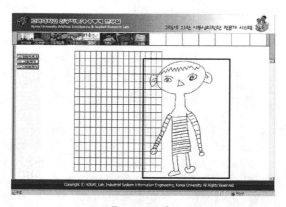

Figure 21.6
A case study of a five-year-old boy with a psychological disorder

A Statistical Regression Model for the Interpretation of Structured Mandala Coloring

For this example, a statistical regression model is used whose dependent variable is the level of dementia as scored by the Mini-Mental State Examination (MMSE) (Folstein, Folstein, and McHugh, 1975), and whose independent (explanatory) variables are the elements of a structured mandala. All of these dependent variables are analyzed using the C_CREATES. The consistency between the MMSE score and the computer system's estimated score is verified statistically. Elderly people with suspected dementia are selected as the subjects of the study. Structured mandala coloring (SMC) is an appropriate art therapy tool for people with notably diminished functions.

A multiple linear regression model is formulated to estimate the level of dementia severity, which is the dependent variable, based on the evaluation of the elements in the SMC, which are the independent variables. The value of the dependent variable (Y) is scored by a test, and the values of the independent variables (X) are evaluated automatically by the system. Several elements that are considered to be important in estimating the level of dementia are selected by stepwise regression.

The regression function derived was as follows:

Y = 4.411 + 14.598 X_1 [*Light green*] - 16.507 X_2 [*Brown*] - 5.145 X_3 [*Green*] + 0.718 X_4 [*Number of clusters*] + 0.095 X_5 [*Accuracy*]

Elements, such as *brown*, *light green*, *green*, the *number of clusters*, and *accuracy*, are identified as important variables for determining levels of dementia. As the *number of clusters* and the *accuracy* increase, the level of dementia becomes less severe. When *brown* or *green* appear to be a *principal color*, the level of dementia becomes more severe. When *light green* is a *principal color*, it becomes lower. The coefficient of determination was R^2 = 0.626, which is only a moderately satisfactory value, but indicates that the model is applicable and relevant.

In Figure 21.6, six SMC samples corresponding to levels of dementia (scores) of 0, 9, 12, 20, 22, and 30, respectively, are shown, and in Table 21.2, the scored and estimated values with other ratings of the independent variables are summarized. The regression functions derived could be used by art therapists without difficulty, since they are only linear equations with statistical concepts of average and standard deviation. The general tendency for the dementia to be less severe (as indicated by an increase in the MMSE-K score and estimated score) correlates with higher *accuracy*. Also, the *number of used colors* and the *number of clusters* become larger except for one drawing (Figure 21.6D). The same results were obtained for *completeness*. The order of the values scored by the test coincided completely with that of the values estimated by the model.

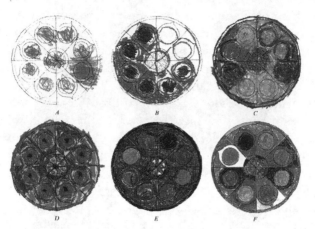

Figure 21.7
SMC samples colored by people with different levels of dementia

Table 21.2 Analysis of mandalas in Figure 21.7

Figure	Accuracy (%)	Number of used colors	Number of clusters	Completeness (rank)	Concentration color	Main score	Dementia estimate
21.6A	11.4	5	0.10	96	Yellow	0	9.1
21.6B	47.7	9	0.68	72	Orange	9	15.4
21.6C	73.3	8	1.0	42	Pink	12	17.1
21.6D	77.8	12	1.0	50.9	Grey	20	20.4
21.6E	86.1	13	1.0	25.8	Blue-green	22	21.9
21.6F	93.1	19	0.96	15	Yellow	30	25.9

Validity of Interpretation

There is still debate among a number of art therapists about whether art interpretation can be objectively measured and whether personal judgments by non-art therapists are allowed for art interpretation (Gantt, 1998). The main difficulties in art interpretation lie in the fact that a drawer's personal and cultural background influences their choice of shapes, colors, and styles of drawing. This implies that even seemingly identical drawings may be subjected to diverse, inconsistent, and sometimes even contradictory interpretations. For example, one study found that persons in a depressed state were likely to draw human figures that are smaller than would persons who are not in such a state (Lewinsohn, 1964), whereas another study reported that there was no relationship between depression and the size of figure drawings (Salzman and Harway, 1967).

One-to-one equivalence of specific drawing elements (signs and symbols) with particular clinical features was arguably doomed from the start (Gantt, 2004). Before interpreting the meaning of signs and symbols, the context is the key to understanding how the signs and symbols function (Gantt, 2004). Kim's expert system interpretation methodology (Kim *et al.*, 2006), having the features of several feedbacks, is not based on one-to-one equivalence, but a process of comprehensive decision-making that considers drawers' various circumstances including the social and cultural backgrounds in which an individual grew up, taking account of diversity and uncertainty. His regression model interpretation methodology (Kim *et al.*, 2009) shows its validity by a statistical measure, the coefficient of determination.

Merits of the CAT for Art Interpretation

In conclusion, the relative merits of the CAT system for art interpretation are: 1) professional—it makes decisions derived from the expertise and experience of experts; 2) comprehensive—it makes decisions through comprehensive knowledge; 3) statistical—it makes decisions probabilistically and objectively based on statistical theory; 4) systematic—it makes decisions based on systematically classified knowledge; 5) testable—it applies various knowledge gained from previous experiments to arrive at results.

Conclusion

In 2016, AlphaGo, the artificial intelligence program developed by Google DeepMind, beat Lee Sedol, one of the greatest players of Go, a game which has a near-infinite number of board positions and, thus, was considered as the ultimate realm of human intuition. IBM's Watson, a supercomputer with artificial intelligence, is changing healthcare, from diagnosing disease to treating it (Smith, 2015), on one occasion correctly diagnosing a patient within minutes, which doctors had failed to do after months (Billington, 2016). In today's world, we often hear terminology common to image mining, such as big data, computer algorithm, machine learning, and artificial intelligence. A number of image mining applications and prototypes have been developed for a variety of domains. It is interesting that art therapy fits the exact definition of image mining but it has been developed as a separate field of image mining. Art therapy can borrow various approaches, methodologies, and techniques of image mining for its improvement and must broaden the definitions of art materials and contexts across a wide spectrum.

Computer technology is changing the way art therapists practice their profession (Peterson *et al.*, 2005). The system can free human experts from the mundane tasks of gathering mechanical information about the drawings so that they can concentrate more on nuanced aspects of evaluation that require professional judgment by humans. Computers can provide human experts with objective information that can assist their decision-making. Also, non-experts such as guardians, teachers, or parents can use the system in ascertaining signs of their clients' psychological problems at an early stage and, therefore, promptly seek the help of professional art therapists. In doing this, the CAT system never shirks its duty, is never fatigued with its responsibility, and never makes a mistake of omission.

Recommendations

- There are a number of possibilities for the CAT. It can be applied to a variety of other art-based standard instruments for evaluating characteristics of drawings and, based on its evaluation results, interpreting the drawer's psychological states.

- The knowledge of expert systems for art-based evaluation can be continuously accumulated and improved. In this process, the CAT can contribute to making art therapy more structured and based on scientific method.

- Consider the CAT as a way to promote the use of various art-based evaluations as well as a means for therapists and researchers to develop their own methodologies to improve the practice and theory of art therapy.

References

Asawa, P. (2009) Art therapists' emotional reactions to the demands of technology. *Art Therapy 26*(2), 58–65.

Betts, D.J. (2003) Developing a projective drawing test: Experience with the Face Stimulus Assessment (FSA). *Art Therapy 20*(2), 77–82.

Billington, J. (2016) IBM's Watson cracks medical mystery with life-saving diagnosis for patient who baffled doctors. Retrieved on April 1, 2018 at www.ibtimes. co.uk/ibms-watson-cracks-medical-mystery-life-saving-diagnosis-patient-who-baffled-doctors-1574963

Brooke, S. (2004) *Tools of the Trade: A Therapist's Guide to Art Therapy Assessments* (2nd edn) Springfield, IL: Charles C Thomas.

Cohen, B.M. (ed.) (1986/1994) *The Diagnostic Drawing Series Rating Guide.* Available from Barry M. Cohen, P.O. Box 9853, Alexandria, Virginia, USA 22304. Inquiries at landmarc@cox.net

Folstein, M.F., Folstein, S.E. and McHugh, P.R. (1975) Mini-mental state: A practical method for grading the cognitive state of patients for the clinician. *Journal of Psychiatric Research 12*(3), 189–198.

Fowler, J.P. and Ardon, A.M. (2002) Diagnostic Drawing Series and dissociative disorders: A Dutch study. *The Arts in Psychotherapy 29*(4), 221–230.

Gantt, L.M. (1990) A validity study of the Formal Elements Art Therapy Scale (FEATS) for diagnostic information in patients' drawings. Unpublished dissertation, University of Pittsburgh, Pittsburgh, PA.

Gantt, L.M. (2004) The case for formal art therapy assessments. *Art Therapy 21*(1), 18–29.

Gantt, L.M. and Tabone, C. (1998) *The Formal Elements Art Therapy Scale: The Rating Manual.* Morgantown, WV: Gargoyle Press.

Gussak, D.E. and Nyce, J.M. (1999) To bridge art therapy and computer technology: The visual toolbox. *Art Therapy 16*(4), 194–196.

Hacking, S. (1999) The psychopathology of everyday art: A quantitative study. Dissertation, University of Keele, UK. Retrieved on April 1, 2018 at http://ethos.bl.uk/OrderDetails.do?uin=uk.bl.ethos.301332

Kaplan, F.F. (1998) Scientific art therapy: An integrative and research-based approach. *Art Therapy 15*(2), 93–98.

Kaplan, F.F. (2000) *Art, Science and Art Therapy: Repainting the Picture.* London: Jessica Kingsley Publishers.

Kim, S.I. (2008) Commentaries [To the editor]. *Art Therapy 25*(1), 41.

Kim, S.I. (2010) A computer system for the analysis of color-related elements in art therapy assessment: Computer_Color-Related Elements Art Therapy Evaluation System (C_CREATES). *The Arts in Psychotherapy 37*(5), 378–386.

Kim, S.I. (2017) *Computational Art Therapy.* Springfield, IL: Charles C. Thomas.

Kim, S.I., Bae, J. and Lee, Y. (2007) A computer system to rate the color-related formal elements in art therapy assessments. *The Arts in Psychotherapy 34*(3), 223–237.

Kim, S.I., Betts, D.J., Kim, H.M. and Kang, H.S. (2009) Statistical models to estimate level of psychological disorder based on a computer rating system: An application to dementia using structured mandala drawings. *The Arts in Psychotherapy 36*(4), 214–221.

Kim, S.I. and Hameed, A.I. (2009) A computer system to rate the variety of color in drawings. *Art Therapy 26*(2), 73–79.

Kim, S.I., Han, J., Oh, Y.J. and Kim, Y.H. (2012) A computer art therapy system for the evaluation of space usage in drawings with application to the analysis of its relationship to level of dementia. *New Ideas in Psychology 30*(3), 300–307.

Kim, S.I., Kim, Y.H., Lee, C.W., Kim, S.K. and Baik, D.K. (1992) An expert system to facilitate the uniform administration of justice in criminal cases. *Expert Systems with Applications 5*(1), 103–110.

Kim, S.I., Ryu, H.J., Hwang, J.O. and Kim, M.S.H. (2006) An expert system approach to art psychotherapy. *The Arts in Psychotherapy 33*(1), 59–75.

Lewinsohn, P.M. (1964) Relationship between height of figure drawings and depression in psychotic patients. *Journal of Consulting Psychology 28*(4), 380–381.

Mattson, D.C. (2012) An introduction to the computerized assessment of art-based instruments. *Art Therapy 29*(1), 27–32.

Munley, M. (2002) Comparing the PPAT drawings of boys with AD/HD and age-matched controls using the Formal Elements Art Therapy Scale. *Art Therapy* *19*(2), 66–76.

Peterson, B.C., Stovall, K., Elkins, D.E. and Parker-Bell, B. (2005) Art therapists and computer technology. *Art Therapy 22*(3), 139–149.

Salzman, L. and Harway, N. (1967) Size of figure drawings of psychotically depressed patients. *Journal of Abnormal Psychology 72*(3), 205–207.

Shin, M.S., Kim, S.K., Kim, J.Y., Park, H.K. *et al.* (2002) *Diagnosis and Understanding of Children through Their Drawings* (in Korean). Seoul, Korea: Hak Ji Sa.

Smith, S. (2015, December 17) 5 ways the IBM Watson is changing health care, from diagnosing disease to treating it. Retrieved at www.medicaldaily.com/5-ways-ibm-watson-changing-health-care-diagnosing-disease-treating-it-364394

Thomson, W. (1889) *Popular Lectures and Addresses.* New York, NY: Macmillan.

Walpole, R.E. and Myers, R.H. (2006) *Probability and statistics for engineers and scientists* (8th edn). New York, NY: Macmillan.

22

DIGITAL MEDIA INCLUSION IN ART THERAPY COURSEWORK

Natalie Carlton

Best practices and educational strategies for teaching digital literacy within art therapy graduate curriculums have become critical social and professional responsibilities and not a choice. Graduate education often requires students to use computers or digital device interfaces to access course materials, register for classes and manage financial aid and tuition, send and receive both informal and formal e-mail communications, source required research materials, and in some cases exchange with professors and other students for online learning. These computer uses engage the student to find, distribute, and interact with information and others, but do not necessarily promote critical thinking for digital readiness skills or literacy (Horrigan, 2016; Miller, 2017). Art therapists must have ongoing education and exposure to the technical, cultural, professional, clinical, ethical, and legal complexities involved in computer use, which can essentially lead to the acquisition of a larger digital humility and skill set for our training and professional work (Choe and Carlton, 2018). Some of these include, but are not limited to the ethical creation, storage, and transmittal of digital communication or art expressions via digital drives and cloud-based technology; digital communication and professionalism on social media; developing digital literacy skills and digital informed consent agreements; and deepening the art therapists' own digital media engagement. The material presented in this chapter is applicable for stand-alone art therapy programs as well as those integrated within creative arts and expressive arts therapy departments and/or mental health counseling and healthcare programs.

After observing media use for both art therapy educational and clinical purposes in the past two decades, both practical and more philosophical questions have arisen, including:

* Who has access to what creative media and how important is it that clients use creative media that they prefer or show interest in?

* How can digital media aesthetics and literacy be elevated but also simplified in classrooms and therapy spaces?

* How can intermedia and hybrid creative forms be further evolved or experienced as adaptive to multiple contexts and social interactivities?

* How are media seen and felt as critical languages, geographical markers, generational differences, larger cultural identifications, and embodied to disembodied experiences?

In this chapter, I attempt to answer critical parts of these questions and provide a preliminary "in process" vision for including digital media in both classroom and experiential use for one graduate art therapy and counseling training program. For Spring 2019, a new course will be added to our Art Therapy and Counseling curriculum titled Digital Media Use in Art Therapy. Specific digital media course content and topic areas to be taught in this future course are identified in this chapter and seem important to include, but those may shift over time and in response to new media and professional developments. Constant changes and updates in digital media present impediments to adoption and inclusion, as well as specific software or hardware suggestions. What is conceptualized and described at the time of writing may or may not turn out to be the whole story of how the projects described within were completed, because digital media are fluid and constantly changing.

Digital Media Use for the Art Therapy Classroom

How Digital Media Break Forms

The beneficial digital media qualities of flexibility in form and relational capacities (Ehinger, 2016; L'Esperance, 2016) critically require more skill building for the art therapy community to explore and understand—and are currently absent in most graduate programs (Choe, 2016; Choe and Carlton, 2018; Ehinger, 2016; Orr, 2012; Partridge, 2016). In one of my recent art therapy graduate classes, a student asked if she could move in front of our classroom because what she had to say about the discussion subject of colonialism in art museum collections across the world was accessible via her body and an Internet music video, not by her words. She turned on a Major Lazer music video from YouTube titled *Get Free* (Major Lazer, 2012) and began to show in movement an exquisite, terrible beauty to black bodies (including her own) being simultaneously freed and empowered, yet potentially minimized and exploited by cultural (mis)appropriation and imagery extraction that can set up for video viewers both limited and unrealistic expectations of the video subjects' social realities and geographical place (Sanchez, 2013). It is challenging to explain now what happened when several students and I absorbed the live performance of movement displayed alongside a video of Jamaican people and dancers engrossed in "authentic" movement and cultural interaction, seemingly both elevated and subjugated via the media effects. The student brought alternative energy and knowledge into the classroom when she embodied her projection and response to the video's powerful imagery, sound, and meaningfulness.

I believe there were important therapeutic digital media literacy factors activated in this classroom moment. For example, I witnessed how this student accessed obfuscated truths for herself and our learning group by envisaging them into the classroom via a media of immediacy (direct experience), merged her self-experience with a media experience (critical engagement), and enacted literacy learning and mastery (evaluating and producing alongside) when her body performance merged with video and music artists who conveyed nuanced forms of communication, infused with the music video (Martin, 2006; Media Smarts, n.d.). Finally, the student told a story via body movements that simultaneously "ordered" and distanced her intimate embodiment and meaning making alongside cascading video moments that held their own parallel and distinct relevance (Carlton, 2015b; Ehinger, 2016).

In the classroom as well as a therapy room, simple structure in art therapy media can override a person's feelings of intimidation by a paper or canvas "blank page" or frustrations and uncertainty of where to start. Far more than that, and from my own applied experiences witnessing student and client applications of digital media critical engagement and production, there are powerful narratives enacted and found, moments of memory made accessible and beautifully layered through the specific qualities of immediacy and spontaneous re-presentation found in photography and video (Carlton, 2014b; Cohen, Johnson, and Orr, 2015). Moreover, such access to familiar Internet content and "projected selves" can bring into the therapy or classroom container several relational and interactivity qualities not found in drawing an image rendered by pencil to paper. In a more simplistic comparison, digital media tools can look like or mimic other creative materials (drawing apps on iPads as compared to tangible charcoal pencils) or display intermedia mixing with other materials (acoustic drum sounds recorded and added to a self-story video) but break typical forms and products through their sensory mixing possibilities, novel presence, and transmedia effects (Carlton, Sit, and Yu, 2018).

The Inequalities of Art Therapy Media

Enhanced digital literacy is critically needed in the art therapy community because cultural communication shifts are continuously occurring via media characteristics (Weigel *et al.*, 2009), innovations in Internet language use and knowledge production, and new applications (Choe, 2016; Choe and Carlton, 2018). The digital divide seems to simultaneously widen and shrink as learning styles and media use adapt (Carlton, 2014a; Horrigan, 2016; Kapitan, 2009; Prensky, 2001), presenting challenges to integrating digital media in both classroom and clinical practices. The digital divide is partly made of generational differences, or inconsistency versus consistency of exposure and "know how" to new media use, but also socio-economic access and interrelated sociocultural schisms and practices with the Internet (Pereyra, 2017). Community educator Pierce (2015) researched the complexities of Internet access and how the socialized spaces contained within illustrated dire advocacy needs as well as provocation for the disenfranchisement of communities of color. The digital divide in art therapy has tended to emphasize the differences between media use over the clinical experiences and digital applications, as both are distinct from and interrelated to the traditions of drawing, painting, and clay (Edmunds, 2012; Orr, 2012; Peterson, 2010), over how new media impact the mind and culture (Carlton, 2015a; Prensky, 2001).

I have yet to teach in an art therapy graduate classroom that has computers or scanners, or video, photography, or audio equipment provided as *creative* media alongside the ample papers, canvases, and painting supplies, sewing notions, collage materials, and adhesives, clay, and drawing inks that they typically supply. The digital media my students have used for art projects have been personal tools and processes they employed at home and brought to class via printed images or posters and on their laptops or cell phones, and projected onto our classroom A/V screen for viewing. Unless there is a dedicated class for digital media use, there is often not enough time to fully discuss and explore the nuanced experiences and context of completing digital media assignments. Phototherapy assignments completed outside the classroom environment versus creatively and collectively built in class are contrasting learning experiences (Wolf, 2007). For example, a recent computer-mediated graphic novel created from student art responses to class readings presented challenges in terms of finding time for full discussion of its construction when compared to other creative media whose processes are better understood and need less explanation.

Digital savvy can be described as the attainment of interrelated "visual vernacular" skills and the development of a "rich vocabulary" (Moon, 2010, p.xvii) for multiple media forms. Working in informed ways with expanded creative palettes is much like being fluently multilingual; in other words, one knows and grasps multiple means of communication and expression through therapeutic materials. This variety creates critical choices for clients but also expands how an art therapist may direct the therapeutic relationship, process, and products towards key communication goals that media can ground and promote (Carlton, 2014a). Talent, interest, exposure, and "know how" in media forms have been major predictors of what materials are used frequently and in what depth by art therapists (Edmunds, 2012; Orr, 2012; Peterson, 2010). Within the majority of multi-stocked graduate art therapy program classrooms, access to certain artistic media and their presumed therapeutic qualities can be seen as reinforcing presumed norms and unconscious preferences (bias), while continually affirming the value of certain imagery possibilities and materials use while negating or underrepresenting others. (Carlton, 2014a; Moon, 2010; Orr, 2010).

Conceptual and experiential choices for art media were characterized by Seiden (2001) as triggering vital relational interactions as well as having symbolic values infused into them by clients and therapists. I believe in a "by any media necessary" approach for both my teaching classrooms and previous clinical work. I have remained critical of stereotypical media approaches that promote aesthetic sensibilities aligned with singularities of perspective or tool usage and privileged socio-economic histories of art valuation. These singularities can subsequently narrow media practices (and art-based assessments) into repetitive rather than expansive, materials use. In art therapy graduate programs, the overreliance on drawing, painting, and strictly "fine art" materials use can serve as a double-edged sword because their normed representations contribute to the success of students learning and valuing "traditional" fine art materials while possibly limiting the breadth and depth of their artistic humility or curiosity in other material valuations, worldviews, and economies. This can also affect the client's experience of art therapy as affirming materials unknown and inaccessible to them, or representative of privilege (Carlton, 2014a). There are many diversity, sociopolitical, and inclusion principles being consciously valued and acted upon when educators provide, experiment with, and discuss contemporary and diverse materials in art therapy education. Such pluralism can nurture critical exchanges and communication between teachers and students, and between clients and therapists, that are frequently underestimated and/or missed (Moon, 2010).

Four Critical Components to Digital Media Educational Inclusion

Ethical Creation, Storage, and Transmittal of Digital Media

The history of technology use in art therapy is variable and not isolated to digital media. One complication with the use of the term "technology" to represent computer-mediated media is that in its most basic meaning, technology can mean any machine or industry invented through applied science. Thus, a sewing machine or a laptop computer are both new technologies (of their eras) advanced from previous media tools. Unlike a sewing machine or a hand-held graphic pen, however, digital media do not stay put (Alders *et al.*, 2011). Digital media are tools, formats, and platforms, and processes of creativity and communication that can be viewed, disseminated, modified, and/or preserved on personal or desktop computers as well as any other devices such as smartphones, iPads (tablets), and iPods. Learning how to ethically create, store, and, in some cases, transmit such digital media is a layered skill set including known and unknown privacy risks, capacities, and protocols often "wired" into certain hardware and software products.

Malchiodi (2000) noted that telehealth, increased communication on the web, and virtual studios were "on the rise" skills for art therapists as early as 2000. To date, the Art Therapy Credentials Board (ATCB, 2016) has added and refined codes related to "electronic" media use between clients and therapists (see Appendix 2 for more information). These codes have required but not specified safeguards against the loss of privacy around confidential exchanges between the therapist and client such as encryption standards and/or firewall protection software options. Staying informed and up to date about security products, encryption options, and other measures to ensure the safety and privacy of "cloud" or external storage devices, software apps, communication platforms, and so on, can be daunting, and the field is in constant flux. Furthermore, the ATCB code accurately states that it is not always possible to use encryption software, and technical failure to the delivery service may occur. Conscious plans and agreements (informed consent) on how to work around such events are baseline ethical behavior and necessitate service delivery models where art therapist and client should explicitly discuss what procedures they will both follow when using digital media for art expressions and communications (Choe and Carlton, 2018) (also see Chapter 2 for more information).

Supporting Digital Literacy Skills and Informed Consent

A complex balance of learning can be struck in how digital literacy skills can be achieved while students engage with media tools, platforms, and processes creatively. While there are consistent definitions of digital literacy in the media studies literature, there are limited examples and discussions in art therapy. Essentially, the meaning in many disciplines has expanded from knowing how to operate machinery or software to understanding, exploring, and producing media to gain interconnected skills of privacy, creativity, and communication (Choe and Carlton, 2018). Enhanced literacy engages technical skill building, but it also incorporates our ability to use information and communication technologies to find, evaluate, create, and communicate information, requiring relational and cognitive skills. For example, a key component to digital media literacy includes an art therapist's ability to assess risks and benefits in engaging digital media with clients and furthering the goals of therapy. The therapeutic capacities of digital media can be determined by weighing the clients' developmental levels, sensory interests and needs, physical and cognitive capacities, and drives against the media's inherent qualities and predictable (or unpredictable) outcomes. Digital literacy skills are important for art therapists to develop to be of service to their clients.

An enhanced aspect of student learning should also include digital media informed consent, confidentiality agreements, and boundaries regarding digital media communications and exchanges between therapists and clients that are critically challenged by fluid qualities on the Internet; these are manageable through conscious means and structure. Digital media informed consent agreements can be added to initial consent forms and discussions with clients and should be updated throughout the course of therapy as needed. A digital media consent conversation may include security and safety in Internet communications, security updates, hardware and artwork storage, precautions to take when clients are using their own devices for digital artwork in sessions, and precautions and limits to sharing artwork via public social media sites (Choe and Carlton, 2018).

Digital Communications and Professionalism on Social Media

Current literature notes the impact of digital media on culture (Carlton, 2014a; Orr, 2010; Sundararajan, 2014), contemporary creative, relational, and e-professionalism activities (Belkofer and McNutt, 2011; Miller, 2016, 2017), and enhanced client communication, media literacy, and life skills (Austin, 2010; Pierce, 2015). Students can assess the various purposes of digital media within art therapy approaches alongside the possible benefits and challenges of varying circumstances and diverse clients and client groups. They can be encouraged to discuss and develop ways to use new media materials to enhance therapy-driven goals and client preferences and interests (Carlton, 2014a; Choe, 2014) while also serving larger media engagement purposes and meaningfulness in clients' lives outside of therapy (Pereyra, 2017).

Seeing the self in the third person has become both a preoccupation and a necessity for participation on the Internet and it is affecting both clients and art therapists alike. In this emerging course, students can practice observing their own "digital footprints" on the Internet and assess how and why they show up in the media and the quality of that engagement. Reflection on how constructions of our digital selves and identities are curated—and should be ethically employed—will be critical course content (Belkofer and McNutt, 2011; Miller, 2017). As with many graduate courses that cover topics in depth, guest teachers and means of accessing experts in particular areas of digital media use are valuable and necessary.

Deepening Art Therapists' Own Digital Media Engagement

Early research and dialogue within both the practical and therapeutic adoption of digital media for art therapists centered on anxieties related to machine malfunction (Asawa, 2009) and general fears regarding the assimilating and automating effects of technology that seemed counter to therapy goals (Kapitan, 2009; Potash, 2009).

Critiques regarding perceptions of missing and intangible thera-peutic qualities (Asawa, 2009; Edmunds, 2012; Klorer, 2009; Orr, 2012; Peterson, 2010) soon followed and paralleled the challenges of confidentiality measures and digital literacy requirements for both clients and therapists (Alders and Allen, 2010; Alders *et al.*, 2011; Belkofer and McNutt, 2011; Choe and Carlton, 2018). Questions regarding low adaptation rates by a majority of art therapists have always circled back to a need for active participation, adaptation, and experimentation that were correlated to differences in media preferences for art therapists and a critical lack of graduate education exposure and experience for digital media ethical, creative, and therapeutic uses (Asawa, 2009; Austin, 2009; Edmunds, 2012; Orr, 2006, 2012; Peterson, 2010). The translation of similar and distinct therapeutic qualities across the "traditional" art therapy media boundaries to digital ones has been continually noted and requires deeper investigation (Carlton, 2015a). For a variety of therapy contexts and clients (adults and older adults as well as youth), digital media qualities have been found to be adaptive to both learning and clinical contexts (Cohen *et al.*, 2015; Mosinski, 2010; Orr, 2010) and to promote increased communication, and relational and self-awareness (Ehinger, 2016; Miller, 2017; Partridge, 2016).

Students deepening their own digital media engagement in graduate studies will utilize computer media devices and combinations of mixed media to explore possible therapeutic applications while designing and executing art-based projects. These assignments will have specific goals of experiential learning and peer-to-peer shared engagement to further learning objectives such as how to engage critical thinking when determining the structure and customizable qualities of digital media as related to client preferences and interests. Students will be able to use encrypted personal devices as well as additional media classroom equipment to expose and heighten new skill development such as green screen, scanography and immersive VR (virtual reality) technologies. Layered media applications and experimentation can encourage "expanded palette" applications and not diminish the use of all the media possible in art therapy. The sum of these experiences augments and deepens students' knowledge of digital and intermedia possibilities as compared to and mixed with the traditional and/or non-virtual, "handmade" tools and material processes of art therapy.

A Digital Media Implementation Example

To move on to how various digital media engagement and literacy skills have served my clinical practices with various clients, I want to share an example from my work with youth. I originated and ran an art therapy studio private practice for 15 years and worked part time for a local youth residential shelter. I was asked to facilitate a fundraising project to decorate a Christmas tree for a nonprofit community auction, with the youth present at that time of year in the emergency shelter. As the youth were being transported to my art therapy studio, I imagined the possible creative uses of old children's books to make paper chains and found objects to make ornaments. I was also considering group dynamics, their previous experiences at Christmas time, and possible feelings of being "forced" to complete such a project. Once the small group of male and female, mixed Hispanic and Native American youth arrived at my art therapy studio, they congregated near my computer and paperwork area (in an otherwise three-room, well stocked art therapy studio of fabrics, drawing, clay, and painting materials), partly due to me being there when they arrived, but also due to a video editing project on screen that immediately attracted them due to their familiarity with the product (videos) and curiosity about the process (video editing).

Once the support staff from the youth residence left, I began to feel the group out for how they felt about the fundraiser project and the task we had been given to do. By the end of our session that night, we had begun to Photoshop® (an image editing program) edit several words and phrases from meaningful hip hop songs known to the youth. We imagined how we could create Christmas ornaments with these words and phrases printed on them.

Overall, the project process took several sessions, with some youth being more engaged in the editing of text and graphics and some more invested in the final decorating of the tree. In the end, they created a black-and-white themed Christmas tree with lyrics affixed to multiple ornaments and a quote from Reverend Sharpton on the 50th anniversary of Martin Luther King Jr.'s March on Washington speech, "we must give our young people dreams again" (Reuters, 2013, para.12), heat-transferred to the cloth tree skirt (Figure 22.1).

Through this multistep project, I witnessed how the clients experienced the hybrid creative forms of digital and tangible media as adaptive and empowering experiences and how these experiences stimulated multiple levels of social interaction within this group's artmaking. The youth were again interacting with each other and interfacing with an unknown community and situation through developing a creative product and complicated emblematic symbol for public auction.

I believe the structural qualities of the digital media facilitated both interest and developmentally appropriate boundaries for the youth to work collaboratively (Austin, 2010; Ehinger, 2015). It also critically ordered and removed any personal narrative or artmaking from the process that may have otherwise felt threatening and revealing. The challenge of unwittingly disclosing one's personal details can be a consistent concern that art therapists working with youth must work into their approaches and methods. This understanding plus a group dynamic where youth members barely knew one another combined with the possible heaviness of memories that any holiday can bring to the surface in youth estranged from their families of origin, were all critical media choice considerations. The task of finding and relating to meaningful song lyrics is a safe and meaningful way for individuals to find agreement and shared perspectives. The lyrics seemed to support and reflect the participants' own messages and lives because they were created by the poets and musicians the youth admired.

A few group members became invested and showed mastery in learning the Photoshop® program and the rudimentary skills of designing words and phrasing that curved around spherical objects and looked "good." There was a general group impression that our tree would stand out very differently from the others, which may look more "Christmas colorful" and typical. That perceived separation felt both healthy and necessary and seemed developmentally appropriate for their group and individual circumstances. I heard later that our tree certainly stood out and was perceived as both poignant and desirable by the person who purchased it.

Figure 22.1
Collaborative Christmas tree skirt project made by residential youth clients

Questions Unanswered and Future Plans

For those whose goal it is to understand the opportunities and limitations of computer technology for creativity and therapeutic uses (Austin 2009, 2010; Carlton 2015a, 2015b, 2016; Ehinger, 2016; Orr, 2010), a key question unanswered by research is whether or not the use of digital media tools or platforms makes significant differences to creative processes and art therapy outcomes (Edmonds *et al.*, 2005). Art therapist Brian Austin previously asserted "Like I said, we have not fully explored what this media is yet, so let us focus on that" (Carlton, 2014b, 26:46). Edmonds *et al.* (2005) described some of the nuance to measuring the impacts of digital media use and particularly in environmental contexts:

> The role that computers might play in the enhancement of creativity is an area that has engaged the authors of this paper for a long time but our experience has demonstrated that the tools in themselves are not the only factors to be considered.

Whether or not creativity can be enhanced in some way may be significantly influenced by the conditions in which it takes place. These conditions might be defined in terms of the environmental (including organizational) factors, and indeed the materials or tools used to achieve the creative outcome. One might hypothesize that the characteristics of any resources, materials, tools or techniques that form a part of the creative work are in themselves critical factors that influence the way it takes place, i.e. the process. (p.456)

As the research into new media grows, art therapists will continue critical research into how these process-oriented and communicative materials might engage therapy-driven goals (Garner, 2016) as well as graduate student learning goals.

Digital media as "interrelated computer-mediated devices, software, and tools that support customizable activities for the creation of on or off-line art forms" (Carlton, Sit, and Yu, 2018, p.74) will be promoted and explored in my role as director and associate professor. When approaching change and curriculum innovation, one has to make small doable goals, gather collaborators, and think big while working incrementally for the long term. I am currently gathering physical resources for a digital media teaching lab on campus and originating curriculum planning with added digital media learning inclusion in multiple course content, as well as developing a specialized elective. Additionally, I am collaboratively creating a 2019 global online symposium titled DICATS (Digital International Creative Arts Therapists) that will bring together digital artists, creative arts and expressive therapists, researchers, community organizers, and software developers from around the world to share research collaborations, exchange with live and prerecorded presentations, and demonstrate educational, therapeutic, and creative innovations regarding digital media use. An overarching goal of all these activities is to continue gathering an invested community that will compare ideas across disciplines and both quantify and qualify digital media properties and emergent edges. Future research that explores questions of media differentials and possibilities, including strengths and weaknesses, will be further articulated and developed so that art therapy graduate programs may continue to provide innovative materials and reflective practices for clientele and our own professional growth.

This chapter was a glimpse into a particular early stage of planning and activation for this author and the shared goals presented in this chapter for the inclusion of digital media in current and future classes. The anticipated implementation of digital media infusion and the content and "how to" for current planning were articulated to ground and raise eternal questions regarding new media's value and interconnectivity to the art therapy of now and the future.

Recommendations

- Generate dialogue between arts therapists and those in adjacent digital media research, and educational and creative communities.

- Further research is needed into how immersive digital media can be seen and felt as embodied and activating experiences.

- Applied curriculum learning goals of enhanced digital media literacy skills and the relational effects of digital media for art therapists need to be implemented and evaluated.

References

Alders, A. and Allen, P. (2010, November) Ethics of representation: Ethical movie making in art therapy. Paper presented at the 41st Annual Conference of the American Art Therapy Association, Sacramento, CA.

Alders, A., Beck, L., Allen, P. and Mosinski, B. (2011) Technology in art therapy: Ethical challenges. *Art Therapy 28*(4), 165–170.

Art Therapy Credentials Board (ATCB) (2016) *Code of Ethics, Conduct, and Disciplinary Procedures.* Retrieved on April 1, 2018 at www.atcb.org/Ethics/ATCBCode

Asawa, P. (2009) Art therapists' emotional reactions to the demands of technology. *Art Therapy 26*(2), 58–65.

Austin, B. (2009) Renewing the debate: Digital technology in art therapy and the creative process. *Art Therapy: Journal of the American Art Therapy Association 26*(2), 83–85.

Austin, B. (2010) Technology, art therapy, and psychodynamic theory: Computer animation with an adolescent in foster care. In C.H. Moon (ed.) *Materials and Media in Art Therapy*. New York, NY: Routledge.

Belkofer, C.M. and McNutt, J.V. (2011) Understanding social media culture and its ethical challenges for art therapists. *Art Therapy 28*(4), 159–164.

Carlton, N.R. (2014a) Digital culture and art therapy. *The Arts in Psychotherapy 41*(1), 41–45.

Carlton, N.R. (Producer) (2014b, October) *Digital Media in Art Therapy Interviews* [video file]. Retrieved on April 1, 2018 at https://vimeo.com/89563621

Carlton, N.R. (2015a) Digital media use in art therapy. Doctoral dissertation. Retrieved on April 1, 2018 at ProQuest Dissertations and Theses database. (UMI No. 3682148)

Carlton, N.R. (2015b) Expansive palettes. In J. Cohen, L. Johnson, and P. Orr (eds.) *Video and Filmmaking as Psychotherapy*. New York, NY: Routledge.

Carlton, N. (2016) Grid + Pattern: The sensory qualities of digital media. In R. Garner (Ed.) *Digital art therapy: Materials, methods, and applications* (pp. 22–39). London: Jessica Kingsley Publishers.

Carlton, N.R., Sit, T. and Yu, D.R. (2018) Transcending media: Tangible to digital and their mixed realities. In R. Corolan and A. Backos (eds.) *Emerging Perspectives In Art Therapy: Trends, Movements and Developments*. New York, NY: Routledge.

Choe, N.S. (2014) An exploration of the qualities and features of art apps for art therapy. *The Arts in Psychotherapy 41*(1), 145–154.

Choe, N.S. (2016) Utilizing digital tools and apps in art therapy sessions. In R. Garner (ed.) *Digital Art Therapy: Material, Methods, and Applications*. New York, NY: Routledge.

Choe, N.S. and Carlton, N.R. (2018) Behind the screens: Informed consent and digital literacy in art therapy. Manuscript in preparation.

Cohen, J.L., Johnson, J. and Orr, P. (eds.) (2015) *Video and Filmmaking as Psychotherapy: Research and Practice*. New York, NY: Routledge.

Edmonds, E.A., Weakly, A., Candy, L., Fell, M., Knott, M. and Pauletto, S. (2005) The studio as laboratory: Combining creative practice and digital technology research. *International Journal of Human-Computer Studies 63*, 452–481.

Edmunds, J.D. (2012) The applications and implications of digital media in art therapy: A survey study. Unpublished master's thesis, Drexel University, Philadelphia, PA.

Ehinger, J. (2015) Filming the fantasy: Green screen technology from novelty to psychotherapy. In J.L. Cohen, L. Johnson, and P. Orr (eds.) *Video and Filmmaking as Psychotherapy: Research and Practice*. New York, NY: Routledge.

Ehinger, J. (2016) Therapeutic technology re-envisioned. In R. Garner (ed.) *Digital Art Therapy: Materials, Methods, and Applications*. London: Jessica Kingsley Publishers.

Garner, R. (ed.) (2016) *Digital Art Therapy: Materials, Methods, and Applications*. London: Jessica Kingsley Publishers.

Horrigan, J.B. (2016) Digital readiness gaps. Pew Research Center. Retrieved on April 1, 2018 at www.pewinternet.org/2016/09/20/digital-readiness-gaps

Kapitan, L. (2009) Introduction to the special issue on art therapy's response to techno-digital culture. *Art Therapy 26*(2), 50–51.

Klorer, P. (2009) The effects of technological overload on children: An art therapist's perspective. *Art Therapy: Journal of the American Art Therapy Association 26*(2), 50–51.

L'Esperance, N. (2016) Art therapy and technology: Islands of brilliance. In R. Garner (ed.) *Digital Art Therapy: Material, Methods and Applications.* London: Jessica Kingsley Publishers.

Major Lazer (Artist) (2012, August 23) *Get Free feat. Amber of the Dirty Projectors* [video file]. Retrieved on April 1, 2018 at www.youtube.com/watch?v=ytIfSuy_mOA

Malchiodi, C.A. (2000) *Art Therapy and Computer Technology: A Virtual Studio of Possibilities.* London: Jessica Kingsley Publishers.

Martin, A. (2006) Literacies for the digital age. In A. Martin and D. Madigan (eds.) *Digital Literacies for Learning.* London: Facet Publications.

Media Smarts (n.d.) The intersection of digital and media literacy. Retrieved on April 1, 2018 at http://mediasmarts.ca/digital-media-literacy/general-information/digital-media-literacy-fundamentals/intersection-digital-media-literacy

Miller, G. (2016) Social media and creative motivation. In R. Garner (ed.) *Digital Art Therapy: Materials, Methods, and Applications.* London: Jessica Kingsley Publishers.

Miller, G. (2017) *The Art Therapist's Guide to Social Media: Connection, Community, and Creativity.* New York, NY: Routledge.

Moon, C. (ed.) (2010) *Materials and Media in Art Therapy.* New York, NY: Routledge.

Mosinski, B.B. (2010) Video art and activism: Applications in art therapy. In C.H. Moon (ed.) *Materials and Media in Art Therapy.* New York, NY: Routledge.

Orr, P.P. (2006) Technology training for art therapist: Is there a need? *Art Therapy: Journal of the American Art Therapy Association 23*(4), 191–196.

Orr, P. (2010) Social remixing: Art therapy media in the digital age. In C.H. Moon (ed.) *Materials and Media in Art Therapy.* New York, NY: Routledge.

Orr, P. (2012) Technology use in art therapy practice: 2004 and 2011 comparison. *Arts in Psychotherapy 39*, 234–238.

Partridge, E. (2016) Amplified voices: Art-based inquiry into elder communication. Doctoral dissertation. Retrieved at Proquest Dissertations Publishing,10190347. Notre Dame de Namur University, Belmont, CA.

Pereyra, P. (2017) The study of media use habits and trends: Rural Latinx media use skills and motivations. Manuscript in preparation.

Peterson, B. (2010) The media adoption stage model of technology for art therapy. *Art Therapy 27*(1), 26–31.

Pierce, J. (2015) *Digital Fusion: A Society beyond Blind Inclusion*. New York, NY: Peter Lang.

Potash, J.S. (2009) Fast food art, talk show therapy: The impact of mass media on adolescent art therapy. *Art Therapy: Journal of the American Art Therapy Association 26*(2), 52–57.

Prensky, M. (2001) Digital natives, digital immigrants. *On the Horizon 9*(5), 1–6.

Reuters (2013, August 27) On Anniversary of King's "Dream" speech, bells to ring for freedom. Retrieved on April 1, 2018 at https://uk.reuters.com/article/us-usa-dream-ring/on-anniversary-of-kings-dream-speech-bells-to-ring-for-freedom-idUKBRE97Q0OH20130827

Sanchez, E. (2013, December 26) Top 10 instances of open and unapologetic celebrity cultural appropriation in 2013! [web blog]. Retrieved on April 1, 2018 at www.autostraddle.com/top-ten-instances-of-open-and-unapologetic-celebrity-cultural-appropriation-in-2013-210371

Seiden, D. (2001) *Mind over Matter: The Uses of Materials in Art, Education, and Therapy*. Chicago, IL: Magnolia.

Sundararajan, L. (2014) Mind, machine, and creativity: An artist's perspective. *Journal of Creative Behavior 48*(2), 136–151.

Weigel, M., Straughn, C., Gardner, H. and James, C. (2009) *Multiple Worlds: Adolescents, New Digital Media, and Shifts in Habits of Mind*. The Developing Minds and Digital Media Project. Retrieved at http://thegoodproject.org/pdf/63-Multiple-Worlds.pdf

Wolf, R.I. (2007) Advances in phototherapy training. *The Arts in Psychotherapy 34*(2), 124–133.

Appendix 1
General Ethical Principles for Potential Cyber Art Therapists

(*Art Therapy and Computer Technology*, C. Malchiodi, 2000, Jessica Kingsley Publishers)

Note: These recommended principles not only provide historical background on the ethics of digital technology and social media, but also form a framework for contemporary ethical questions and challenges in using new media in art therapy practice.

In addition to online confidentiality, electronic storage, disposition of digital images, and other issues of ethics with regard to computer technology, there are a few other general points that the potential "cyber art therapist" should consider. These include, but are not limited to, the following:

1. Obtain a basic reference about the Internet and programs you plan to use. If you plan to use computer technology in your work, you will find that you need to stay current in your working knowledge of computer technology, just as you would do with ethics, legal issues, and practice issues relevant to your work.

2. Establish a philosophy about your plan to use computer technology for therapeutic purposes. If you integrate computer technology into your practice it is important that you consider how you personally see it as useful to the therapeutic process and how clients can benefit from this type of interaction or experience. Competence is necessary not only in computer or digital technology, but also in

text-based communication. Style and knowledge of how to communicate with people through e-mail is intrinsic to the quality of online exchange.

3. Be sure to tell clients about the reservations of online therapy. What you do not like about computers and e-communication is as important as identifying the benefits of this technology.

4. Experiment with various components of computer, electronic, and digital technology yourself. It is now possible to get supervision from some people who are using this technology and material on competencies for telehealth and telemedicine are available. Peer supervision with other therapists interested in this area of work is also an option.

5. Consider the research on computer-mediated communication and therapy. For example, one study concluded that a greater use of the Internet might be associated with declines in people's communication with family members, decreases the size of their social circle, and increases depression (Kraut *et al.*, 1998). But others have observed the use of computer-mediated communication for social skill building and increased social networks, and that the Internet has made possible a global community. Computers have been successfully used to enhance already existing communities, such as neighborhoods, schools, and support groups (Michaelson, 1996). Research on computer-based counseling and therapy is extremely limited at present; outcome research on the use of art therapy via the computer is non-existent.

6. Explore the less tangible issues of cyber art therapy. For example, does overexposure to this type of technology make children less creative because it essentially "seduces" them away from hands-on activities such as art making (Kramer *et al.*, 1995)? Are there diversity and socioeconomic issues involved, such as equal access or cultural preferences? Although many professions, including those in healthcare, require that one be proficient in navigating the digital world, access or right to the Internet has not been universal due to socioeconomic factors and other influences. This obviously raises questions about those who do not have the privilege of access to this technology and those who do.

Consider when computer technology can be culturally appropriate and helpful in treatment and communication. Earlier in this book I related my experience of using e-communication with a group of teens at a homeless shelter. Computers, along with video games and other electronic media, are part of the language and day-to-day life of increasing numbers of adolescents, but adults as well. For that particular group of adolescents, Internet communication was an effective way to engage them with a therapist.

7. Don't be quick to judge online therapy too harshly. Be open to how technology can benefit your practice, as well as its disadvantages and drawbacks.

References

Kramer, E., Gerity, L., Henley, D. and Williams, K. (1995, November) Art and art therapy and the seductive environment. Panel presented at the 26th annual conference of the American Art Therapy Association, San Diego, CA.

Kraut, R., Lundmark, V., Patterson, M., Kiesler, S. and Scherlis, T. (1998) Internet paradox: A social technology that reduces social involvement and psychological well-being? *American Psychologist 53*(9), 1017–1031.

Michaelson, K. (1996) Information, community, and access. *Social Sciences Computer Review 14*(1), 57–59.

Appendix 2

Sections of the Art Therapy Credentials Board (ATCB) *Code of Ethics, Conduct and Disciplinary Procedures* that address digital communication and social media

[reprinted with permission of ATCB]

2.9.1 Art therapists must inform clients of the benefits, risks, and limitations of using information technology applications in the therapeutic process and in business/billing procedures. Such technologies include but are not limited to computer hardware and software, faxing, telephones, the Internet, online assessment instruments, and other technological procedures and devices. Art therapists shall utilize encryption standards within Internet communications and/or take such precautions to reasonably ensure the confidentiality of information transmitted, as in 2.9.5.6.

2.9.2 When art therapists are providing technology-assisted distance art therapy services, the art therapist shall make a reasonable effort to determine that clients are intellectually, emotionally, and physically capable of using the application and that the application is appropriate for the needs of clients.

2.9.3 Art therapists must ensure that the use of technology in the therapeutic relationship does not violate the laws of any federal, provincial, state, local, or international entity and observe all relevant statutes.

2.9.4 Art therapists shall seek business, legal, and technical assistance when using technology applications for the purpose of providing art therapy services, particularly when the use of such applications crosses provincial, state lines or international boundaries.

2.9.5 As part of the process of establishing informed consent, art therapists shall do the following:

> 2.9.5.1 Inform clients of issues related to the difficulty of maintaining the confidentiality of electronically transmitted communications, and the difficulty in removing any information or imagery that has been posted electronically if consent is later revoked.

> 2.9.5.2 Inform clients of all colleagues, supervisors, and employees (including Information Technology [IT] administrators) who might have authorized access to electronic transmissions.

> 2.9.5.3 Inform clients that, due to the nature of technology assisted art therapy, unauthorized persons may have access to information/art products that clients may share in the therapeutic process.

> 2.9.5.4 Inform clients of pertinent legal rights and limitations governing the practice of a profession across state/provincial lines or international boundaries.

> 2.9.5.5 Inform clients that Internet sites and e-mail communications will be encrypted but that there are limitations to the ability of encryption software to help ensure confidentiality.

> 2.9.5.6 When the use of encryption is not possible, art therapists notify clients of this fact and limit electronic transmissions to general communications that are not client specific.

2.9.5.7 Inform clients if and for how long archival storage of transaction records are maintained.

2.9.5.8 Discuss the possibility of technology failure and alternate methods of service delivery.

2.9.5.11 If a client wishes to access insurance coverage for technology-assisted distance art therapy services, art therapists shall advise clients that it is the client's responsibility to confirm coverage before beginning services.

2.9.5.12 Inform clients that communication will be included in client documentation as mentioned in 2.7.3.

2.9.6 Art therapists maintaining sites on the Internet shall do the following:

2.9.6.1 Regularly check that electronic links are working and professionally appropriate.

2.9.6.2 Provide electronic links to the ATCB and other relevant state, provincial, and or international licensure and professional certification boards to protect consumer rights and facilitate addressing ethical concerns.

2.9.6.3 Strive to provide a site that is accessible to persons with disabilities

2.10.1 Art therapists who maintain social media sites shall clearly distinguish between their personal and professional profiles by tailoring information specific to those uses and modifying who can access each site.

2.10.2 Art therapists do not disclose or display confidential information through social media.

Appendix 3
Samples of Electronic Transmissions Statements

Note: Be sure to check with your agency or institution and the regulations established by the jurisdiction in which you live (country, state, or province) for any additional information that is required for electronic transmission statements.

Sample 1: *Confidentiality Notice*: The information contained in this telecommunication message is privileged and confidential, and intended only for the use of the individual(s) named above. Federal and state regulations, including but not limited to the Electronic Communications Privacy Act and the Health Insurance Portability and Accountability Act (HIPAA), prohibit interceptions of any electronic communications without written consent of the person to whom it pertains. Therefore, if you have received this transmission in error, please immediately notify me to arrange for return or destruction of the materials.

Sample 2: IMPORTANT: This facsimile transmission contains confidential information, some or all of which may be protected health information as defined by the federal Health Insurance Portability and Accountability Act (HIPAA) Privacy Rule. This transmission is intended for the exclusive use of the individual or entity to whom it is addressed and may contain information that is proprietary, privileged, confidential, and/or exempt from disclosure under applicable law. If you are not the intended recipient (or an employee or agent responsible for delivering this facsimile transmission to the intended recipient), you are hereby notified that any disclosure, dissemination, distribution, or copying of this information is strictly prohibited and may be subject to legal restriction or sanction. Please notify the sender by telephone (number listed above) to arrange the return or destruction of the information and all copies.

Appendix 4
Questions to Consider When Developing a Social Media Policy

Some ethics codes now encourage or require that therapists who use social networking platforms have a social media policy and include it in their informed consent. This policy should cover client expectations about interacting with therapists via social networks, clearly explaining possible risks, confidentiality issues, and possible benefits. The following questions will help you consider what to address in your social media policy and informed consent document.

- Do you have any restrictions or privacy settings to prevent access to your professional and personal information on social media platforms?
- What is your position on "friending" and "fanning" by clients? Do you permit or not permit this and why?
- What is your position on text messaging to/from clients?
- Do you use search engines to as a matter of normal practice activity, researching clients, or in emergency situations only (e.g. suspicion of client self-harm or harm to others)?
- Is your professional profile on sites that review your practice or business?
- How do you handle client testimonials? Do you accept testimonials from former clients?
- What is your position on electronic mail received from/sent to clients?
- What is your position on clients posting art created during treatment on social media?

- Can you guarantee that your computer, cell phone, or other digital devices you use for client interactions are secure?
- If you conduct distance therapy, what do you share/receive via digital communication?
- Is the language used in your social media user friendly/understandable by the general public?
- If you have a social media presence, such as a blog or website, do you discuss the nature of it with clients?
- Do you maintain separate personal and professional e-mails?

There are two excellent resources for further information on the development of a social media policy:

References

Dr. Keely Kolmes' website, www.drkkolmes.com; see "My Private Practice Social Media Policy." Retrieved on April 1, 2018 at http://drkkolmes.com/social-media-policy

Natwick, J. (2017) Boon or bother? Social media marketing and ethics. *Counseling Today, 59*(7), 22–23.

CONTRIBUTORS

Brian Austin, MPS, is the founder and program director of The Animation Project (TAP), a program that utilizes animation and video to help at-risk youth to focus on their future and skills to improve their lives as well as their careers. Based in New York, Austin is also a professional three-dimensional (3D) animator and art therapist.

Christopher Belkofer, PhD, ATR, LPC, is the director of the Graduate Art Therapy Programs at Mount Mary University in Milwaukee, WI.

Kristin Belkofer, MA, LPC, is a licensed professional counselor at Shoreside Therapies in Milwaukee, WI.

Natalie Carlton, PhD, ATR-BC, LPCC, is an associate professor and director of Drexel University's Art Therapy and Counseling program in Philadelphia, PA. She has published chapters on the diverse subjects of digital culture, sensory qualities of digital media, and graphic novel use in art therapy.

Donald J. Cutcher, MA, LCAT, ATR-BC, is a founder and honorary life member of the Buckeye Art Therapy Association (BATA) and is also a co-founder and board member of Art Therapy Without Borders, Inc. He recently retired from providing services to clients experiencing physical and/or psychological trauma from workplace injuries in Ohio.

Olena Darewych, PhD, RP, RCAT, is a registered psychotherapist and art therapist and serves as adjunct faculty at Adler University and Wilfrid Laurier University in Waterloo, Ontario. She is a past president of the Canadian Art Therapy Association. Currently, Dr. Darewych facilitates digital art therapy group sessions for adults with autism spectrum disorder.

Bryce Evans is an award-winning Canadian artist currently living in Thailand and is the founder of The One Project as the first photography community for people suffering from depression and anxiety. He is a presenter on therapeutic photography, including a TEDx talk on how photography impacts mental health.

Bronwen Gray, MA AT, JD, PhD, is a freelance artist, art therapist, and educator who has worked in a multitude of creative settings and served on the faculty of Whitecliffe College of Art and Design in Auckland, New Zealand, and Phoenix Institute in Melbourne, Australia. Her digital storytelling projects have been accepted into the permanent collection of the Australian Centre for the Moving Image in Australia and into Nga Taonga Sound and Vision archive in New Zealand.

Jeffrey Jamerson, PhD, has over 20 years of experience in the public sector and has served at-risk youth in various capacities. He is an expressive arts therapist and currently is the Vice President of Programs and Services at Aviva Family and Children's Services in Los Angeles, CA, where he oversees foster family agency and adoption, community mental health, relative support services, and wraparound services.

J. Lauren Johnson, MSc, PhD, is a psychologist working in Edmonton, Alberta, Canada. Dr. Johnson spends the majority of her time working with Indigenous Canadians as well as victims of trauma and has built a steady practice using the video-based creative method of therapeutic filmmaking in her comprehensive psychological approach.

Debra Johnson-Fuller is an enrolled member of the Fond du Lac Band of Lake Superior Chippewa in Cloquet, MN, and is a cancer health educator. Ms. Johnson-Fuller has presented nationally on topics ranging from digital storytelling to traditional medicine.

Gudrun Jones, MPhil, Reg ATh, has worked as an art therapist in mental health, oncology, and palliative care in Wales. She is an original member of the Wales Arts Therapies Advisory Forum (WATAF) and has a special interest in the use of video conferencing to provide psychological support.

Seong-in Kim, PhD, is a professor emeritus of Industrial Management Engineering at Korea University in Seoul. His recent focuses have been on developing computer systems in art therapy, including the C_CREATES (Computer_Color-Related Art Therapy Evaluation System) and an app to evaluate drawings.

Joe Kavitski, MA, is an award-winning filmmaker and artist whose work includes the integration of digital technology with art therapy. As adjunct faculty at New York University, he teaches *Multimedia in Art Therapy* as part of their Adaptive Techniques in Art Therapy course. He currently serves as Director of Admissions and Outreach for Fusion Academy in Rockville, MD.

Mary K. Kometiani, MA, ATR-BC, LPCC, is an art therapist, licensed professional clinical counselor, lecturer, and author in art therapy. She is the owner of Art Therapy Heals, LLC in Ohio, and is collaborating with organizations and health services, and educating the public about art therapy and its benefits.

Alexander Kopytin, PhD, is a psychiatrist and professor in the psychotherapy department at Northwest Medical I.I. Mechnikov University, and head of postgraduate training in art therapy at the Academy of Postgraduate Pedagogical Training at St. Petersburg, Russia. He is the chair of the Russian Art Therapy Association and has written and co-edited several books including *Clinical Art Psychotherapy with War Veterans.*

Jeff Lohrius, MA, is an art therapist in Boulder, CO, who provides individual and group virtual reality art therapy sessions, workshops, and private consultations to other art therapists who wish to integrate VR tools into their own practice.

Shaun McNiff, PhD, is a university professor and founder of the Expressive Therapies and Integrated Arts in Education graduate programs at Lesley University, Cambridge, MA. He is an exhibiting painter who wrote *Art-Based Research,* the first book on the subject, and currently serves as an editor for the Beijing-based journal *Creative Arts Education and Therapy.*

Rachel Rahman, PhD, FHEA CPsychol, AFBPsS, is a senior lecturer in the psychology department at Aberystwyth University, Aberystwyth, Wales.

Martine Robson, PhD, FHEA, is a lecturer in the psychology department at Aberystwyth University, Aberystwyth, Wales.

Jedediah Walls, PhD, is a media psychologist studying how technology can be used to improve society and human lives. He has worked with the Telehealth Subcommittee of the American Psychological Association and hosted presentations on how psychologists can best utilize telehealth technologies.

Elizabeth Warson, PhD, ATR-BC, LPC, NCC (Texas Comanche, Eastern Band Cherokee), is the executive director of American Indian Art Therapy and a former professor at George Washington University and Eastern Virginia Medical School. She has more than 20 years of clinical experience in a variety of settings and currently has a private practice in Fort Collins, CO.

Alan Young, PhD, has been a design practitioner and educator for over 15 years and has worked on award-winning community-based social justice projects. He has had works exhibited at The Powerhouse Museum and installed as part of the permanent collection of the Australian Centre for the Moving Image, and is currently a senior lecturer in Communication Design at Auckland University of Technology, New Zealand.

ABOUT THE EDITOR

Cathy Malchiodi, PhD, ATR-BC, LPCC, LPAT, REAT, is an art therapist, expressive arts therapist, research psychologist, and clinical mental health counselor as well as a recognized authority on art therapy and expressive arts therapy with children, adults, and families. She has given more than 400 invited presentations on art therapy around the world and has published numerous articles, chapters, and books, including *What to Do When Children Clam Up in Psychotherapy, Understanding Children's Drawings, Handbook of Art Therapy* (2nd edn), *Art Therapy Sourcebook* (2nd edn), *Creative Arts and Play Therapy for Attachment Problems*, and *Creative Interventions with Traumatized Children* (2nd edn). A sought-after educator, Cathy has served as a professor at seven universities throughout the US and as a lecturer and consultant for a variety of national and international organizations, foundations, and governmental agencies on the use of art therapy and expressive arts therapy for disaster relief, mental health, and public health and wellness.

Cathy is the founder and executive director of the Trauma-Informed Practices and Expressive Arts Therapy Institute, an organization dedicated to service, education, and research on trauma-informed intervention for children, adults, families, and communities. She has served on numerous boards of professional organizations including the American Counseling Association (ACA), Art Therapy Without Borders (ATWB), American Art Therapy Association (AATA), and Association for Humanistic Counseling (AHC) among others, and on the editorial boards of *The Arts in Psychotherapy, Creative Arts in Education and Therapy* (China), and *Academic Journal of Creative Arts Therapies* (Israel). In recognition of her contributions to art therapy, Cathy was given the Honorary Life Member award from AATA (2002) and Kennedy Center Honors (1987) for her international art therapy work in China.

Cathy's interest in digital technology spans several decades, including training in documentary filmmaking and animation, digital storytelling, and computer-generated art. As a visual artist, her artwork often integrates traditional and digital images to create mixed-media pieces that depict personal narratives. More recently,

Cathy's work with the Department of Defense has involved the use of virtual reality (VR) and augmented reality (AR) with returning combat military and various forms of digital art therapy with children, adolescents, and adults who are recovering from medical illnesses or traumatic brain injury. As a recreational pilot, she also enjoys her time in flight simulators (VR technology) to learn more about how to be an excellent aviator.

Cathy has also been actively involved in online communities and social networking platforms as an advocate and activist for the role of art therapy in health since 1995. In 2008, *Psychology Today* selected her as one of ten individuals to blog on the topic of "Arts and Health"; her column currently has a readership of over 4.4 million. One of the initial founders of the Art Therapy + Happiness Project, an online art-making community, she continues to explore and envision how social networking platforms can improve the lives of individuals through the positive psychology principles of connection, compassion, courage, and contribution.

INDEX